'In the vaults ben[

Archaeological recording at St George's Church, Bloomsbury

by Ceridwen Boston, Angela Boyle, John Gill,
and Annsofie Witkin

with contributions by
Jennifer Kitch, Louise Loe, Jane Phimester, Ian Scott, Richard Wright

Illustration and design
Magda Wachnik, Georgina Slater and Laura Kirby

Oxford Archaeology
Monograph No. 8
2009

'In the vaults beneath'
Published by Oxford Archaeology as part of the Oxford Archaeology Monograph series

Designed by Oxford Archaeology Graphics Office
Cover design by Lucy Martin and Georgina Slater

Edited by Ian Scott

ISBN 978-0-904220-53-7

© 2009 The Oxford Archaeological Unit Ltd

For more information visit: http://thehumanjourney.net

Figure 1.1 is reproduced from the Ordnance Survey on behalf of the controller
of Her Majesty's Stationery Office, © Crown Copyright, AL100005569

Typeset by Production Line, Oxford
Printed in Great Britain by Information Press, Eynsham, Oxford

Contents

List of Figures vii

List of Plates ix

List of Tables xi

Summary xiii

Acknowledgements xvi

Chapter 1: **Introduction** *by Ceridwen Boston and Angela Boyle*

PROJECT BACKGROUND 1

Location and topography 1

Restoration programme 1

ARCHAEOLOGICAL PROGRAMME 1

Desk-based assessment 1

Archaeological mitigation 3

Project aims 3

Archaeological aims 3

Osteological aims 3

Recording system 3

Plans 4

Photographic record 4

Recording the coffins 4

Coffins and coffin fittings 4

Sealed coffins 4

Osteological methodology 4

Low resolution recording 4

High resolution recording 4

Ethical and legal considerations 4

Health and safety 5

Structure of the report 5

Chapter 2: **Historic buildings recording of the crypt and archaeological watching briefs within the churchyard** *by Jon Gill, Ceridwen Boston and Jane Phimester*

INTRODUCTION 7

RECORDING THE CRYPT 7

Background 7

Aims, objectives and methodology 7

Summary history of the building 7

Description of vaults 8

Introduction 8

Vault 1 8

Vault 2 13

Vault 3 14

Vault 4 15

Vault 5 15

Vault 6 15

Vault 7 17

Vault 8 (context 9001) 17
Vault 9 (context 9002) 18
Vault 10 (context 9003) 18
Vault 11 (context 9004) 20
Vault 12 (context 9005) 20
Conclusion 20
ARCHAEOLOGICAL WATCHING BRIEFS IN THE CHURCHYARD AND CRYPT 20
Test pits 1 and 2 20
Areas 7 and 8 21
Area 7 22
Area 8 22
Stairwell on the south side of the tower (Test pit 3 and Area 5) 22
Test pit 4 23
Area 6 23
Listed building description 27

Chapter 3: The spatial distribution of the coffins within the crypt *by Ceridwen Boston*

INTRODUCTION 29
VAULTS 1 TO 6 29
VAULT 7 31
SPATIAL ARRANGEMENT OF THE COFFINS WITHIN THE VAULTS 33
CONCLUSION 35

Chapter 4: The church, the parish and parishioners *by Ceridwen Boston and Ian Scott*

THE PARISH OF BLOOMSBURY AND ITS PARISH CHURCH 61
Parish of Bloomsbury in the 18th and 19th centuries 61
The need for a new church 61
Construction of the new church 63
PARISHIONERS 66
Introduction 66
Coffin plate inscriptions 67
Memorial plaques 68
Other sources 68
Parish registers, related records and civil registration 68
Wills 73
Census records 73
Trade directories, Post Office directories, and professional registers or lists 74
Death notices and obituaries, and other sources 74
The professions and occupations of the crypt population 74
The law 74
The church 76
The army, navy and merchant marine 78
Members of Parliament and politicians 80
Imperial administrators and civil servants 82
Merchants, bankers, stockbrokers, etc 82
Artisans, tradesmen and business men 84
Principal librarians and staff of the British Museum 88
Doctors of medicine and surgeons 89
The arts 89
Abodes and social stratification 90
Church and charity: joining and giving 92
Bloomsbury a cosmopolitan parish 93
Conclusion 94

Chapter 5: Demography *by Ceridwen Boston*

INTRODUCTION 95
AGE DISTRIBUTION 95
SEX DISTRIBUTION 98
SEASONALITY OF DEATH 98
CAUSES OF DEATH 99

Chapter 6: The human bone assemblage *by Ceridwen Boston, Annsofie Witkin, Angela Boyle and Jennifer Kitch*

INTRODUCTION 103
THE NAMED SAMPLE 103
    Methodology 103
        Preservation and completeness 103
        Skeletal inventory 103
        Determination of sex 103
        Estimation of osteological age 104
        Estimation of stature 105
        Comparative assemblages 105
    Results 105
        Quantification 105
        Preservation and completeness 106
        Demography 108
        Osteological age and sex 108
        Chronological age and sex 109
        Stature 111
        Dental pathology 111
        Dental interventions 114
        Skeletal pathology 117
THE UNNAMED SAMPLE 128
    Introduction 128
    Methodology 128
    Results 128
        Preservation and completeness 128
        Composition of the sample 129
        Skeletal pathology 132
        Dental pathology 134
        Dental interventions 134
DISCUSSION OF THE NAMED AND UNNAMED SAMPLES 137
    Demography 137
    Health status 137

Chapter 7: Examination of methods used to estimate osteological age and sex *by Ceridwen Boston and Louise Loe*

AGE AT DEATH METHODS 139
    Adults 139
        Auricular surface 139
        Cranial suture closure 141
        Dental attrition 141
        Pubic symphisis 141
        Sternal rib ends 141
        Statistical analysis 141
        Discussion of ageing methods 142

Subadults 143
   Discussion of ageing methods 143
   Sexing methods 144

Chapter 8: Burial practice and material culture *by Ceridwen Boston*

BURYING THE DEAD OF THE PARISH 147
  The burial ground 147
  The crypt 147
MATERIAL CULTURE 148
  Historical background 148
  Early 19th-century perceptions of death 148
  Coffins 149
    Coffin materials and construction 149
    Lime in the coffin 151
    Preservation of the coffins 151
  Coffin fittings 151
    Introduction 151
    Symbolism of motifs used on coffin fittings 152
    Upholstery and stud-work 163
    Depositum plates 164
    Grips and grip plates 165
    Lid motifs and escutcheons 166
    New coffin fitting types from St George's crypt 167
  Grave clothes and grave goods 170
    Textiles: shrouds and coffin linings 170
    Grave goods 170
    Death masks 171
  CONCLUSION 171

Chapter 9: Discussion and conclusions *by Angela Boyle and Ceridwen Boston*

INTRODUCTION 173
RESEARCH ISSUES IN POST-MEDIEVAL BURIAL 173
THE ARCHAEOLOGICAL AND HISTORICAL VALUE OF THE ST GEORGE'S
  ASSEMBLAGE 173
  Completeness 173
  Condition 173
  Rarity 174
  Group value 174
  Research potential 174
THE REBURIAL DEBATE 174
  Recent relevant developments 175
CONCLUSION 176

Appendices

  Appendix 1: Alphabetical list of named individuals known from coffin plates 177
  Appendix 2: Statistical testing of osteological dating methods *by Richard Wright* 221

Bibliography 227

List of Figures

Chapter 1
Figure 1.1   Site location 2

Chapter 2
Figure 2.1   Plan of crypt showing brickwork and ashlar work. 10
Figure 2.2   Cross-section through east side of vaults in crypt 11
Figure 2.3   Plan of church and churchyard showing the location of test pits and boreholes
              and excavation areas 19
Figure 2.4   Test pit 1: S-facing section; Test pit 2: S-facing section 20
Figure 2.5   Areas 7 and 8: plans of excavation 21
Figure 2.6   Area 5 and Test Pit 3: excavation of the stairwell 9000 S of the tower: Plans
              and sections. 23
Figure 2.7   Test pit 4: NW-facing section 24
Figure 2.8   Area 6: Plan of north-eastern extension showing location of well 10007 25
Figure 2.9   Area 6: Section 500: Elevation showing blocked arch 10016; Section 501: Elevation
              showing blocked arch 10017 26

Chapter 3
Figure 3.1   Plan of the crypt showing locations of Vaults 1-7 30
Figure 3.2   Vault 1: the uppermost layer of coffins on racks and in stacks A-G 32
Figure 3.3   Vault 1: Matrix of the coffins on the racks 34
Figure 3.4   Vault 1: Matrix of the coffin stacks- Row A 35
Figure 3.5   Vault 1: Matrix of the coffin stacks- Row B 36
Figure 3.6   Vault 1: Matrix of the coffin stacks- Row C 37
Figure 3.7   Vault 1: Matrix of the coffin stacks- Row D 38
Figure 3.8   Vault 1: Matrix of the coffin stacks- Row E 38
Figure 3.9   Vault 1: Matrix of the coffin stacks- Alcove F 39
Figure 3.10   Vault 1: Matrix of the coffin stacks- Alcove G 39
Figure 3.11   Vault 2: the uppermost layer of coffins in stacks A-D 40
Figure 3.12   Vault 2: Matrix of the coffin stacks- Row A 41
Figure 3.13   Vault 2: Matrix of the coffin stacks- Row B 42
Figure 3.14   Vault 2: Matrix of the coffin stacks- Rows C and D 43
Figure 3.15   Vault 3: The uppermost layer of coffin in stacks A-F 43
Figure 3.16   Vault 3: Matrix of the coffin stacks- Row A 44
Figure 3.17   Vault 3: Matrix of the coffin stacks- Row B 45
Figure 3.18   Vault 3: Matrix of the coffin stacks- Row C-F and the private tomb 3500 46
Figure 3.19   Vault 4: The uppermost layer of coffins in stacks A-E 47
Figure 3.20   Vault 4: Matrix of the coffin stacks- Row A 48
Figure 3.21   Vault 4: Matrix of the coffin stacks- Row B 49
Figure 3.22   Vault 4: Matrix of the coffin stacks- Row C 49
Figure 3.23   Vault 4: Matrix of the coffin stacks- Row D 50
Figure 3.24   Vault 4: Matrix of the coffin stacks- Ledge E 51
Figure 3.25   Vault 5: The uppermost layer of coffins in stacks A-G 51
Figure 3.26   Vault 5: Matrix of the coffin stacks- Row A 52
Figure 3.27   Vault 5: Matrix of the coffin stacks- Row B 52
Figure 3.28   Vault 5: Matrix of the coffin stacks- Rows C-G 53
Figure 3.29   Vault 6: The uppermost layer of coffins in stacks A-F 54
Figure 3.30   Vault 6: Matrix of the coffin stacks- Row A 55
Figure 3.31   Vault 6: Matrix of the coffin stacks- Row B 55
Figure 3.32   Vault 6: Matrix of the coffin stacks- Row C 56

Figure 3.33   Vault 6: Matrix of the coffin stacks- Row D 56
Figure 3.34   Vault 6: Matrix of the coffin stacks- Row E 57
Figure 3.35   Vault 6: Matrix of the coffin stacks- Row F 58
Figure 3.36   Vault 7: Matrix of the stacked coffins found at the back of the vault 59

Chapter 4
Figure 4.1   Map taken from Rocque's Plan of the Cities of London and Westminster and
               Borough of Southwark (1746). 62
Figure 4.2   Map taken from Horwood's Plan of the Cities of London and Westminster
               (3rd Edition 1813) 64
Figure 4.3   Map taken from Bacon's large-scale Ordnance Atlas of London and Suburbs (1888) 65

Chapter 5
Figure 5.1   Bar graph showing the number of interments within the crypt between 1803
               and 1856 96
Figure 5.2   Mortality curve of the crypt population shown as a percentage of the
               population 97
Figure 5.3   Mortality curves of the crypt population and the wider London population
               based on Bills of Mortality of 1848 97
Figure 5.4   Piechart showing sex distribution of subadult and adults based on *depositum*
               plate inscriptions (N = 707) 98
Figure 5.5   Mortality curves of the total crypt population and for males and for females 98
Figure 5.6   Piechart showing seasonality of death 99

Chapter 6
Figure 6.1   Recovery of skeletal elements (percentage of total bones of each element) 107
Figure 6.2   Named sample: Mortality profile based on osteological age (N=72) 109
Figure 6.3   Named sample: Mortality profile based on chronological age (N=72) 110
Figure 6.4   Named sample: Comparison between mortality profiles based on osteological
               and chronological age (N=72) 110
Figure 6.5   Named sample: Mean stature of males and females (N=15 and 20 respectively) 111
Figure 6.6   Named sample: True prevalence of osteoarthritis 118
Figure 6.7   Named sample: True prevalence of Schmorl's nodes on the thoracic and
               lumber spines. 120
Figure 6.8   Named sample: True prevalence of periostitis according to element 122
Figure 6.9   Unnamed sample: Mortality profile (N = 39) 130
Figure 6.10   Unnamed sample: True prevalence of osteoarthritis 132
Figure 6.11   Named and unnamed samples combined: Mortality profile based on osteological
               age (N=111) 137

Chapter 7
Figure 7.1   Skeleton 7081: comparison of age determinations using different ageing methods 142
Figure 7.2   Skeleton 2008: comparison of age determinations using different ageing methods 142
Figure 7.3   Skeleton 7045: comparison of age determinations using different ageing methods 143
Figure 7.4   Bar graph showing percentage accuracy in ageing methods (N=52) 143
Figure 7.5   Percentages of adult males and females estimated using different methodologies
               (N = 63) 144

Chapter 8
Figure 8.1   The elaborate coffin of the Duke of Wellington, displaying a full suite of coffin
               fittings (after May, 1996, 28) 152

Appendix 2
Figure A2.1   Regression: ageing using pubic symphysis (Todd) . . . .
Figure A2.2   Regression: ageing using pubic symphysis (Suchey & Brooks) 223
Figure A2.3   Regression: ageing using dental attrition 223
Figure A2.4   Regression: ageing using sternal rib end 224
Figure A2.5   Regression: ageing using cranial suture closure 224
Figure A2.4   Regression: ageing using auricular surface 225

List of Plates

Chapter 2

Plate 2.1   Main central vault looking S. The doorway leads through to the E-W vault and the main stairs. 9

Plate 2.2   E-W Vault to the S of the main central vault of the crypt, showing one of the main stairways at the E end of the vault 9

Plate 2.3   Central vault, N end, showing inserted modern stairs with Vault 7 to the left. To either side of the main vault, the fillets or buttresses in front of the main arch springs can be seen clearly. 9

Plate 2.4   Vault 1 looking E. Note the two cast iron uprights originally designed to support the racking for coffins. 12

Plate 2.5   Detail of iron strut from former shelving in Vault 1. 12

Plate 2.6   Stone post bases and extant cast iron posts for shelving in Vault 1. 12

Plate 2.7   Vault 2 looking E, showing recess with raised sill and blocked window 13

Plate 2.8   Vault 2 looking N, showing to the left the brick blocking of the opening through to Vault 1. 13

Plate 2.9   Vault 2, later features: to the left an iron bar supporting inserted brickwork, and to the right is a blocked rectilinear opening with an iron lining. 14

Plate 2.10   Vault 3 looking E, showing slightly skewed window recess with private tomb 3500 beneath. The semi-circular lid of the tomb is lying on the floor. 14

Plate 2.11   Vault 3 looking N, showing brick blocking between Vault 3 and Vault 2 14

Plate 2.12   Vault 4 looking W. The skewed window recess in the apse at the end of the vault is clear. 15

Plate 2.13   Vault 5 showing exposed brickwork where the 19th-century sealing wall has been removed 15

Plate 2.14   Vault 5 looking W, showing square end of vault and blocked window. To the left is the block archway to Vault 4. To the right the fillet or buttress in front of the arch spring can be seen clearly. 16

Plate 2.15   Vault 6 looking W. The block doorway to the base of the tower is clear. 16

Plate 2.16   Vault 6, details of the stone quoins of the archway to the tower. 16

Plate 2.17   Vault 7 looking N. The original wall and vault to the left are primary the wall to the right is a 20th-century insertion. The awkward positioning of the window at the north end of the vault is clear. 17

Plate 2.18   Vault 7 looking S. The S wall is built of 19th-century bricks, the E wall to the left is built of 20th-century bricks. 17

Plate 2.19   Vault 8 containing kitchen. View looking W. Note the apsidal end and skewed window opening. 18

Plate 2.20   Vault 8 looking E. 18

Chapter 3

Plate 3.1   Vault 2: Coffin stacks before removal 29

Plate 3.2   Vault 7: Arrangement of the coffins within the vault. 31

Chapter 4

Plate 4.1   St George's, Bloomsbury in c 2001 - viewed from Bloomsbury Way. 63

Plate 4.2   St George's, Bloomsbury from Hart Street (later renamed Bloomsbury Way) 66

Plate 4.3   Gin Lane by William Hogarth (1751), the spire of St George's church is clearly visible in the background. 67

Chapter 6

Plate 6.1   Skeleton 3027: real tooth crown on a gold peg 117
Plate 6.2   Skeleton 3027: Congenital hip displacement 118
Plate 6.3   Skeleton 5041: rheumatoid arthritis of the left foot 120
Plate 6.4   Skeleton 1041: DISH 121
Plate 6.5   Skeleton 5068: rickets and fracture of the fibular shaft 126
Plate 6.6   Skeleton 4032 wearing a gold partial denture 136
Plate 6.7   Skeleton 3044 wearing one set of swagged dentures. A second pair was found within
             his coffin 136

Chapter 5

Plate 8.1   Inner breastplate of Ann Porral (coffin 2013) showing the error in her Christian name.
             Mary has been deleted and Ann inserted. 150
Plate 8.2   Lid motifs BBM 13 (left) and BBM 8 (right) 161
Plate 8.3   Grip plates CCS 3 (left) and BBM 3 (right). 161
Plate 8.4   Lid motifs CCS 13 (left) and CCS 6 (right). 162
Plate 8.5   Grips BBM 1 (top left), BBM 2 (top right), and CCS 4 (bottom) 162
Plate 8.6   Lid motifs BBM 11 (left) and CCS 4 (right) 163
Plate 8.7   Lid motif BBM 1 (top) and BBM 12 (bottom). 164
Plate 8.8   Examples of wooden coffin cases showing coffin fittings and upholstery 165
Plate 8.9   Escutcheons CCS 13 (top left), CCS 12 (top right), BBM 8 (bottom left) and BBM 1
             (bottom right) 167
Plate 8.10   Discovery of the death masks in the coffin of Anna Stringfield (coffin 3064) 170
Plate 8.11   Plaster death masks and the cast of a hand found within the coffin of Anna
             Stringfield (coffin 3064) 171

List of Tables

Chapter 4

Table 4.1   Transcripts of selected memorial inscriptions from wall plaques within the interior
of the church of St George, Bloomsbury 68–9

Table 4.2   Summary memorial inscriptions from wall plaques within the interior of the church
of St George, Bloomsbury 70–73

Table 4.3   The Law 75

Table 4.4   Nineteenth-century rectors of St. George's, Bloomsbury (from George Clinch,
*Bloomsbury and St Giles's: past and present; with historical and antiquarian notes of the
vicinity*, London 1890, 129) 76

Table 4.5   The Church 77

Table 4.6   Army, Royal Navy, East India Company service and merchant marine 78

Table 4.7   Members of Parliament and politicians 81

Table 4.8   Diplomats, imperial administrators and civil servants 82

Table 4.9   Merchants, bankers, stockbrokers, etc 83

Table 4.10   Artisans, tradesmen and businessmen 85

Table 4.11   Librarians and staff of the British Museum 88

Table 4.12   Doctors of medicine and surgeons 89

Table 4.13   The Arts 90

Table 4.14   Distribution of known abodes of selected professions. (Street names in bold are
located to the south of the British Museum and Great Russell Street) 91

Chapter 5

Table 5.1   The number of interments of known date within the crypt of St. George's in each
decade between 1803-1856 (n = 682), based on *depositum* plate inscriptions, and
the total number of burials in the parish, recorded in parish registers between
1801 and 1840 (London Metropolitan Archives). (The figures in brackets give
numbers and %ages of crypt burials distributing undated burials proportionally) 95

Table 5.2   Distribution of age-at-death in the St. George's crypt population, in total and by
sex (N = 652). Percentages of males, females and total population are shown for
each age category. 96

Table 5.3   Comparative mortality rates within selected named burial assemblages and from
London Bills of Mortality 97

Table 5.4   Number of deaths per calendar month. Data from coffin plate inscriptions (n = 637) 99

Table 5.5   Recorded causes of death (n=263). The information is largely derived from the records
of the Bloomsbury searchers (LMA P82/GEO1/62) 100

Chapter 6

Table 6.1   Human bone: Age categories 104

Table 6.2   Quantification of coffins by vault, showing numbers of coffins in the named and
unnamed samples 105

Table 6.3   Named sample: Completeness and preservation (N = 72) 106

Table 6.4   Named sample: Preservation and location within the crypt 106

Table 6.5   Named sample: Completeness and location within the crypt 107

Table 6.6   Named sample: Osteological age and sex (includes two adults who have been
assigned sex based on biographical and not osteological data) 108

Table 6.7   Named sample: Chronological age and sex (redistributed totals) taken from
depositum plate inscriptions 109

Table 6.8   Stature in four contemporary skeletal assemblages 110

Table 6.9   Comparison of prevalence of dental disease (per tooth) in five contemporary
osteological assemblages 112

Table 6.10   Named sample: True prevalence of osteoarthritis in different joints 119
Table 6.11:   Named sample: True prevalence of affected vertebrae 119
Table 6.12:   Named sample: Summary of fractures by element 121
Table 6.13   Named sample: True prevalence of periostitis by element (lefts and right sides
              combined) 122
Table 6.14   Unnamed sample: Summary of the age, sex, stature, completeness and
              preservation (N = 39) 129
Table 6.15   Unnamed sample: Osteological age and sex (N = 39) 130
Table 6.16   Unnamed sample: Summary of the skeletal pathology (N = 39) 131
Table 6.17   Unnamed sample: True prevalence of osteoarthritis in different joints 133
Table 6.18   Unnamed sample: Summary of the dental pathology and dental interventions 135

Chapter 7
Table 7.1   Quantification of age assessment methods used per skeleton (N= 52) 139
Table 7.2   Quantification of ageing methods used (N= 52) 139
Table 7.3   Chronological age of adults compared with biological age (N = 52). All ages are
              given in years. 140
Table 7.4   Chronological age of subadults compared with biological age 144
Table 7.5   Sex determination per method used (N=63) 145

Chapter 8
Table 8.1   Overall level of preservation of triple coffins (N = 775) 151
Table 8.2   Summary of coffin fittings from the 18th and 19th century churches in England,
              based on typologies from Christ Church, Spitalfields 151–60
Table 8.3   Summary of known metals used for coffin fittings (N = 1623) 166
Table 8.4   New types of coffin fittings from St. George's church, Bloomsbury, and St. Luke's
              church, Islington, that could be matched stylistically (N = 9). N represents the number
              of examples found, with the number of dated examples shown in brackets. 168
Table 8.5   Date ranges of the new types of coffin fittings identified at St George's. N refers to
              total numbers found, with the number of dated examples in brackets 169

Appendix 2
Table A2.1   Multiple Linear Regression: weights of the age indicators 221

Summary

Oxford Archaeology (OA) undertook archaeological recording at the Grade I listed St George's Church, Bloomsbury, London, from April to June 2003, on behalf of the Parochial Church Council (PCC) of St George's Church, Bloomsbury, in advance of redevelopment of the crypt.

The work involved recording the structure of the crypt, and small scale investigations in the churchyard and recording of funerary architecture. The major work was the record of the 781 burials found in seven vaults leading off the central chamber of the crypt. These were recorded prior to their removal for reburial by Burial Ground Services.

All 781 coffins were triple coffins, mostly comprising an upholstered wooden case, a lead shell and an inner wooden coffin. The coffins and their associated fittings were recorded in full. The names of 86% of the assemblage were identified from *depositum* plate inscriptions, although some of these had become detached from their coffins.

Osteological analysis of 111 skeletons recovered from open lead coffins was undertaken on site. Where the identity of individuals was known (named sample; n=72) detailed analysis was undertaken, but where the identity was unknown (unnamed sample; n=39), a lower level of analysis was carried out.

The burials dated from 1804 to 1856, after which date the crypt was sealed. Documentary research was carried out on the named individuals. This confirmed that the burial population largely represented the wealthy upper middle classes residents of Bloomsbury, and numbered amongst them were many lawyers, doctors, M.Ps, imperial administrators, and Army and Navy officers. The population also included members of the staff of the nearby British Museum, including one Principal Librarian. In addition to the wealthier middle classes there were a number of tradesmen including butchers, grocers, builders, wine merchants and carpenters and a servant.

Palaeodemographics and disease patterns are consistent with this social picture. An interesting feature of this group was the wealth of evidence for dental surgery and prostheses and as such, the affluent population of St George's crypt, Bloomsbury provides a rare insight into this early period in the history of dentistry.

Acknowledgements

The project was managed by Angela Boyle who was also responsible for the project design. David Score ran the work in the field. Molyneux-Kerr Architects was the consultant on behalf of the Parochial Church Council of St George's, Bloomsbury. We are indebted to John Schofield, Archaeological Advisor to the London Diocesan Advisory Commitee, for his help and advice during the course of the project.

The burial clearance company was Burial Ground Services and we would particularly like to thank Peter Mitchell, Tony McHale, Karen McHale, Roy Lander and their team of Albanian workers for their hard work and co-operation under pressured working conditions. Osteological recording was carried out by Annsofie Witkin, Ceridwen Boston, Angela Boyle and Jennifer Kitch. Much of the day to day site work was carried out by Diana Mahoney, Jennifer Kitch, Tim Powers, Tom Davies, Chris Naisbett and Ali Yildirim. Illustrations were produced by Magda Wachnik, Georgina Slater and Laura Kirby.

The work was carried out on behalf of the Parochial Church Council of St George's church, Bloomsbury, whom Oxford Archaeology would like to thank for funding the project. The Report was edited by Ian Scott of Oxford Archaeology.

Chapter 1: Introduction

by Ceridwen Boston and Angela Boyle

PROJECT BACKGROUND

The Parochial Church Council (PCC) of St George's Church, Bloomsbury, commissioned Oxford Archaeology (OA) to undertake an archaeological desk-based assessment in advance of major restoration of the church. The proposed works comprised the clearance of coffins within the crypt and restoration of the crypt to its original form; reinstatement of the steps to the south of the tower; installation of a wheelchair platform lift; demolition of the sacristy; the siting of gate piers; modification of existing drainage within the north churchyard, and the excavation of six 75 mm diameter boreholes and four test pits within the churchyard and crypt, the latter to done be under archaeological supervision. Between April and June 2003, during a ten-week crypt clearance programme, 781 early 19th-century coffins were recorded by Oxford Archaeology (OA) and removed for reburial by Burial Ground Services (BGS). OA undertook archaeological watching briefs during the excavation of the four test pits and in four other areas within the churchyard (Areas 5-8). This report presents the results of these archaeological interventions.

Location and topography

The Grade I listed church is located in the parish of St George, Bloomsbury, in the London Borough of Camden at NGR TQ 3025 8150. It is bounded to the south-east by Bloomsbury Way (formerly Hart Street), to the south-west by Museum Street, to the north-west by Little Russell Street and to the north-east by Bury Place (Fig. 1.1).

The geology of the area is Lynch Hill gravel (BGS Sheet 256), which is one of a number of gravels forming part of the post-diversionary Thames River Terrace deposits; gravel, sandy and clayey in part. Test Pit 4 within the crypt of the church confirmed that the foundations of the church rest on gravel at a depth of 1.38 m below the present level of the crypt floor (see Fig. 2.7). This geology was overlaid by alluvial clay.

Restoration programme

Prior to restoration, the church was in a bad state of repair. Restoration works commenced in the spring of 2003. The work programme comprised the following elements:

- The main standing fabric of the church would not be altered but would be repaired. The structure of the church had already been subject to non-destructive analysis and a full digital survey including ashlar joints.

- The steps to the south of the tower, constructed as part of the original design but later removed, were to be reinstated.

- A wheelchair platform lift would be installed adjacent to the steps.

- The existing 1870s sacristy building to the north-east of the site was to be demolished and a new building, designed to allow full access to the undercroft and church level from Little Russell Street, was to be constructed in its place.

- The gate piers and railings to Bloomsbury Way were to be reinstated in their original location.

- New gates and railings were to be sited at the boundary of the North Courtyard.

- Some modifications to the existing drainage within the north courtyard would be made in order to drain new WCs within the Little Russell Street entrance building and the undercroft. Otherwise, it was proposed that the existing extensive service runs were reused.

- New electrical, gas and water services were to be laid in from Little Russell Street across the north courtyard.

- Four 75 mm diameter boreholes and six 600 mm^2 trial pits were to be excavated in the positions shown on Figure 2.3. The latter works were to be undertaken under archaeological supervision.

- The undercroft was to be restored to close to its original form. This involved the removal of all interments from within the crypt and removal of later brick walls sealing the vaults from the central chamber, and separating adjacent vaults.

ARCHAEOLOGICAL PROGRAMME

Desk-based assessment

In the first instance, the Parochial Church Council (PCC) of St George's Church, Bloomsbury, commissioned OA to undertake an archaeological desk-based assessment of the proposed restoration works at the church. This document formed an initial stage of archaeological investigation that was intended to inform any future mitigation strategies. As requested, OA supplied a proposed archaeological mitigation strategy as part of this document. The assessment also included a site visit, which was carried out on 8th January 2003. The probable number of interments within the crypt could not be established from parish burial records as these did not distinguish between those buried within the crypt and those interred in the burial ground. A number of memorial plaques recorded in the church explicitly stated that the deceased had been interred within the crypt but these represented only a handful of individuals.

Small holes were made in the brick walls sealing three of the seven vaults prior to the commence-

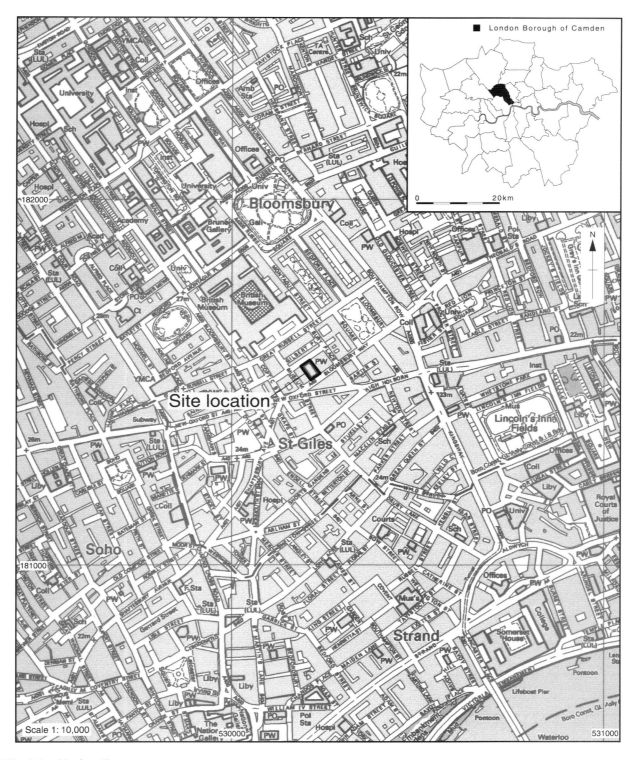

Fig. 1.1   *Site location*

ment of site works. The outlines of multiple layers of coffins were clearly visible in Vault 1. They appeared to be aligned west-east and were covered by a layer of charcoal, sand and rubble. Charcoal and considerable quantities of rubble were clearly visible in Vault 2, although there were no coffins visible. A number of north-south aligned coffins could clearly be seen in Vault 3. Again they were covered by charcoal and rubble. Details of a triple shelled wood-lead-wood coffin could be discerned. Coffin stud decoration was clear and the condition of the coffin appeared to be good. The total number of coffins could not be determined on the basis on these explorations.

Archaeological mitigation

OA undertook the archaeological recording at the church of St George, Bloomsbury, between April and June 2003.

The mechanical excavation of four test pits was archaeologically monitored by OA and the findings are reported in Chapter 2. The structure of the church had already been the subject of non-destructive analysis and a full digital survey including a record of ashlar joints. Because the vaults had not been not accessible when this survey was carried out, additional limited recording of the structure of the crypt was undertaken by OA prior to and following the removal of the coffins. The results of this work are also presented in Chapter 2.

The archaeological recording action within the crypt took place between 21st April and 20th June 2003. OA were in attendance on Burial Ground Services (BGS). All archaeological and osteological recording took place during site works prior to re-interment of the 781 coffins and human remains at St Pancras cemetery, East Finchley.

Project aims

The main aim of this archaeological recording action was to record and interpret as much detail as possible within the parameters of a relatively rapid exhumation and re-interment exercise. It was believed that the archaeological data collected would contribute to the history and development of late Georgian and early Victorian funerary trends and the demography of the population of the crypt.

Archaeological aims

Specific objectives of the archaeological work included:

- The osteological recording of the human remains from breeched coffins prior to their removal by BGS.

- Recording of coffins, fittings and contents of breached coffins that will contribute to the understanding of the history and development of funeral trends.

- Creation of an updated typology of coffin fittings.

- Collection of documentary data from *depositum* plate inscriptions that will contribute to the understanding of the demography of the population of the crypt.

- The creation of a database of the inscriptions and assessment and analysis of the inscriptions data.

- Documentary research to enhance and augment information recorded from memorial plaques within the church, the International Genealogical Index (IGI) and the Trade Directories.

- Establishment of the stratigraphic sequence of burials.

- Recording of the vault structures and their contents.

- Full reporting and dissemination.

Osteological aims

The osteological aims are detailed below.

- To establish the biologically determined demographic structure of the sample.

- To investigate and interpret pathological manifestations and patterns within the sample.

- To compare the biological profile of the sample with the historical picture of the group provided by documentary sources.

- To compare the mortality and morbidity of the sample with other populations similar in date and type.

- To blind test osteological ageing and sexing methods in the named sample.

- To provide a detailed record of the skeletal group prior to its re-interment.

Recording system

A single context recording system was not thought to be appropriate for the coffin record. Therefore, the focus of recording became the coffin. Each interment was assigned a unique number from a continuous running sequence. The same number was assigned to the coffin, any associated fittings, skeleton and grave goods. This system had previously been applied successfully during the archaeological watching brief at St Bartholomew's, Penn, Wolverhampton (Boyle 2004), and the archaeological excavation of the churchyard and crypt clearance at St Luke's church, Islington (Boyle *et al.* 2005), which were carried out by OA in attendance upon Necropolis.

All other contexts (i.e. structures, overlying soil layers and iron and wooden coffin supports) within the crypt were assigned individual context numbers. These were numbered according to their provenance within each of the seven vaults, the first digit of the context number signifying the vault in which it was discovered. Specialised recording forms were available for the recording of both coffins and skeletons. Written descriptions were recorded on *proforma* sheets and comprised both factual data and interpretative elements. Charnel and disarticulated remains were not recorded although they were carefully collected for reburial by the enabling contractor, BGS.

Plans

The uppermost layer of the coffin stack within each vault was recorded in plan at a scale of 1:20. Coffins lower in the stacks were not individually recorded in plan. Matrices of their stratigraphic position relative to other coffins, however, were recorded and are presented in Chapter 3. In this way the vertical and horizontal relationship between the coffins was documented. After each vault had been emptied of coffins, it was planned at a scale of 1:50. A register of plans was kept.

Photographic record

A black and white and colour (35 mm transparency) photographic record was maintained. The photographic record also included shots to illustrate more generally the nature of the archaeological work. In addition, a digital photograph of each coffin was taken. Unfortunately due to the poor lighting and the excessive charcoal dust within the crypt, the quality of much of the photography was poor. Photographs were recorded on OA Photographic Record Sheets, and digital photographs were renumbered with their context number.

Palaeopathology of particular interest was photographed on site before reburial, as were well preserved coffin fittings and previously unidentified fitting types.

Recording the coffins

Coffins and coffin fittings

Wooden and lead coffins and any associated fittings, including fixing nails, were recorded on a *proforma* coffin recording sheet. All surviving coffin fittings were recorded in detail by reference to the published corpus of material from Christ Church, Spitalfields (Reeve and Adams 1993) as well as the unpublished catalogues of material from St Nicholas, Sevenoaks (Boyle 1995), St Bartholomew's, Penn (Boyle 2004) and St Luke's church, Islington (Boyle *et al.* 2005). Where individual types could not be paralleled, they were drawn and/or photographed, and assigned a style number, prefixed by BBM (eg. BBM 1). In addition, there are detailed coffin recording sheets with supporting illustrative and photographic records.

Sealed Coffins

It was anticipated that there would be very few fully intact sealed coffins, due to the environmental conditions, time and vandalism. Each coffin was inspected prior to lifting. Where coffins have already been perforated due to collapse, oxidisation or vandalism, and the decency of the occupant has already been compromised, the remains were collected and analysed on site by osteoarchaeologists. In the event that some coffins remained largely intact, irrespective of whether they were sealed or not, these coffins were not be opened. Burials with substantial soft tissue survival were not osteologically analysed.

Osteological methodology

Low-resolution recording

Skeletons that could not be identified by name, age and/or sex were subjected to low-resolution recording. This includes a skeletal and dental inventory, age and sex assessments, gross pathological observations, and basic metrical recording for use in the determination of stature and sex. The primary aim was to provide enough information to reconstruct the demography of the skeletal assemblage. These skeletons formed the Unnamed Sample discussed in subsequent chapters.

High-resolution recording

Individuals whose names were recorded on *depositum* plates were recorded in more detail. This entailed compiling a skeletal and dental inventory, analysis of skeletal preservation and completeness, age and sex estimation, detailed metrical recording, detailed descriptions of pathology and differential diagnosis, and a study of the non-metric traits. These individuals formed the Named Sample.

Ethical and religious considerations

The crypt has not been used for burial since its prohibition in 1856. However, as the church is still consecrated it was necessary to obtain a faculty prior to commencement of works. The Desk Based Assessment was submitted in support of the application for a faculty.

For reasons of decency and dignity, the faculty stipulated that sealed coffins should not be opened and that such coffins should be sleeved on site and removed for reburial. The ethical and religious implications were of primary concern throughout the project. The entire site was secured from the general public and controlled access was in operation for the duration of the site works. All staff involved in the exhumation of the remains were expected to behave with care and attention, showing respect for the dead at all times.

The burials represented the remains of past parishioners of the church of St George and thus particular consideration had to be afforded to the sensitivities of any individuals who have connections with St George's during all excavation and reinterment works. All sealed or substantially sealed lead coffins were to remain unopened, were sleeved on site prior to removal for reburial, as stipulated in the faculty. Ethical considerations – opening undamaged coffins was unnecessarily invasive in the case of such recent burials – lay behind this condition in the faculty.

The contents of open or badly damaged coffins were inspected by archaeologists, subject to a health and safety evaluation. Human remains were then collected for osteological examination. All attempts were made to re-unite the skeletons that had undergone osteological analysis with their coffin. The coffin and skeleton were sleeved together and were reburied as an entity. All grave goods and personal effects (eg. dentures) were reinterred with the rest of the burial. In this way the integrity of each burial was maintained.

Health and safety

OA was required to demonstrate that that they had planned safe working practices by providing the Planning Supervisor and Principal Contractor with a Risk Assessment and developed Health and Safety plan of all work to be undertaken by the archaeological team, a current Health and Safety policy, and detailed specification for the archaeological watching brief. The Health and Safety at Work Act 1974, under which the Personal Protective Equipment at Work Regulations are made, was complied with at all times by OA. All work was carried out according to the requirements of *Health and Safety at Work, etc. Act 1974*, *The Management of Health and Safety Regulations 1992*, the OA Health and Safety Policy, any main contractor requirements and all other relevant Health and Safety regulations.

Funerary archaeology presents a specific and complex range of hazards. Human remains, particularly soft tissue, have the potential to pose infection risks to those who handle them (Healing *et al.* 1995), but the use of appropriate protective clothing and observance of *Control of Substances Hazardous to Health* regulations should protect handlers. Disease present in the 18th and 19th centuries included plague, cholera, typhoid and tuberculosis (all notifiable diseases today), but these are unlikely to survive long in a buried cadaver (ibid.). The risks posed by smallpox and anthrax are less easily defined. Contracting smallpox is remote possibility but the potential threat to the population at large is such that it must be taken seriously (Young 1998; Kneller 2003, 18). The risk of contracting anthrax from cadaveric human tissue is as yet unproven but is unlikely to be significant, but well-preserved horsehair or woollen materials used in the coffin pads, pillows and packing may pose a greater health risk.

During the crypt clearance, all staff wore protective clothing at all times when handling coffins, coffin contents and human remains. This included chemical protection suits and latex gloves. The highest health risk from body tissue is presented by those individuals within sealed lead coffins and where preservation of soft tissue may be good. In addition, the increased risk of post-traumatic stress disorder (Reeve and Cox 1999, 168), made it undesirable to deliberately open sealed lead coffins.

The presence of lead coffins in all the burials ensured that in many cases some soft tissue and/or coffin liquor was present within the unsealed coffins. For the most part, individuals were largely or completely skeletonised, with soft tissue restricted to hair and toenails. Coffin liquor was found in the majority of coffins. This viscous black liquid was mixed with the remains of textile coffin linings, shrouds, sawdust and bran and pads lining the base of the coffins. These hazards were treated as potentially severe and appropriate protective systems were employed.

A potential respiratory health risk identified during the crypt clearance was charcoal dust encountered when charcoal layers that sealed sand and overlay all coffin stacks was disturbed. In order to minimise the risk facemasks were worn during any disturbance. Attempts to dampen down the charcoal were made. The disturbance of so many lead coffins within the confined space of the vault created the risk of lead dust inhalation, and the accumulation of toxic levels of lead within the body. Serum blood levels were not taken on archaeological staff, as the duration of the works was deemed too short. Sanitary and washing facilities were provided on site and strict hand washing before meals and before leaving site was observed. Strict adherence to the site Health and Safety policy produced by Burial Ground Services was observed at all times. Personal protective clothing worn on site was not worn outside the compound area.

Coffin liquor, disposable paper suits and respiratory protection equipment are all classified as clinical waste and were collected and incinerated by approved contractors. Lead can be stored and recycled. Rotting wood from coffins can be disposed of by agreement with the local waste regulation authority. The disposal of decontaminating fluids into sewers requires approval and possibly a licence. All of the above were the responsibility of BGS. Lead coffins may weigh up to one third of a ton. Their removal was undertaken by BGS.

Structure of the report

Chapter 1 provides the background to the project, aims of the current restoration project and of the archaeological mitigation programme. Chapter 2 describes the structure of the church crypt and the archaeological watching briefs undertaken within the churchyard. Chapter 3 describes the stratigraphic arrangement of the coffins within Vaults 1-7. Chapter 4 discusses the historical evidence for the individuals buried in the crypt and identified from *depositum* plates. Chapter 5 considers the demography of the crypt population. Chapter 6 presents the osteological analysis of the skeletal assemblage. Chapter 7 examines the reliability of the methods used for ageing skeletons. Chapter 8 considers funerary practice and looks in detail at the coffins and their fittings. Finally, Chapter 9 presents some overall conclusions about the data and evaluates the success of the particular methodological approach applied to St George's, particularly in relation to the reburial debate.

The main text is supported by four appendices, two print appendices – Appendix 1: Alphabetical lists of named individuals known from coffin plates with supporting evidence; Appendix 2: Statistical analysis discussed in Chapter 7 – and two appendices available via the internet only – Appendix 3: New coffin fitting styles recovered from St George's church (Figs. A3.1–A3.49); Appendix 4: Catalogue of all coffins and fittings recorded in the crypt.

Chapter 2: Historic buildings recording of the crypt and archaeological investigations within the churchyard

by Jon Gill, Ceridwen Boston and Jane Phimester

INTRODUCTION

This chapter presents the results of the historic building investigation within the crypt, and the evidence recorded in the four test pits and four small area excavations (Fig. 2.3). The test pits formed part of the restoration works, and were excavated to ascertain the underlying geology and below-ground structures within the church and churchyard.

RECORDING THE CRYPT

Background

St George's in Bloomsbury is a Grade I listed building and is therefore by definition of national significance for its architecture and history. Although the archaeological works undertaken at St George's principally centred on recording the burials, which were cleared from the crypt, they included an investigation of the fabric of parts of the church itself.

The proposed construction works largely comprised repairs and minor alterations to the church rather than substantial changes, particularly to the primary fabric. The works included the reinstatement of a set of steps at the south end of the building, which had been part of the church's primary layout but which had been removed subsequently, the insertion of a wheelchair platform adjacent to the south steps, and the demolition of a Sacristy dating from the 1870s to the north-east of the site.

Aims, objectives and methodology

The principal aim of the work was to produce a record of the Church's crypt, (together with several other smaller areas) after the clearance of the vaults, but before the start of the principal conversion works. This work was intended both to record the structure and to enhance understanding of the building through investigating its construction, use and alteration. The other principal aim of the work was to make the results of the investigation and the archive publicly accessible.

The historic building investigation was limited in scope and was not intended to provide a fully comprehensive record of the entire church. The recording was entirely internal and did not include the main body of the church. A comprehensive architectural survey had previously been undertaken by Michael Gallie and Partners, Chartered Measured Building Surveyors, but much of the crypt had been inaccessible because of the sealed vaults. OA was only required to investigate the crypt. The results of this survey are presented below. It concentrated on the main areas directly affected by the development works and, in particular, the church's crypt and the individual vaults which were cleared and exposed during the works. Interred coffins were cleared from seven previously sealed vaults in the crypt and, although the structural recording centred around these areas it was also extended to the rest of the crypt and the other vaults which were not sealed with coffins.

The main recording was undertaken after the burials had been removed from the vaults and comprised drawn, photographic and descriptive elements. The drawn survey was partly based on an existing architect's survey plan of the crypt with descriptive annotation added to explain and interpret the construction, phasing and use of the crypt.

In addition to the plan, a cross section through several of the vaults was produced to further record the structure. The photographic survey of the church was undertaken using 35 mm film (black and white prints and colour slides) and each film was given a unique number to correspond with the wider archaeological project at St George's. The written survey provided further analytical and descriptive detail.

In addition to the record of the crypt and vaults a series of structural recording works were also undertaken within the churchyard where excavations revealed features. Each of these were planned, photographed and described (see Archaeological watching briefs, below).

Summary history of the building

St George's is an architectural masterpiece built to the designs of Nicholas Hawksmoor under the Fifty New Churches Act of 1711. Construction began in 1716 (Cherry and Pevsner 1998, 257-58) and the church was consecrated in January 1730 although it was only fully completed in 1731. The site of the church was already hemmed in by houses when it was originally constructed and Hawksmoor's design was therefore dictated by the restrictions of the space. A grand Corinthian portico faces south onto Bloomsbury Way although the main entrances to the building are to the west side, on the north and south faces of St Georges' famous west tower. The tower has a stepped spire which was inspired by antiquity, and in particular by Pliny the Elder's description of the mausoleum of Halicarnassus (*Natural History*, 36, iv, 30-31), and at its top is a statue of George I.

In 1781 the church underwent alterations, which included the removal of the altar from the east to the north side and the replacement of a north gallery with one to the east. Due to the expanding population of the parish and the limited space available in the churchyard it was decided in 1803 to allow bodies in lead coffins to be interred in the previously unused crypt and vaults of the church. Due to the poor condition of many of the coffins it was decided in 1844 to seal them into a side vault with brickwork. This was taken further in 1856 when further burials in the crypt were prohibited and the entrances to the vaults with coffins were sealed. The crypt has since been used for a variety of purposes including a boys' club meeting place and more recently for storage.

The Church underwent a further restoration in 1870-1 by George Edmund Street, one of the giants of the Victorian Gothic movement. These works included the removal of the east gallery which had been added in 1781 as well as a primary west gallery and also the removal of statues of lions and unicorns from the base of the stepped west tower. These statues have been reinstated during the current works to the church.

Description of the vaults
(Figs 2.1-2.2; Plates 2.1-2.)

Introduction
The main body of the crypt comprises a long, vaulted north to south room along the spine of the building with five smaller vaults to each side (Plate 2.1). In addition there is a further, separate east to west vault at the south end of the crypt (Plate 2.2), which incorporated a staircase at either end. These stairs form the main entrance to the crypt. There is a short passageway between this east-west vault and the main body of the crypt (Plate 2.1). At the north end of the crypt there is also a single set of concrete steps at which was inserted in the 20th century (Plate 2.3) together with a further contemporary vault (7). Vault 7 was immediately to the west the new stairs.

Prior to the restoration works six of the ten side vaults were sealed and contained coffins interred in the 19th century. Vault 7, was created in the 20th century, apparently to house coffins moved from elsewhere in the crypt. The vault numbering system used in the building recording follows that of the rest of the project so that Vaults 1-7 are those which contained interments. A further five vaults, numbered Vaults 8-12 (context numbers 9001-9005),

have also been recorded as part of the project.

The main structure of the vaults and crypt is primary and generally comprises yellow stock bricks with some pink elements (Fig. 2.1). Most of the primary brickwork has a stone skirting or plinth, and a string course (15 cm high, 2.03 m above ground) at the height of the arch springs or imposts (Fig. 2.2). The side walls of each vault are supported by full length fillets or buttresses built of brick constructed in front of the arch springs where the vaults are supported (see Plates 2.3 and 2.14) . The skirting and string courses do not continue around these fillets giving the impression that they are secondary additions to strengthen the structure, but, on close inspection it is clear that they are keyed into the rest of the primary structure and are original features. The 19th-century brick walls, which had sealed the vaults, had been almost entirely removed prior to recording.

The floor of the crypt and the individual vaults was largely covered with stone flags of various sizes (e.g. 40 cm x 70 cm) in an irregular, but not totally random, pattern. In a few small areas these stones had been removed and towards the south-east corner (adjacent to Vaults 2 and 3) they had been replaced by brick pavers.

Vault 1 (Plates 2.4-2.6)
Vault 1 is at the centre of the east side of the crypt and other than the central room is the largest vault (*c.* 6 m wide x 9 m deep x 4 m tall). It has a shallow basket-arch vault and a semi-circular east end, in the form of an apse, within which are two blocked former windows (Plate 2.4). These have moulded stone sills, semi-circular heads and primary ashlar quoins although the quoins are partially obscured by plaster (probably primary) which covers much of the walls and vault. The windows were almost certainly blocked in the first half of the 19th century when the coffins were interred and the vault was sealed. The plaster has come away from parts of the walls but it remains largely intact to the ceiling. This plaster was abutted by the mid 19th-century wall which sealed the vault and therefore clearly pre-dates the blocking. Vault 1 would originally have been linked to the adjacent vaults to the north and south by tall semi-circular arched passages but each of these has been blocked. The passage to Vault 2 to the south was blocked with 19th-century stock bricks which probably date to when the vault was sealed. The passage to the north has older, probably 18th-century, red bricks, which abutted the plastered jambs of the passage. Unlike the passage to the south this infill wall is plastered.

Despite the fact that the coffins had been entirely removed from the vault when the building recording was undertaken some evidence of the former shelves and racking which supported the coffins did survive. This included six tapering, full-height, circular section cast-iron posts (8 cm diameter at the base, 5 cm diameter at mid point) on

Plate 2.1   Main central vault looking S. The doorway leads through to the E-W vault and the main stairs.

Plate 2.2   E-W Vault to the S of the main central vault of the crypt, showing one of the main stairways at the E end of the vault

Plate 2.3   Central vault, N end, showing inserted modern stairs with Vault 7 to the left. To either side of the main vault, the fillets or buttresses in front of the main arch springs can be seen clearly.

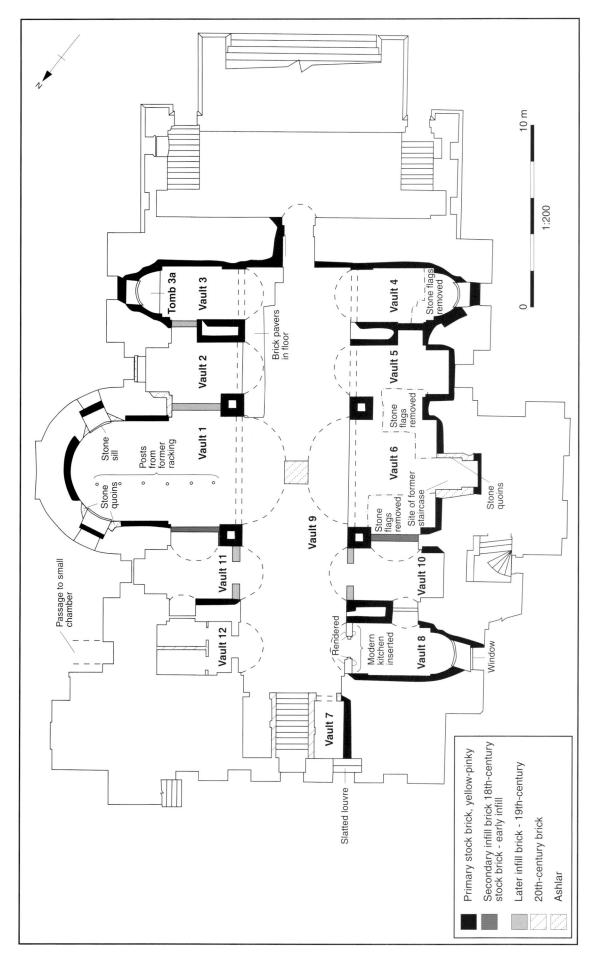

Tomb 3a

Vault 3

Vault 2

Vault 1

Stone
sill

Stone
quoins

Posts
from former
racking

Passage to small
chamber

Vault 11

Vault 12

Slatted louvre

Vault 7

Rendered

Modern
kitchen
inserted

Vault 8

Window

Vault 10

Vault 9

Stone
flags
removed

Site of former
staircase

Stone
quoins

Vault 6

Stone
flags
removed

Vault 5

Vault 4

Stone flags
removed

Brick pavers
in floor

N

0   1:200   10 m

Primary stock brick, yellow-pinky

Secondary infill brick 18th-century
stock brick - early infill

Later infill brick - 19th-century

20th-century brick

Ashlar

Fig. 2.1 Plan of crypt showing brickwork and ashlar work

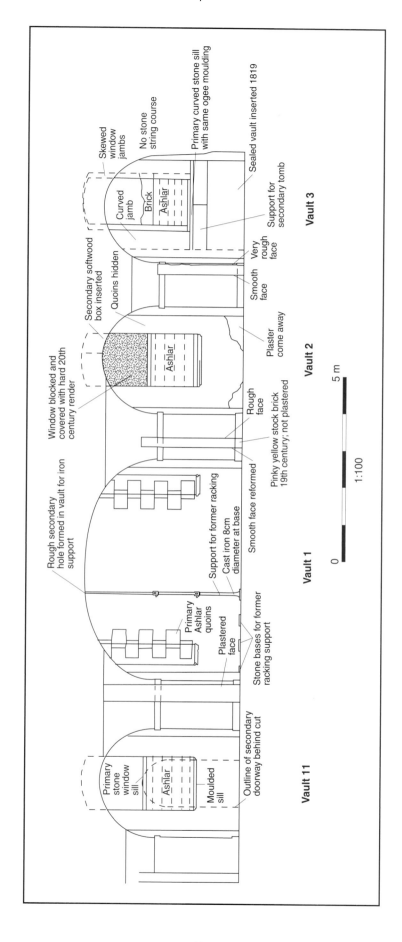

Fig. 2.2   Cross-section through east side of vaults in crypt

Plate 2.4   Vault 1 looking E. Note the two cast iron uprights originally designed to support the racking for coffins.

Plate 2.5   Detail of iron strut from former shelving in Vault 1

Plate 2.6   Stone post bases and extant cast iron posts for shelving in Vault 1

the north side of the central line of the vault (Plate 2.4). Each post has two brackets (at 1.17 m and 2.3 m above the floor) that would have supported shelves to hold the coffins (Plate 2.5). The posts are set on inserted, shallow stone bases, and their tops continued vertically through small holes cut into the ceiling of the vault. In the northern half of the room are 15 further similar stone bases on which further cast iron posts would presumably have sat (Plate 2.6). Each base has a square hole for the former post but there are no corresponding holes in the vault ceiling above each base. It may be that the main structural supports were those posts that survive and the shelving was additionally supported by lesser struts that did not continue to the ceiling.

Vault 2 (Plates 2.7-2.9)

Vault 2 immediately to the south of Vault 1, is substantially smaller (2.4 m wide x 5.1 m long x 3.6 m tall) and, unlike Vault 1, has a semi-circular vaulted ceiling. The vault has a rectangular plan and at its east end it has a recess with a deep stone sill at the base with a moulded lip and a higher stone sill indicating the base of a former window which was blocked with bricks almost certainly when the vault was sealed in the mid 19th century (Plate 2.7). The vault again has a stone plinth and

string course around the primary walls but these did not extend around the infill walls blocking the archways to the two adjacent vaults to the north and south (Plate 2.8). The northern archway is smaller than that to the south, and reflects the relative size of the adjacent vaults. The blocking is 19th-century brickwork. The blocking wall to the south has smooth faced brickwork in Vault 2, but the opposite face in Vault 3 was rough suggesting that Vault 3 was sealed before Vault 2. The west wall, which sealed the vault from the main crypt, was formed of similar 19th-century bricks and the removal of this in the current works has shown that the historic plaster continued beneath it.

Among the minor features of interest in Vault 2 include two secondary alterations in the vault ceiling towards the south-east corner (Plate 2.9). The first alteration is located at the intersection of the wall and the barrel vault and appears to comprise a wrought iron bar below an area of brick infill 45 cm wide. This brickwork does not appear to be rebuilding or patching due to a structural fault, but rather the filling of a hole. Presumably the hole was formed after the vault was sealed to give access into the vault. The second feature is in the vault ceiling itself and appears to be a sheet-iron lining around a former opening or feature (e.g. vent or shaft). The lining is bolted to the ceiling and forms a square with a large square hole (now blocked) in the centre.

Plate 2.7   Vault 2 looking E, showing recess with raised sill and blocked window

Plate 2.8   Vault 2 looking N, showing to the left the brick blocking of the opening through to Vault 1

Plate 2.9 Vault 2, later features: to the left an iron bar supporting inserted brickwork, and to the right is a blocked rectilinear opening with an iron lining

Another feature is a small iron candle holder in-situ on the primary wall adjacent to the blocked archway to the north.

Vault 3 (Plates 2.10-2.11)

This vault, which is at the south-east corner of the crypt, has a semi-circular vaulted ceiling and is 3 m wide by 5.75 m long by 3.6 m tall. It has a semi-circular, apse-like east end with a curved, ogee-moulded sill and a former window that would have been blocked when the vault was sealed (Plate 2.10). The jambs of the window are skewed slightly south-wards so that the window fits into the building's external, architectural composition and the base of the window itself is 90 cm above the main deep sill (reflecting the external ground level). Between the deep sill with the moulded lip and the window sill itself is primary ashlar. The former window continues up in a light well and there is a somewhat awkward intersection created by the semi-circular apse, the vault and the skewed window. There are curved ashlar quoins to the window jambs but these have been plastered over and are largely hidden. The former base of the window is indicated by a plain sill and above this are 19th-century yellow/pink bricks with chalky mortar. This brick is contemporary with the blocked passage to Vault 2 (detailed above) (Plate 2.11).

The vault is largely covered with probable primary plaster and this continues beneath the now removed wall, which sealed the west end of the vault.

Within the semi-circular apse at the east end of the vault are the remains of an early 19th-century family tomb (Plate 2.10) and the walls within the tomb are plastered, unlike the brick insertions associated with the tomb (for example for the lintel). The fact that the plastered walls continued into the

Plate 2.10 Vault 3 looking E, showing slightly skewed window recess with private tomb 3500 beneath. The semi-circular lid of the tomb is lying on the floor

Plate 2.11 Vault 3 looking N, showing brick blocking between Vault 3 and Vault 2

tomb confirmed that the plaster pre-dated the tomb. The three interments in this tomb were dated 1806, 1811 and 1819.

Vault 4 (Plate 2.12)

Vault 4 is at the south-west corner of the crypt and is opposite Vault 3. The two vaults are similar. It is 3 m wide by 5.6 m long and it has a semi-circular apse-

Plate 2.12   Vault 4 looking W. The skewed window recess in the apse at the end of the vault is clear

like west end with a blocked window the jambs of which is again skewed slightly to link with the external opening (Plate 2.12). The window again has stone quoins, a low sill with moulded lip, a higher sill, which indicated the former base of the window, and 19th-century brick infill above this. Beneath the brick infill and the window sill is primary ashlar. The stone flags have been largely removed from the west end of the floor and replaced with brick pavers. The primary passage to Vault 5 to the north had been blocked with rough 19th-century pinky yellow stock bricks. At the former location of the mid 19th-century wall which sealed the east side of the vault there are only faint traces of the former plaster pre-dating the sealing of the vault and much less than in the other vaults.

Vault 5 (Plates 2.13-2.14)

Vault 5 is immediately to the north of Vault 4, on the west side of the crypt and has similar detailing – stone-flag floor, stone plinth and string course – to the other vaults. The walls and ceiling of the vault are plastered but as in Vault 4 there is relatively little plaster on the walls and ceiling where the sealing wall has been removed (Plate 2.13). The west end of Vault 5 is squared and has a blocked window, as in the other vaults, but unlike elsewhere, the brick infill is flush with the wall and there is no recess or sill (Plate 2.14). Furthermore, the former window has no stone quoins. There are two surviving iron candle holders in Vault 5, one on the north wall and one on the south. These comprise an L-shaped bar strapped to the wall with a loop at the furthest point from the wall in which the candle would have sat.

Vault 6 (Plates 2.15-2.16)

Vault 6 is the large vault at the centre of the west side of the crypt. It has a similar profile to Vault 1 with a tall, flattened basket arch (6 m wide by 4 m tall) but it is less deep (4.75 m) and its west end is

Plate 2.13   Vault 5 showing exposed brickwork where the 19th-century sealing wall has been removed

Plate 2.14   Vault 5 looking W, showing square end of vault and blocked window. To the left is the block archway to Vault 4. To the right the fillet or buttress in front of the arch spring can be seen clearly

Plate 2.15   Vault 6 looking W. The block doorway to the base of the tower is clear

squared rather than semi-circular (Plate 2.15). At the centre of the west wall is an opening and a 2.3 m long vaulted passage which is blocked at its west end (Plate 2.15). There is a large patch of render towards the top of this blocking and this passage led to the base of the tower and to the curved stair-case giving access to ground level. The passage has stone quoins and stone voussoirs to the arch (Plate 2.16). At the west end of Vault 6 is a 25 cm^2 hole in the crest of the main, tall vault with a hard cement surround which clearly must have linked to something on the floor above (possibly a vent). As with the other vaults, there were originally two open passages linking with the adjacent vaults but only that to the south remained open. The northern passage has been blocked with a relatively early, probably 18th-century, infill brick. As elsewhere, much of the floor is covered with stone flags but these have been removed from around the two former passages to the adjacent vaults. On the north side of the vault is a small looped candle holder, similar to that in Vault 5.

Plate 2.16   Vault 6, details of the stone quoins of the archway to the tower

Vault 7 (Plates 2.17-2.18)

Vault 7 is a small vault located at the northern end of the crypt immediately to the west of the central staircase at this end of the building (see Plate 2.3). Both the staircase and vault are of mid 20th-century date and subdivide the northern 3.5 m of the main vaulted crypt. The ceiling and west wall of Vault 7 are primary and plastered (Plate 2.17). The east wall is formed with mid 20th-century bricks but the south wall is formed with reused 19th-century bricks (Plate 2.18). It may be that the vault was originally open at its south end and that it was later blocked with the reused bricks. Regular holes in the west and east walls may be evidence of a former racking system for supporting coffins.

The northern end of the western wall of Vault 7 awkwardly abuts a window despite these both apparently being primary features (Plate 2.17). This must reflect the conflict between the internal layout, based on the practical needs and use of the crypt, and the desired external aesthetics or architectural composition. The window in the west part of the north wall continues to the west behind the primary west wall of the vault. This window has a primary moulded stone sill but it is only the width of the opening in Vault 7. The east jamb of the window has stone quoins and the window has a set of louvre

slats fixed shut, rather than being sealed with brick infill.

The fact that the window is blocked with slats rather than being permanently sealed with bricks is clearly a reflection of the fact that this vault is a 20th-century alteration, constructed long after the end of interments in the crypt. Presumably the vault was created to accommodate coffins moved here from elsewhere in the crypt; the most likely place being the adjacent vault 8 (context 9001) to the south-west.

Vault 8 (context 9001) (Plates 2.19-2.23)

Vault 8 is the northernmost vault on the west side of the crypt. Unlike Vaults 1-7 it did not house coffins prior to the current works and was not sealed. It had been converted into a small kitchen in recent decades. It appears likely that coffins were removed from this area to Vault 7 when the kitchen was installed.

In plan Vault 8 is similar to Vaults 3 and 4 at the south-west and south-east corners of the crypt and has a semi-circular apse-like west end. Unlike the other vaults previously described, the window at the west end was not blocked but was of later 20th-century date with a grill over it and is probably

Plate 2.17   Vault 7 looking N. The original wall and vault to the left are primary, the wall to the right is a 20th-century insertion. The awkward positioning of the window at the north end of the vault is clear

Plate 2.18   Vault 7 looking S. The S wall is built of 19th-century bricks, the E wall to the left is built of 20th-century bricks

contemporary with the kitchen (Plate 2.19). It may be that the window was blocked in the 19th century when coffins were interred, but that it was unblocked in the mid to later 20th century when the kitchen was installed.

The two primary stone window sills, which were similar to those in the other vaults, survived: the lower one was deeper and had a moulded lip while the higher one, which formed the base of the window was plain. Immediately beneath the window were ashlar blocks above the deep sill. The plaster had been removed from the main walls and vaulted ceiling although the east wall which flanked the main central vault was covered with hard cement render. This wall appears to be of 20th-century brick and was presumably contemporary with the conversion of the vault to a kitchen.

The removal of plaster had exposed the structure of the walls and confirmed several common details less visible in other vaults (Plates 2.19-2.20). Among these details were the edges of the intersecting vaults at right angles to each other, which were formed with special, fine bricks clearly distinct from the stock bricks that form the main walls and vaults. The other feature revealed was that the long buttresses which flank the walls supporting the vault were keyed into the rest of the structure and were clearly primary despite the fact that the string course and skirting did not continue around them.

In the other vaults the lack of string course or skirting suggested that these buttresses could have been secondary additions. In the northern side of the apse was a small blocked opening 25 cm by 50 cm and 75 cm above the floor, which had a rough brick arch over it. The feature looked primary.

Vault 9 (context 9002)

Vault 9 is the main central vault, which extends north to south for the main length of the crypt. Interments were not made in this area and it was not sealed prior to the current development. It has a wide, flattened basket-arch profile, with intersecting groin vaults to each of the side bays, and at its centre is a square plan ashlar pillar (1.3 m²) which supports the vault. The southern half of the crypt has plaster in the vault, but below the string course the walls are just painted. Any plaster and paint had been removed from the northern half of the crypt prior to the current works. The removal of this plaster was probably undertaken relatively recently, perhaps when the kitchen was inserted into Vault 8.

Vault 10 (context 9003)

Vault 10 is towards the northern end of the west side of vaults; it had not contained interments and was not sealed at the start of the current investiga-

Plate 2.19 Vault 8 containing kitchen. View looking W. Note the apsidal end and skewed window opening

Plate 2.20 Vault 8 looking E.

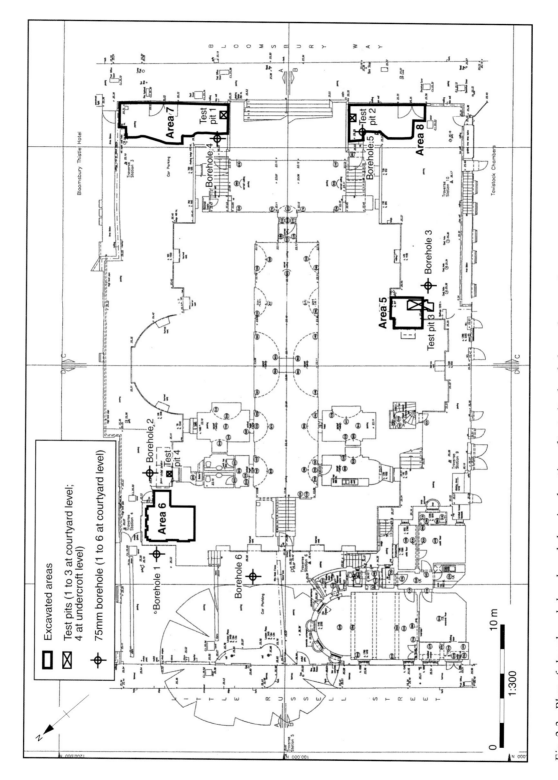

Fig. 2.3   Plan of church and churchyard showing location of test pits, boreholes and excavations areas. Survey drawing of supplied by Michael Gallie and Partners

tion. The vault has a squared west end but there is no window here due to the location of a staircase on the outside of the building in this area. The wall, which closes the vault on its east side is of relatively old brick, possibly of 18th-century date, with a soft chalky mortar but the arch formed over the doorway has later 20th-century mortar. The doorway itself appears to be primary to the wall as the jambs have not been reformed. The internal primary walls are still plastered although the wall which blocks the former passage to the adjacent vault is painted.

Vault 11 (context 9004)

Vault 11 is immediately north of Vault 1 on the eastern side of the crypt and it was open at the start of the current investigation. It has a squared east end and originally had a window but this was covered with black plastic. (Possibly the window had been removed). The stone window sills survive and have a similar form to those in the other vaults together with the ashlar immediately below. The walls and ceiling of the vault were formerly plastered but this had been removed prior to the current works. The west wall of the vault is of old brick (18th century), probably contemporary with the east wall of Vault 10, but the jambs of the doorway have been roughly reformed confirming that this door is a secondary insertion. The passages to the two adjacent vaults are both blocked and the infill brickwork rendered.

Vault 12 (context 9005)

Vault 12 is located immediately north of Vault 11 at the north-eastern corner of the crypt and it had been subdivided into two small WC cubicles by the insertion of modern partitions. The older arrangement partially survives at the east end of the vault beyond the WCs where there is a curved apse-like alcove, similar to the other corners of the crypt, with curved ashlar quoins and a louvred opening. However, below the louvre is an arched passage which projects to a small chamber or cavity beyond the footprint of the church. The cavity and the arched passage appear to be primary, although a concrete slab has been added above the arch and a 20th-century boiler and flue has been inserted into the chamber.

Conclusion

St George's in Bloomsbury is a nationally significant building designed by one of the country's most important architects and having been on the official list of the world's 100 most endangered sites as recently as 2002, it is now being rescued and restored. The clearance works within the crypt have enabled a programme of building recording in this area, which has enhanced our understanding of the building and of the alterations undertaken since the church's construction in the early 18th century.

The main alteration was clearly the use of several of the vaults of the crypt for interments in the first half of the 19th century and the subsequent sealing of these vaults in the mid 19th century. The present record has detailed the vaults that were sealed, as well as the other main vaults, and various minor, earlier, probably 18th-century, changes to the primary arrangement of the building.

ARCHAEOLOGICAL WATCHING BRIEFS IN THE CHURCHYARD AND CRYPT

Test pits 1 and 2 were located to the west and east of the main steps, and were then extended and a number of brick-built structures were recorded (Areas 7 and 8) (Fig. 2.3). Test pits 3 was located south of the tower on the west side of the church, and the trench was extended to investigate the stairs that originally led down to the base of the tower (Area 5). Test pit 4 was on the east side. In addition, OA was requested to undertake archaeological recording of a well and associated structures discovered during ground reduction works within a later extension to the church in the north-eastern churchyard (Area 6).

Test pits 1 and 2 (Fig. 2.4)

Test pits 1 and 2 were located respectively immediately to the east and west of the main entrance to the church (Fig. 2.3). The deposits and stratigraphic sequence in the two test pits were the same. The layer 3 = 6 was a backfill against the brick foundations (4 = 7) for the front steps leading up to the main

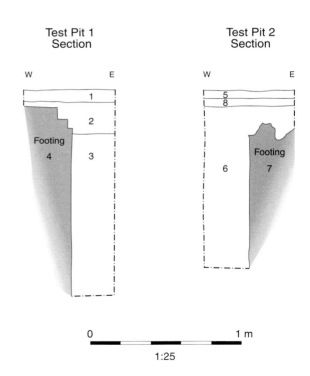

Fig. 2.4   Test pit 1: S-facing section; Test pit 2: S-facing section

entrance of the church. This fill comprised compact reddish light- brown sandy clay with brick, mortar and charcoal fragments. It was excavated to a depth of 1.10-1.30 m in the test pits, and borehole data indicated that it continued for a further 0.40-0.60 m. It was overlaid by a levelling layer 2 = 8, which comprised dark brown friable clay sand with brick, mortar and charcoal fragments up to 0.22 m deep. This in turn was overlaid by paving slabs (1 = 5).

Areas 7 and 8 (Fig. 2.5)

Areas 7 and 8 were located immediately to the south of the principal south façade, at the east and west of the broad flight of steps respectively (Fig. 2.3). Several brick piers were exposed and these are described below. These structures are thought to date from the 19th century and are evidence of the foundation piers of structures that are no longer extant.

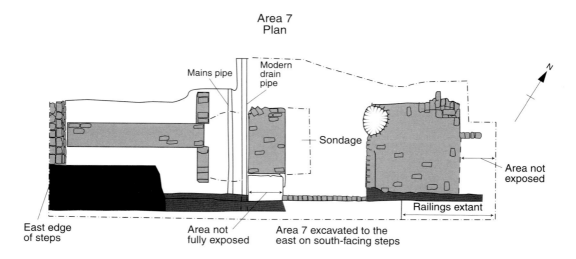

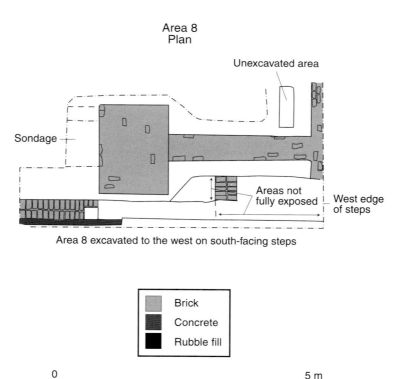

Fig. 2.5   *Areas 7 and 8: plans of excavation*

Area 7

The Area 7 to the east of the steps revealed a number of brick features. Test pit 1 had been excavated previously against the E side of the steps (see above, Fig. 2.4). At the west end of the trench were the brick-built footings of the steps. Running east from just west of the steps was a long rectangular brick pier just 0.30 m below the present ground level. The red bricks measured 0.23 by 0.07 m, which were excavated to a depth of four courses (*c.* 0.31 m). The bricks were bonded with a white chalky mortar with small inclusions and a further layer was also extant on the surface of the pier.

At the east end of this long brick feature were two smaller red brick structures which extended to the north and south respectively, which were excavated to a depth of 0.23 m. Modern pipes running north to south separate these features from a N-S orientated rectangular brick pier again 0.30 m below ground level. This is of a similar red brick construction to the rectangular E-W pier described above. Two course were revealed. A test pit was dug to a depth of 0.88 m to the east side of this pier. The pit revealed that the red brick extends to a depth of 0.51 m and sits on a concrete raft. These bricks were similar to those of the elongated rectangular structure described above.

At the east end of the excavated area a large red brick pier was revealed which was also covered in a thin layer of mortar and situated 0.30 m below present ground level. A shallow pit roughly lined in brick lies at the north-west corner of this area.

Area 8

The area to the west of the main entrance steps also revealed substantial brick piers. Previously Test pit 2 had been excavated against the W side of the steps (see above, Fig. 2.3). At the east end of the trench were the footings of the steps. These were excavated to a depth of 0.42 m or *c.* 5 courses. Running west from these footings was a long brick-built pier or footing. This was revealed to a depth of 0.45 m or *c.* 4 courses. It was constructed of red bricks similar to those already described in Area 7.

At the W end of the elongated pier was a large rectangular pier which was revealed to a depth of 0.34 m (*c.* 4 courses) which was constructed from the same bricks and mortar as previously described. There was a layer of mortar on the surface of the pier. A test pit was dug at the west side of this pier, which revealed further courses of red brick extending to a depth of 1.08 m and built on a concrete raft. Along the south edge of the trench part of a platform built of red brick overlaid by concrete was exposed. It is likely to have extended further to the south.

Stairwell on the south side of the tower (Test Pit 3 and Area 5) (Fig. 2.6)

On the north side of the tower there is an extant flight of stairs rising up to give access to the tower. Through the wall supporting these steps is a door which gives onto a curved flight of steps leading down into the base of the tower. Originally on the south side of the tower there was a similar arrangement, which was later demolished. Test pit 3 was excavated to establish whether there were any surviving steps leading down to the base of the tower mirroring those to the north. The small rectangular trench was excavated in the angle between the west wall of the church and the south wall of the tower. The trench, which measured 2.6 m x 1 m, was excavated from pavement level, and revealed part of the remains of the original stairs leading down to the basement of the tower and the wall supporting the stair up to the tower. Area 5 was later opened to fully investigate the stairwell leading to the basement.

The stone paving (11) revealed in Test pit 3, consisted of a single course of square and rectangular slabs of varying dimensions, the depth of which did not exceed 0.14 m. This layer rested on a 0.08 m deep levelling layer of loose grey-brown silty sand (12) that included a small proportion (5%) of ceramic building material (CMB), stone and mortar. These contexts were removed to reveal two parallel brick and mortar walls (structures 13 and 16), at a right angle to the south wall of the west transept. Only the uppermost courses of the two walls were revealed. Wall 13 was the more substantial of the two, being 0.5 m wide. It consisted of an inner and outer facing of bricks, with a core of less regularly laid bricks and brick fragments set in cream-coloured mortar. This wall would appear to have been the main foundation wall for the demolished stair to the south side of the tower. The thinner outer wall 16 was located approximately 0.1 m to the south-west of wall 13, and was constructed of an inner and an outer facing of brick with a mortar and rubble core. The wall was 0.25 m wide. Further investigation during the excavation of Area 5 revealed a substantial wall footing 9002 which formed the north side of the stairwell and was constructed of brick (brick dimensions 0.06 m x 0.11 m x 0.20 m). Wall 9002 was 0.54 m wide. Walls 13 and 16 appear to have been built on footing 9002.

Three dressed stone slabs that formed the second, third and fourth steps of the staircase (structure 10 = Area 5 structure 9000) to the crypt were revealed in Test Pit 3. Each of the steps had two square hollows in its upper surface at its outer edge, and these are interpreted as evidence for a cast iron banister rail. Further investigation which revealed the complete curving stair which comprised steps of machine-tooled limestone ashlar (9000), and was set on a brick base (9001). Structure 9001 was built of dark orange bricks – measuring 0.11 m x 0.06 m x 0.20 m – in English bond with bright white lime-rich

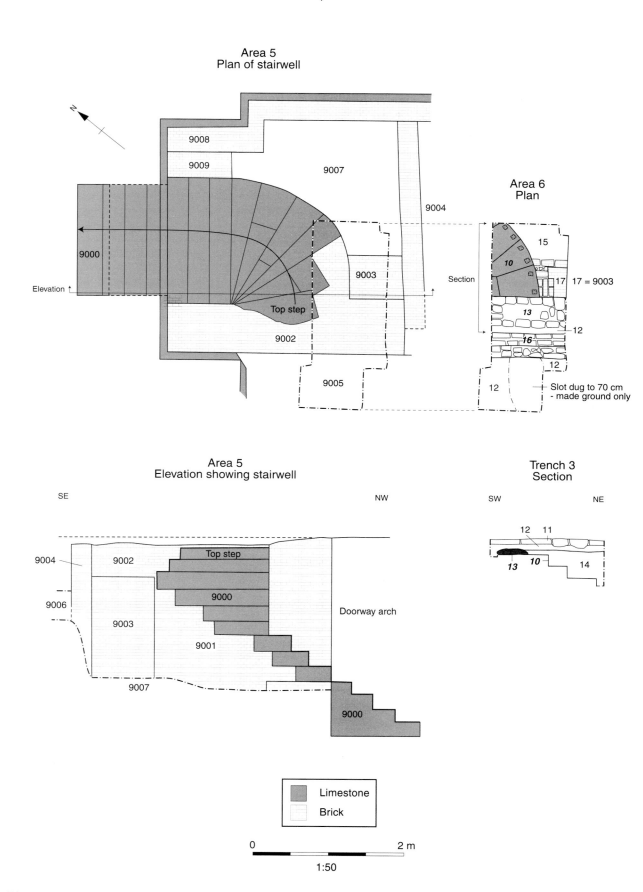

Area 5
Plan of stairwell

Area 6
Plan

Area 5
Elevation showing stairwell

Trench 3
Section

Limestone
Brick

0   2 m
1:50

Fig. 2.6   Area 5 and Test Pit 3: excavation of the stairwell 9000 S of the tower: Plans and sections

mortar. The upper steps were supported by an additional brick and mortar structure 17 = 9003, which abutted wall 9002.

The limestone of the steps was very similar to that used in the rest of the church structure and was presumably part of the original construction of *c.* 1730s. The first six extant steps curved from the SW to NW as they descended. There were three further steps to the archway through the wall of the tower. The base of the entrance arch measured 0.61 m deep through the wall. Four further steps, each measuring 1.22 m long x 0.22 m deep x 0.16 m tall, descended through this archway into the base of the tower. Inserted between the NW side of the steps and supporting structure 90009001 and the plinth (9008) of the nave wall of the was a platform of orange brick (9009), which presumably provided additional support.

The S wall of the stairwell was probably formed by the NE-SW wall 9004 built of orange bricks (0.06 m x 0.11 m x 0.22 m) in English bond with lime mortar. The wall was 0.22 m wide and >2.5 m long. It was revealed to a height of 1.78 m. Its north end butted against the nave wall plinth (9008), but its south end was overlaid by rubble (9005).

The space between the steps and brick support 9000/9001, the southern brick wall 9004, and structure 17=9003, was filled with a fairly compact medium to dark brown silty sand containing small to medium sized fragments of CBM and mortar (10%) (context 15). This deposit, which was at least 1.8 m deep, appears to constitute the original fill dating from the construction of the stairwell in the 18th century. It colour and composition contrasted with the later material (14) used to backfill after the demolition and levelling of the southern tower stair superstructure. Fill 14 was a loose pink-orange deposit of large and medium sized CBM fragments and mortar, probably derived from the demolished superstructure. It sealed the stone steps and had a maximum depth of 0.36 m.

Test pit 4 (Fig. 2.7)

Test pit 4 was located immediately against the eastern foundation wall of the church outside Vault 8. The test pit was excavated to a depth of 1.38 m from the level of the crypt floor and measured 0.4 m by 0.5 m. The natural gravel on which the foundations of the church rest was a grey-yellow layer composed of small to medium sized gravel (70%) within a matrix of yellow clay (context 21). Overlying the gravel was a 1.15m deep compact layer of yellow sandy clay containing minimal inclusions (context 20). The latter layer was natural clay. It was in turn sealed by a compact brown-grey sandy clay deposit containing charcoal flecks and small fragments of CBM and mortar (5%) (context 19). This deposit was 0.15 m deep, and seems to be an intermediate layer between the natural clay (20) and the levelling layer (context 18), which was the uppermost deposit in this trench. Context 18 was a

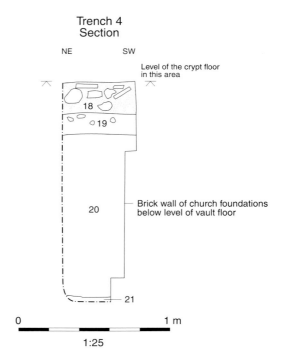

Fig. 2.7 *Test pit 4: NW-facing section*

very compact deposit of dark grey to black silty sand containing mortar and fragments of CBM of varying sizes (10%). The dark colour was probably derived from the presence of charcoal within this fill. Context 18 formed the surface of the crypt floor in this area, but it may originally have been sealed by the stone flooring that was found in other parts of the crypt.

Area 6 (Figs 2.8-2.9)

In March 2004, OA undertook an archaeological watching brief during ground reduction in the eastern churchyard within a 19th-century brick built extension (10016), which abuts the eastern wall (10015) of the church near its north corner. Earlier structures revealed during excavation included an 18th-century well (10007), three brick and mortar walls (10003, 10004 and 10005) and two blocked arches (10016 and 10017) (Fig. 2.8).

The earliest of the three brick-built walls was wall 10004. This abutted the stone plinth of the church wall 10015, and was orientated north-south. The wall had been cut short at its north, to make room for wall 10016 of the later extension. Wall 1004 was built of red bricks (0.215 m x 0.104 m x 0.75 m) in stretcher bond and bonded by lime mortar. The east face was pointed and the west face was roughly finished. Reduction of the ground level revealed a blocked archway (10017) through the wall (Fig. 2.9). The archway was keyed into the church wall (10015), and the span of the arch extended beyond wall 10003 to the north, and clearly predated the building of wall 10003. The archway had been blocked up by brickwork 10018, which was pointed on the eastern face and rough on the west. This brickwork rested on an original floor surface of blackened York paving (10010). A short length of brick wall (10005) orientated E-W was inserted to the W of wall 10004 between it and the church wall 10005. Precisely when this occurred is unclear.

Following the blocking of archway 10017, wall 10003 was built of red bricks (0.22 m x 0.104 m x 0.075 m) in stretcher bond and bonded with lime mortar. This wall was an L-shaped insertion abutting the E side wall 10004 and the blocking 10018 of arch 10017. The wall measured approximately 2.8 m from wall 1004 to the corner at its east end. Here it turned south and ran for 3.1 m to a second return, where it turned back towards the church wall. The wall formed an L-shaped room. The internal southern and western faces were pointed and whitewashed.

Ground reduction revealed a blocked arch 10016 located beneath the modern doorway of the later extension. This east-west orientated arch spanned between wall 10003 and church wall 10015 (Fig. 2.9). The arch had been blocked by red brick (0.215 m x 0.104 m x 0.075 m) and lime mortar brickwork in stretcher bond (context 10006). The north-face wall

was smooth pointed, and the southern face was rough. The doorway is thought to have been blocked up when the footings for the 1870s extension were laid. The base of this brickwork 10006 had been pierced (cut 10011) for a large metal pipe (10012) to pass through.

Wall 10003 was clearly earlier than the upstanding Victorian extension, and has been interpreted as an external access to a cellar or the undercroft. A stone step (10014) was found cut into the southern-most visible part of wall 10003. It may have been part of a stairway leading down to a cellar through archway 10016.

To the north of the room formed by wall 10003, a roughly built brick-lined well (10007) was discovered when the wooden boards supporting made ground 10000 collapsed. The well was constructed of red brick (0.21-0.22 m x 0.10 m x 0.65 m) in stretcher bond. The cylindrical, vertically faced brickwork had originally been capped by square York stone slabs (0.6 m x .06 m), which were flush with floor slabs 10010. The well had an internal diameter of 1.39 m and an estimated depth of at least 1.20 m. The well appears to have predated the extension, the brickwork suggesting an 18th-century date. A gully was observed leading off

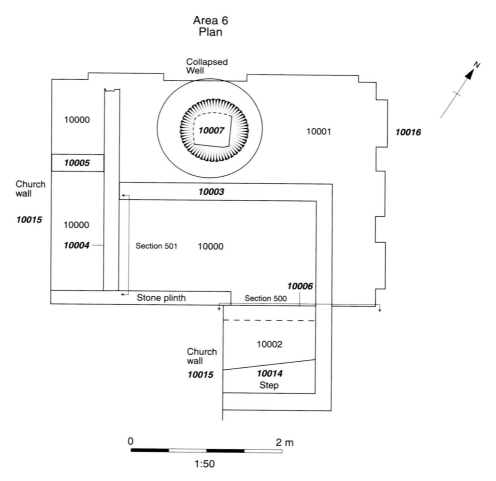

Fig. 2.8   *Area 6: Plan of north-eastern extension showing location of well 10007*

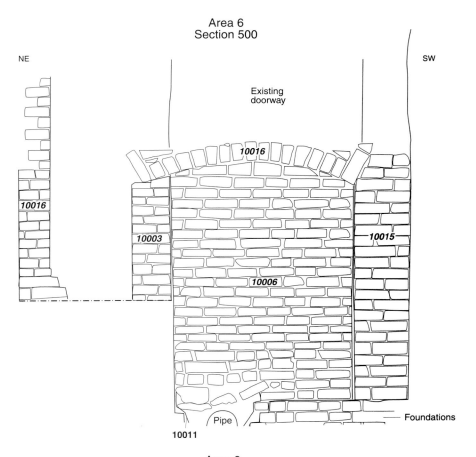

Area 6
Section 500

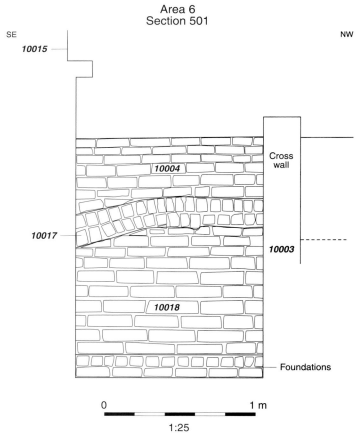

Area 6
Section 501

Fig. 2.9 Area 6: Section 500: Elevation showing blocked arch 10016; Section 501: Elevation showing blocked arch 10017

towards the church. The well and floor had been sealed with rubbly fill 10001. This layer appeared to be deliberate infilling layer of the cellar, probably laid down in preparation for the construction of the extension in the 1870s. This is probably contempo-rary with made ground 10002, located in the vicinity of the modern doorway to the extension. The well was enclosed within the later extension (dating to the 1870s), the walls (10016) of which were upstanding at the time of recording.

Listed building descriptions

IoE number:	476747
Location:	CHURCH OF ST GEORGE AND ATTACHED RAILINGS, GATES AND LAMPS, BLOOMSBURY WAY (north side)
	CAMDEN TOWN, CAMDEN, GREATER LONDON
Photographer:	N/A
Date Photographed:	N/A
Date listed:	24 October 1951
Date of last amendment:	24 October 1951
Grade	I

CAMDEN

TQ3081NW
798-1/100/113

BLOOMSBURY WAY
(North side)

Chapter 3: The spatial distribution of the coffins within the crypt

by Ceridwen Boston

INTRODUCTION

Nicholas Hawksmoor's original design for the crypt of St George's was never intended as a place of burial. The original open space, was divided by brickwork blocking arches to create 10 vaults leading off from a central open area (Fig. 3.1). Coffins were found within seven of the vaults (Vaults 1 to 7). A kitchen had been built into Vault 8 and lavatories inserted into Vault 12. Vaults 9-11 were devoid of coffins. Vault 11 adjacent to Vault 1 contained a pile of loose coffin fittings. Most legible inscriptions from *depositum* plates could be matched to inscriptions on coffins redeposited within Vault 7.

The fronts of Vaults 1 to 7 were sealed by brick walls of a single thickness. Vaults 1 to 6 appeared to have been bricked up in the mid-Victorian period, whilst the presence of a copy of *The Sun* newspaper found within Vault 7 gave a *terminus post-quem* of 1991. The arrangement and treatment of the coffins within Vaults 1 to 6 and Vault 7 were markedly different.

VAULTS 1 TO 6

These vaults contained neatly stacked coffins, arranged directly one on top of another in piles up to eight deep. There appears to have been an attempt to arrange the coffins roughly in accordance with size, with large adult coffins occupying the lower stacks, and smaller coffins (such as infants' coffins) being placed on the top (Plate 3.2). In most of the vaults, infants' and children's coffins also occupied alcoves or bricked-up window ledges. The coffin stacks had been covered over with a layer of sand. This served to stabilise the stacks and to prevent them from collapsing sideways. Most of the damage to the coffins was due to vertical pressure, resulting from the weight of the lead coffins,

Plate 3.1   Vault 2: Coffin stacks before removal

29

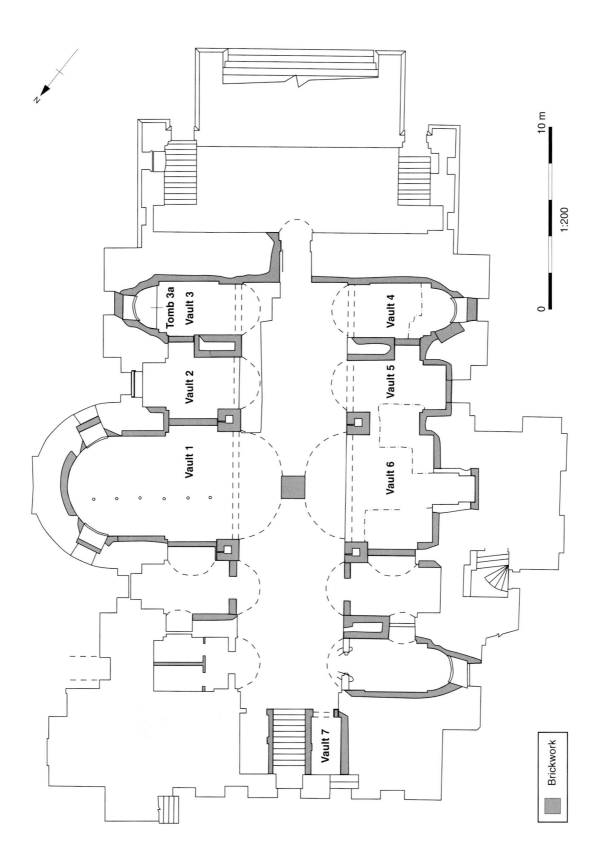

Fig. 3.1 Plan of the crypt showing locations of Vaults 1-7

causing many coffin sides and lids to collapse inwards. The sand layer was overlaid by a thick layer of charcoal. This served to absorbed the miasma resulting from putrefaction of the corpses within breached coffins.

In many other church vaults of this period, coffins were not placed directly one on top of the other, but rested on wooden or iron racks. In these cases, the footplate inscription was particularly important in identifying the name of each individual interred. In St George's crypt, Vault 1 was the only vault to have extant racks. Here, the iron racks took up the northernmost third of the vault. The racks consisted of six vertical solid iron posts set 1.2 m apart (see Plates 2.4-2.5) and aligned parallel to the north wall of the vault. The bases of the posts were cemented into sockets cut into the flagstone floor. The central two posts were fixed into the ceiling, thereby anchoring the structure into place. Three 'shelves' were created by the use of horizontal slats of sheet iron. Fourteen coffins were accommodated horizontally on each shelf. Vertically, between two and three coffins were stacked directly on top of one another on each shelf. However, in several parts of the racks, fewer coffins were thus stacked, the space being backfilled with sand. It is possible that these rack spaces originally were occupied by individuals whose coffins had been reclaimed in 1853, and reburied elsewhere. In total, sixty-three coffins occupied the racks and spaces beneath.

The number of coffins within the vaults varied, largely as a factor of the different sizes of each vault. Two hundred and twenty-five coffins were found within Vault 1; 69 in Vault 2; 94 in Vault 3; 85 in Vault 4; 80 in Vault 5, and 139 in Vault 6. A further 89 coffins were found in Vault 7. The total number of coffins found was 781.

Each vault contained individuals from many different families. The only private family burial area was the small tomb of the Ford family (3500), constructed against the eastern wall of Vault 3, and containing the coffins of four members of the family: Randle Ford (coffin 3502), his wife Elizabeth (3503) and two grandchildren (coffins 3501 and 3504) (see above Fig. 2.1, Tomb 3a).

VAULT 7 (Plate 3.2)

This small vault was located beneath the chancel to the left of inserted modern steps. The coffins and human remains found in Vault 7 had been treated very differently. Eighty-nine lead coffins were found within this small vault. Twenty-seven lead coffins were arranged at the rear of the vault in three neat stacks. The orderly arrangement of these coffins was not dissimilar to the treatment of coffins in the other six vaults, although they lacked a covering of sand and charcoal. Spaces in the brick-work of the vault side walls suggest that originally this vault had contained either iron or wooden racks, which have since been removed. It is possible

that originally the stacked coffins been placed on the racks, but after the decay or deliberate dismantling of the racks, had been re-arranged directly on top of one another in the rear of the vault. However, no clustering of surnames was noted from the named coffins. This re-organisation would have made more space available in the vault and probably occurred when many more coffins were crammed into the Vault 7 (Plate 3.2). This may have happened as recently as 1991. What is clear is that very much less care was taken over the re-deposition of the remaining 62 lead coffins and the human remains originally within them.

On opening the vault, it was evident that the sole intention had been to cram as many coffins into this confined space as possible. To achieve this end, coffins had been torn up, folded in half, and twisted to accommodate all of the available space. Plastic bags, including old fertiliser bags, filled with charnel and human hair had been forced into any remaining spaces. Cross-bars of wooden planking and iron piping had been placed across the entranceway to stabilise the heap. The vault had then been bricked up, plastered and painted black on the exterior. Owing to the disorder in which the coffins were found in Vault 7 it was not practical to produce a coherent plan, although limited recording of the sequence of deposition was possible (Fig. 3.36).

Plate 3.2   Vault 7: Arrangement of the coffins within the vault

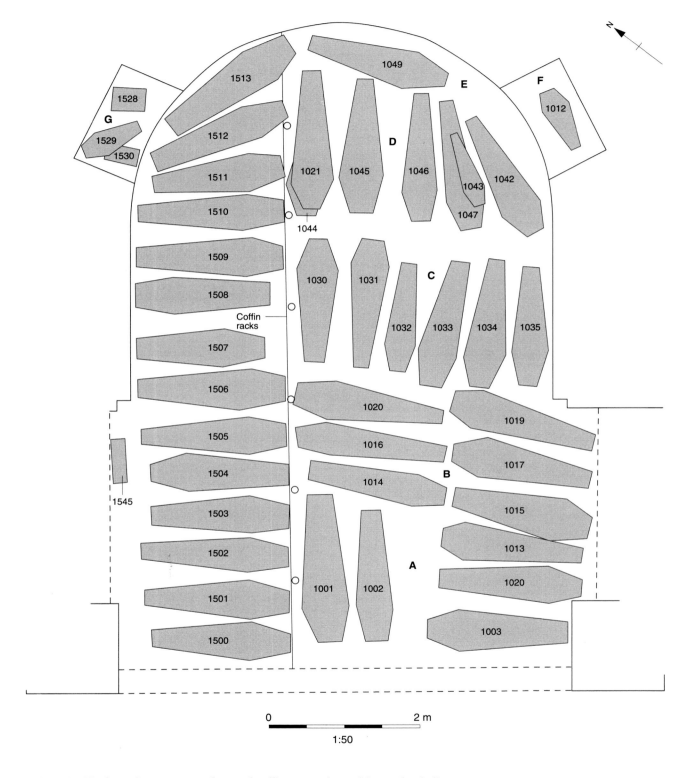

Fig. 3.2 Vault 1: the uppermost layer of coffins on racks and in stacks A-G

SPATIAL ARRANGEMENT OF THE COFFINS WITHIN THE VAULTS (Figs 3.3-3.36)

Because 78.1% of coffins from the crypt had legible *depositum* plates, it was possible to analyse the spatial relationships between individuals with the same surname, who presumably were related, and also the sequence of deposition, based on the year of death.

In the late Georgian/Victorian period, considerable emphasis was placed on interring or burying family members together. Hence, the popularity of family plots in graveyards, and the use of both intra and extra-mural brick-lined shaft graves. In many churches, such as St Luke's Church, Islington, and Christ Church, Spitalfields, the crypts of the churches were divided into small family vaults, usually containing between one to ten coffins (Boyle *et al* 2005). At St Luke's the large central area of the crypt was also crammed with coffins of many different families. However, even in the darkness and chaos of this crypt, it was evident that considerable effort had been made to seek out the coffins of family members of the recently deceased, in order that they might be interred with their kin. Indeed, some Victorians made a living out of descending into the dark crypts of churches to seek out the coffins of relatives of the newly dead for this purpose.

The uppermost level of the coffin stacks within each vault was recorded in plan, and a matrix of each stack has been constructed, showing the name and year-of-death of each coffin. These are shown in Figures 3.2-3.36. What becomes immediately apparent from the *depositum* plate inscriptions is that the coffin stacks were not simply added to incrementally over time, with later coffins being stacked on top of earlier ones. Early interments were as likely to be found towards the top of the stacks, as they were to be located in the middle levels, or towards the base of stacks. Conversely, later burials were found throughout the stacks. It is clear that considerable re-arrangement of the coffins had taken place, and that this had occurred after the crypt had ceased to be used for further burial, but before the outer wooden cases of many of the coffins had decayed extensively. In all likelihood, this occurred in 1856 when the church issued a directive 'hermetically to seal the entrance to the vaults' (Meller 1975, 23). To some extent, consideration of coffin size also influenced the spatial arrangement of the coffin stacks with smaller coffins frequently being found towards the top and within alcoves and on ledges.

With the exception of the Ford family tomb (3500), there were no areas marked out for the exclusive use of any one family. Although clustering of coffins with the same surname was not as clear at St George's as in the crypt of St Luke's church, Islington, it seems nonetheless that some attempt had been made to keep family members together or close. For example, three members of the Yenn family (coffins 1517, 1534, 1550) were located one above the other in the racks in Vault 1 (Fig. 3.3).

Similarly, four members of the Atkinson family (coffins 1553, 1573, 1574 and 1575) were alongside or above one another in the racks. All six members of the Jeakes family (coffins 1013, 1015, 1024, 1057, 1075, and 1079) were in close proximity in Vault 1 (Figs 3.4-3.5). The Jeakes family lived at 36 Little Russell Street, the street directly behind the church. The burial register entry for Thomas Jeakes (burial 1057) reports that he died of inflammation of the liver, and that he worked as a carpenter.

In Vault 4, the redoubtable family of barristers and judges, the Hely Hutchinsons (coffins 4063, 4070, and 4083) are stacked one above the other in row D (Fig. 3.23). Separated from the rest of the family, but in the same vault was the coffin of Maria Louisa Hely Hutchinson (aged 1 year 5 months) (coffin 4005). Her coffin had been placed at the top of stack A (Figs 3.19-3.20).

It appears to have been common practice to stack family members one on top of another, rather than laying them side by side in a horizontal plane. However, this coffin sorting was by no means carried out consistently. For example, all four members of the Meabry family (coffins 2007, 2014, 2022 and 2032) were interred within Vault 2 (Figs 3.11-3.14). The Stringfield family (coffins 2067, 3064, 6033, 6039, 6040, 6071, 6109 and 6110), were largely concentrated in Vault 6. Four family members (coffins 6033, 6039, 6040 and 6071), a daughter-in-law Anna Stringfield (coffin 6110) and a son-in-law Bisse Phllips Sanderson (coffin 6109) all being located there. Another Stringfield, an adult male (coffin 2067), probably William Stringfield, was interred in Vault 2 (Fig. 3.13), and seven year-old Anna Stringfield (burial 3064) in Vault 3 (Fig. 3.17). The Stringfield family are discussed more fully in Chapter 4.

A similar pattern of deposition was noted with the Keysell family. In this instance at least six members of the family (coffins 6007, 6019, 6020, 6069, 6119 and 6138) were located in Vault 6 (Figs 3.29, 3.32-3.33), whilst Richard Keysell (aged 10 months) (coffin 1092) was found in Vault 1. Another member of the family is Miss [Catherine] Ele[an]or [Key]sell (burial 6085) whose coffin was immediately beneath that of Henry Keysell (burial 6069) in Vault 6 (Fig. 3.33). John Keysall (coffin 6008) was a banker and was probably not related although he was interred in Vault 6.

Four members of the Sanders family were interred in the crypt. Francis William Sanders (coffin 1073), his wife (coffin 1080) and his mother (coffin 1137) were interred in Vault 1, but Elinor the young daughter of the family (coffin 6044) was interred in Vault 6. There appears to be no reason chronological or otherwise why some members of a family are found apart from their family group. It seems likely that young children are more likely to be separated, perhaps because their coffins were smaller and could not be stacked in the normal way.

More evidence for the re-arrangement of coffins within the crypt is the fate of the coffin of Dame

1513 Charles John Harrison Batley *1841*	**1527** Thomas James Tatham *1850*	**1544** Sarah Tatham *1847*	**Sand**	**1576** James Ogle *1823*	**1579** Edward Ogle *1819*
1512 Alexander Auldjo *1821*	**1526** Harry Herman Luard *1816*	**1543** Emily Angelica Platt *1825*	**1560** Mary Portia Williams *1828*	**1561** Edward Bullock *1835*	**1562** Isabella Sophia Stevenson *1816*
1511 Joseph Littledale *1842*	**1525** John Jortin *1843*	**1549** John Bearpacker Jortin *1827*	**Sand**	**Sand**	**Sand**
1510 Elizabeth Mary Roche *1833*	**1524** Barbera Gray *1831*	**1548** Mary Gray *1825*	**Sand**	**1551** Sarah Bayley Jortin *1840*	**1575** Margaret Atkinson *1825*
1509 Richard Smith *1830*	**1523** William Gray *1842*	**1540** William Henry Manley *1813*	**Sand**	**1552** Sarah Martin *1817*	**1574** Thomas Atkinson *1836*
1508 Unnamed	**1522** Unnamed	**1539** Ann Martin *1810*	**1547** Sophia Manley *1823*	**1553** Martha Atkinson *1837*	**1573** John Atkinson *1828*
1507 Elizabeth Children *1839*	**1521** Unnamed	**1538** John Lee Martyn *1836*	**1546** Hannah Martyn *1810*	**1554** Catherine Elwell Beaumont *1826*	**1572** John Percival Beaumont *1844*
1506 Thomas Bland *1825*	**1520** Mary Martyn *1835*	**1537** Unnamed	**1542** Susannah Day *1810*	**1555** Unnamed	**1571** Daniel Beaumont *1821*
1505 Elizabeth Planta *1821*	**1519** Ansell Day *1808*	**1536** William Day *1807*	**Sand**	**1556** Philadelphia Wood *1851*	**1570** Anne Day *1827*
1504 Mary Williams *1835*	**1518** Emily Charlotte Donne *1823*	**1535** Thomas Day *1815*	**1541** Ann Catherine Day *1818*	**1557** Unnamed	**1569** Thomas ----- *1811*
1503 Miles Booty *1815*	**1517** Susannah Maria Yenn *1845*	**1534** Elizabeth Yenn *1806*	**1550** John Yenn *1821*	**1558** Harriet Tatischeff *1843*	**1568** Robert Nares *1829*
1502 Jane Maria Pearce *1819*	**1516** Mary Susan Holmes *1829*	**1533** Anne Young *1830*	**Sand**	**Sand**	**1567** Harriet Agnew *1815*
1501 John Hutchinson *1815*	**1515** Eleanor Pope *1831*	**1532** Mary Newcombe *1836*	**Sand**	**1564** William Agnew *1828*	**1566** Mary Agnew *1831*
1500 Sophia Fuseli *1832*	**1514** Elizabeth Beckwith *1814*	**1531** Lettia Beetson *1830*	**Sand**	**1563** Jane Addison *1856*	**1565** Ralph Addison *1840*

Floor

34

Fig. 3.3   Vault 1: Matrix of the coffins on the racks

Caroline Alecia Briscoe of Wimpole Street and Crofton Hall, Cumbria (coffin 3078). A memorial plaque within the church explicitly states that the lady was interred in the crypt within a private vault beneath the chancel. Nonetheless, Dame Caroline Briscoe's coffin was discovered within Vault 3 (Fig. 3.16). Like so many others, she had clearly been moved from her original resting place at a later date.

CONCLUSION

Unlike many churches with crypt interments of this date, the crypt of St George's did not appear to have been sub-divided extensively into small family vaults. The Ford family tomb (3500) and the Briscoe vault are the two exceptions.

Within the crypt, two major re-organisations of the coffins appear to have occurred. The coffins in Vaults 1 to 6 were re-arranged in very much the

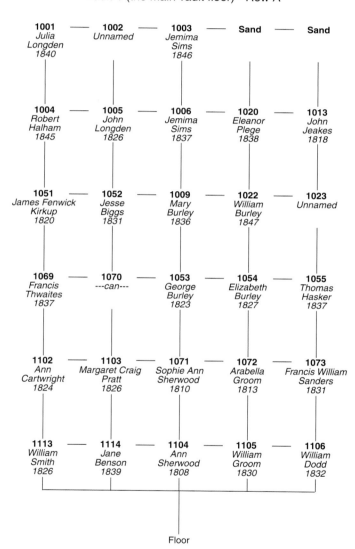

Vault 1 (the main vault floor) - Row A

Fig. 3.4   Vault 1: Matrix of the coffin stacks – Row A

same manner, suggesting that the re-organisation of the crypt was undertaken as a single event, probably around 1856. It is unclear whether the central open area of the crypt had originally housed coffins, but based on comparisons with contemporary church crypts, such as St Luke's church, Islington, this seems highly likely. They were probably removed to the vaults during the reorganisation, leaving the central area clear. It is probable that the vaults were bricked up at the same time.

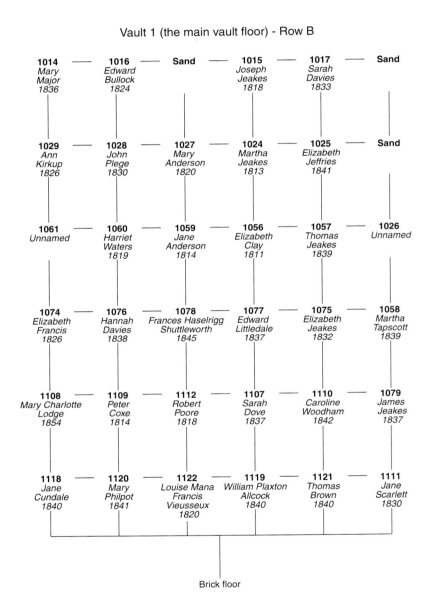

Fig. 3.5 *Vault 1: Matrix of the coffin stacks – Row B*

The re-arrangement of coffins within Vault 7 was undertaken at a much later date (in 1991). It is probable that most of the coffins within the vault were cleared from the northern end of the crypt (the area now occupied by the kitchen, lavatories and two empty vaults) when the facilities were installed, and this area was re-used as a boys' club.

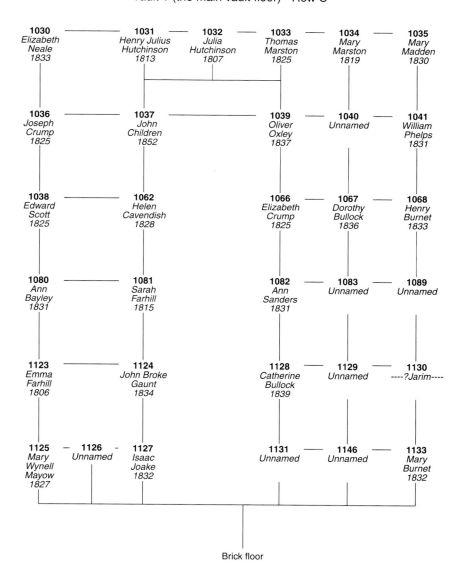

Vault 1 (the main vault floor) - Row C

Fig. 3.6   Vault 1: Matrix of the coffin stacks – Row C

Vault 1 - Row D

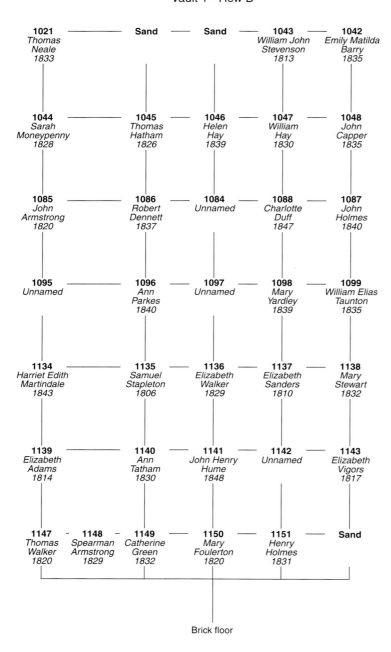

Fig. 3.7   Vault 1: Matrix of the coffin stacks – Row D

Vault 1 - (Main vault floor) Row E

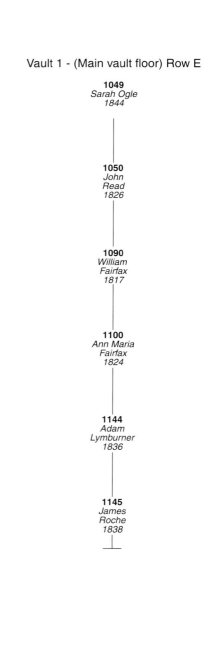

Fig. 3.8   Vault 1: Matrix of the coffin stacks – Row E

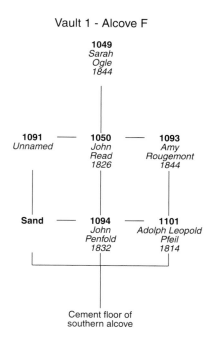

Vault 1 - Alcove F

1049
*Sarah
Ogle
1844*

1091 —— **1050** —— **1093**
Unnamed   *John*   *Amy*
       Read   *Rougemont*
       1826   *1844*

Sand —— **1094** —— **1101**
       John   *Adolph Leopold*
       Penfold   *Pfeil*
       1832   *1814*

Cement floor of
southern alcove

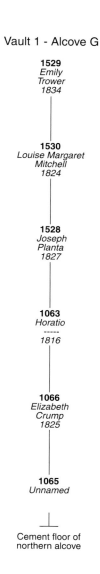

Vault 1 - Alcove G

1529
*Emily
Trower
1834*

1530
*Louise Margaret
Mitchell
1824*

1528
*Joseph
Planta
1827*

1063
*Horatio

1816*

1066
*Elizabeth
Crump
1825*

1065
Unnamed

Cement floor of
northern alcove

Fig. 3.9   Vault 1: Matrix of the coffin stacks – Alcove F   *Fig. 3.10   Vault 1: Matrix of the coffin stacks – Alcove G*

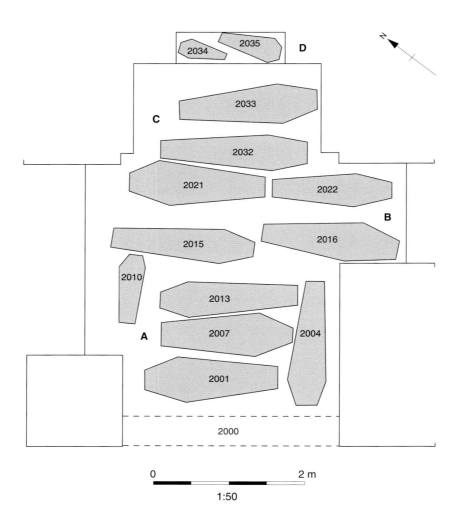

Fig. 3.11 Vault 2: the uppermost layer of coffins in stacks A-D

Vault 2 - Row A

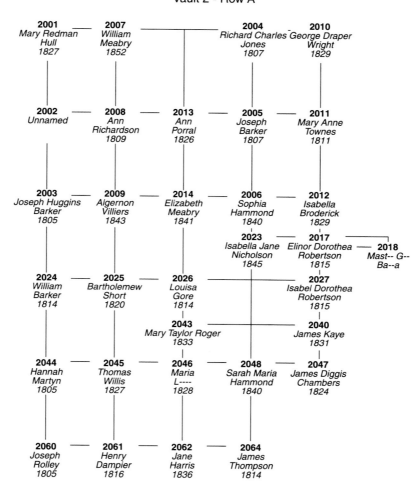

Fig. 3.12   Vault 2: Matrix of the coffin stacks – Row A

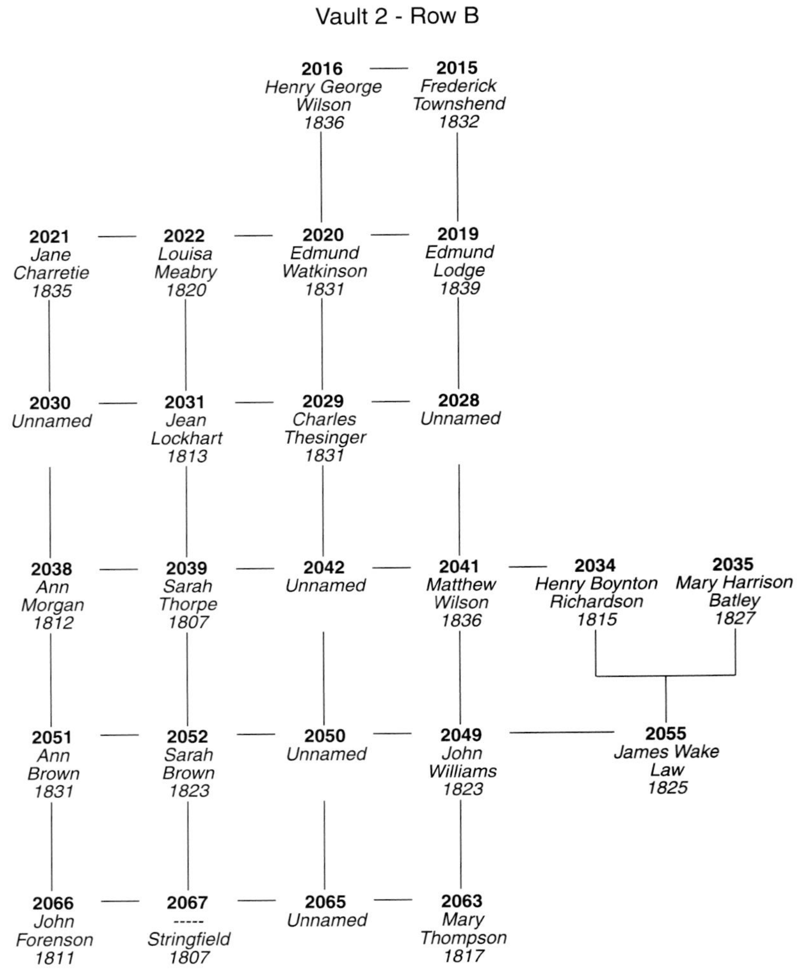

Vault 2 - Row B

2016 — **2015**
Henry George | Frederick
Wilson | Townshend
1836 | 1832

2021 — **2022** — **2020** — **2019**
Jane | Louisa | Edmund | Edmund
Charretie | Meabry | Watkinson | Lodge
1835 | 1820 | 1831 | 1839

2030 — **2031** — **2029** — **2028**
Unnamed | Jean | Charles | Unnamed
| Lockhart | Thesinger |
| 1813 | 1831 |

2038 — **2039** — **2042** — **2041** — **2034** **2035**
Ann | Sarah | Unnamed | Matthew | Henry Boynton | Mary Harrison
Morgan | Thorpe | | Wilson | Richardson | Batley
1812 | 1807 | | 1836 | 1815 | 1827

2051 — **2052** — **2050** — **2049** — **2055**
Ann | Sarah | Unnamed | John | James Wake
Brown | Brown | | Williams | Law
1831 | 1823 | | 1823 | 1825

2066 — **2067** — **2065** — **2063**
John | ----- | Unnamed | Mary
Forenson | Stringfield | | Thompson
1811 | 1807 | | 1817

Fig. 3.13   Vault 2: Matrix of the coffin stacks – Row B

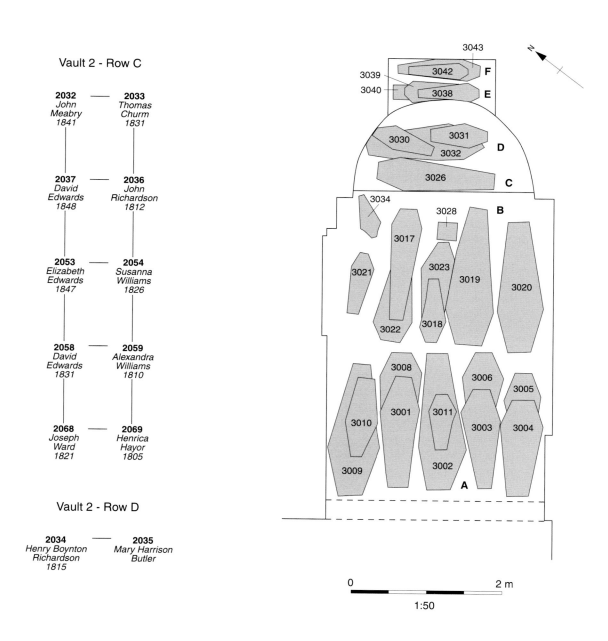

Vault 2 - Row C

2032 John Meabry 1841	—	2033 Thomas Churm 1831
2037 David Edwards 1848	—	2036 John Richardson 1812
2053 Elizabeth Edwards 1847	—	2054 Susanna Williams 1826
2058 David Edwards 1831	—	2059 Alexandra Williams 1810
2068 Joseph Ward 1821	—	2069 Henrica Hayor 1805

Vault 2 - Row D

| 2034 Henry Boynton Richardson 1815 | — | 2035 Mary Harrison Butler |

Fig. 3.14   Vault 2: Matrix of the coffin stacks – Rows C and D

Fig. 3.15   Vault 3: The uppermost layer of coffin in stacks A-F

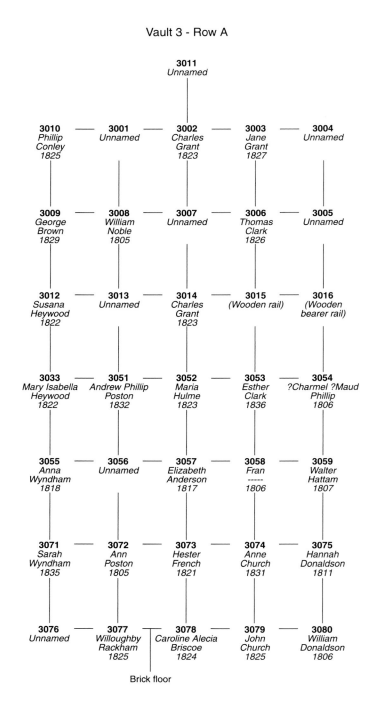

Fig. 3.16   Vault 3: Matrix of the coffin stacks- Row A

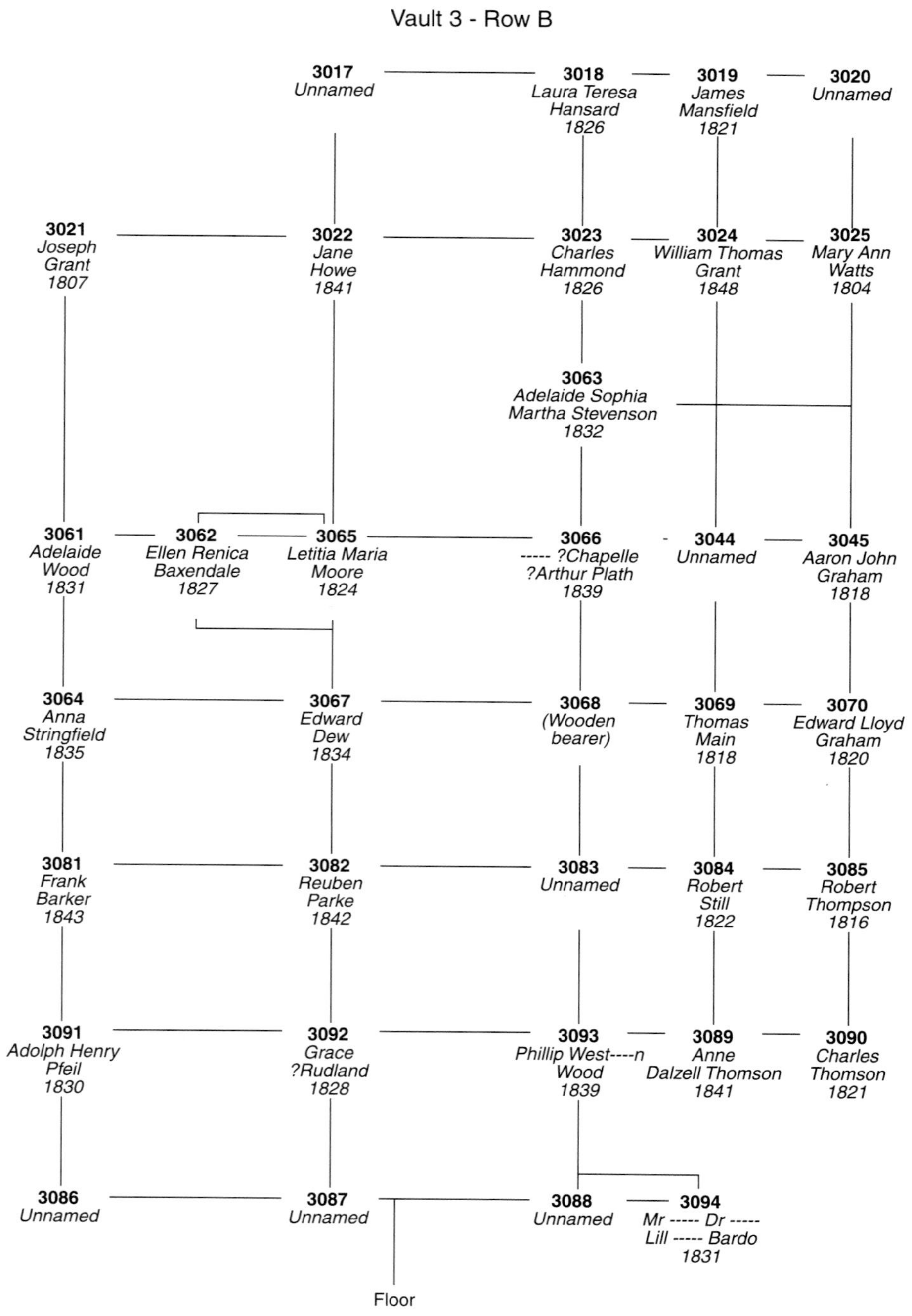

Vault 3 - Row B

	3017 *Unnamed*	**3018** *Laura Teresa* *Hansard* *1826*	**3019** *James* *Mansfield* *1821*	**3020** *Unnamed*
3021 *Joseph* *Grant* *1807*	**3022** *Jane* *Howe* *1841*	**3023** *Charles* *Hammond* *1826*	**3024** *William Thomas* *Grant* *1848*	**3025** *Mary Ann* *Watts* *1804*

3063
Adelaide Sophia
Martha Stevenson
1832

3061 *Adelaide* *Wood* *1831*	**3062** *Ellen Renica* *Baxendale* *1827*	**3065** *Letitia Maria* *Moore* *1824*	**3066** *----- ?Chapelle* *?Arthur Plath* *1839*	**3044** *Unnamed*	**3045** *Aaron John* *Graham* *1818*
3064 *Anna* *Stringfield* *1835*		**3067** *Edward* *Dew* *1834*	**3068** *(Wooden* *bearer)*	**3069** *Thomas* *Main* *1818*	**3070** *Edward Lloyd* *Graham* *1820*
3081 *Frank* *Barker* *1843*		**3082** *Reuben* *Parke* *1842*	**3083** *Unnamed*	**3084** *Robert* *Still* *1822*	**3085** *Robert* *Thompson* *1816*
3091 *Adolph Henry* *Pfeil* *1830*		**3092** *Grace* *?Rudland* *1828*	**3093** *Phillip West----n* *Wood* *1839*	**3089** *Anne* *Dalzell Thomson* *1841*	**3090** *Charles* *Thomson* *1821*
3086 *Unnamed*		**3087** *Unnamed*	**3088** *Unnamed*	**3094** *Mr ----- Dr -----* *Lill ----- Bardo* *1831*	

Floor

Fig. 3.17   Vault 3: Matrix of the coffin stacks- Row B

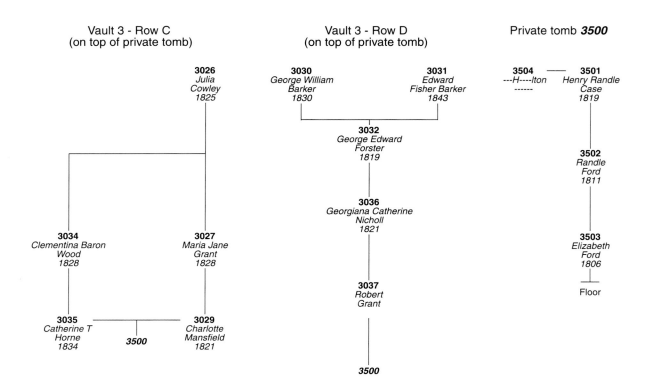

Fig. 3.18 Vault 3: Matrix of the coffin stacks- Row C-F and the private tomb 3500

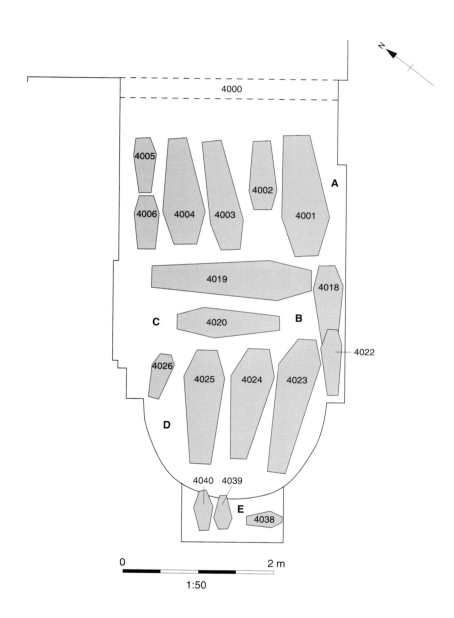

Fig. 3.19   Vault 4: The uppermost layer of coffins in stacks A-E

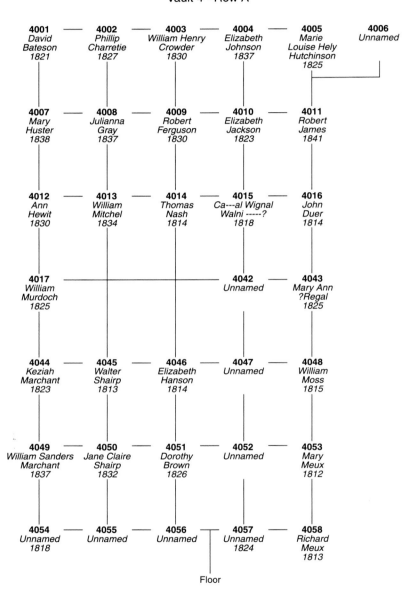

Fig. 3.20   Vault 4: Matrix of the coffin stacks- Row A

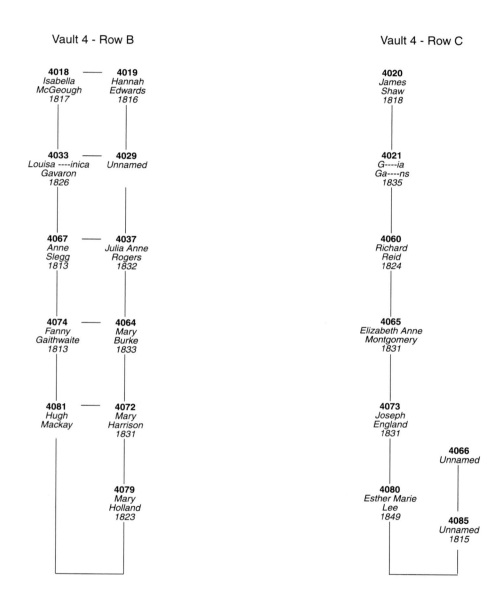

Fig. 3.21   Vault 4: Matrix of the coffin stacks- Row B   *Fig. 3.22   Vault 4: Matrix of the coffin stacks- Row C*

Vault 4 - Row D

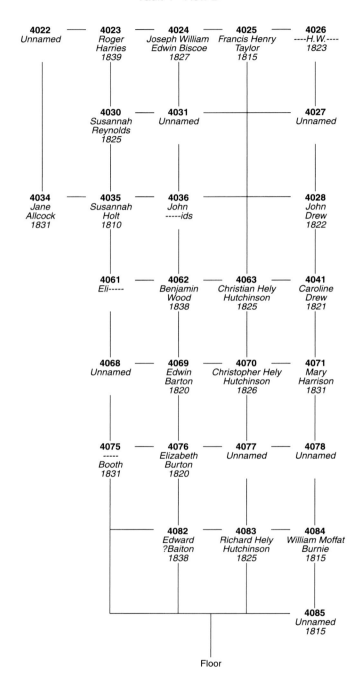

Fig. 3.23   Vault 4: Matrix of the coffin stacks- Row D

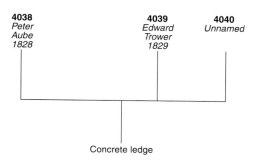

Vault 4 - Ledge (E) (Infant Coffins)

Fig. 3.24 Vault 4: Matrix of the coffin stacks- Ledge E

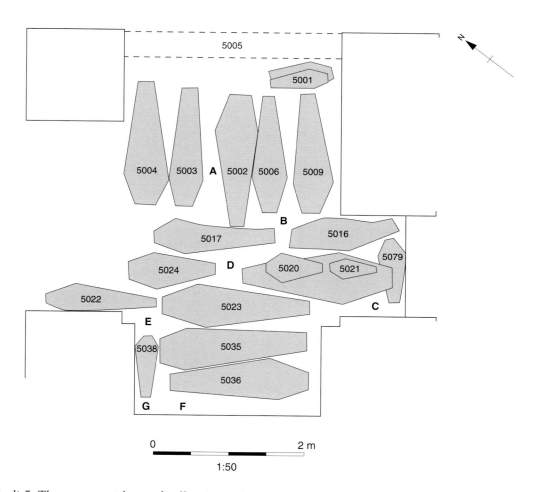

Fig. 3.25 Vault 5: The uppermost layer of coffins in stacks A-G

Vault 5 - Row A

Vault 5 - Row B

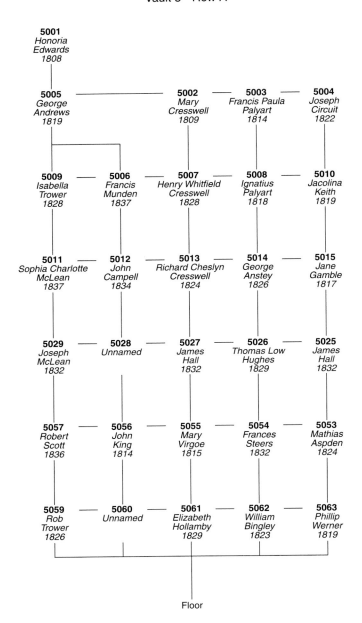

Fig. 3.26   Vault 5: Matrix of the coffin stacks- Row A   *Fig. 3.27   Vault 5: Matrix of the coffin stacks- Row B*

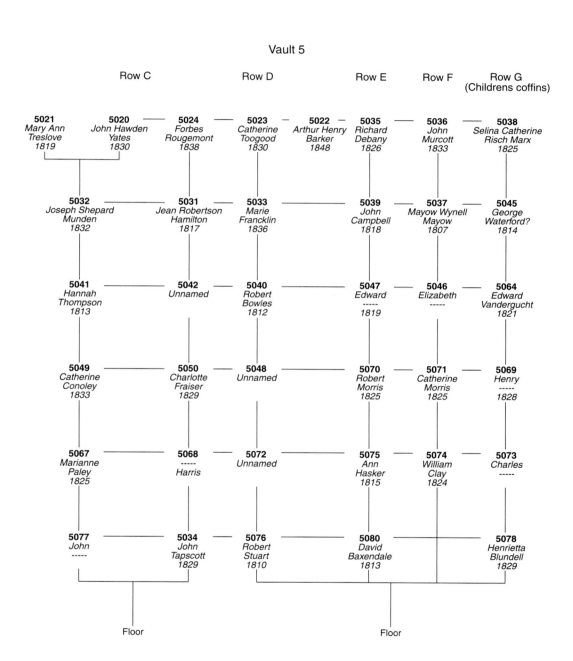

Vault 5

Fig. 3.28   Vault 5: Matrix of the coffin stacks- Rows C-G

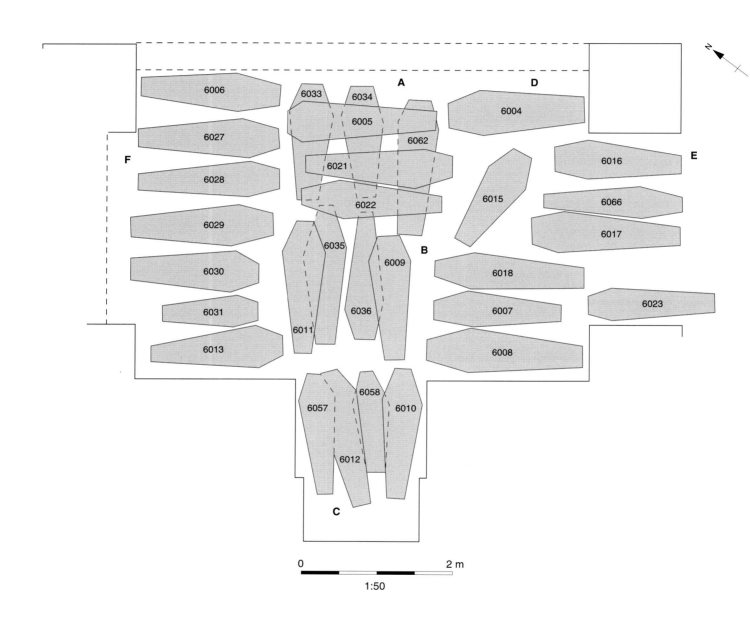

Fig. 3.29   Vault 6: The uppermost layer of coffins in stacks A-F

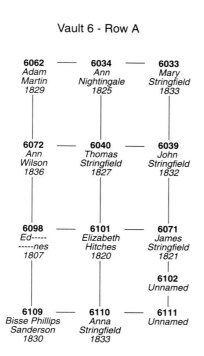

Vault 6 - Row A

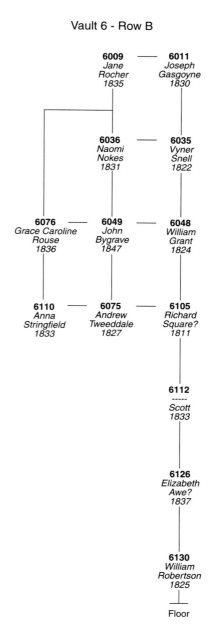

Vault 6 - Row B

Fig. 3.30   Vault 6: Matrix of the coffin stacks- Row A   *Fig. 3.31   Vault 6: Matrix of the coffin stacks- Row B*

55

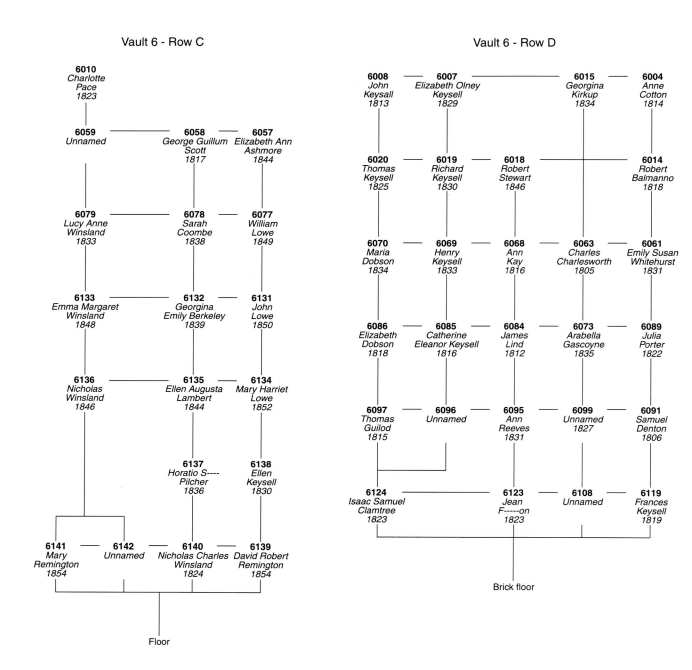

Fig. 3.32   Vault 6: Matrix of the coffin stacks- Row C   *Fig. 3.33   Vault 6: Matrix of the coffin stacks- Row D*

Vault 6 - Row E

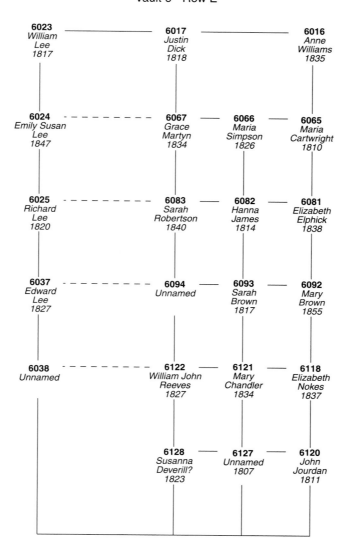

Fig. 3.34   Vault 6: Matrix of the coffin stacks- Row E

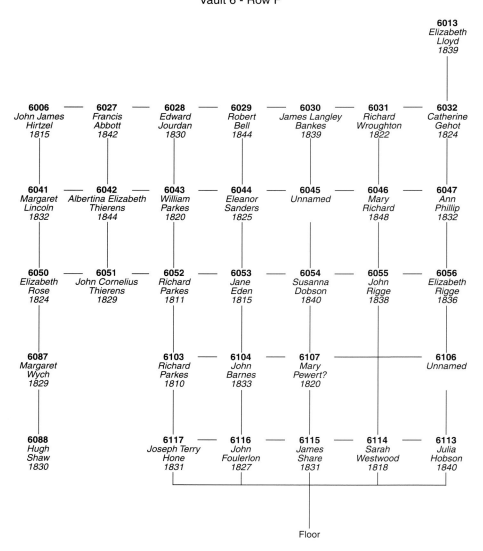

Vault 6 - Row F

Fig. 3.35   Vault 6: Matrix of the coffin stacks- Row F

Vault 7

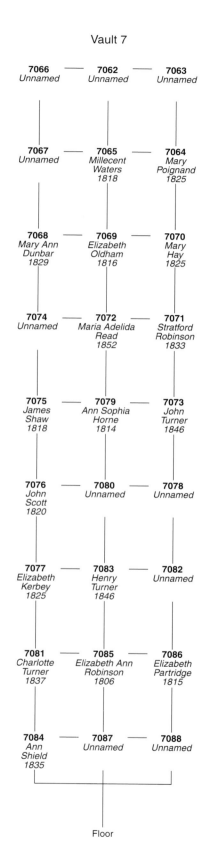

Fig. 3.36   Vault 7: Matrix of the stacked coffins found at the back of the vault

Chapter 4: The church, the parish, and the parishioners

by Ceridwen Boston and Ian Scott

THE PARISH OF BLOOMSBURY AND ITS PARISH CHURCH

Parish of Bloomsbury in the 18th and 19th centuries

In the early 18th century, the area of Bloomsbury comprised a growing number of residences of the 'middling sort' and a few mansions of the aristocracy. The genteel classes were attracted by its location away from the industrial areas of the City and East End (Fig.4.1).

Much of the land was owned by the Dukes of Bedford, and their association with Bloomsbury is reflected in many street names, such as Bedford Place, Bedford Square, and Little and Great Russell Streets. Other place names, such as Cardington Street, Goldington Street and Goldington Crescent, and Woburn Square, refer to their estates in Bedfordshire, Taviton Street, Tavistock Square, Endsleigh Gardens and Endsleigh Street to their Devon estates, and Thornhaugh Street evokes their Northamptonshire property (Fig. 4.2).

Bloomsbury owes much of its current layout to a systematic housing development undertaken by the Duke of Bedford in the later 18th century. Whilst major urban development of the West End burgeoned in the mid- to late-18th century, the 3rd Duke was slow to build. Locations further to the west had already become more fashionable. The area never received the caché of slightly earlier experiments in town planning, such as Grosvenor Square, and remained resolutely middle class, with a reputation for being somewhat staid (White 2008, 71-3). Nevertheless, successive Dukes were so determined to uphold the tone of the area, that they restricted the number of shops, did not allow taverns, and erected gates at the entrances. (Porter 1994, 112, 220)

Bedford Square and Gower Street began in 1776, becoming desirable quarters for the professional classes. Their proximity to a number of the Courts of Law made them particularly popular among lawyers (White 2008, 71, 73). This is strongly reflected in the population interred within the crypt at St George's (see below). Urban expansion continued northwards towards Euston Road. The Foundling Hospital for the care of abandoned children and babies (Figs. 4.3), founded by Thomas Coram in 1739, was sited in the fields north of Grays Inn, and opened to receive its first children in 1741. Fund raising at the hospital soon established it as a

venue where the fashionable world went to enjoy pictures and hear music, such as Handel's Messiah, which was performed there in 1749 (Picard 2000, 257). Another centre for culture, the British Museum in Great Russell Street was created in Bloomsbury in 1753, only a street away from St George's church. A number of librarians and scholars of the Museum were buried within the vaults of St George's church (see below).

Urban development in and around Bloomsbury continued apace in the early 19th century (Figs 4.2-4.3), with Bloomsbury soon enclosed to the north by the parishes of St Pancras and Clerkenwell. The Regents Canal was responsible for industrialisation of St Pancras and the Tottenham Court Road areas, with timber being towed up the canal to supply a thriving building and carpentry trade, and piano and furniture making (Porter 1994, 218). A number of carpenters and cabinet makers were interred in the crypt of St George's church. Associated slums mushroomed. The workhouse of St Giles in the Fields and St George's Bloomsbury was described by philanthropist Jonas Hanway as 'the greatest sink of mortality in these kingdoms, if not on the face of the whole earth' (ibid, 149).

Sandwiched between these less salubrious areas, Bloomsbury represented a genteel oasis of middle class respectability. In the 1820s, anxious to maintain the tone, the Duke of Bedford erected a cordon sanitaire around Bloomsbury by blocking up streets and erecting gates at the entrance onto Euston Road. These remained in place until the 1890s (ibid, 220).

The need for a new church

Although the origins of Bloomsbury can be traced to the 13th century when William Blemund was made Lord of the Manor, it did not attain parochial status until the 18th century (Meller 1975). Until the early part of the 18th century, Bloomsbury lay within the parish of St Giles in the Fields. Originally founded by Queen Matilda as a leper hospital in 1101, the hospital chapel and succeeding churches of St Giles served as the parish church.

This arrangement proved satisfactory until the late 17th century, when Bloomsbury began to expand rapidly. The number of houses increased from 136 in 1623, to 954 in 1739. One reason for this growth is given by Strype who, in 1720, wrote, 'this place by physicians is esteemed the most

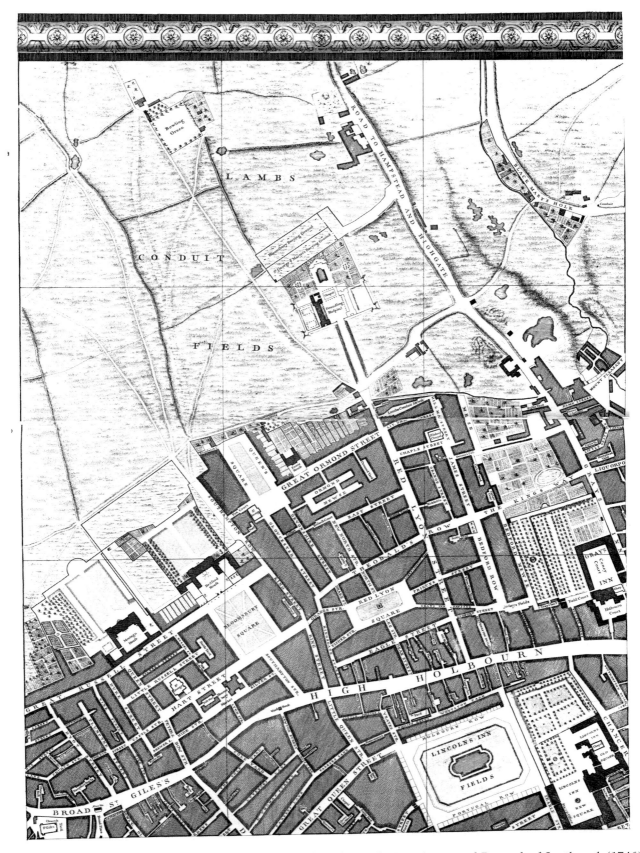

Fig. 4.1   Map taken from Rocque's Plan of the Cities of London and Westminster and Borough of Southwark (1746). The extract from The A to Z of Georgian London, *is reproduced by kind permission of the publishers, Harry Margary at www.harrymargary.com in association with The Guildhall Library, Aldermanbury, London, and at http:collage.cityoflondon.gov.uk.*

healthful of any in London'(ibid.), lying as it did on the outskirts of the city, far from the pollution and overcrowding of the City to the east (Fig. 4.2). The parish of St Giles in the Fields included not only the great mansions of the Duke of Monmouth, the Earl of Thanet and the Dukes of Bedford (the primary landowners of vast tracts of land in Bloomsbury) (Meller 1975) and a growing number of respectable middle class dwellings, but the infamous slums known as the Rookery. Located close to today's Tottenham Court Road (Porter 1994, 267) they were a hot bed of crime and vice. The destitution and hopelessness of the poor of the Rookery is immortalised in Hogarth's 1751 engraving of 'Gin Lane' (Plate 4.1), a critique of the evils of gin consumption at the height of the Gin Craze. The spire of St George's church, is depicted in the background of the plate. Respectable residents of the northern part of the parish of St Giles in the Fields increasingly objected to having to pass through this notorious district in order to attend church, and petitions were made to build another church within the parish.

By the 18th century, London was expanding rapidly, but continued to rely on existing parish churches to serve the religious needs of its burgeoning population. In 1711 the Act for the Building of Fifty New Churches was passed in order to address the shortfall in church numbers. Of the 50 new churches proposed, only a dozen were ever constructed. These included six churches designed by Nicholas Hawksmoor: St Alfege in Greenwich, St Anne, Limehouse, Christ Church, Spitalfields, St George-in-the-East, Stepney, the City church of St Mary Woolnoth, and St George's, Bloomsbury. A new church designed by Henry Flitcroft was also constructed on the site of the earlier churches of St Giles-in-the-Field as part of this scheme (Porter 1994, 124). Even with these new churches, London's pews could hold only a quarter of the population – a factor implicated in a reduction in religious observance in the Georgian period.

Figures for the population of the parish of St Giles in the Fields gathered by the Commissioners for the Act illustrate the social heterogeneity of the parish. It was found to contain 2999 housekeepers, of whom 269 were gentlemen, 1923 tradesmen and 807 poor housekeepers. The Commissioners assumed that an average of seven people inhabited each house, so that the church had to serve a population of approximately 20,000 people (Meller 1975, 2), and that additional places of worship were sorely needed.

Construction of the new church

The Commissioners chose Nicholas Hawksmoor as the architect of the new church of St George, rejecting designs by such illustrious architects as Vanbrugh and James Gibb (Meller 1975). The site chosen for the church (known as the *Plowyard*) had been purchased for £1000 from Lady Russell, widow of Sir John Russell, late Duke of Bedford. As it stands today, the plot fronted onto Bloomsbury Way (then Hart Street) to the south, and was hemmed in by existing buildings. The constricted space made design of the traditional east-west orientation of a church difficult, but Hawksmoor was able to overcome these restrictions and place the altar to the east. Work on the church began in June 1716 and continued for 16 years, punctuated by periods of inactivity when funding for the project was temporarily exhausted. The Commissioners had resolved in 1712 that all the churches were 'to be built with stone on the outside and lined with brick on the inside' (ibid.). The vaults, accessible from doors either side of the portico steps, are the only part of the church where this brickwork is clearly to be seen, as stone facing was dispensed with in this area.

Stonework was particularly expensive. The estimated cost of building the church was £9,790 17s. 4d, but by the time it was completed in 1731, the total project (including the Minister's House) had cost approximately £31,000. Almost half this sum had been paid to the stonemasons. In 1730, before work on the interior was complete, the church was consecrated by Edmund Gibson, Bishop of London (ibid.).

Hawksmoor is thought to have based the grandiose Neo-Classical façade of the main portico (Plates 4.1 and 4.2) on the Roman Temple of Baalbek (now in Lebanon) illustrations of which had been published by the explorer Henry Maundrell in 1703.

Plate 4.1   St George's, Bloomsbury in c 2001 – viewed from Bloomsbury Way

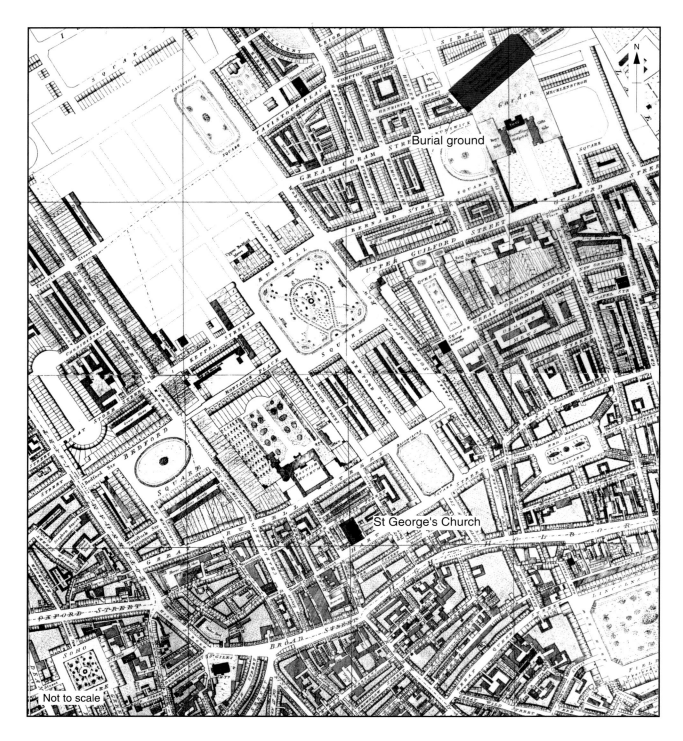

Fig. 4.2 Map taken from Horwood's Plan of the Cities of London and Westminster (3rd Edition 1813).
The extract from the The A to Z of Regency London, *is reproduced by kind permission of the publishers,*
Harry Margary at www.harrymargary.com in association with The Guildhall Library, Aldermanbury, London,
and at http:collage.cityoflondon.gov.uk

Fig. 4.3 (opposite)   Map taken from Bacon's large-scale Ordnance Atlas of London and Suburbs (1888)
The extract from the The A to Z of Victorian London, *is reproduced by kind permission of the publishers,*
Harry Margary at www.harrymargary.com in association with The Guildhall Library,
Aldermanbury, London, and at http:collage.cityoflondon.gov.uk

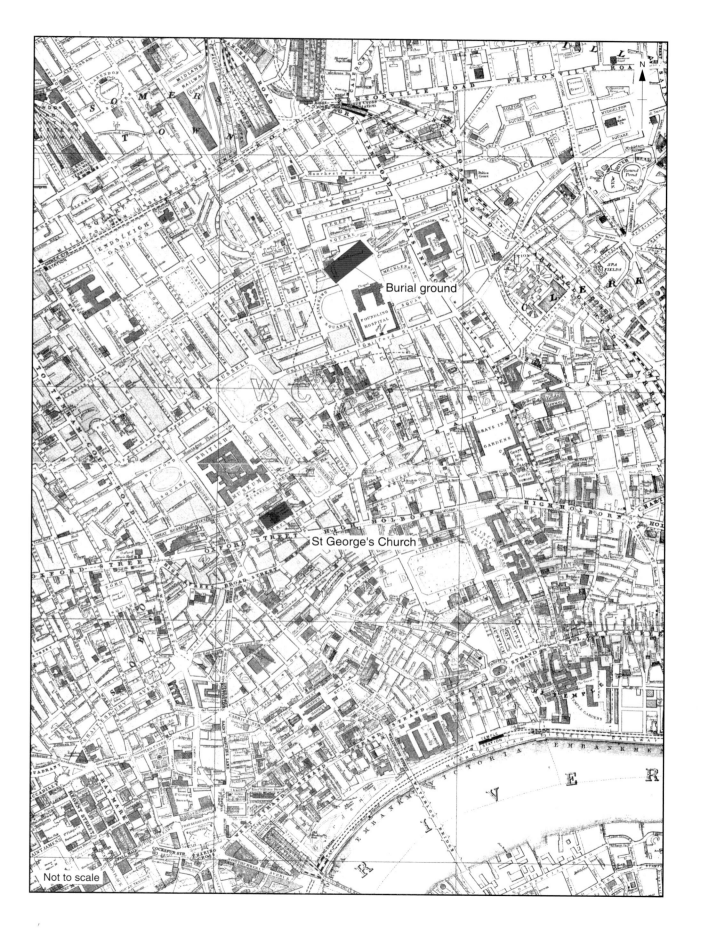

Not to scale

Plate 4.2 St George's, Bloomsbury from Hart Street (later renamed Bloomsbury Way)

The extraordinary steeple of the tower on the west of the church was also influenced by classical architecture. Inspired by Pliny's description of the Mausoleum at Halicarnassus (modern Bodrum, Turkey), it is stepped like a pyramid (as can be clearly seen in the background of Hogarth's *Gin Lane* (Plate 4.3). Hawksmoor decorated the steeple with 'lions, unicorns, festoons and crowns' evidently without the permission of the Commissioners, who were horrified at the expense (Meller 1975). By 1871 the lions and unicorns originally placed at the steeple's base were crumbling away and were removed. A statue of George I in Roman dress, posing as St George on the top of the steeple, was the gift of parishioner William Hucks, brewer, whose brewery was in Duke Street. From 1715 he was brewer to the Royal Household, and was a Member of Parliament. He served as MP for Abingdon (1709-10), and then for Wallingford (1715-40).

The original main entrance to the church was via steps leading up to doors on the north and south sides of the church tower. These steps and doors led a traditional west entrance to the church interior. Only the steps to the north of the tower survived, the southern steps having been removed to make way for a car park. Wall foundations and a sealed staircase were discovered in Test pit 3 and investigated in Area 5 (Fig. 2.6) (see Chapter 2 above).

The Vestry Minutes for the 18th and 19th centuries record numerous repairs and modifications to the church. During the reordering of 1781, the north gallery was replaced by an east gallery. A west gallery had already been added in 1731. In 1870, major restoration was carried out by George Edmund Street and further re-ordering of the interior was undertaken, during which the east and west galleries were removed. In 1930 Street's tiles were removed, and in 1972-74 (under Laurence King) the church was redecorated and a glass screen added below the south gallery.

The major programme of works aimed to restore the church to much of its original splendour. This included restoration of the original decorative plaster ceiling, which was pulling away from its support. The exterior was badly weathered, and the roof, windows, railings, floors and furnishings all required refurbishment. The church was on the World Monuments Fund's List of 100 Most Endangered Sites (Amery 2002).

PARISHIONERS

Introduction

The inscriptions on the *depositum* plates found in the crypt of St George's are a very valuable addition to historical records already available for this population. Record of burials in the parish do exist but do not differentiate between individuals buried within the vaults and those buried in the churchyard, which was situated north-east of Brunswick Square in the parish of St Pancras (Meller 1975).

Other sources of information are the mural memorials in the interior of the church. Although they commemorate only a few of the more prominent citizens buried in the parish, many of them were interred within the vaults beneath and the commemorative inscriptions supplement the information found on coffin plates.

The demographic information derived from coffin plates is considered in Chapter 5 below. In this section the historical evidence for the composition of the population is consider. It has not been possible, as part of the Bloomsbury project, to undertake a comprehensive search of the available historical sources for the history of the crypt population. Nonetheless an attempt has been made to identify the individuals buried in the crypt, to establish their social standing and, where applicable, their professions. A number of notable figures were buried in the crypt and brief accounts of some of these are also included. Families of some tradesmen were interred in the crypt and some account of these is published. Amongst the crypt population were some of Huguenot descent and a number of foreigners, or aliens, who were living in Bloomsbury and these are briefly considered. Finally the evidence for abodes of the of the crypt population and the distribution of different occupational groups is discussed briefly

Coffin plate inscriptions

The crypt assemblage comprised 781 coffins and 146 loose coffin plates. The coffins included 644 with plates still attached. The plates on 10 coffins had no legible name and only limited age or date information, and the plates on a further 24 coffins had only partial names which could not be identified. A total of 610 coffins (78.1%) had clearly identifiable names (Appendix 1).

The 146 detached coffin plates were found mainly in Vault 7. Some of the plates could be identified with named coffins, but others provided the names or identities of a further 63 individuals, giving a total of 673 identified individuals. These include two still born babies apparently buried in a single coffin and commemorated on plate 3109.

The inscriptions provide a wealth of valuable historical data about the professional classes of Bloomsbury in the late Georgian/Early Victorian period. All breastplate inscriptions included the title, name, date and age at death of the deceased, and occasionally provided additional data, such as their place of birth or abode, their profession, and details of family connections. Several brass outer breastplates also bore crests. Footplates and headplates were less informative, usually giving only the title, name and year of death of the deceased.

The main limitations of this resource are usually due to poor preservation of the coffin fittings, and human error in transcribing inscriptions. Overall, preservation at St George's church was excellent, and most of the inscriptions were clearly legible. Exceptions were brass outer breastplates, which were often difficult to read, due to the fineness of the inscription and oxidation of the brass. Of the lead breastplates, the worst corroded plates were from the lowest levels of the coffin stacks, especially in Vaults 4 and 5. It is to be expected that a certain unavoidable level of human error did occur in reading the inscriptions, but this is unlikely to have been significant, given the overall excellent condition of the *depositum* plates. The inscriptions are listed in Appendix 1. An attempt has been made to confirm identify of the individuals interred in the crypt from other sources, and this has revealed some transcription errors, which have been silently corrected.

Plate 4.3   Gin Lane by William Hogarth (1751), the spire of St George's church is clearly visible in the background

Memorial plaques

On the walls of the interior of the church are stone plaques commemorating many of the faithful who died within the parish in the 18th and 19th centuries. Due to inaccessibility and poor lighting six memorials on the north side of the altar, and three to the west of the altar, could not be read. The names and details of the individuals recorded on the memorials are listed in Tables 4.1 and 4.2. The majority of the memorials are contemporary with the period when the crypt was in use for burial, and several explicitly state that the mortal remains of those commemorated were deposited in the vaults below. The plaques vary in detail, but tend to give similar information to the breastplate inscriptions, but in some instances they do give additional details of the relationships between family members, and sometimes link different surnames of families joined by marriage.

Not all the individuals identified from the mural plaques could be matched to *depositum* plate inscriptions from the crypt. There are a number of possible reasons for this. Firstly, it is not always clear from the memorial plaque that the individuals commemorated on the plaque were interred within the vault. The Honourable and Right Reverend Henry Montague Villiers, Bishop of Durham, was commemorated because he had been rector of St George's as his memorial records. He was buried in the chapel of the Bishop's palace at Bishop Auckland, County Durham. Mary Madden (coffin 1035), who died in childbirth, aged 26, was survived by her spouse Frederick Madden by many years. Sir Frederick Madden died in 1873 long after burial in the crypt had ceased. Indeed he had remarried and was buried with his second wife at Kensal Green cemetery. It is also possible that some individuals commemorated within the church were buried in the nearby churchyard rather than within the vaults.

Secondly, it is likely that some coffins were removed when interment in the crypt ceased. The 1856 vestry minutes which include the decision to seal the crypt also state that 'parties whose connec-tions lie in the vaults should take the necessary steps for the removal of the remains of their connec-tions' (Meller 1975, 23). There is no written record of how many followed this directive. One memorial plaque in the church explicitly states that Mrs Sophia . . . (name illegible) was removed to the family vault at Kensal Green in 1853. At a time when burial within crypts and churchyards was being abandoned in favour of burial within the modern, spacious new municipal cemeteries, such as Highgate and Kensal Green (Curl 2003), it is unclear how many others, like Sophia, originally interred in St. George's crypt were relocated to these new burial sites.

Finally, it may simply be that individuals interred in the crypt have not been identified, because their *depositum* plates were illegible.

Other sources

A number of sources have been used to help to identify the crypt population and to attempt to establish relationships between individuals, partic-ularly those sharing the same surname. These sources are listed in the bibliography. It is not proposed here to discuss all the available sources that might be used, but rather to indicate which sources were used, and their strengths and weaknesses.

Parish registers, related records, and civil registration

Burial in the crypt was limited to the first half of the 19th century a period during which there were significant changes in the way that data about the population was collected. Before 1837 and the introduction of civil registration, births, marriages and deaths were recorded in parish registers, and the information recorded could vary in quality and detail. It has not been possible as part of this project to undertake an extensive search of the parish registers to establish the identity of individ-

Table 4.1: Transcripts of selected memorial inscriptions from wall plaques within the interior of the church of St George, Bloomsbury

Memorial no.	Surname	Forename	Inscriptions on memorial plaques within the church	Coffin No
1	Lowe	Eliza	Sacred to the Memory of **William Lowe** Esqre. of Montague Street, Russell	n/a
	Lowe	William	Square, and Tenfold Court, Inner Temple; born 5th April 1770, died 21st	6077
			December 1849. Also of **Eliza**, his wife, who died at Medina Villas, Hove,	
			Sussex, and is buried in the churchyard of that parish, born 5th February 1781,	
			died 12th March 1858	
2	Stringfield	Thomas	Sacred to the Memory of Mr **Thomas Stringfield**, more than 50 years an inhabitant	6040
	Stringfield	Mary	of this parish, who died Novr 15th 1827, aged 68. And of Mrs **Mary Stringfield**,	6033
	Stringfield	James	his wife, who died Novr 4th 1833, aged 71. Also of Mr **James Stringfield**, their son,	6071

Table 4.1 (continued): Transcripts of selected memorial inscriptions from wall plaques within the interior of the church of St George, Bloomsbury

Memorial no.	Surname	Forename	Inscriptions on memorial plaques within the church	Coffin No
	Stringfield	John	who died May 9th 1821, aged 21. Also of Mr **John Stringfield**, their son, who died	6039
	Stringfield	William	Septr 2nd 1832, aged 37. Also of Mr **William Stringfield**, their son, who died July	n/a
	Sanderson	Bisse Phillips	23rd 1837, aged 38. Also of Mr **Bisse Phillips Sanderson**, their son-in-law, died Feby	6109
	Stringfield	Anna	12th 1830, aged 42. Also of Mrs **Anna Stringfield**, wife of the above John	6110
	(née Frickelton)		Stringfield, who died July 9th 1833, aged 25. Also of **Anna**, daughter of the above	
	Stringfield	Anna	John and Anna Stringfield, who died Decr 6th 1835, aged 7.	3064
3	Jourdan	John	In the vault under this church are deposited the remains of **John Jourdan**, Esquire,	6021
	Jourdan	George	late of Bedford Place, died 6th October 1811, aged 63 years. **George Jourdan**, late	n/a
	Jourdan	Edward	of Gower Street, died 8th December 1823, aged 66 years. Major **Edward Jourdan**,	6028
			late of Devonshire Street, who died 26th September 1830, aged 79 years	
4	Hull	James Watson	Sacred to the Memory of **James Watson Hull** Esqe of the County of Down, Ireland,	8051
	Hull	Margaret Redman	died April 5th 1831, at Farquhar House, Highgate, aged 72. Also **Margaret Redman**	2001
	Hollamby	Elizabeth	**Hull**, third daughter of the above J.W.Hull, died June 4th 1827, aged 33. Also of	5061
			Elizabeth Hollamby, died April 30th 1829, aged 72	
5	Pilcher	Jeremiah	Sacred to the memory of	**Jeremiah Pilcher**, Esqre. J.P.	of Russell Square, London,	n/a
	Pilcher	Mary Rebecca		and Worthing, Sussex;	died April 11th 1790, died July18th 1866,	aged 76 years.	n/a
				"The Memory of the Just is Blessed." Proverbs x, 7.	**Mary Rebecca Pilcher**		
			widow of Jeremiah Pilcher Esq	daughter & Co heiress of	Walter Swaine, Esq.		
			of Leverington, Cambs,	born 8th Nov. 1803, died 25th July 1885.	For a space the	
			tired body	lies with feet towards the dawn	till there breaks the last and brightest	
			Easter morn	on that happy Easter morning	all the graves their dead restore		
			father, sister, child and mother meet once more.	
6	Beckwith	Elizabeth	In the chancel vault under this tablet are deposited the remains Mrs **Elizabeth**	1514
	Sutherland	Frances	**Beckwith**, late of the City of York, widow, who departed this life the 2d January	n/a
	Sutherland	A. P.	1814, aged 76 years. Also of her daughter, Mrs **Frances Sutherland** wife of A.H.	n/a
			Sutherland Esqr of Gower Street, Bedford Square, who departed this 19th	
			November 1808, aged 47 years.	
7	Debary	Richard	In the vault beneath this church are deposited the remains of **Richard Debary**,	5035
	Debary	Anne Phoebe	Esqre. of Lincolns Inn Fields, who departed this life on the 8th of January, 1826,	5043
			aged 58. Also of **Anne Phoebe**, his wife, second daughter of the late Lieutt Colonel	
			Downman, she died on the 15th of February, 1829, aged 51	
8	Addison	Ralph	In memory of **Ralph Addison**, Esqre., Late of Temple Bar, and of Montague Street,	1565
	Addison	Jane	Russell Square, who departed this life on the 6th of August 1840, in the 70th year	1563
			of his age. Also of **Jane Addison**, wife of the above, who departed this life on the	
			14th of February 1850, in the 77th year of her age.	
9	Mansfield	James	In the vault	under this church are deposited	the mortal remains of the Rt	3019
			Honorable	**SIR JAMES MANSFIELD** KNT	Late Chief Justice of	the Court	
			of Common Pleas.	And one of His Majesty's most honourable Privy Council		
			To his memory	this tablet is erected by his surviving children	in token of their	
			sense	as well of his private virtues	adorned by a conciliating and lively		
			simplicity of manner, as of his eminent talents,	and learning, energy, and integrity		
			successfully displayed in the profession in the Law,	by which he attained	to that	
			elevated station	wherein he was esteemed and honoured	as one of it's (sic) most	
			distinguished ornaments.	He was born X May MDCCXXXIV,	and died XXIII	
			November MDCCCXXI.	
10	Day	Thomas	Sacred to the memory of **Thomas Day**, Esqre. who died 12th July 1841, aged 71.	n/a
	Day	Mary	Also of **Mary**, his widow, who died 3rd July 1836, aged 80	n/a
11	Ellis	Frances Jane	Sacred to the Memory of **Frances Jane Lady Ellis**, wife of **Sir Henry Ellis** K.H.,	n/a
	Ellis	Sir Henry	Principal Librarian of the British Museum, born Augt 16th 1779, died Octr 12th	n/a
			1854, *'In daily piety to God: in the desire to do good: in Affection: and in*	
			Meekness: None could exceed her.'	

Table 4.2: Summary memorial inscriptions from wall plaques within the interior of the church of St George, Bloomsbury

Memorial number	Surname	Forename	Date	Age at death
12	Smith	Jane	-	-
13	Nash	Thomas	died 30th May 1814,	60 years
14	Bell	Robert	died 20th March 1844,	86 years
15	Donaldson	Hannah Bell	died 8th September1811	72 years
	Donaldson	William	died 28th February 1806	70 years
16	Martindale	Harriet Catherine	died 6th February 1848.	-
17	Villiers	Henry Montague	died 9th August 1856.,	68 years
18	Abbott	Francis	died 19th November 1842	75 years
19	Meabry	Elizabeth	died 5th August 1842	70 years
	Meabry	John	died 7th September 1842	76 years
20	Thompson	Isabel Barclay	died 14th February1906	67 years
21	Parry	Edward	-	-
22	Smoult	J.T.	died 6th April 1830	33 years
23	Kirkup	Joseph	1st May 1815	53years
	Kirkup	James Fenwick	28th June 1820	26 years
	Kirkup	Ann	died14th January1826	66 years
24	Groom	William	died 24th April 1839	54 years
	Groom	Arabella	died 8th March 1848	64 years
25	Littledale	Edward	died 20th April 1837	58 years
26	Grant	Charles	died 31st October 1823	78 years
27	Planta	Joseph	died 3rd December	n/a
	Planta	Elizabeth	11th February 1821	n/a
28	Robertson	Francis	died 18th April 1814	5 years
	Robertson	Ebena Dorothea	died 25th April 1815	10 months
29	Dove	Sarah	died 20th May 1837	46 years
	Dove	William	died 8th April 1854	57 years
30	Edwards	David	died 3rd April 1831	51 years
31	Bankes	James Langley	died 8th May 1839	42 years
	Lloyd	Elizabeth	2nd May 1839	40 years
32	Yenn	Elizabeth	born 1757, died 1806	
	Yenn	John	born 1754, died 1821	
	Yenn	Susannah	born 1786, died 1845	
33	Sanders	Francis William	died 1st May 1831	62 years
	Sanders	Anne	16th February 1831	63 years
	Sanders	Elizabeth	-	-
	Sanders	Francis William	died 27th December 1829	16 years
	Sanders	Eleanor	died 15th June 1823	21 years

Relationships and other details	Coffin No
widow of Thomas Smith	n/a
late of Guilford Street, London	4014
General, Commandant of the HEI Company's Madras Military	6029
relict of William Donaldson	3075
(husband of Hannah Bell Donaldson)	3080
'beloved wife of Chas Montague Martindale, Esq. Erected by her two children of a former marriage' [Georgiana and Percy Lousada].	1134
'Hon. Right Rev. Henry Montague Villiers, D.D., Lord Bishop of Durham, for 15 Years rector of this parish'	n/a
late of Brunswick Square, whose remains are deposited in the vault beneath,	6027
of Museum Street .'They were married for 48 years, and their mortal remains rest in the vault beneath'.	2014
'over fifty years resident in Bloomsbury'	n/a
'for many years the director of the East India Company, in which capacity he laboured chiefly for God and for the establishment of Christianity in India.'	n/a
'In the middle aisle of this church are deposited the remains of J.T. Smoult, Esq., who died in London. Lamented as a son, brother and friend . . .'	n/a
'In the vaults beneath this church are deposited the remains of Joseph Kirkup, Esquire., late of Harpur Street . . .	8043
Also, **James Fenwick Kirkup** (son of the above) who drowned whilst bathing . . . Also Ann Kirkup, widow of	1051
Joseph Kirkup, and daughter of the late Seymour Stocker, Esq. of Limehouse . . '	1029
late of Russell Square, husband of Arabella Groom	1105
wife of William Groom	1072
Edward Littledale, Esq	1077
To the memory of Charles Grant for fifty years employed in the service of the civil government of India or in the directing of its affairs in England, in four successive parliaments the representative of the County of Inverness . . . who in his private life was beloved for every domestic affection and social virtue and revered for integrity, devotion and charity. This memorial is consecrated by the East India Company as a tribute of respect and affection . . . Born Aldourie in Invernesshire . . . Died in London	3002
chief librarian, British Museum	1528
wife of Joseph Planta	1505
'In the vault beneath are deposited the remains of Francis, eldest son of Mr Francis Robertson of Lincoln's Inn Fields . . .	n/a
And Ebena Dorothea, youngest daughter of the above Francis'	2017
wife of William Richard Dove of this parish	1107
interred at the cemetery at Kensal Green	n/a
'In the vault beneath are deposited the remains of Mr **David Edwards** late of King Street of this parish'	2058
'**James Langley Bankes** Esq. of Upper Bedford Place . . . his sister-in-law, Elizabeth, daughter of the late Robert Lloyd, Esq., of Ince Hall, Lancashire . . . Their remains were deposited in the vaults of this church May 8th 1839'	6030 / 6013
'In the vaults beneath repose the remains of **Elizabeth Yenn** . . . Also of her husband John Yenn, Esq . . . Their grateful children have erected this tablet to their much cherished memories. . . Also of Susannah Mary Yenn, their beloved daughter'	1534 / 1550 / 1517
Francis William of Lincoln's Inn, Esq.. ' . . . an eminent lawyer and a profound and distinguished writer on legal isubjects, and was one of the Commissioners appointed by His Majesty George IV . . . **Anne** his wife, who he survived but a few weeks' 'Also in the same vault are interred his mother, **Elizabeth Sanders**, wife of John William Sanders of the Island of Nevis, Esq., and two of his children, **Francis William Sanders** . . . and **Eleanor Sanders**'	n/a / n/a / 1137 / n/a / n/a

Table 4.2 (continued): Summary memorial inscriptions from wall plaques within the interior of the church of St George, Bloomsbury

Memorial number	Surname	Forename	Date	Age at death
34	Alexander	William	Died 18 January 1814	61 years
	Rose	Elizabeth	died 29th February 1824	78 years
	Rose	Charles	-	-
35	Creswell	Mary	10th April 1809	51st year
	Creswell	Richard Cheslyn	died 11th February 182	70th year
	Creswell	Henry Whitfield	died 17th February	36th year
36	Partridge	Elizabeth	[14th] February 1815	-
37	Martyn	Nicholas	17th June 1807	46 years
	Martyn	Hannah	31 May 1810	70 years
	Martyn	Grace	2nd October 1834	64 years
	Martyn	Hannah	3rd December 1856	81 years
	[Martyn]	Nicholas	-	-
38	Briscoe	Carolina Alicia	died 27th December 1822	66th year
39	------	Sophia	-	-
40	Madden	Mary	26th February 1830	-
	Madden	Frederick Hayton	-	5 days

uals, but some information was extracted from parish registers. The quality of recording in St George's parish is very variable over time, and poor preservation of the primary records has rendered parts illegible.

St George's parish records do not distinguish between individuals interred within the crypt, and those buried within the churchyard off Brunswick Square, which was in use between 1713 and 1855 (Meller 1975, 20-23). Someone, evidently with a passion for figures, and possibly one of the rectors, was particularly helpful in neatly summarising the annual numbers of baptisms, marriages and deaths for the years between 1731 and 1840. For the decade of 1831-1840, he also summarised the annual number of burials by age. This information gives fascinating palaeodemographic insights into the inhabitants of St George's parish throughout much of the time that the crypt was in use. This information is discussed in Chapter 5 below.

With the introduction of civil registration in 1837, the information recorded was more standardised and is more complete, but detailed information can only be obtained by ordering individual certificates, which was not practical for a project such as this. The indices of the General Register Office are accessible on-line and can be used to check the date of the registration of births, marriages and deaths to within a particular quarter, and to identify potential spouses. The use of information from post 1837 civil registration has been very limited.

Perhaps the most useful sources available for Bloomsbury are the records of the Bloomsbury searchers, which survive for the period 1771-1834 (LMA P82/GEO1/63). These records contain the information collected by the parish searchers. The Parish Clerk had to be notified of any deaths in a parish. The parish searchers, often elderly female paupers, were employed by parishes to visit the recently deceased to determine whether or not there was any need for further official action. The searchers recorded the date of the visit, the name and age of the deceased, their disease, their abode (usually the street name), where they were to be buried, and, very occasionally, additional notes were added. So far as the crypt population is concerned the data recorded by the searchers is fullest for the 1820s, but there are still some individuals buried in the crypt in that decade, who are not listed by the searchers. Nonetheless the data recorded is amongst most the most useful since it provides information on causes of death, and on abodes, and confirmation of dates of death. The data regarding causes of death is considered in the next chapter.

The International Genealogical Index (IGI) (of the Church of the Latterday Saints) was also consulted on-line. This provides information regarding baptisms and marriages largely derived from parish registers. The IGI is only an index, and does not give the full information available in the parish registers. It gives the dates of marriages, the names of the

Relationships and other details	Coffin No
'In the vaults below this spot are deposited the remains of **William Alexander Esq**. . . . He was many years Provost Marshal General of the Mainland of St. Vincent, the duties of which office he discharged with honour to himself and satisfaction of the public. . . . Also of his sister **Elizth Rose**, relict of **Dr Charles Rose** LLD and rector of Graffam in Sussex'	1143 6050 n/a
'**Mary**, the beloved wife of Richard Cheslyn Creswell Esq., . . . Also of the said **Richard Cheslyn Creswell**, Esquire, one of the Deputy Registrars of the Prerogative Court of Canterbury, late of Queen's Square, Bloomsbury, and of Doctor's Commons . . . Also of **Henry Whifield Creswell** Esquire, late of Doctor's Commons, their third son . . . Whose bodies repose in the vault beneath.'	5002 5013 5007
'. . . daughter of the late William Partridge of Nottingham, whose remains are deposited in the vault of this church . . .'	7086
'Nicholas Martyn, Esq, late of Southampton Row of this parish . . . . Hannah, widow of the above . . . Grace Martyn, daughter of the above . . . Their mortal remains are deposited in the vault of this church. Hannah Martyn, daughter of Hannah and Nicholas, . . . Nicholas -------- (illegible)'	1546 6067 n/a n/a
'In the private chancel vault beneath . . . relict of Mr John Briscoe of Wimpole Street and Crofton Hall, Cumberland . . .'	3078
'The remains of **Mrs Sophia** ---------- were removed to the family vault in Kensall Green Cemetery in 1853'	n/a
'Mary, the beloved wife of Frederick Madden, Esq., of the British Museum and daughter of Robert Hayton, Esq. of Sunderland in the county of Durham . . . born June 7th 1803, married 18th April 1829 died 26th February 1830, after giving birth to an infant son Frederick Hayton, who survived only 5 days and lies with his deeply lamented mother in the vaults beneath' Anne his wife, who he survived but a few weeks	n/a n/a

couple and the church. The witnesses are not given. For baptisms, the names of the parents are listed. Unfortunately coverage of London Parishes is far from complete.

Finally Pallot's Marriage and Baptism Indices were consulted, again on-line. Both cover the period 1780 to 1837. The marriage index includes the vast majority of marriages in London, but the baptism index is far from complete. Pallot's Marriage Index gives the names of the couple, the church and the year of the marriage. Very rarely a marriage date is given. But the index often does show whether either party is a widow or widower, indicates if either party was a minor, and notes which parish either party is from if they are not local. The baptism index gives the parents names.

Wills

During Victorian times a surprisingly large proportion of the population, even the poor, made wills. Wills had to be proved in an ecclesiastical court. There was a hierarchy of ecclesiastical courts, and the appropriate court depended upon the wealth of the individual and the location of any property held. Since most of the individuals interred in St George's were wealthy many of the wills were proved in the senior ecclesiastical court, the Prerogative Court of Canterbury. Copies of the wills of many of those interred in St. George's church can be found in the Prerogative Court records, which

are held in the National Archives. The indices can be consulted on-line and can provide useful information, such as where individuals lived and their occupation, without the necessity of accessing individuals wills. Only a very small number of individual wills have been consulted.

Census records

In England, censuses were taken on 10 March 1801, 27 May 1811, 28 May 1821 and 30 May 1831, but these usually record only the numbers of people living in each parish, the number of houses and some indication of occupations or professions. Some census returns were retained, but the coverage is patchy.

The first census for which records were retained as a matter of course was that taken in 1841. This records the names, sex and occupations of individuals within households. Ages of adults were rounded up or down to the nearest 5 or 10 years. Relationships between the various household members were not recorded. The census also recorded whether or not the individuals were born in the county in which they were recorded. The 1841 census is useful in identifying the occupations of individuals and where they lived. It has more limited use in establishing family relationships.

The 1851 census included fuller details of individuals, such as name, sex, occupation and age, whether married or single, and relationship to the head of the household. The census also shows where individuals were born. This census fell right at the end of the period in which burial taking place in the crypt of St George's. Nonetheless the 1851 and later censuses can provide information about the descendants of the crypt population.

Trade directories, Post Office directories, and professional registers or lists

A number of trade and post office directories have been consulted. These are particularly useful in identifying the occupation of individuals. Trade directories and some Post Office directories provide lists of tradesmen, commercial enterprises and professional people, and little more. Other directories including some Post Office directories, have separate trade and professional listings, street directories and alphabetical listings of individuals. The *Post Office London Directory for 1841* is one such directory. Other directories that have been consulted extensively are *Kent's Directory for the Year 1794. Cities of London and Westminster, & Borough of Southwark*; *The Post Office Annual Directory for 1808*; *Holden's Annual London and Country Directory for the year 1811*, and *The Post Office London Directory for 1829*.

There are various published lists and directories for Army and Navy officers, for the Clergy and the Law and Courts. Lists were also published for the Bombay and Madras establishments of the East India Company.

Death notices and obituaries, and other sources

Finally death notices and obituaries of many of those interred in the crypt can be found in *The Gentleman's Magazine* and other periodical publications (see List of Sources in Appendix 1). These give details of abode, sometimes provide information about near relations, and often indicate a profession. *The Times* archive, which is accessible on-line, was also consulted. Finally the *Dictionary of National Biography* provided more detailed biographies of some of the more eminent occupants of the crypt.

The professions and occupations of the crypt population

The majority of the crypt population represented the wealthy professional classes resident in the parish of Bloomsbury. This included numerous lawyers from the nearby Inns of Court, doctors of medicine and surgeons, army and navy officers, imperial administrators, and curators and librarians of the British Museum, and their families. However, a number of tradesmen and their families were also interred, and even one servant, Mary Huster (4007) who was interred in a triple coffin no less lavish than the rest.

Members of various professions are listed in Tables 4.3, 4.5-4.13 below. Because in the first half of the 19th century the professions were almost exclusively a male preserve, the only women listed below

are the wives and daughters of professional men. Those denoted with an asterisk are individuals known from the memorial plaques within the church. More detail about the individuals listed, together with the sources of information can be found in Appendix 1.

The law (Table 4.3)

Practitioners of the law, including solicitors, barristers, proctors and judges, were the most numerous single professional group identified from the population interred in the crypt of St George's. The majority were barristers and solicitors, but there were senior judges, most notably Sir Joseph Littledale, Judge of the Court of Queen's Bench (appointed 1824) and Privy Counsellor (Hamilton 2004), Sir William Elias Taunton, Judge of the Court of King's Bench (appointed 1830) (Carr 2004), and Sir Henry Dampier, Judge of the Court of King's Bench (appointed 1813) (Oldham 2004).

Samuel Heywood, Sergeant at Law and judge of the Carmarthen circuit, was an important figure because he was a dissenter, and one of the few to be appointed a national office before the repeal of the Test Act. He was born in Liverpool, and later attended Cambridge University. He did not take his degree, because to graduate he had to subscribe to the Thirty-Nine Articles of the Church of England, which as a dissenter he refused to do. He studied at the Inner Temple. He wrote pamphlets and campaigned actively for the repeal of the Test and Corporation Acts. His friend John Lee, is quoted as saying of him: 'Well, Sam … thou art, in Truth a Dissenter! dissenting more than anybody I ever knew! – for thou agreest with nobody about anything!' (Lincoln and McEwen, 1960, 112, quoted in Ditchfield 2004). Lee was another Dissenter, like Heywood a Unitarian, and remarkably he became an MP and served briefly as solicitor general under Rockingham in 1782, and as solicitor general and then as attorney general in the Fox-North coalition of 1783. Heywood was a friend of Charles James Fox and contributed to his *History of the Early Part of the Reign of James II* (1808). He was also an expert on electoral law and published two works: *Digest of the Law Concerning County Elections* (1790) and *Digest of the Law Respecting Borough Elections* (1797). He died in 1828 at Tenby while on circuit. He was buried in Bristol. His wife and daughter were interred in the crypt of St George's.

Charles Thomson was one of the Masters in Chancery (appointed 1809; Haydn 1851, 241). He died of a 'paralytic stroke' in his house in Portland Place (*Gentleman's Magazine*, July 1821, 93). Henry and Richard Cresswell were both eminent figures in the ecclesiastical courts (Court of Arches). Richard Cheslyn Cresswell was a Deputy Registrar of the Prerogative Court of Canterbury (*The London Magazine*, March 1824, 336). Other notable figures were Francis William Sanders, described on his memorial in St George's church as 'an eminent

Table 4.3: The Law

Surname, Forename	Notes	Died	Burial no.
Addison, Ralph	of Temple Bar	6/8/1840	*1565
Addison, Jane	wife of Ralph Addison	14/2/1850	*1563
Ashmore, Elizabeth Ann	daughter of **James Ashmore**, barrister	27/7/1844	6057
Atkinson, Thomas	of Lincoln's Inn Fields and Bedford Place	4/8/1836	1574
Barker, Arthur Henry	son of **George Barker**, attorney, 1 Gray's Inn	1/7/1848	5022
Barker, Edward Fisher	son of **George Barker**, attorney, 1 Gray's Inn	17/3/1843	3031
Barnes, John	of the Inner Temple	-/4/1833	6104
Barry, Emily Matilda	wife of **Charles Upham Barry**, solicitor	24/11/1835	1042
Baxendale, Ellen Renica	daughter of **Lloyd Salisbury Baxendale**, solicitor	30/4/1827	3062
Berkeley, Georgina Emily	2nd daughter of **Charles Berkeley**, 53 Lincoln's Inn Field	27/3/1839	6132
Bullock, Catharine	wife of **Edward Bullock**, of the Inner Temple	11/6/1839	1128
Burley, George	solicitor, Messrs Beardsworth, Burley and Moore, Lincoln's Inn	25/12/1823	1053
Burley, Mary	wife of **George Burley**, solicitor	14/7/1836	1009
Cresswell, Richard Cheslyn	of Doctor's Commons, one of the Deputy Registrars of the Prerogative Court of Canterbury, Registrar of the Court of Arches	11/2/1824	*5013
Cresswell, Henry Whitfield	Supernumerary Proctor excercent in the Ecclesiastical Courts in Doctor's Commons	17/2/1828	*5007
Dampier, Sir Henry	Justice of His Majesty's Court of Kings Bench	3/2/1816	2061
Debary, Richard	of Lincoln's Inn Fields	8/1/1826	*5035
Debary, Ann Phoebe	wife of **Richard Debary**	15/2/1829	*5043
Dennett, Robert	of 39 Lincoln's Inn	14/5/1837	1086
Donaldson, William	of Temple Bar	23/2/1806	3080
Donaldson, Hannah	?wife of **William Donaldson**	8/9/1811	3075
Ford, Randle	Barrister, of Wexham, Buckinghamshire	1/1/1811	3502
Ford, Elizabeth	wife of **Randle Ford**	23/6/1806	3503
Groom, William	solicitor for the Board of Control for the Affairs of India; Richard and William Groom solicitors	25/-/1830	1105
Groom, Arabella	wife of **William Groom**		
Heywood, Susanna	wife of **Samuel Heywood**, Sergeant at Law	19/1/1822	3012
Heywood, Mary Isabella	daughter of **Samuel Heywood**, Sergeant at Law	16/10/1822	3033
Hobson, Julia	wife of **Campbell Wright Hobson**, of Gray's Inn	20/9/1840	6113
Hone, Joseph Terry	barrister at law	18/8/1831	6117
Hutchinson, Henry Julius	L.L.B	19/11/1813	1031
Lambert, Ellen Augusta	daughter of **Richard Lambert**, attorney and solicitor	25/2/1844	6135
Lambert, Mary Hannah	daughter of **Richard Lambert**, attorney and solicitor	13/12/1843	5052
Littledale, Sir Joseph	Kt, Judge of the Court of Queen's Bench and member of the Privy Council	1842	1511
Littledale, Edward	bibliophile, and founder member of the Roxburghe Club, brother of **Sir Joseph Littledale**	20/4/1837	1077
Lowe, John	attorney at law and solicitor	21/9/1850	6131
Lowe, Mary Harriet	wife of **John Lowe**	16/10/1852	6134
Lowe, William	of Tenfold Court, Inner Temple	21/12/1849	*6077
Mansfield, Sir James	Kt, Lord Chief Justice of the Court of Common Pleas	23/111821	*3019
Mansfield, Charlotte	2nd daughter of **Sir James Mansfield**	3/4/1821	3029
Martyn, Grace	daughter of **Nicholas Martyn**, of Lincoln's Inn Fields	7/10/1834	6067
Rackham, Willougby	of Lincoln's Inn	-/3/1825	3077
Robertson, Francis	eldest son of **Francis Robertson** of Lincoln's Inn Fields	18/4/1814	*7056
Robertson, Elinor Dorothea	daughter of **Francis Robertson** of Lincoln's Inn Fields	28/4/1815	*2017
Rogers, Julia Anne	daughter of **Francis James Newman Rogers**, Queen's Counsel, judge, author, and Deputy Judge Advocate General to Her Majesty's Forces	8/1/1832	4037
Sanders, Francis William	of Lincoln's Inn Fields	1/5/1831	*1073
Sanders, Ann	wife of **Francis William Sanders**	16/2/1831	*1082
Sanders, Eleanor	daughter of **Francis William Sanders**	15/6/1825	*6044
Taunton, Sir William Elias	Kt, Judge of the Court of King's Bench	11/1/1835	1099
Thomson, Charles	Master in Chancery	5/7/1821	3090
Thomson, Anne Dalzell	wife of **Charles Thomson**	9/1/1841	3089
Wilde, Charles Robert Claude	son Thomas Wilde, 1 st Baron Truro, Solicitor general, Attorney general and Lord Chancellor	29/8/1810	2049

lawyer and a profound and distinguished writer on legal subjects'. William Groom acted as solicitor for the Board of Control for the Affairs of India (Elmes 1831, 70).

Sir James Mansfield, Lord Chief Justice of the Common Pleas and Privy Counsellor was undoubtedly the most prominent member of the legal profession interred in the St George's crypt (Davis, MT 2004). Sir James Mansfield is best remembered for his achievements in the reformation of many civil liberties. His memorial in the church records that his 'eminent talents and learning, energy and integrity' in his profession rendered him 'one of its most distinguished ornaments'.

Mansfield's stance on slavery was very different from that of Charles Grant and the Clapham Sect, although his ruling in 1772 in the case of the slave James Somerset considerably stoked the growing moral uneasiness regarding the slave trade. In this case, the highest lawyers in the land debated whether slaves from Africa and the Colonies remained slaves when they were brought to England. Chief Justice Mansfield upheld the judgement that the sale of a slave in England was valid, but that forcible detention of a slave with the view to selling him/her abroad was unacceptable, and that the slave should be discharged (Picard 2000, 114). In this way, James Somerset won his freedom. However, considerable ambivalence existed over the question of slave ownership in England, with Mansfield himself ruling in 1785 that black slaves in Britain were not entitled to be paid for their labours, but free blacks should be paid.

Despite his reputed liberalism, Sir James Mansfield supported the use of press-gangs as a means of recruitment for the Royal Navy. Between 1756 and 1788, he took the view that it was a practice 'founded upon memorial custom allowed for ages' and that it was necessary for the defence of the realm (Picard 2000). It should be remembered, however, that he was merely echoing the pervasive view held by the propertied classes of his time.

The daughter of Francis James Newman Rogers, Queen's Counsel and also Deputy Judge Advocate General to Her Majesty's Forces (Hughes 1845, 222), was interred in the crypt of St George's Church. Newman Rogers was born in Dorset the son of a clergyman. He married Julia Eleanora Yea in June 1822. Rogers had lived in Woburn Place, but when he died on 19 July 1851 his home was in Wimpole Street (Boase 2004).

The young son of Thomas Wilde, 1st Baron Truro, was also buried in the crypt. He served as Solicitor General, Attorney General and finally as Lord Chancellor. Wilde was called to the bar in 1817. He had made his reputation as a defence lawyer for Queen Caroline in her trial of 1820. In gratitude, Queen Caroline made Wilde one of the executors of her will. He married Mary Devayne, daughter of Thomas Wileman and widow of a banker William Devayne in 1813. The couple had a daughter and three sons. Mary died in 1840, and Wilde married his second wife Augusta Emma D'Este, daughter of the 4th earl of Dunmore, in 1845. There were no children from the second marriage. Wilde was MP for Newark on Trent and then Worcester in the Whig interest (Rigg 2004).

The church (Tables 4.4-4.5)

A small number of clergymen were interred in the crypt of the church. Only one rector of the Parish was interred in the crypt (Table 4.4). This was the Rev Thomas Willis (1754-1827), who was the rector of St George's from 1791 to 1828, and also prebendary of Rochester and rector of Wateringbury, Kent. He was born in Lincolnshire in 1754, and was the son of the Rev Francis Willis. Frances Willis began his career as a clergyman, but took up medicine and became a doctor specialising in the treatment of the insane. His most famous patient was George III, whom he treated at Kew in 1788. He worked in partnership with his son Dr John Willis. John Willis and his younger brother Dr Robert Darling Willis treated the King again in 1801. The Rev Thomas Willis met the King through this connection and visited Kew Palace (Cannon 2004).

A second incumbent of St George's was the Hon and Right Rev Henry Montague Villiers, who is commemorated by a mural monument in the church. He was rector at St George's Bloomsbury from 1841 to 1856. His young son Wilbraham Edward, who died aged three and half months, was interred in the crypt. In 1856 Villiers was appointed Bishop of Carlisle, and then in 1860 he was translated to the see of Durham. Unfortunately the following year he became ill and died aged only 48 years old (Munden 2004). A younger brother, the

Table 4.4: Nineteenth-century rectors of St. George's, Bloomsbury (from George Clinch, Bloomsbury and St Giles's: past present; with historical and antiquarian notes of the vicinity, *London 1890, 129)*

Name	Inducted	Notes
Thomas Willis, LL.D.	March 16th, 1791	died 9 Nov 1827
John Lonsdale, B.D.	February 8th, 1828	Bishop of Lichfield 1843-1867
Thomas Vowler Short, B.D.	February 22nd, 1834	Bishop of St Asaph 1846-1870
Hon. Henry Montagu Villiers, M.A.	July 9th, 1841	Bishop of Carlisle 1856-60; Bishop of Durham 1860-61
Sir John R. L. E. Bayley, M.A.	May 24th, 1856	died 4 Dec 1917

Table 4.5: The Church

Surname, Forename	Notes	Died	Burial no.
Bingley, Rev. William	clergyman, naturalist and writer on botany, topography and zoology	-/3/1823	5062
Hume, Rev. John Henry	vicar of Figheldean and Hilmartin, Wiltshire; vicar of Calne; chaplain to the Earl of Rosslyn	22/1/1848	1141
Martyn, Rev. John Lee	rector of St George the Martyr, Queen Square	19/8/1836	1538
Nares, Rev. Robert	clergyman and philologist	23/3/1829	1568
Poston, Rev. Andrew Philip	clerk	13/5/1822	3051
Rose, Rev. Dr. Charles	rector of Graffham, Sussex		*
Rose, Elizabeth	relict of **Rev. Dr. Charles Rose**, sister of **William Alexander**	29/2/1824	*6050
Villiers, The Right Hon. Rev. Henry Montague	Lord Bishop of Durham (1860-61), Bishop of Carlisle (1856-60), and rector of St George's Bloomsbury (1841-56)	9/8/1856	*
Villiers, Wilbraham Edward	son of **Henry Montague Villiers**	21/11/1845	3038
Williams, Mary	widow of **John Williams**, vestry clerk of St. Dunstan in the West	9/3/1835	1504
Willis, Rev Thomas	L.L.D., rector of St George's, Bloomsbury	9/11/1827	2045
-------, Rev. Francis		23/4/1806	3058

Hon Algernon Villiers, a lieutenant in the Royal Navy, was interred in the crypt of St George's (see 'The army, navy and merchant marine' and Table 4.6 below).

The Rev John Lee Martyn who was interred in the crypt had been the incumbent of St George's Hanover Square (*The Clerical Guide or Ecclesiastical Directory*, 1817, 117). The other clergymen interred in the crypt include the Rev William Bingley, who was minister of Fitzroy Chapel (St Saviour's) in Charlotte Street from 1816 to 1823. He was a naturalist and a writer on botany, topography and zoology. His most popular work was *Animal Biography*, published in 1802, which went into many editions and was translated into a number of European languages (Courtney 2004).

The other notable clergyman interred in St George's was the philologist the Rev Robert Nares (Wroth 2004). He held several of ecclesiastical appointments. In 1787 he was chaplain to the Duke of York, and from 1788-1803 was an assistant preacher for the Honourable Society of Lincoln's Inn. In 1798 he was appointed a cannon residentiary at Lichfield a post he held till his death. He was also a prebendary at St Paul's Cathedral, and Archdeacon of Stafford. He was vicar of St Mary's, Reading, for a time, and then from 1818 to 1829 he was rector of All Hallows, London Wall. In addition he was appointed assistant librarian in the department of manuscripts at the British Museum in 1795, and in 1799 was made to keeper of manuscripts.

He published theological works, including his Lincoln's Inn *Sermons* (1794), a work on political science comparing the French and British systems of government, *Principles of Government* (1792), but is best remembered for *A Glossary; or a collection of words, phrases, names and allusions to customs, proverbs, &c. which have been thought to require illustration in the works of English authors particularly Shakespeare and his contemporaries* (1822) and *Elements of Orthoepy, containing a distinct view of the whole analogy of the English language as far as it relates to pronunciation, accent and quantity* (1784), He died at his house, No. 22 Hart Street, Bloomsbury, London, on 23 March 1829

Some of the clergy interred at St George's were clearly well-connected socially. The rectory itself was wealthy, and the patron of the parish was the monarch (*The Clerical Guide or Ecclesiastical Directory*, 1817, 117). Three of the Rev Willis's successors as incumbent went on to become bishops (Table 4.4). The Rev Willis had contact directly with George III through his father and brothers who treated the King's madness. Henry Montague Villiers was a member of the aristocracy. His brother was the 4th Earl of Clarendon and foreign secretary. Villiers was an 'evangelical' in doctrine and a very hard working parish priest, who worked well with the non-conformists. As a bishop he was active in promoting clerical piety and attempted to raise the academic standards of clerical appointees .

John Henry Hume was the grandson of the Right Rev John Hume, Bishop of Salisbury and his wife Lady Mary Hay, daughter of George 7th Earl of Kinnoul. His father Thomas Henry Hume was Canon Residentiary and Treasurer of Sarum, and vicar of Stratford sub Castrum, Wiltshire and of Kewstoke, Somerset. John Henry Hume was vicar of Calne and Figheldeane and chaplain to the Earl of Rosslynn. Robert Nares, had slightly less exalted connections than Hume. His father was organist at York Minster, but his uncle Sir George Nares was a judge, and a cousin Edward Nares, was Regius professor of modern history at Oxford University (Wroth 2004). William Bingley seems to be an exception. His father was a clergyman in Doncaster, and he attended Cambridge University. After graduation he was ordained a deacon, and became a curate in North Yorkshire. His prominence depended more upon his writing than on his clerical preferments, which were modest.

The army, navy and merchant marine (Table 4.6)

A number of officers from the army, navy and East India Company service were interred in the crypt of St George's church. Many of them, such as John Percival Beaumont (captain half pay, 30th Regiment of Foot), John Covell (formerly major, 76th Regiment of Foot), William Dunbar (formerly captain, 40th Regiment of Foot) and Joseph MacLean (major, half pay, the late 3rd West India Regiment of Foot) had clearly retired from service. It has not been possible to identify with certainty Major Joseph MacLean, of the 3rd West Indian Regiment of Foot, nor William Dunbar, formerly Captain in the 40th Regiment. Nor can Major Sam Stapleton or Colonel Matthew Wilson be identified.

Thomas Draper, whose wife Elizabeth was interred in the crypt rose to the rank of Inspector General of Army Hospitals. He began his career as a Hospital Assistant in April 1795, was promoted Assistant Surgeon in April 1799, and Regimental Surgeon on 17th April 1804. He served in Sicily in 1806, in Egypt in 1807 and in the Corunna Campaign with Sir John Moore. He had been surgeon with the 78th Foot when he was promoted to Staff Surgeon on 1 September 1808 (*Gazette*, Issue 16178, 3 Sept 180, 1196). He served in Portugal in 1811 and was in Holland in 1814. He was awarded the Peninsula Medal, but not the Waterloo medal, although there is evidence that he was in Belgium in 1815. On June 25th he wrote a letter from Ostend to Dr Dick in London giving him news of his son Colonel Robert Dick of the 42nd Regiment. In 1816 Draper was promoted to Deputy Inspector General of Army Hospitals, and in February 1840 he was promoted to

Table 4.6: Army, Royal Navy, East India Company service and merchant marine:

Surname, Forename	Notes	Died	Burial no.
Army			
Beaumont, John Percival	Captain, half pay, 30th Regiment	25/2/1844	1572
Buchanan, Elizabeth Dundas	4th surviving daughter, of **Colonel Buchanan**, Royal Engineers	27/6/1836	8054
Covell, John	formerly Major, 76th Regiment of Foot	17/9/1834	7055
Covell, Jane Dennis	widow of **Major Covell**	9/5/1838	*7045
Draper, Elizabeth	wife of **Thomas Draper**, Inspector General of Army Hospitals	30/9/1834	3099
Dunbar, William	formerly Captain 40th Regiment	21/3/1842	8086
Dunbar, Mary Anne	wife of **William Dunbar**	11/4/1829	7068
MacLean, Joseph	Major, half pay, of the late 3rd West India Regiment of Foot	25/2/1832	5029
Stapleton, Samuel	Major	16/8/1806	1135
Wilson, Matthew	Lieutenant Colonel	15/7/1836	2041
Wilson, Ann	widow of Colonel Matthew Wilson	23/8/1836	6072
Royal Navy			
Denton, Samuel	Purser, R.N.	27/3/1806	6091
Duer, John	Commander, R.N.	17/11/1814	4016
Graham, Edward Lloyd	Captain, R.N.	27/5/1820	3070
Share, James	Commander, R.N.	11/2/1831	6115
Villiers, The Hon. Algernon	Lieutenant R.N., Knight of Isabella the Catholic (Spain)	13/7/1843	2009
Young, Ann, Dowager Lady	relict of the late **Admiral Sir George Young**, K.C.B.	16/10/1830	1533
East India Co.			
Bell, Robert	General, Madras Artillery, in the Hon. East India Co. service	26/3/1844	*6029
Bowles, Robert	Major General, Hon. East India Co. service	6/9/1812	5040
Gasgoyne, Joseph	Lieut. Colonel in the Hon. East India Co. service	21/3/1830	6011
Gascoyne, Arabella	wife of **Joseph Gascoyne**	8/4/1835	6073
Jourdan, Edward	Major , 2nd Cavalry, Madras Army, in the Hon. East India Co. service	26/9/1830	*6028
Vigors, Elizabeth	relict of **Lt. Gen. Urban Vigors**, in the Hon East India Co. service	22/7/1817	1143
Jeakes, James	Commodore, Bombay Marine	8/4/1837	1079
Merchant navy			
Fairfax, William	Captain of the *Hugh Inglis* in the Hon. East India Co. service	19/3/1817	1090
Foulerton, John	Captain, (not R.N); Elder Brother of Trinity House	16/11/1827	6116
Foulerton, Mary	?daughter of **John Foulerton**	18/9/1820	
Uncertan			
Biscoe, Joseph William Edwin	Captain, uncertain, not RN	24/3/1827	4024
Fraser, . . .	daughter of **Capt. Fraser**, unknown service	26/5/1832	5025

Inspector General (Hart, 1841, 414, 423 note 4*). He died aged 76 at Instow, near Barnstaple on 28 June 1850 (*Gentleman's Magazine*, August 1850, 225).

General Robert Bell and Major General Robert Bowles, both of the East India Company service had also retired. General Bell served with the Madras artillery (Philippart 1823, 128-30; Dodwell and Miles 1838, 8-9). He fought at Mallavelly and Seringapatam (1799), and had commanded the Indian artillery that served with Sir Ralph Abercrombie in the expedition to Egypt in 1801. In 1809 the then Colonel Bell was in command of the garrison of Seringapatam when the officers of the Madras Army mutinied against Sir George Barlow, the governor of Madras. Barlow had dismissed two officers from army following a dispute with the outgoing commander in chief of the Madras Army. Many officers showed their support for the dismissed men, and Barlow attempted to remove a number of these officers including Lieutenant Colonel Robert Bell (British Library, IOR/H/696, IOR/H/700). This led to mutinies of Hyderabad and Jaulna Brigades and the Seringapatam garrison amongst others. Eventually these units surrendered, and the mutiny ended. Most officers were offered an amnesty but a small number were cashiered and others were dismissed the service. Sir George Barlow was recalled. Bell was promoted to Major General in July 1810, and was re-appointed to command the Madras Artillery and to a seat on the military board (British Library IOR/F/4/389/9876). He was made a Lieutenant General in August 1819 and General in 1837. It is uncertain when he left India, but by 1821 he was living at No. 80 Guilford Street.

Major General Bowles served with the Bombay Presidency. In 1798 he was a Major General, Commandant of the Bombay Presidency, a member of its military board, and on Lt General Stuart's staff representing the Company's military establishment (Adjutant General's Office, 1798, unpaginated). He was born in about 1744 and would have been 54 in 1798. Little more is known about him.

Colonel Joseph Gascoyne had entered the East India Company' military service as an ensign in 1778. He served in the 4th Regiment of Bengal Native Infantry, until his promotion to lieutenant colonel in 1803, when he was posted to the 21st Regiment. He retired from the Company's service in 1809 (Welch 1852, 401). He married Arabella Denton, widow of Samuel Denton, in 1808.

Five Royal Navy officers were interred in the crypt of St George's. John Duer, and Edward Lloyd Graham both served during the Napoleonic Wars and both were young enough when they died to be serving officers. Duer, who died in 1814, was commissioned lieutenant in 1802, promoted to commander in 1804 and made post rank in 1806. In 1808 en route for the West Indies in command of the *Aurora* he captured a French privateer *La Vengeance* (*Gazette* 16162, 12 July 1808, 908) and in 1809 he was one of the officers who negotiated the surrender of Santo Domingo to British forces (*Gazette* 16294, 2 Sept

1809, 1418-21). He was also present at the surrender of Guadeloupe on 6 February 1810. His ship the *Aurora* was part of the squadron commanded by Sir Alexander Cochrane (Allen, 1852, 310).

Edward Lloyd Graham who died in 1820 aged only 38, was a lieutenant in 1797, commander in 1802 and promoted to post captain in 1804. He served as Sir Edward Pellew's flag captain in the *Caledonia* in 1814 (James 1837, 255). His father Aaron Graham knew Pellew from his time in Newfoundland (see 'Imperial administrators and civil servants' below)

The third officer Royal Navy officer was the Hon. Algernon Villiers, brother of the Bishop of Durham and of the 4th Earl of Clarendon. He died aged 25 in 1843. He had been commissioned lieutenant in 1838, and had served in the Royal Navy squadron that supported the Spanish government in the First Carlist War in Spain. He was made a Knight of Isabella the Catholic for his part in the war. James Share, R.N. was commissioned as a lieutenant in June 1782 and died aged 79 in 1831. No more is known of his service.

James Share, R.N. was commissioned as a lieutenant in June 1782 and died aged 79 in 1831. No more is known of his service.

Samuel Denton was at one time a purser in the Royal Navy (*Naval Chronicle*, **20**, 493). He served as purser on the 28 gun frigate *Aurora* (Captain James Cumming) in her service in the West Indies from July 1777 until her return to Britain in December 1779. Captain John Duer (see above) was later to command the *Aurora*. However Denton was also working as a prize agent (eg. *Gazette*, **12614**, 18 Jan 1785, 42; **12893**, 9 June 1787, 281-82; **13106**, 16 June 1789, 443) in partnership with Isaac Clementson. Prize agents were employed by naval officers to deal with disposal of ships and cargoes taken as prizes of war (Hill 1998, chapter 14). By 1796 the partners were based at No. 14 Clement's Inn (*Gazette*, **13875**, 15 March 1796, 262). In 1800 Denton was purser of the *Fortitude* a former 3rd rate 74 line of battleship, which had been a prison ship since July 1798 (TNA ADM 36/12803), and also working as a prize agent (*Gazette*, **15260**, 24 May 1800, 525; **15285**, 16 Aug 1800, 937). In 1801 the partnership between Denton and Clementson was dissolved and Denton continued the business alone (*Gazette*, **15356**, 18 April 1801, 424).

Denton lived in Russell Square, but was resident at Turnham Green, Middlesex at the time of his death (TNA PROB 11/1446). He was married to Arabella, and the couple had a daughter Arabella Phillis Denton born in 1791 and christened at St Clement Danes (IGI). Denton died in March 1806 aged 47 years, and in 1808 his widow married Lt Col Joseph Gascoyne (*Naval Chronicle*, **20**, 1808, 493; *Gentleman's Magazine*, Dec 1808, 1125).

James Jeakes served with the Bombay Marine, the naval service the East India Company, and retired as commodore. In 1809 he commanded a detachment of the Bombay Marine in the Persian Gulf. A force comprising two Royal Navy Frigates, *Chiffonne* (Capt. Wainwright) and *Caroline* (Capt. Gordon) and a detachment of India Company cruisers, *Mornington* (Capt. Jeakes) and *Aurora, Nautilus, Prince of Wales, Fury* and *Ariel* (Lts Conyers, Watkins, Allen, Davidson and Salter) was sent to deal with pirates at Ras-al-Khyma. On board the cruisers were with troops under Lieutenant Colonel Smith. On 13th November this force took the town of Ras-al-Khyma, which had for a 'some time been a nest for numerous desperate pirates' (Allen, 1852, 302; *The Asiatic Journal and Monthly Miscellany*, July 1826, 88-89). Jeakes returned to England in 1829 (*The Asiatic Journal and Monthly Miscellany*, June 1829, 802). (For the Jeakes family see below)

Amongst the other men were a number of merchant captains. William Fairfax was the master of the India Company ship the *Hugh Inglis*. The ship was launched in 1799 and made its first voyage in 1799-1800 under the command of Fairfax (British Library, IOR/L/MAR/A-B, Ships' Journals, *Hugh Inglis*). His last voyage in the *Hugh Inglis* was made in 1815 -1816 from China to the Downs. Fairfax died in 1817 at home in Southampton Row.

John Foulerton was probably another merchant captain. His *depositum* plate was transcribed as reading 'Captain John Foulerton, RN' but no record of any service in the Royal Navy can be found. He is not listed in 'Commissioned Sea Officers of the Royal Navy, 1660-1815, a manuscript compilation held at the National Maritime Museum and now accessible on-line. In 1797 he was present at a meeting of merchants, ship-owners and insurers organised by the Marine Society under the chair-manship of Hugh Inglis, in response to the Nore mutiny (*The Times*, Monday 12 June 1797).

He was an Elder Brother of Trinity House Deptford (Cotton, 1818, 244). In 1824 he was one of the Central Committee of the 'Royal National Institute for the Preservation of Life from Shipwreck', later known as the 'Royal National Lifeboat Institution'. In the list he is simply named as Captain Foulerton with no RN after his name unlike his fellow committee member Captain Deans Dundas RN (Hillary, 1825, 47). John Foulerton, of Upper Bedford Place, also patented a number of improvements to buoys (*Annual Register for 1816*, 347; *The Repertory of patent inventions and other discoveries and improvements*, Vol **X**, 1830, 63). In 1819 it seems that John Foulerton of Upper Bedford Place, merchant and elder brother of Trinity House was declared bankrupt (*The Literary Panorama and National Register*, Vol **VII**, 1819, 315; *The Times* Friday 10 Sept 1824). He died in November 1827.

Members of Parliament and politicians (Table 4.7)

Two members of Parliament – Charles Grant and the Honourable Christopher Hely-Hutchinson – were interred in St George's crypt. Two of the children of another Member of Parliament – Charles Harrison Batley – were also buried there.

Charles Grant (1746-1823) is commemorated by a large and ornate mural memorial in the church. The coffin containing his mortal remains was recovered from Vault 4 of the crypt, but was not opened. Grant, was four times MP for Invernesshire and Director of the Honourable East India Company. He was best known for his tireless campaigning against social injustice in India, England and Scotland (Carson 2004).

Charles Grant was born in Aldourie, Scotland, in 1746, the third of seven children. Grant's father Alexander Grant fought as Jacobite solder, was badly wounded at Culloden and went into hiding. In 1756 he joined a regiment raised for service in America, and died in Havana in 1762. The family's fortunes were impoverished as result of Alexander's Jacobite activities. Fortunately Charles was supported at school and after by his uncle John. His uncle's support was not forgotten.

He was first apprenticed to William Forsyth a Cromarty shipowner and merchant, and then obtained a position through his cousin Captain Alexander Grant, who was partner in London merchant house. He worked his way up to become head clerk. He wished to restore his family's fortune, and felt that India would provide the best opportunity. Through contacts he obtained an appointment as cadet in the Honourable East India Company's Bengal Army. He served for two and half years before his health broke down and he returned to Britain.

On his return to Britain he set up in business but not with any great success. His fortunes took a turn for the better when a merchant friend procured him a place as a writer in the Honourable East India Company (HEIC) in 1772. He married the beautiful seventeen year old Jane Fraser, daughter of Thomas Fraser of Balnain, just before leaving for India. It was to be a long and happy marriage.

He remained with the company for many years rising to become company director. During his time in India, Grant witnessed gross civil injustices practiced upon natives of the country, both by the British but also by their own countrymen. Whilst resident in North India, Grant and his wife were shattered by the loss of their two young daughters Elizabeth and Margaret who both died of smallpox in 1776. Macaulay records that in their extreme affliction the couple turned to God, and remained fervent Christians thereafter. Grant, who had lost heavily at gambling, regarded the deaths as a punishment for his ungodly life. The Grants with their five children left India in 1790.

Grant's Christian faith compelled him to confront the many injustices he had witnessed in India, where corruption was rife and natives were shown little respect or humanity. Together with Brown and Bentinck, Grant pressurised the Company and the British government to right these injustices and was instrumental in the abolition of the traditional Indian practices of suttee and infanticide. In 1813 the British Government published Grant's *Observations of the*

Table 4.7: Members of Parliament:

Surname, Forename	Notes	Died	Burial no.
Grant, Charles	M.P. for Invernesshire, director of the Hon. East India Co.	31/10/1823	*3002
Grant, Jane	wife of **Charles Grant**	23/1/1827	3003
Grant, William Thomas	son of **Charles Grant**	15/5/1848	3024
Harrison Batley, Mary	daughter. of **Charles Harrison Batley**, M.P. for Beverley, Yorkshire	13/8/1827	2035
Harrison Batley, John Charles	son of **Charles Harrison Batley** M.P. for Beverley, Yorkshire	30/1/1841	1513
Hely Hutchinson, the Hon. Christopher	M.P. for the City of Cork	26/8/1826	4070
Wilde, Charles Robert Claude	see Table 4.3	-	-

state of society amongst the Asian subjects of Great Britain, in which he criticised the denigration of Britain's Indian subjects. Under his directorship a criminal justice system was introduced in India, and the spread of Christianity encouraged. Circumventing the wishes of the company he encouraged missionaries to spread the Word in India. His philanthropy was remembered by Mangalwadi in his book *India: the Grand Experiment* (1997) when he wrote: 'Did you know that the first manifesto for India's freedom was published 77 years before Mahatma Gandhi was ever born? And by a Britisher? . . . Charles Grant of the British East India Company? He led the assault on the Company's misrule of India for four decades, articulated a grand vision for India and built a team to implement it'.

Grant did not confine his philanthropy to Indians but also included his native Highland Scots, who had suffered tremendous hardships as a result of the Highland clearances following Bonnie Prince Charlie's disastrous rebellion. As MP for Invernesshire he 'laboured effectively for the improvement of his native country where he was prime mover of these noble works which have changed the face of the Scottish Highlands' (memorial inscription).

It is perhaps for his involvement with the Clapham Circle that Charles Grant is best remembered. The Clapham Sect, which included William Wilberforce, was a group of philanthropists that met between 1790 and 1830 to lobby against the slave trade. After a series of major campaigns, public pressure and the support of the Whigs, they finally brought about a ban on the slave trade in 1803, followed by the Abolition of Slavery and the Emancipation Acts passed in 1833 (Gardiner and Wenborn 1995). Grant's anti-slavery stance also involved him in the founding of a colony for freed slaves in Sierra Leone (Meller 1975).

The achievements of Charles Grant's two sons, Charles and Robert, were by no means contemptible. Born in India, they returned to England where they studied at Magdalene College, Cambridge. Charles junior entered politics and rose to become Lord Palmerston's Colonial Secretary, and was made Lord Glenelg. He died in 1866, and hence, was not interred in St George's crypt with his father.

Robert was admitted to the bar in 1807. He then entered politics, winning a seat in parliament, aged 29 years. Like his father, he was deeply concerned with social issues. It was through his persistence that a bill was passed which emancipated England's Jews. He also returned to India where he became Governor of Bombay. A deeply religious man, Robert also spent time writing hymns, twelve of which were posthumously published by his brother Charles. His hymn 'Oh worship the King' was written in 1838 and remains one of the most beautiful and popular hymns today. He died in India.

Christopher Hely-Hutchinson was the fifth son of John Hely Hutchinson and Christiana Nikson, and a younger brother of Richard Hely-Hutchinson, 1st earl of Donoughmore, and John Hely-Hutchinson, 2nd earl of Donoughmore. He was called to the Irish Bar in 1792, entered the Irish Parliament in 1795. He opposed the Union with England. He fought in The Helder expedition and was wounded at Alkmaar. In 1801 he was promoted Lieutenant Colonel and served with his brother Richard under Sir Ralph Abercrombie in Egypt. In 1802 he became MP for Cork, and continued to represent the city until his death, except for the period 1812-18. Christopher Hutchinson was never wealthy and was fiercely independent. He died in Hampstead in 1826 after a long lingering illness (Dunlop 2004).

Richard Hely-Hutchinson, 1st earl of Donoughmore was also interred in St George's crypt. He is remembered best as an advocate of Catholic emancipation. He sided with George IV in the trial of Queen Caroline, when the King tried to divorce his wife on the grounds of adultery with Pergami. The divorce was an attempt by the King to prevent Caroline claiming her rights as Queen Consort, after he was crowned. The King rewarded him with a British peerage as Viscount Hutchinson. He died on 22 August 1825 at 4 Bulstrode Street, Manchester Square, Marylebone, Middlesex. The Catholic Association hailed him as their hereditary patron (Thorne 2004).

John Charles Harrison Batley, who was interred in the crypt of St George's Bloomsbury, was the son and heir of Charles Harrison Batley who was MP for Beverley, and his wife Anna (*Gentleman's Magazine*, Vol 97 Part 1, 1827, Supplement, 640). Charles Harrison Batley himself died in 1835 at St Omer in France aged only 49 (*Gentleman's Magazine*, Dec 1835, 667).

Imperial administrators and civil servants (Table 4.8)

A small number of civil servants and imperial administrators were buried in the crypt. William Alexander and Charles Thesiger both had connections with the Island of St Vincent in the West Indies. Alexander had been Provost Marshall General (Table 4.2, memorial 34), and Thesiger the collector of customs. According to *Burke's Peerage*, Thesiger's estate on the island was destroyed by a volcanic eruption in 1812.

Aaron Graham had been Secretary to the Governors of the Island of Newfoundland from 1779–1791, and in that capacity had known Captain Edward Pellew (Privy Council 1927, vol IV, 1919-23).

Edward Dew was 'late Examiner of the King's Duties, and Collector of the City Dues, at the Custom House' (*Gentleman's Magazine*, June 1834, 666). Charles Montague Martindale, whose daughter Harriet Edith was interred in the crypt, lived at No. 4 Montague Street and worked in the Paymaster General's office (Census 1841 and 1851).

Merchants, bankers, stockbrokers, etc (Table 4.9)

Significant numbers of merchants, bankers and stockbrokers are represented in the crypt population. Amongst them was Mathias Aspden, who left the United States because of the War of Independence.

Mathias (or Matthias) Aspden, was born in Philadelphia on 21 November 1746. He was the only child son of Matthias Aspden, senior (b. Padiham, Lancashire 4 May 1693 or 1695; d. 23 August 1765, Philadelphia) and his second wife Rebecca Packer (b. 1705, Burlington, New Jersey; d. 10 Oct 1773, Philadelphia) who was a widow. Matthias Aspden senior was a Quaker and a merchant. The younger Aspden was educated in England, and at the outbreak of the War of Independence he left America for England.

Aspden along with a number of other men was declared a traitor to the Commonwealth of Pennsylvania by a proclamation of 27th July 1778, and was strictly charged and required to present himself to a magistrate to be tried for treason (*Pennsylvania Archives*, Series 3, **X**, 537-9). He was attainted a traitor on the 27th July 1780 (*Pennsylvania Archives*, Series 4, **III**, 774-777) and subsequently his property was confiscated (eg. *Pennsylvania Archives*,

Series 6, **XII**, 193-95, 496, 582-82; *Pennsylvania Archives*, Colonial Records, **XIII**, 209).

Aspden settled in London and was a successful merchant. He was a shareholder in the East India Company and one eligible to be a director (*List of Members 1815; The Times*, 1 Dec 1823). In the 1815 list his address was given as Richmond, Surrey. Although Aspden appears to have settled in Britain and died in England in 1824, he did return to the United States on at least two occasions. The first time was immediately after the War of Independence. In 1786 the State of Pennsylvania proposed to lift the attainder on Aspden (*Pennsylvania Archives*, Colonial Records, **XIV**, 621, 625). That he was pardoned is confirmed by his old school friend Charles Biddle, who wrote that

> At this time there was an application from my old friend and schoolmate, Mr Mathias Aspden. . . for a pardon. It gave me great pleasure to have an opportunity of serving this worthy man. I sent him a pardon, January 19, 1786, and he soon came to Philadelphia. After he had been here a short time, he called on a gentleman of the law to know if, by the treaty of peace, he was secure from arrest. The gentleman not knowing, and Mr Aspden not telling him, that he had a pardon from the Executive Council, told him that he did not think so. As soon as he got this opinion, without seeing any of his friends he immediately set off for New York, and embarked on board a packet, then ready to sail for England, where he now is, 1804. . . . He lives very retired in London. (Biddle 1883, 211).

According to Henry Graham Ashmead (1884, 637-38) Aspden had returned to America in 1785. He made his will while in America. The will was dated 1791 in Philadelphia, which would suggest that he had stayed for some time before sailing for England.

His second visit was in about 1816 or 1817. Samuel Mickle, clerk to the Quaker Meeting in Woodbury, New Jersey, made the following entry in his diary for the 18 May 1817:

> [1817] 5/18. Mathias Aspden at meeting says he was taken away from ye country to England at ye time of Revolutionary war and kept as a prisoner at large and returned to America

Table 4.8: Diplomats, imperial administrators and civil servants:

Surname, Forename	Notes	Died	Burial no.
Alexander, William	Provost Marshall General of the Mainland of St. Vincent	18/1/1814	*
Dew, Edward	late Examiner of the King's Dues and Collector of City Dues	22/1/1834	3067
Martindale, Harriet Edith	wife of **Charles Montague Martindale** of the Paymaster General's Office	-/2/1843	1098
Palyart, Ignatius	Portuguese Consul General and merchant	22/12/1818	5008
Thesiger, Charles	collector of His Majesty's Customs of the Island of St Vincent	18/2/1831	2029

about 18 mo[nth]s. ago after an absence of 40 years. Enquired of me after many persons many years in their graves (Stewart 1917, 205).

Aspden died in August 1824. He had never married and had no children, and his enormous fortune was left to his 'heir-at-law'. This brief phrase was the cause of a legal dispute which lasted for nearly 30 years. Aspden had numerous cousins, both in England and America. It has been suggested that the number of claimants was as high as 200 (Ashmead, 1884, 637-38). By the time the dispute was finally settled in 1853 many of the original protagonists had died. Judgement was in favour of his American cousins. One of the English claimants was John Aspden. Prior to the final decision of the court the American cousins had offered him an out of court settlement of $250,000, which he had refused. Following the judgement, John Aspden

> fell dead, at a tavern in Carter's alley, of disease of the heart, supposed to have been induced by disappointment and mortification. At the time of his death, his pockets contained a solitary cent, his entire fortune. To-day, the man that might have been the possessor of a quarter of a million of dollars, will be borne to his grave from an obscure part of the district of Southwark. (*The New York Times*, Wednesday, March 25, 1853).

Matthias Aspden left a fortune estimated to be about $500,000.

Alexander Auldjo, who was born in Aberdeen, made his fortune in Canada, where he arrived in about 1778. Initially he invested in the fur trade. He formed a partnership with William Maitland in 1785, and the company became Auldjo, Maitland and Co. by 1800. His brother John Auldjo was a merchant in London and seems to have supplied some of the goods in which Auldjo and Maitland traded. Auldjo was a leader of the Montreal business community, a militia officer, J.P. and an active member of the Scottish Presbyterian Church in Montreal. He briefly served in the House of Assembly. In 1804, he married Eweretta Jane Richardson, probably sister of John Richardson, who was leading Canadian businessman and politician. The couple had two sons and a daughter. Unfortunately Jane died shortly after giving birth to the daughter who also died.

In 1813 Auldjo returned to Britain and its seems that shortly afterwards he retired from his business, his nephew George Auldjo becoming a partner in Auldjo, Maitland and Company in his place. The company changed its name to Maitland, Garden and Auldjo in 1815 (Tuchinsky 1966).

Jeremiah Pilcher who served as Sherriff of London and Middlesex was the director of a number of company, including the New Zealand Company (*Colonial Gazette*, 28th August, 1839) and the Argus Life Assurance Company (*The Scotsman*, Saturday, 20th May 1843). Another insurance company director was John Slegg, who served on the board of the Royal Exchange Assurance Office.

Table 4.9: Merchants, bankers, stockbrokers, etc

Surname, Forename	Notes	Died	Burial no.
Aspden, Matthias	merchant, of Philadelphia, USA	9/8/1824	5053
Auldjo, Alexander	merchant and banker,	21/5/1821	1512
Balmanno, Alexander	son of **Alexander Balmanno**, of Alexander Balmanno & Co., Merchants, 78 Queen St, Cheapside	11/3/1818	6014
Bankes, James Langley	silk merchant	4/5/1839	6030
Brown, James	merchant	26/11/1829	6012
Cundale, John	merchant, Hart Street	8/7/1819	1019
Cundale, Jane	wife of John Cundale	30/4/1840	1118
de la Chaumette, Lewis Andrew	stockbroker	1/1/1836	Vlt 2,11
Hirtzel, John James	merchant	13/10/1815	6006
Keysall, John	banker	2/5/1813	6008
Murdoch, William	merchant	11/4/1825	4017
Parry, Edward	of Gower Street, director of the Hon. East India Co	-	*
Pilcher, Jeremiah	Sheriff of London and Middlesex and company director	18/7/1860	*
Pilcher, Mary Rebecca	wife of **Jeremiah Pilcher**	25/7/1885	*
Remington, David Robert	stockbroker	26/10/1854	6139
Remington, Martha	wife of David Robert Remington	23/11/1854	6141
Rougemont, Forbes	son of Francis Frederick Rougemont, merchant	17/11/1838	5024
Rougemont, Amy	dau. of Francis Frederick Rougemont, merchant	19/8/1842	1093
Shuttleworth, Frances Haselrigg	wife of John Bradley Shuttleworth, merchant	12/8/1845	1078
Slegg, John	director, Royal Exchange Assurance Office	15/7/1830	1581
Wood, Benjamin	stockbroker	16/11/1838	4032

Artisans, tradesmen and business men (Table 4.10)

In addition to the wealthy of independent means, the lawyers, merchants and others, who formed the majority of those interred in St George's crypt, there were also a number of people who provided services to the wealthy inhabitants of Bloomsbury. Most notable amongst these were the Jeakes (carpenters, builders and ironmongers), the Meabry (grocer), the Stringfield (butchers) and the Keysell (cheesemongers) families. Several members of each of these families were interred in the crypt of St Georges Church, and the Stringfields are remembered by a mural memorial within the church.

Other tradesmen included Joseph England, builder of Wilmot Street, and Nicholas Winsland, builder, Robert Stuart, stone mason of Hyde Street, and Thomas Churm, plumber of 4 Hyde Street. Two young sons of the Pfeil family, who were ironmongers in Broad Street, were interred in the crypt. David Bateson, an upholder and cabinet maker of Holborn, James Thompson cabinet maker of King Street, David Edwards dressing case manufacturer of King Street, and Richard Harrison upholsterer.

Suppliers of food and drink included Joseph Circuitt, a butcher at No. 5 Bloomsbury Market. The Circuitt family seems to have had connections with Woburn and with the Dukes of Bedford. Richard Reid baker of Little Russell Street, Thomas Guillod wine and brandy merchant, Isaac Tooke and William Moss, both wine merchants, and John Harrison victualler. Thomas Guillod was probably a wine and brandy retail merchant, rather than a wholesale merchant. In 1808 his business was located at No. 3 Cockspur Street, and this street was clearly given over to retail premises. In 1810 his premises were at No. 27 Craven Street, which street provided a comparable range of services. In *Holden's Directory for 1811* he is listed at No. 7 Hart Street which was almost certainly his residential address.

In addition there was William Davis a bookseller, and Laura Hansard the daughter of the printer Luke Graves Hansard. Joseph Kirkup, auctioneer and diamond dealer and his members of his family were interred in the crypt. His son James Fenwick Kirkup 'drowned while bathing'. Oliver Oxley of 16 Russell Court seems to have traded in various items. In 1809, he was a dealer in ready-made linen (SUN MS 11936/448/825859, 20 January 1809), in 1817 he was described as a dress maker (SUN MS 11936/476/931307, 3 June 1817), and finally in 1828 he described himself as a picture dealer (*Old Bailey Proceedings* 21 Feb 1828, Ref No. t18280221-18).

Four families however dominate the record from the crypt: the Stringfield family of Duke Street, the Meabry family of No. 1 Broad Street, the Keysells of No. 7 Broad Street, and the Jeakes family of Little Museum Street and Great Russell Street.

The Stringfields were butchers, and had premises in Duke Street, Bloomsbury. Thomas Stringfield (b. c 1759, d. 1827) had his premises at 27 Duke Street in 1820 (SUN MS 11936/483/970381, 10 August 1820), but by 1823 the business had moved 32 Duke Street (SUN MS 11936/498/1005041, 14 May 1823). The property which was leased comprised a house, shop and slaughterhouse. Thomas and his wife Mary had at least four sons – John (b. 1795), William (b. 1799), James (b. 1800) and George (1805) – and one daughter, Mary, who married Bisse Phillip Sanderson in 1814. James (d. 1821) predeceased his father. John the eldest married, but neither James nor William appear to have married before their early deaths, and George the youngest and only surviving son did not marry.

The father, Thomas, died in Hart Street in 1827 (LMA P82/GEO1/63), and left all his money, stocks and securities, 'household furniture and also all other my Estate and effects whatsoever . . . unto my dear wife Mary Stringfield' (TNA PROB 11/1734). Mary herself died in 1833. The butcher's business had been taken over by John and William on Thomas's death. Unfortunately John died in Duke Street aged 37 in 1832. It is clear from John's will, that he and his brother had had equal shares in the business and the leasehold of the premises, and that they had purchased jointly the lease on an adjoining yard and buildings (TNA PROB 11/1806). Under the terms of John's will, it seems that it was his wish that William should pass his share of the butcher's business and lease on the butcher's premises to John's widow Anna, and in return William would receive John's share of the lease on the adjoining premises. It seems that this is what happened, because John's wife, Mrs Anna Stringfield, clearly took over the butchery side (SUN MS. 11936/539/1157324, 24 July 1833) since in her will she leaves the business and its goodwill to William provided he sells the same to his younger brother George for a price to be agreed between them (TNA PROB 11/1819). William meanwhile traded from the adjoining yard as a skin and hide salesman (SUN MS 11936/539/1157325, 24 July 1833; TNA PROB 11/1883). Anna Stringfield died of consumption in 1833 aged only 25. William Stringfield died in 1837 aged 38. George Stringfield (b. 1805, d. 1881) the youngest brother took over the butchery business on Anna's death in 1833 and continued to operate out of 32 Duke Street until at least 1851. By 1861 he had given up the business and was living at Billingshurst, Sussex with his nephew John William Stringfield and his family. John William was the son of John and Anna Stringfield. He was a 'Lime, Slate & Cement merchant, and George was described as a 'House proprietor' in the 1861 census. The butchery business had been given up by 1861.

It is clear from William Stringfield's will (TNA PROB 11/1883) that the family had accumulated considerable capital to invest in stocks, funds and securities. They do not seem to have invested in freehold property, until George gave up the butcher's business and became a 'house proprietor'. In addition to the premises in Duke Street, members of the family had occupied a property in Hart Street

Thomas insured a property at No. 43 Hart Street in 1827 (SUN MS 11936/516/1065593, 18 October 1827). It is where he died (LMA P82/GEO1/63). Mary Sanderson (née Stringfield) occupied this property between 1832 and 1834 (SUN MS 11936/538/1143963, 11 October 1832; MS 11936/544/1184264, 22 October 1834). It is probable that the family lived at No. 43 Hart Street in the late 1820s and 1830s. The 1841 census records show that Mary Sanderson was living with her brother George in Museum Street, although the business was still operating out of Duke Street.

The only mention of property in the wills of the Thomas, John, William or Anna Stringfield, is the reference to leases on the Duke Street premises in the wills of John Stringfield and Anna Stringfield. The Stringfields were a family of some wealth and standing; seven members of the family were interred in the crypt of St George's church, and a mural memorial was erected to the memory of eight family members.

John Meabry (coffin 2032, b. 1766, d. 1841) was a tea dealer and grocer with premises at No 1 Broad Street, Bloomsbury, and Francis Keysell (b. 1789, d. 1849) was a wholesale cheesemonger at No 7 Broad Street. Both businesses are listed in *Kent's Directory 1794*, the *1808 Post Office London Directory*, and in *1841 Post Office London Directory*. Next door to Keysells in 1841, at Nos 5 and 6 Broad Street, were the premises of the ironmonger Adolph Pfeil. Adolph Leonard Pfeil (coffin 1101) and Adolph Henry Pfeil (coffin 3091) were the young sons of this family.

John Meabry and his wife Elizabeth (or Eliza) Rishforth married in 1793 (Pallot's Marriage Index). They had a number of children, including Mary Eliza (b. *c.* 1797) who married George Maber in 1820 (*The Times*, May 17 1820) and Jane Meabry, who married John Oakley, of St Paul's Covent Garden, in 1827 (*The Times*, June 4 1827). Both couples married at St George's Bloomsbury. George Maber was a grocer in partnership with James Charles Farr. In 1816 to 1819 their premises were 110 Fleet Street

Table 4.10: Tradesmen and artisans:

Surname, Forename	Notes	Died	Burial no.
Bateson, David	upholder and cabinet maker	19/3/1821	4001
Churm, Thomas	plumber, 4 Hyde Street	8/7/1831	2033
Circuit, Joseph	butcher, Bloomsbury Market	11/3/1825	5004
Davis, William	bookseller	23/6/1827	8117
Edwards, David	dressing case manufacturer	3/4/1831	2058
England, Joseph	carpenter and builder	14/10/1831	4073
Guillod, Thomas	wine and brandy merchant	10/3/1815	6097
Hansard, Laura Teresa	4th daughter of **Luke Graves Hansard**, printer	4/5/1826	3018
Harrison, John	victualler	21/9/1841	5065
Harrison, Richard	upholsterer	28/1/1812	8079
Jeakes, John	builder and carpenter – see text		
Jeakes, Thomas	builder and carpenter – see text	20/12/1839	1057
Keysell, Francis	cheesemonger – see text		
Kirkup, Joseph	auctioneer and diamond merchant	1/5/1815	8043
Kirkup, Ann	wife of **Joseph Kirkup**	14/1/1826	1029
Kirkup, James Fenwick	son of **Joseph Kirkup**	28/6/1820	1051
Kirkup, Georgiana	?daughter of **Joseph Kirkup**	24/11/1834	6015
Meabry, John	Grocer – see text		
Meux, Richard	brewer, owner of the Griffin Brewery	2/7/1809 2/7/1813	4058
Meux, Mary	?wife Richard Meux	8/12/1812	4053
Moss, William	wine merchant	24/7/1815	4048
Oxley, Oliver	dealer in ready-made linen (1809), dress maker (1817) and picture- dealer (1828)	10/2/1837	1039
Pfeil, Adolph Leonard	son of **Adolph Leonard Pfeil**, ironmonger	16/3/1814	1101
Reid, Richard	baker	1/7/1824	4060
Stringfield, Thomas	butcher – see text	15/11/1827	*6040
Stringfield, John	butcher – see text	2/9/1832	*6039
Stuart, Robert	stonemason	31/10/1810	5076
Thompson, James	cabinet maker	3/2/1814	2064
Thompson, Hannah	wife of James Thompson King's Street Hollow	29/1/1813	5041
Winsland, Nicholas	builder	27/1/1846	6136
Winsland, Emma Margaret	daughter of Nicholas Winsland	31/3/1848	6133
Winsland, Lucy Anne	daughter of Nicholas Winsland	15/8/1833	6079
Winsland, Nicholas Charles	son of Nicholas Winsland	30/5/1824	6140

(SUN MS 11936/467/919290 15 May 1816; *The Times*, Oct 15, 1819), but by 1824 they were at 32 Chiswell Street (SUN MS 11936/503/1019959 15 September 1824). In 1829 George Maber was trading on his one behalf at 10 Aldgate High Street (*1829 PO London*). By 1841 George and Mary Eliza Maber were farming in Havant, Hampshire (1841 census). In 1851 they were at Hambleton, Hampshire farming 561 acres and employing 14 labourers (1851 Census) and by 1861 they were at Great Park Farm, Titchfield, Hampshire, farming 791 acres and employing 23 labourers and 8 boys (1861 census).

John Oakley was a tea and wine merchant. In 1841 and 1851 John and Jane Oakley were living at 182-183 Piccadilly, which formed part of Fortnum and Mason's premises. In 1834 the buildings in Piccadilly occupied by Fortnum and Mason had been rebuilt, and in 1838 and 1840 the business was reconstituted and John Oakley and his neighbour at 181 Piccadilly, George Scorer, were both given one-eighth share of the profits. The controlling interest was retained by Richard Fortnum who was unmarried. When Fortnum died he bequeath his share of the business to his nephew, but Scorer and Oakley were both given the opportunity to buy a further eighth share if they agreed to renew the partnership until 1869 (*Survey of London*, 1960).

Sarah and Martha both married into the Keysell family in 1822, and that both weddings took place in St George's Bloomsbury (The Times, Sep 3, 1822, & May 17, 1822 respectively). Other children were William (coffin 2007, b. c 1807, d. 1852), Charles (b. c 1808, d. 1872), Louisa (coffin 2022, b. c 1812, d. 1820), and Ellen (b. c 1814, d. 1889). Neither William nor Charles followed their father into the grocery business. William never married, and in the 1851 census is described as having 'no business'. He died aged 45 the following year. Charles married in 1843, and in 1851 was living with his wife Ann and children in Mitcham, Surrey and was described as a 'Fund holder'. He died in 1872. The youngest sister Ellen married Thomas Oakley, almost certainly the younger brother of her brother-in-law John Oakley, in 1843 (The Times, May 22, 1843). Both men were born in Shrewsbury (IGI). Thomas Oakley was a master currier with premises in St Martin's Lane, St Martin in the Fields (1851 Census). By 1851 the former Meabry premises were occupied by another grocer William Palmer. Four members of the Meabry family were identified in the crypt.

At least seven, and probably eight, members of the Keysell family were interred in the crypt of St George's church. John Keysall (coffin 6008) was a banker who lived in Queen Square and is probably not a relation.

In 1794 the premises at No. 7 Broad Street were occupied by the firm of Keysell and Rice, cheesemongers (*Kent's 1794 Directory*). Francis Keysell (d. 1804; LMA P82/GEO1/63) was then the head of the family. Mrs Frances Keysell (coffin 6119, b. c 1755, d. 1819) was probably his wife. His daughter Catherine Eleanor died in 1816 aged 21 (*The Times*,

6th Aug 1816) and was interred at St George's (coffin 6085, b. c 1795). She appears to have had at least one sister, Mary Ann, who married Henry Robert Wylie, at St George's church in 1819 (Pallot's Marriage Index). Thomas Keysell (coffin 6020, b. c 1788, d. 1825) and Richard Keysell (coffin 6019, b. c 1793, d. 1830) were her siblings, and Henry Keysell (coffin 6069, d. 1833) was probably another. Richard and Henry both married into the Meabry family. Richard married Martha Meabry and Henry married Sarah Meabry. Both marriages took place at St George's church in 1822. Thomas, Richard and Henry all died at a comparatively young age, and it is recorded that Richard and Henry died of consumption (LMA P82/GEO1/63).

By 1808 Francis's remaining son, also Francis Keysell, was trading in his sole name at No. 7 Broad Street (*PO London 1810*). This second Francis married twice, first, in 1814, to Eliza Olney Price (coffin 6007) who died in 1829 aged 34 (*The Times*, 3rd July 1829), and then to Margaret (d. 1856). Francis and Eliza had at least five children: Mary Ann (b. c 1817, d. 1895, aged 78), Eliza (b. c. 1819, d. 1900, aged 80), Sarah Olney (b. c 1821, d. 1879, aged 58), Francis Price (b. c 1824, d. 1898, aged 74) and Ann Bye (b. c 1826). Richard Keysell (coffin 1092) who died aged 10 months in 1827 may have been another child of the marriage. Ellen Keysell (coffin 6138) who died aged 4 months 19 days in November 1830 was born too late to be a child of the marriage of Francis and Eliza. It is uncertain who her parents were.

By 1829 the business was trading as F and R Keysell, and seems to have expanded to occupy both Nos 7 and 8 Broad Street (*The Times*, Thursday 8th Oct, 1829, 1). This suggests that Francis had been joined in the business by his brother Richard. Unfortunately Richard Keysell died in 1830 leaving Francis to run the business alone until he died in September 1849.

Francis Price Keysell then took over the business and traded as F. P. Keysell. At the time of the 1851 census F. P. Keysell and his sisters, all unmarried, appear still to have been living in Broad Street, but in the *PO London Directory 1852*, their home was listed as Sycamore Villa, Carlton Hill, St John's Wood. Francis and his sisters were still in Sycamore Villa at the time of the 1861 census, but in 1866, Francis Price married Hannah A. Sandford (b. c 1830, d. 1913, aged 83), and in 1881 he and his new family were living in Grove House, College Road, Cheshunt, Hertfordshire. The couple had three children – Francis, Folliot and Amy – and a household comprising a governess and four servants. In 1871, Francis's sisters – Mary Ann, Eliza, Sarah Olney and Ann Bye – were living together in Hampstead, and were described as living on 'English funds'. In the 1881 and 1891 census Francis still described himself as a provision merchant. His sisters continued to live together in Hampstead.

The Jeakes family, at least 6 of whose members were interred in the crypt of St George's church, has a fascinating history. The first known member of the family was John Jeakes (coffin 1013), who was a carpenter and builder operating from No. 3 Little Museum Street (*Holden's 1811*; *PO London 1808*). His wife was Martha Crochet, whom he had married in February 1768 (IGI). Martha died in 1813 and was interred in St George's (coffin 1024). John died of 'apoplexy' in 1818. Martha and John had at least eight children, four boys and four girls. The coffins of four of the children were identified in the crypt. The eldest known child was James Jeakes (coffin 1079, b. 1773, d. 1837), followed by Elizabeth (coffin 1075, b. 1775, d. 1832), then Joseph (coffin 1015, b. Nov 1778, d. 1818) and Thomas (coffin 1057, b. 1782, d. 1839). The next three children were Mary (b. *c* 1788), Martha (b. c. 1789) and Ann (b. *c* 1792). None of these three was interred in the crypt. The youngest child was William (b. before 1798).

James the eldest son became an officer in the Bombay Marine, the naval force of the East India Company (see above). He ended his career as a commodore. He returned from India in 1829, and retired to Lower Halliford, Middlesex. The next child, Elizabeth, never married and died in Little Russell Street of 'apoplexy'. Joseph the third child was an engraver of some note, but unfortunately died of a fever in 1818 at the age of 39. Joseph Jeakes specialised in topographical and naval aquatints. He produced prints of the '*Chesapeake* and *Shannon*' (published 1815) and 'After the battle between his Majesty's frigate *Endymion* and the U.S. frigate *President*' (published 1815). He also provided the aquatint plates for William Thorn's *Memoir of the conquest of Java*, published in London in 1815.

The next three children were Mary, Martha and Ann. Mary married Thomas Allerson, described as a 'Freeholder and Leaseholder' in the 1851 census. Neither Martha nor Ann married.

The seventh child William set up as an ironmonger at 51 Great Russell Street (*PO London 1829*). He married Sarah Pool from Suffolk in 1816 (Pallot's Index of Marriages) and in 1817 their son John William was born (Pallot's Index of Baptisms). William is absent from 51 Great Russell Street in the 1841 census, although his son John William is listed, as William junior. William developed and expanded his ironmongery business, and specialised in the manufacture and supply of cooking equipment; the company proudly advertised its patent 'Metastatic Fire grates' which were 'a perfect remedy for that worst of all nuisances the smokey chimney' (*The Times*, Saturday, Jul 28, 1810, 1, Thursday, Jul 20, 1815, 2) and the 'newly invented Patent Retentive Plate, for all purposes of Cooking . . . with this great advantage . . . much less consumption of fuel, at the same time keeping the kitchen perfectly cool' (*The Times*, Monday, July 29, 1822, 2). The business supplied ranges and cooking equipment to country houses (Sambrook 2006, 185), but also heating systems, gas fittings and hot water systems. Jeakes supplied fittings to a number houses in Grosvenor Square, for example the gas fittings and hot water system for No.20, and a hot water system, galvanised iron

cistern, bell pulls and a speaking tube for No.21 (*Survey of London*, 1980). The company also supplied fixtures for and fitted out the kitchen and scullery of the House of Lords refreshment rooms and supplied heating and ventilation systems for the new Houses of Parliament (TNA WORK 11/16/3). They also built a drying cabinet for Florence Nightingale, for use in the military hospital at Scutari (Sambrook 2006, 185). William Jeakes had a number of patents to his name, and in the Catalogue of the Great Exhibition of 1851, he was described as an inventor (loc. cit.). William died in 1850 and his son John William took over the business. John William soon retired from the business and in the 1861 Census he described himself as a 'retired engineer'. He bought Winchester Hall at the corner of Highgate Hill and Hornsey Lane. He served as a magistrate and was colonel of 37th Middlesex Rifle Volunteer Corps until 1863 when he resigned (*Colburn's United Services Magazine*, Sept 1863, 143). Indeed he was frequently referred to as Colonel Jeakes in the press. John William died suddenly in 1874. His son was not interested in the business which was sold William Clements and continued to trade until the 1927 as Clement Jeakes.

Thomas Jeakes the youngest son had joined his father John in the building business in Little Russell Street by 1816 (SUN MS 11936/471/915263, 12 February 1816). Thomas continued in the business after his father's death, until his own death in 1839, when the business seems to have ceased to operate. It is clear from Thomas's will that he had not married (TNA PROB 11/1921). He divided his estate, which included three houses, Nos 11-13, in Charles Street, between his surviving siblings Martha, Ann, Mary, James and William.

The Jeakes family are almost a microcosm of late Georgian and early Victorian society, with James Jeakes the naval officer and imperial administrator, Joseph the artist, who died young, William the entrepreneur and engineer, and Thomas the builder. The surviving brothers – William and James – both prospered and moved out of Bloomsbury.

This section is perhaps the place to consider three men who represent larger businesses. They are Thomas Bland, Richard Meux and Nicholas Winsland. Thomas Bland (coffin 1506) who died of smallpox in 1825 aged 22, was a member of the brewing family of the same name. The firm of Bland and Martineau had their brewery in Chiswell Street and it was there that Thomas Bland is reported to have died (*Gentleman's Magazine*, August 1825, 187). Apparently he contracted the disease from his friend Richard Martineau (*Gentleman's Magazine*, November 1826, 438). In 1812 Bland and Martineau set up a partnership with Samuel Whitbread, eventually leading to a merger of the two concerns.

Richard Meux (coffin 4058) with his original partner Mungo Murray built the Griffin Brewery in Liquorpond Street now part of Clerkenwell Road. In 1793 Andrew Reid a wealthy City merchant invested in the company and a few years later Sir Robert Wigram an East India merchant provided further investment in the company. The brewery became one of the largest in London.

Richard Meux married Mary Brougham in 1767 and couple had a daughter and three sons. Mary died in 1812 and Richard in 1813. He had ceased to be active in the business for some time before he died. Reid and Wigram were not in a position to oversee the day to day running of the brewery, which fell to Meux's three sons, who fell out over business. Eventually, as a result of disagreements between the partners, the business was sold in 1809 and Reid became the senior partner. The brewery continued to operate until 1899 when the company merged with Watney and Combe (Wilson 2007).

The final tradesman who can briefly be discussed is Nicholas Winsland. In 1818 in a case heard at the Old Bailey, William Rice was accused of stealing 2lbs of white lead from Winsland (*Old Bailey Proceedings*, 28 Oct 1818, Ref No. f18181028-1). In his testimony Nicholas Winsland described himself as a painter and glazier. He lived at No. 18 Queen Street (*Holden's 1811 Directory*). By 1829 Winsland is living at No. 44 Great Russell Street, and by 1841 he had moved to No. 84 Great Russell Street. Winsland was listed in *The Times* as one of the builders tendering to build the New Royal Exchange and described as one the 'principal builders of London'. Winsland's tender was for £134,219 for building in Portland stone, or £136,620 for building in Magnesium limestone. He did not win the job which went to Thomas Jackson, who tendered £115,900 and £124,700 respectively (*The Times*, 2nd September 1841).

Principal librarians and staff of the British Museum (Table 4.11)

Given that St George's Bloomsbury is the nearest church to the British Museum it is not surprising that a number of prominent, and not so prominent, members of the Museum's staff were buried at St George's. Joseph Planta, Principal Librarian of the British Museum 1799-1827 and his wife were both interred in the church. There is also a memorial plaque in Latin to the couple. Planta was originally from the Grisons in Switzerland. His father brought

the family to England when he became minister of the German Reformed church in London. Planta senior also worked as an assistant librarian at the British Museum. Joseph also became an assistant librarian at the British Museum then under-librarian in the department of manuscripts. He married Margaret Atwood in 1778. In 1799 he became Principal Library. Under his guidance the Museum grew and its collections expanded. Amongst other publications Planta produced his *An Account of the Romansh Language* (1776). Romanish was the language of the natives of the Grisons (Harris 2004).

Joseph Planta's successor Sir Henry Ellis was not interred in the crypt, but his wife was and again there is a commemorative mural plaque (see Table 4.2). Ellis was born in the parish of St Botolph without Bishopsgate, London. He worked at the Bodleian library for a short time after University. He then moved the British Museum, eventually becoming secretary to the trustees of the Museum. When Planta died Ellis successfully lobbied to succeed him. He was not a particularly successful appointment as Principal Librarian. He eventually retired in 1856, and died 1869 at his home at No. 24 Bedford Square in 1869 (Borrie 2004a).

Mary, the first wife of Frederick Madden, who died in childbirth, was buried in the crypt and is remembered with a mural plaque. Madden was an extremely fine scholar, and much of his work set new standards for subsequent scholarship. He became keeper in the department of manuscripts. Amongst his many achievements was the discovery and publication of *Sir Gawayne and the Grene Knight* (1839). He courted Mary Hayton, who eventually became his wife, for 10 years. Her family did not approve of the match. They married in March 1829. She died giving birth to a son less than a year later. Frederic Hayton Madden died shortly after his mother. Madden eventually remarried (Borrie 2004b)

Another eminent member of the Museum's staff was John Children, Assistant Librarian and Keeper of Zoology. He and his third wife Eliza were both interred in the crypt. Children was a chemist. He was appointed to the post of assistant librarian in

Table 4.11: Librarians and staff of the British Museum:

Surname, Forename	Notes	Died	Burial no.
Bygrave, John	attendant, British Museum	19/4/1847	6049
Children, John George	Assistant Librarian and Keeper of Zoology, the British Museum, Fellow and Secretary of the Royal Society	10/1/1852	1037
Children, Elizabeth	2nd wife of **John Children**	1/9/1839	1507
Ellis, Sir Henry	Principal Librarian of the British Museum,1827-1856; Kt of Hanover		*
Ellis, Frances Jane, Lady	relict of **Sir Henry Ellis**, Kt,	12/10/1854	*
Madden, Frederick	Keeper of Manuscripts of the British Museum		*
Madden, Mary	wife of **Frederick Madden**	26/2/1830	*1035
Planta, Joseph	Principal Librarian of the British Museum 1799-1827	9/12/1827	1528
Planta, Elizabeth	wife of **Joseph Planta**	2/2/1821	1505

the department of antiquities, but then transferred to the department of natural history (Forgon 2004).

Less exalted is John Bygrave, who was an attendant in the Museum (1841 Census). He died aged 94.

Doctors of medicine and surgeons (Table 4.12)

There is a small number of doctors amongst those buried in St George's crypt, although little is known of most of them. Thomas Draper, whose wife was interred in St George's crypt, and who was Inspector General of Army Hospitals has already been mentioned above (see 'The army, navy and merchant marine' above). The most famous name amongst the doctors is James Lind. This is not the James Lind (1716-1794) who was a naval surgeon and is famous for his work on scurvy, but rather his nephew. Early in his career Lind had sailed as a ship's surgeon to India, the East Indies and China. In 1772 he went on an expedition to Iceland with Sir Joseph Banks. He was interested in science, and particularly astronomy and meteorology. He was a close friend of James Watt. Lind became physician-in-ordinary to the Royal Household. Fanny Burney wrote that 'with his taste for tricks, conundrums, and queer things' people were 'fearful of his trying experiments with their constitutions, and think him a better conjuror than physician'. At Windsor he took under his wing the young Shelley, who was then a schoolboy at Eton. Lind died in the house of his son-in-law William Burnie, in Russell Square, London, on 17 October 1812 (Cooper 2004). Burnie's young son, William Moffat Burnie (coffin 4048), who died aged only 3 days, was interred in the crypt in 1815.

Another doctor interred in the crypt is Ely Stott, who was an 'electrical practitioner'. He died in Upper Islington in 1821. He was described as formerly of Hart Street. He died of 'apoplexy' according the records of the Bloomsbury searchers (LMA P82/GEO1/63). He became notorious because of his treatment of his only daughter Charlotte Dew (née Stott). Stott's left 'real and personal property to

the value of 40,000*l*. and upwards.' His widow, who was his second wife, was left £400 per annum for her lifetime, and his daughter was to receive about £100 per annum. The residue of the estate after some small legacies was left to his nephews Thomas and Valentine Clark. Charlotte Dew challenged the will in the Prerogative Court. It seems that Stott had taken against his daughter almost from her birth and made allegations about her behaviour which were clearly false. The case was reported in the *Annual Register of the Year 1826* ('Law cases and narratives', 6*-12*). In February 1821 Stott's wife 'applied for a commission of lunacy against him; the inquisition was executed accordingly, and the deceased was found to be of unsound mind from the preceding January'. Unfortunately the will in dispute was dated May 1818. The case hinged on whether or not the deceased was of unsound mind when he made the will. The judgement was given in favour of his daughter Charlotte Dew. Dr George Man Burrows, who had seen the patient wrote that Stott's constitution was 'singularly robust' and that his 'passions at all times appear to have been extremely violent' so as to 'have induced a suspicion of his sanity' (1828, 271-72). Stott had had a slight 'stroke of paralysis from which he had perfectly recovered, except that his temper appeared more irritable than before'. 'When about seventy years old he experienced an attack of hemiplegia', and although he largely recovered his muscular powers 'his intellects were evidently now deranged' (loc.cit.). He died about a year later.

The arts (Table 4.13)

Amongst those interred in the crypt of St George's were a number of people eminent in the art world. Thomas Brown of High Holborn was an artists' colourman. He took over the business of William Legg in 1805 or 1806. In *Holden's 1811* and the *PO London 1829 directories*, Thomas Brown is listed as 'Colourman to Artists, 163 High Holborn'. He was known sometimes as Old Brown to distinguish him from his son also called Thomas, who was known as

Table 4.12: Doctors of medicine and surgeons

Surname, Forename	Notes	Died	Burial no.
Armstrong, John	M.D.	12/12/1829	1085
Draper, Elizabeth	wife of **Thomas Draper**, Inspector General of Army Hospitals – see Table 4.7 above)	30/9/1834	3099
Halham, Robert	M.D.	24/11/1845	1004
James, Robert	surgeon	17/2/1841	4011
Lind, James	M.D. F.R.S.	17/10/1812	6084
Scott, John	M.D.	30/7/1849	8010
Stott, Ely	surgeon, and practitioner in Medical Electricity	18/11/1821	vlt 2, 10
Turner, Henry	surgeon, King St, brother of **John Turner**, surgeon	9/2/1846	7083
Turner, John	surgeon, King St, brother of **Henry Turner**, surgeon	1/3/1846	7073
Werner, Phillip	late of Gibraltar	2/5/1819	5063
Williams, Robert	M.D.	24/11/1845	3107

Table 4.13: The Arts

Surname, Forename	Notes	Died	Burial no.
Brown, Thomas	artist, colourman, High Holborn	25/9/1840	1121
Coxe, Peter	poet and auctioneer	22/1/1844	1109
Fuseli, Sophia	wife of **Henry Fuseli**, artist and keeper of the Royal Academy	1832	1500
Jeakes, Joseph	engraver	16/7/1818	1015
Munden, Joseph Shepherd	comic actor	6/2/1832	5032
Munden, Frances	wife of **Joseph Shepherd Munden**	20/9/1837	5006
Reeves, William John	colourman, Holborn Bridge	-/9/1827	6122
Reeves, Ann	wife of **William John Reeves**	8/-/1831	6095
Yenn, John	architect	1/3/1821	1550
Yenn, Elizabeth	wife of John Yenn	-/3/1806	1534
Yenn, Susannah Mary	daughter of John Yenn	19/1/1845	1517

Young Brown. Old Brown died in 1840 and left the business to his son. The firm supplied many famous artists ((NPG British Artists' suppliers, 1650-1950, 'Thomas Brown, 163 Holborn, London'). Thomas Brown).

Another artists' colourman was William John Reeves, whose name is still known today for artists' materials. William John was the son of the founder of the firm Thomas Reeves. From 1784 the business traded as Thomas Reeves & Son. Thomas died in 1799, and William soon after went into partnership with William Woodyer trading as Reeves & Woodyer. In the *Holden's 1811 Directory* the firm is listed as 'Reeves & Woodyer, superfine colour manufacturer to her Majesty and the Prince Regent, 80, Holborn Bridge'. In 1818 the partnership with Woodyer was dissolved, and so after the business was trading as W J Reeves & Son. In the *PO London 1829 directory* the company was listed as 'Reeves W. J. & Son, superfine Colour Preparers, Fancy Stationers and Manufacts. of Drawing-materials, 80 Holborn bridge'. Later its name was changed to W J Reeves & Sons, under which name it traded until 1890. Thereafter it was known as Reeves & Sons. William John Reeves died in 1827 (NPG British Artists' Suppliers, 'Thomas Reeves, Fetter Lane, London').

Sophia Fuseli, the widow of the Swiss born artist Henry Fuseli was also interred in the crypt. Sophia Fuseli (née Rawlins) (coffin 1500) married Fuseli in 1788; she was more than twenty years younger than her husband. Fuseli was elected as a Royal Academician in 1790, and professor of painting in 1799. He became keeper of the Royal Academy in 1804. He died in 1825, and Sophia died in 1832 (Weinglass 2004).

Joseph Jeakes the engraver (coffin 1015) was a member of the Jeakes family, who were builders, carpenters and ironmongers and are discussed above (see 'Artisans, tradesmen and business men' above). Born in November 1778 he died of a fever in Little Russell Street in July 1818.

Perhaps the most notable people were the architect John Yenn, and the comic actor Joseph Sheppard Munden. John Yenn was clerk of the

works at Somerset House from 1776, designed the Temple of Health (1789) at Blenheim Palace, and with Henry Hake Seward rebuilt the west façade of the King Charles Block at Greenwich Hospital. He also served as Surveyor of the Hospital. Munden was a celebrated comic actor. The essayist Charles Lamb composed a short essay 'On the acting of Munden' in which he wrote that 'he is not one, but legion, not so much a comedian, as a company'. He was also described as 'by far the greatest comedian we ever saw', and as 'one of the best comic actors that ever trod the stage' (quoted in Davis, J, 2004).

Abodes and social stratification

The assumption has been that the individuals and families interred in the crypt were largely drawn from the upper echelons of Bloomsbury society. The presence of peers, senior judges and members of parliament together with members of their families tends to provide support for the assumption.

It might be possible to provide more concrete support for the idea if consideration is given to identifying where families and individuals lived within the Parish and adjacent districts. One problem has been removing from consideration work or professional addresses. Many lawyers for example are known to be 'of Lincoln's In Fields', or 'of Gray's Inn', but often they have separate home addresses. Another problem is that individuals did move within the district. General Robert Bell is known to have lived at No. 80 Guilford Street (1821-22), at No. 1 Doughty Street (1823), and in his will his address is given as Russell Square.

The sample of individuals of known abodes forms a quite small proportion of the crypt population. Rather than attempt to look at all known abodes, it was decided to sample by taking a selection of the professional or occupational groups. The groups chosen were the legal profession (Table 4.3), military and naval officers (Table 4.6), and artisans and tradesmen (Table 4.10). These three were the largest occupational groups. In addition the 'Arts' group (Table 4.13) was also included although it was only small in number. Only one member of each household was counted for each professional group. The Jeakes family for example feature in three occupational groups, army and naval officers, trade and arts, but the Meabry, Keysell and Stringfield families feature only once each in the trade category.

The distribution of occupations and addresses is remarkable. The addresses of tradesmen, lawyers and those involved in the arts appear to be largely mutually exclusive (Table 4.14). The distribution of Army and Navy officers is only slightly less distinct. Two points need to be made. Firstly, it must be stressed that the numbers used are small and therefore these figures may not be truly representative of the distribution of the occupational groups of the crypt population. Nonetheless the patterns are suggestive. The second point is more serious. If, as has been assumed, the crypt population is a self-selecting elite from within the overall population of the parish and district, then the distribution pattern will reflect the distribution of that elite. It does not give the complete picture for the social composition of the parish. Nevertheless the distribution in Table 4.14 shows that smaller tradesmen and retailers were largely concentrated in the streets to the south of Great Russell Street in the older part of the parish, whereas by contrast the lawyers were largely concentrated in the newer streets and squares built by the Duke of Bedford to the north.

An alternative approach to understanding the social make-up of Bloomsbury, which permits a look at that large portion of the population not represented in the crypt of St George's is to look at Census records and Street listings in Post Office directories. The problem is that the earliest available census records are for 1841, near to the end of the phase of interment in the crypt. Fortunately there is the *Post Office London Directory for 1841*, which includes a street directory, and this can be used for comparison.

Three samples were selected from the streets around St George's Church. The first sample is drawn from Hart Street, on which St George's fronts, and which is now called Bloomsbury Way. The sample comprises properties numbered Nos 1-11, 11a and 12-13 in the *Post Office London Directory for 1841*. In the 1841 Census records there is an additional property (John Edwards, coal merchant) inserted between house No.8 (Thomas Bagg, engraver) and house No. 9 (Timothy Francis Power, merchant). This gives a total of 16 properties in the sample. The second sample comprises Nos 1-16, Broad Street, where the Meabry and Keysell families had their businesses. The third sample comprises 12 properties – Nos 1-12 – in Duke Street, near Lincoln's Inn Field.

In Hart Street the 16 properties housed 21 households with a total of 107 individuals, of who 30 were servants. The average number of households per property was 1.31, and the average household comprised 5.09 individuals including servants. The average number of individuals per property was

Table 4.14: Distribution of known abodes of selected professions. (Street names in bold are located to the south of the British Museum and Great Russell Street)

Street	Trade	Law	Arts	Army/Navy	Total
Broad Street	4				4
Little Russell St	3		1		4
King St	3				3
'St George Bloomsbury'	2	1		1	4
Southampton Row	2	1		1	4
Hart St	2				2
Hyde St	2				2
Montague Place	1	4	1		6
Bloomsbury Square	1	2			3
High Holborn	1	1			2
Bedford Square	1				1
Bloomsbury Market	1				1
Browns Lane, Spitalfields	1				1
Duke Street	1				1
Great Russell Street	1			1	2
Harpur Street	1				1
Holborn	1				1
John Street, Oxford Street	1				1
Oxford Street	1				1
Russell Court	1				1
Wilmot Street	1				1
Russell Square		4		1	5
Bedford Place		3			3
Montague Street		3		1	4
Bloomsbury Place		2			2
Guilford St		1			1
Portland Place		1			1
Torrington Square		1			1
Torrington Street		1			1
Woburn Place		1			1
Bernard Street			1	1	2
Charlotte Street			1		1
Holborn Bridge			1		1
Kensington Palace Green			1		1
'St Marylebone'				1	1
'St Pancras'				1	1
Cheltenham, Glos				1	1
Devonshire Street				1	1
Kent House, Knightsbridge				1	1
Kenton Street				1	1
Liverpool Street, Middlesex;				1	1
Manchester Street				1	1
Queen Square				1	1
Somers Town				1	1
Tavistock Square				1	1
Upper Bedford Place				1	1
Upper Fitzroy Street				1	1
	32	25	6	20	83

6.69, with a minimum of two people and a maximum of 13. The ratio of servants to others was 1:2.56. The occupations of the household included five lawyers, five surgeons, a merchant, a clergyman, an architect, an auctioneer and a diamond merchant. A number of people who lived in Hart Street were interred in the crypt of St George's.

In the 16 properties in Broad Street there were 144 individuals, including 19 servants, living in 35 households. The average number of households per property was 1.84, and the average size of households was 4.11. The average number of individuals per property was exactly nine. The minimum number in any house was two, and the maximum was 13. The ratio of servants to other inhabitants was 1:6.58. The occupations included a grocer, a cheesemonger, clockmakers, provision merchants, a chemist and druggist, a tailor, a boot maker, a coach trimmer, a carver and gilder and a professor of music. The occupations, household size and number of servants all show that the inhabitants of this part of Broad Street was less well-off than the occupants of Hart Street, but were still essentially middle class and prosperous. They were largely retailers and craftsmen providing services for the inhabitants of the district. The retailers included the Meabry, Keysell and Pfeil families, members of which families were interred in the crypt.

The final sample is drawn from Duke Street. Twelve properties were studied. The occupants of these properties number 197 and formed 64 apparently separate households. The number of households per property averaged 5.33, and the households comprised on average 3.07 individuals. There were 16.42 people per property on average. The minimum number in any property was 9, and the maximum was 26. There were only 6 female servants and it is possible that none was working as a servant in the street, but rather were servants working elsewhere. Many of the households clearly comprised single individuals lodging together. The occupations included builder and bricklayer, coachman, dairyman, shoe maker, tailor, pianoforte maker, musician, straw bonnet maker, tallow chandler, police constable, smith, whitesmith, nurse, carpenter, needlewoman and stay maker. An attendant and an assistant working at the British Museum also lived in the street.

The only individuals interred in the crypt who had a connection with Duke Street were the Stringfield family (see 'Artisans, tradesmen and business men' above). They operated their butchers business initially from 27 Duke Street, then from about 1823 from 32 Duke Street, but seem to have lived for a period in the late 1820s and 1830s in Hart Street where the father of the family Thomas died in 1827. In 1841 the remaining son George was living in Museum Street with his sister Mary although the business was still in Duke Street. The butchers business included a slaughter house and in 1834 John Stringfield was operating as a skin and hide salesman from the adjacent premises.

It is clear that Hart Street had the smallest number of households per property but the largest average household size. By contrast Duke Street had the smallest household size and the largest average number of households per property. Duke Street also had the densest occupancy per property.

What the samples show is that there was marked social stratification within the parish, and that was reflected in the occupations and households found in different streets. This is no more than would be expected. It tends to confirm that the streets around St George's church were occupied by trades people and artisans. It also shows that a good number of lawyers were to be found in areas other than those shown in Table 4.14. Clearly within the legal profession there were social distinctions.

Church and charity: joining and giving

What linked the people who were interred in St George's crypt was status, perhaps a confidence in their own status, and a desire to be accepted as being of the certain standing in the community. It is interesting to note that in addition to the obvious occupants of the crypt – the judges, wealthy merchants and bankers, members of the aristocracy – there was a substantial group of solid trades people, in particular the Meabry, Keysell, Stringfield and Jeakes families which are discussed in some detail above (see 'Artisans, tradesmen and business men'). Nicholas Winsland can be included to this group.

What marks out this group is that they strove to improve their status. The oldest surviving son of the Meabrys, Charles was never involved in the family business, but instead invested in funds and moved eventually to Mitcham in Surrey and lived off his investments. Frances Price Keysell after running the family business for a number of years, eventually moved away from Bloomsbury and latterly lived on his investments. George, the youngest Stringfield son, and the only one to survive into old age, eventually sold the family business, invested in property and retired to Sussex where he lived with his nephew and his family. The Jeakes family were more remarkable. One son – William – was an engineer and entrepreneur, who created a substantial and thriving business. His son sold the business and retired to the life of a gentleman, becoming a JP and colonel of Rifle Volunteers. Another son made his way in the Navy of the East India Company before retiring to a riverside property in Lower Halliford, Middlesex. Joseph was a gifted engraver, but unfortunately died young. Thomas joined the family carpentry business and ran it until his death in 1839.

The desire to improve their status was not simply manifested through business success. This group were active in local charities and in their church. In 1829 John Meabry, Frances Keysell and Nicholas Winsland were all members of the joint Vestry of the Parishes of St Giles in the Fields and St George Bloomsbury. Other members included John Jortin (coffin 1525), Henry Ellis of the British Museum, William Groom (coffin 1105) and Luke Graves Hansard the printer. One of the church wardens was Thomas Brown (coffin 1121) colourman of High Holborn (Dobie 1829, 416-19).

In 1822 and again in 1823, Frances Keysell was one of the stewards at the Anniversary Dinner of the Middlesex Hospital presided over the Duke of Northumberland (*The Annual Subscription Charities and Public Societies in London*, London, 1823, 29; *The Times*, Friday, 3rd May, 1822, 4). Another steward was a fellow Bloomsbury resident, the builder, Nicholas Winsland. Winsland was also a steward at the dinner held at the London Tavern following the Anniversary Meeting of the Charity Schools within the cities of London and Westminster (*The Annual Subscription Charities and Public Societies in London*, London, 1823, 54).

Winsland clearly had social pretensions. In a bond relating to the construction of a chapel of ease at Hersham Surrey, he is described as 'builder to Sir Richard Frederick of Burwood Park, Walton upon Thames, Bart, and Sir Henry Fletcher of Ashley Park, Bart' (Surrey Heritage, Ref 2843/4/20). He would no doubt have been delighted to have witnessed the marriage of his second daughter Mary Elizabeth, to James Hannen of the Middle temple and to have known that his son-in-law would become Baron Hannen (Polden 2004). As a result his grandchildren would be known as the Hon. Mary Lucy Hannen, the Hon. Margaret Ellen Hannen, the Hon. James Chitty Hannen and the Hon. Henry Arthur Hannen.

Bloomsbury a cosmopolitan parish

The inhabitants of Bloomsbury were cosmopolitan, drawn from across Britain and Ireland and including a sizeable group of foreign extraction. Many of the wealthier members of the community had come to the Parish from outside London and retained houses out of town. Many of the lawyers and judges had been drawn in by the presence of the Inns of Court and law courts; Sir James Mansfield was born in Hampshire, and Sir Joseph Littledale, and his brother Edward, in Lancashire of a Cumberland family; another brother, John, was collector of Customs at Whitehaven. Sergeant at Law Samuel Heywood was from Liverpool. These people were clearly drawn to London, by the opportunities available in the capital and Bloomsbury was the parish in which they chose to settle amongst similarly successful professional and commercial classes.

There were a number of foreign merchants and members of the families of foreign descent interred in the crypt of St George's. Mathias Aspden, from Philadelphia has already been noted. Ignatius Palyart (coffin 5008), was a merchant, with premises at 9 London Street, Fenchurch Street, as well as being the Portuguese Consul General. Both he and his wife (coffin 5003) were interred in the crypt of St George's. The family resided at 10 Bedford Place and at Strand on the Green near Kew (*Holden's 1811 Directory*).

Theodore Gavaron, 52 Woburn Place, was another foreigner living in London. What his profession was is not known. His wife Maria Magdalen, and at least two daughters were born in Gibraltar. The eldest daughter Maria married Francisco Rebellio, 'provisional Portuguese consul-general' at St George's Bloomsbury in September 1820 (*The Annual Register for the year 1820*, 561; Pallot's Index of Marriages). Her sister Catherine married William Weishaupt, who is described in the 1851 census as the 'manager of a foreign merchants house'. Weishaupt was born in Trieste, then within the Austrian Empire. The youngest daughter of the family, Augusta was born in Middlesex in 1818. Louisa, who died aged 13 years and 9 months and was interred in the crypt (coffin 4033), may have been born in Middlesex too.

Charles de Constant (plate 8070) was a native of Geneva. His full name was Charles de Constant de Rebecque. He was known as 'Le Chinois' because of his travels in the Far East between 1779 and 1789 (Dermigny 1964). His cousin was Benjamin de Constant, a French-Swiss novelist and political writer, who had a twelve year relationship with Madame de Staël. In August 1798 Charles de Constant married Anne Louise Renée Achard, the daughter of the banker Jacques Achard, who was also from Geneva (IGI).

Of course there were also families of Huguenot descent. One such family was the Jourdans. Three members of the family – John, Edward and George – are recorded on a mural tablet in the church (Table 4.1) and the coffins of two of these men – John (coffin 6120) and Edward (coffin 6028) – were identified in the crypt. The three brothers were the sons of Antoine and Rachel Jourdan. This couple had at least eight children, seven boys and one girl. The first five children – born between 1747 and 1753 – were christened in a Huguenot church in Westminster, and their parents' names were recorded as Antoine and Rachel Jourdan (IGI). John and Edward were christened Jean and Edouard respectively. The final three children, including George, were born between 1754 and 1757 and were christened in the Anglican church of St Martin's in the Fields, and their parent's names were recorded as Anthony and Rachel Jourdan (IGI). It may be that the family had moved home, and that it was convenient to use the church of St Martin in the Field. But possibly Antoine and Rachel had made a conscious decision to become more integrated into English or British society.

Nevertheless, John and Edward Jourdan both married women of foreign descent. They married respectively Susannah and Elizabeth Zornlin, who were Swiss, and whose father was John Jacob Zornlin, a partner in the firm of Battier, Zornlin and Co., merchants, 10 Devonshire Square (*Kent's Directory 1794*). Their mother was Susannah Maria Battier, the daughter of John Rudolph Battier of Basle, who was Zornlin's partner. Battier, Zornlin and Co. went bankrupt in late 1799. It was one of a number of London firms that failed in 1799 as part of wider crisis which began in Hamburg where 152 houses went bankrupt (Schulte Beerbühl, 2008, 75).

George Jourdan married into the Huguenot Mesman family. His wife Mary Jourdan (née Mesman) died on 31 October 1793 aged just 23 and was interred in Christchurch Spitalfields, together with their baby son Charles Daniel who survived his mother by just 2 weeks and died on 12 November 1793 aged 3 weeks (Molleson and Cox 1993, fig. 8.2, fiche 6.1, p.3; Cox 1996, 121). John and George were both silk weavers, and worked out of 14 Spital Square (*PO London 1808*; *Holden's 1811*).

Although it would appear that integration of John and George into English society was limited, it should be noted that by the time of their deaths they had moved away from Spitalfields. John was living in Bedford Place, and George, according to his will, was living in Wanstead, Essex. The third brother, Major Edward Jourdan would appear to have become more integrated into English society. He was as an officer in the service of the East India Company's Madras Army. He fought in the 2nd Mysore War against Hyder Ali and by 1786 was commanding the 2nd Cavalry. He retired from the service in 1788 (Philippart 1828, 261; Dodwell and Miles 1838, 92-3) and returned to England. By 1808 he was living at 43, Devonshire Street, Portland Place (*Holden's 1811*) and he died there in 1830. He was a shareholder in the East India Company (*List of names 1815*) and he was a member of the wealthy upper middle class with notices of his death in the *Gentleman's Magazine* (Oct 1830, 380) and *La Belle Assemblée* (Nov 1830, 231). It is clear that all three brothers had become well integrated into upper middle class society in Bloomsbury. All three are commemorated on their mural monument in St George's.

Conclusion

The crypt population represents part of the elite of Bloomsbury society. Lawyers, civil servants, army and navy officers, MPs, wealthy merchants and bankers, but also up and coming tradesmen intent on improving their position in society, were interred in the crypt of St George's in the first half of the 19th century. The data recovered from the *depositum* plates on their coffins provides a window into their shared history. The potential for historical research into the population interred within the crypt is considerable. The notes presented here have by no measure tapped the full historical potential of the data on the crypt population.

Chapter 5: Demography

by Ceridwen Boston

INTRODUCTION

Coffin plates were found attached to 644 of the 781 coffins recovered from the crypt. Of these some 610 had clearly identifiable names. In addition 146 detached coffin plates were found (Appendix 1). Some of the loose plates could be matched to *depositum* plates inscriptions attached to coffins, but many could not be matched. It is assumed that the detached plates that could not be matched had originally been attached to the poorly preserved coffins found in Vault 7. The detached plates provided the names of a further 63 people.

The demographic information on the *depositum* plate inscriptions is a valuable historical resource. St. George's is unparalleled in the proportion of named individuals in the total crypt population. In the analysis which follows, this population is compared to the records for the parish as a whole, and with two broadly contemporary crypt populations of comparable social class from Christ Church, Spitalfields (Molleson and Cox 1993), and from St. Bride's Church, Fleet Street (Scheuer and Bowman 1995).

Interments in the crypt of St George's spanned the period from 1801 to 1856. The numbers interred in each decade varied with peak in the 1820s (Table 5.1)

AGE DISTRIBUTION

The ages of the crypt population of St. George's ranged from newborn to 99 years (Table 5.2). The mortality curve (Fig. 5.2) demonstrates the age distribution within this population. Infant mortality (the first year of life) was high, in keeping with the high risk of complications associated with childbirth,

congenital abnormalities, problematic infant feeding and most importantly, exposure to the infections so rife in industrialised centres of this era (Roberts and Cox 2003). It is interesting to note, however, that only a small proportion of these infants were newborn or stillborn (n = 7). Two of these were the still born twins of Charles and Clar. . . . Martyn, buried together in a single coffin (plate 3109).

The low proportion of neonates would suggest either that many newborns were buried elsewhere, or that infant mortality associated with complications of childbirth or congenital anomalies was indeed low in this population. In this middling population, it is not unreasonable to assume that maternal health overall would have been better than amongst the poorer classes. Hence, the tendency to premature delivery, low birth weight infants, developmental anomalies and complications in childbirth, associated with maternal ill health and deleterious social practices such as excessive alcohol consumption, would have been lower. The attendance of competent obstetricians and midwives may have reduced the risks of labour to both mother and child. However, medical intervention was frequently linked to the transmission of *streptacoccus* bacteria to mothers during and after labour, resulting in the dreaded pueperal fever (*streptococcal* septicaemia), the greatest killer of young women in this period (Codell Carter 1999, 265). At St George's crypt, the mortality curve in the young adult years showed no rise, either in the death of young women or men, as is commonly found in pre-modern societies. There is nothing to suggest that death due to childbirth was a signifi-

Table 5.1: The number of interments of known date within the crypt of St. George's in each decade between 1803-1856 (n = 682), based on departum plate inscriptions, and the total number of burials in the parish, recorded in parish registers between 1801 and 1840 (London Metropolitan Archives). (The figures in brackets give numbers and %ages of crypt burials distributing undated burials proportionally)

Decade	Interments in crypt	Total burials in St George's parish	Crypt burials as a %age of total burials in each decade
1803-1810	57 (65.27)	2910	1.96% (2.24%)
1811-1820	151 (173)	1953	7.73% (8.9%)
1821-1830	219 (250.79)	2093	10.46% (11.98%)
1831-1840	180 (206.12)	1700	10.59% (12.12%)
1841-1850	64 (73.29)	no data	-
1851-1856	11 (12.6)	no data	-
Total	682 (781)	8656	

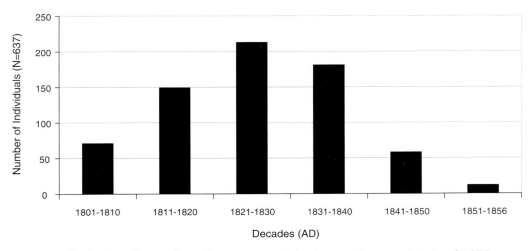

Fig. 5.1   Bar graph showing the number of interments within the crypt between 1803 and 1856

cant factor amongst this population. Death in childbirth was recorded as the cause of death in the case of Harriot Lent of Kings Street (plate 8116) and Mary Madden (coffin 1035), both of whom died aged 26 in 1830.

In the crypt sample, there was a rapid decrease in the number of deaths, after the first most vulnerable year, presumably as children became more immune

to the multitude of infectious diseases endemic in this pre-modern industrial city. Being a wealthy population, it is unlikely that the children in this assemblage suffered the malnutrition and poor living conditions so pervasive in the lower orders during this period, and nor the resulting high exposure to and poor recovery from such environmental insults. On the periphery of the metropolis,

Table 5.2: Distribution of age-at-death in the St. George's crypt population, in total and by sex (n = 652).
Percentages of males, females and total population are shown for each age category.

Age category	Males	%age males	Females	%age females	Unknown	Total	%age total
still	2	9.15		5.18		2	7.21
Neonate	4		1			5	
1m-12m	23		16		1	40	
13m-23m	6	3.79	7	4.57		13	4.14
2y-5y	6	3.15	8	2.74		14	2.91
11y-15y	9	2.84	12	3.66		21	3.22
16y-20y	5	1.58	16	4.88		21	3.22
21y-25y	8	2.52	9	2.74		17	2.61
26y-30y	8	2.52	17	5.18	1	26	3.99
31y-35y	6	1.89	15	4.57	1	22	3.37
36y-40y	14	4.42	21	6.40		35	5.37
41y-45y	13	4.10	12	3.66		25	3.83
46y-50y	7	2.21	23	7.01	1	31	4.75
51y-55y	16	5.05	15	4.57		31	4.75
56y-60y	25	7.89	21	6.40		46	7.06
61y-65y	45	14.20	21	6.40	2	68	10.43
66y-70y	28	8.83	30	9.15		58	8.90
6y-10y	10	9.46	9	6.40		19	7.98
71y-75y	30	7.89	21	7.32	1	52	7.52
76y-80y	25	5.05	24	5.49		49	5.21
81y-85y	16	3.15	18	2.44		34	2.76
86y-90y	10	0.32	8	0.91		18	0.61
91y-95y	1	3.79	3	0.30		4	0.15
96y-100y			1	4.57		1	4.14
Total	317		328		6	652	

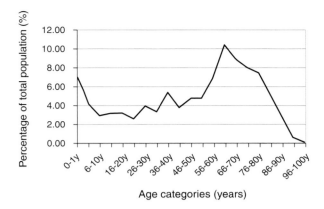

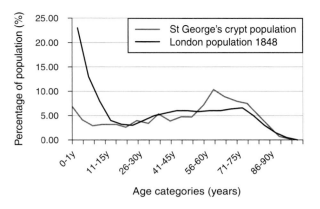

Fig. 5.2   *Mortality curve of the crypt population shown as a percentage of the population*

Fig. 5.3   *Mortality curves of the crypt population and the wider London population based on Bills of Mortality of 1848*

upwind from the major industry of the East End, the position of the new urban development of Bloomsbury was deliberately chosen because as a 'place by physicians [it] was esteemed the most healthful of any in London' (Strype 1720, cited in Meller 1975, 1). From the analysis below, these healthful effects appear to have played their role in the mortality patterns of the crypt population.

There are marked differences between the demography reflected in the London Bills of Mortality of 1848 and that compiled from the coffin plate inscriptions (Fig. 5.3) from St George's crypt. Childhood mortality below the age of five years was very much lower in the latter group (11.35% compared to 40%). This was probably due to the environmental and socio-economic factors discussed above. Similarly, mortality figures for the first 20 years of life are dramatically lower (20.71%) compared with those for the wider London population (50%). Lastly, adult longevity was much greater in the St George's population, with a far higher proportion of the population surviving beyond 70 years of age (24.23% compared to 6% of the general London population.

These results are similar to those of other named assemblages from London (Table 5.3) which also reflect low mortality among the under fives and longevity among those over 70 years. The explanation for the apparent under-representation of children at Christ Church, Spitalfields, was

explained in terms of differential treatment of some deceased children - that some children were not interred with family members within the crypt but were buried elsewhere, possibly within the church-yard (Cox 1996, 20).

However, in an era when there was excessive sentimentality surrounding the death of children (Rugg 1999) considerable efforts were made to ensure that family members were interred together. It is unlikely that the dearth of subadults within the Spitalfield's crypt indicates a lower value was accorded to a child than to an adult. Nor are discrete post-medieval infant and child burial grounds, such as the *cillini* of Ireland (Donnelly and Murphy 2008), known in England.

It is very much more probable that the apparent dearth of subadults in the middle class named assemblages shown in Figure 5.3 reflects demographic reality, and not age-specific burial practices, and that the differences in child mortality between the London Bills of Mortality and the crypt assemblages are very much more likely relate to differences in longevity and health which can be associated with the highly stratified society that was late Georgian England.

This conclusion is supported by the findings of Edwin Chadwick's 1840 study on childhood mortality in nine different locations in England (Rugg 1999, 219). He concluded that the average child mortality amongst the gentry and profes-

Table 5.3: *Comparative mortality rates within selected named burial assemblages and from London Bills of Mortality*

Assemblages	Mortality below the age of five years	Mortality below the age of 21 years	Survival > 70 years
St George's crypt, Bloomsbury	11.35%	20.71%	24.23%
St Luke's Church, Islington	14%	22.8%	27.2%
St Brides, Fleet St	-	28%	-
Christ Church, Spitalfields	19.2%	23%	21.8%
London Bills of Mortality	40%	50%	6%

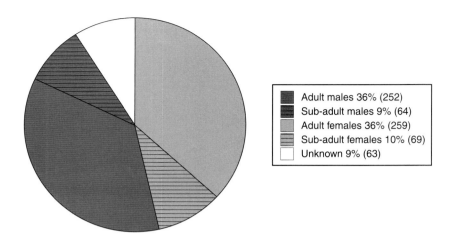

Fig. 5.4   Piechart showing sex distribution of subadult and adults based on departum plate inscriptions (N = 707)

sionals was 20%, whereas amongst labourers, artisans and servants the rate was approximately 50%. The childhood mortality rate of the St George's Church assemblage (as with St Luke's, Islington, and Christ Church, Spitalfields) approximates Chadwick's middle and upper classes. Similarly, the high proportion of the population surviving beyond 70 years is more typical of the middle and upper classes of the day.

Using mortality figures from nine different locations in 1840, Edwin Chadwick (quoted in Rugg 1999) calculated that in these places on average one in five children of the gentry and professional classes did not survive to adulthood, whilst amongst labourers, artisans and servants this figure leapt to one in two. St. George's crypt population, like Christ Church, Spitalfields, and St. Bride's church, Fleet Street, represented the wealthier middle classes of the metropolis, and had a child mortality rate in keeping with their class in other locations in England at that time.

At St. George's church, mortality rates do not change substantially over later childhood, adolescence or early adulthood, but begin to increase more acutely after 40 years, peaking in the 61-65 year old age bracket. After this there is a decrease in the number of deaths in the years following, but these do remain elevated until 85 years, after which there is a rapid decline, with only 21 individuals surviving beyond 85 years, and 6 individuals beyond 90 years of age. Nevertheless, the survival of so many individuals into advanced old age is itself eloquent of the good quality of life enjoyed by the St. George's church population.

SEX DISTRIBUTION AND MORTALITY

The distribution of males (n = 317) and females (n = 328) in the St George's crypt population was 49.15% and 50.85%, respectively of the burials of known sex. This is broadly reflects the proportions quoted

in the London Bills of Mortality (50.86% and 49.14% respectively) (quoted in Molleson and Cox 1993). This would seem to suggest that in the St George's crypt assemblage, the slight sexual inequality in distribution appears not to be due to preferential inclusion of males over females but to a wider demographic reality. It is interesting to note from parish records, that between 1801 and 1840 the proportion of females to males in the whole burial population within St George's parish was almost exactly the same. Males constituted 49.83 % and females 50.17 %. Figure 5.4 show the proportions of male and female adults and subadults and burials of unknown age and/or sex amongst the burials known from *depositum* plates.

Figure 5.5 shows the number of deaths in each age category for the entire population and for males and females. The pattern of mortality for males and females are slightly different. Very young male children suffered markedly higher death rates than their female counterparts. Thereafter females tend to have slightly higher mortality rates until late adulthood. Between the ages of 56 and 80 men have

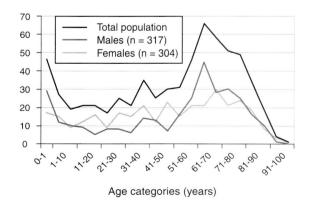

Fig. 5.5   Mortality curves of the total crypt population and for males and for females

higher mortality rate. Thereafter the mortality rate for men and women is the same.

SEASONALITY OF DEATH

The month of death is shown on most coffin plates. Table 5.4 shows the distribution of deaths by calendar month. No marked patterning could be discerned, other than that January was the month with the highest number of deaths, probably reflecting an exacerbation of respiratory diseases in the winter months. June was the month when deaths were at their lowest. Investigating the seasonality of death in 18th-century London, Bradley (1982) found that amongst children the peak months were June, July and November, whilst May, June and July were peak months for adult deaths. This was probably due to the increased prevalence of epidemics in the summer months and of respiratory diseases in the winter. This patterning was not found to be the case in the St. George's population.

The months of the year were divided into the four seasons of three months each. The proportion of deaths in each season is displayed in Figure 5.6 below. As hypothesised, winter shows a slightly higher mortality rate, but this is by no means marked. It is possible that the lack of seasonality of deaths in this population is due to the buffering effects of good nutrition, housing and medical care.

Table 5.4: Number of deaths per calendar month.
Data from coffin plate inscriptions (n = 637).

Month	No of burials
January	71
February	58
March	61
April	58
May	62
June	38
July	55
August	49
September	56
October	32
November	49
December	48
Total	637

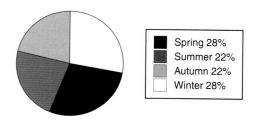

Fig. 5.6 Piechart showing seasonality of death

Spring 28%
Summer 22%
Autumn 22%
Winter 28%

CAUSES OF DEATH

The cause of death is seldom cited either in the *depositum* plate inscriptions or on the memorial plaques within the church. The breastplate inscription of Gilbert Gollan (coffin 7043), aged 62 years, 'late of the Island of St. Vincent died after a most painful and ...ious illness which he bore with Christian fortitude and resignation' suggests a chronic and painful end, but gives no further details of his malady. The records of the Bloomsbury searchers record only that he died of consumption (LMA P83/GEO1/63). Two memorial plates within the church interior are more specific. The Kirkup family memorial states that James Fenwick Kirkup (coffin 1051), son of Ann and Joseph Kirkup, aged 26, drowned whilst bathing. The poignant memorial to Mary Madden (coffin 1035), aged 26, tells of her death whilst giving birth to an infant son. The infant son, Frederick Hayton Madden, lived for only five days after birth. Harriot Lent (plate 8116) also died in childbirth aged 26.

The records of the Bloomsbury searchers for the period 1771–1834 survive in the London Metropolitan Archives (P82/GEO1/63). Prior to the introduction of civil registration, the parish clerk had to be informed of all deaths within his parish. The searchers, often elderly female paupers, were employed by parishes to visit the recently deceased to ensure that no further action was required. The data from the Bloomsbury searchers' records has been transcribed and is accessible on-line. From this source the causes of death of over 250 individuals have been found. The searchers records are not comprehensive and by no means all deaths in the period are recorded. The data is best for the 1820s. Additionally the causes of death of eight individuals have been found in the parish records. In total the causes of death of 267 individuals have been found, and are summarised in Table 5.5. The most common recorded causes of death are consumption (72 cases), 'inflammation' (39 instances) and dropsy (22 cases), together with old age (18 cases).

Victorian medical diagnoses are rarely directly comparable to their modern equivalents. Given the limited tools for diagnosis at the time, they are frequently less specific than today. For example, the 'natural decay' or 'decay of nature' experienced by Sophia Hammond (coffin 2006), Jane Howe (coffin 3022) and Mary Huster (coffin 4007) usually refers to the ageing process. The 'arthralgia' experienced by the latter is a term analogous to painful arthritis. In the case of Jane Howe, the natural decay was accompanied by 'effusion of the chest'. The 'inflammation of the liver' suffered by Thomas Jeakes (coffin 1057) suggests hepatitis, possibly due to infection of the liver by viruses, bacteria or parasites; or to a complication of prolonged alcohol misuse. As a carpenter, a lifetime of exposure to varnish, paint and glue might also have caused this condition.

The widespread nature of the disease suffered by Robert James (coffin 4011) suggests some form of

Table 5.5: Recorded causes of death (n=263). The information is largely derived from the records of the Bloomsbury searchers (LMA P82/GEO1/62)

Cause of death	Females	Males	Total
abcess	1	1	2
apoplexy (7F; 5M); apoplectic attack (1M)	7	6	13
asthma	1	5	6
'asthma, disease of the heart and dropsy'		1	1
cancer	7		7
'child bed' (1F), child birth (1F)	2		2
'complications of disease of the brain, bowel and bladder'		1	1
consumption	38	34	72
convulsions	4	7	11
croup	1		1
decay of nature	1		1
'decay of nature attended with arthralgia'	1		1
died suddenly	2	2	4
disease of the heart		1	1
diseased liver	1		1
dropsy	14	8	22
dropsy brain (1M); 'dropsy in the brain' (1M)		2	2
'drowned while bathing'		1	1
'enlargement of the heart'		1	1
fever	2	2	4
gout	2		2
hernia (sic)	1		1
infl[amed] lungs		1	1
'inflammation'	15	24	39
inflammation of the liver		1	1
inflammation of the throat	1		1
jaundice		1	1
liver complaint		1	1
measles		1	1
'mortification'	2	4	6
'natural decay and effusion of the chest'	1		1
old age (8F, 8M), aged (2M)	8	10	18
'ossification of the heart'	1		1
palsy		3	3
paralysis		1	1
paralytic [stroke] (2M); paralytic stroke (1M)		3	3
scarlet fever	1		1
smallpox		2	2
spasm (2F, 1M); spasms (1F, 2M)	3	3	6
stone		3	3
'stoppage in the stomach'		1	1
suicide		1	1
teeth (1F); teething (1M)	1	1	2
thrush		1	1
tumour	1	1	2
typhus fever		1	1
'water head' / 'waterhead' (2F, 1M), 'water on the head' (4F)	6	1	7
whooping cough	2	3	5
Total	126	138	267

metastatic cancer, whilst Thomas Tatham's symptoms suggest cardiac failure (coffin 1527). Untreated congestive cardiac failure is often attended by peripheral oedema (the hands and legs becoming swollen). 'Dropsy' was a catch-all diagnosis, referring to the accumulation of fluid within the body. This occurs in kidney failure, when the body no longer excretes water and salts efficiently, or as ascites, associated with liver failure (Estes 2003, 100-105). However, the most common cause of dropsy was heart failure. In Thomas Tatham's case, this would seem the most likely explanation. His 'asthma' may well not have been 'asthma' as we know it today, but rather respiratory distress brought about by poor cardiac function, possibly with attendant pulmonary oedema.

Unlike the chronic conditions described above, Charlotte Turner (coffin 7081) appears to have died of an acute infection, evidently not differentially diagnosed. The underlying cause for Jane Covell's 'throat inflammation' is unknown, but may have ranged from infectious diseases, such as diphtheria or tuberculosis, to throat cancer (coffin 7045).

The commonest cause of death was consumption, which was the cause in over a quarter of the recorded cases. Just how devastating consumption could be is illustrated by the Stringfield family, who are commemorated on a mural plaque in the Church (see Table 4.1 above). Thomas Stringfield the father was a butcher. He and his wife Mary had four sons – John, William, James, and George – and a daughter Mary. Between 1821 and 1835 eight members of the family died: Thomas and Mary, their sons John, William and James, John's wife Anna, their son-in-law Bisse Phillips Sanderson who had married their daughter Mary, and Anna the young daughter of John and Anna Stringfield. The cause of death is known in five cases, and of these three – Thomas, his son James and daughter in law Anna – died of consumption. Mary died from 'inflammation' and John of 'dropsy'. The only members of the family to survive seem to be the youngest son George, who never married, his sister Mary Sanderson now a widow, Mary's daughter Sarah, and John and Anna's son John William. Three members of the Keysell family – the brothers Richard and Henry, and their sister-in-law Eliza Olney Keysell, first wife of Francis Price Keysell – died of consumption. The Stringfields and Keysells were traders who lived and worked in the most populous south part of the parish of St George

Bloomsbury, but those who live in the newer properties north of Great Russell Street were not immune to tuberculosis. Samuel Heywood, Sergeant at Law and Judge of the Carmarthen Circuit, lost his wife Susannah and his daughter Mary Isabella to consumption. The Heywood family lived in Bedford Place. Two young daughters of the Waters family of Russell Square died of consumption in 1818 and 1819. George Burley, solicitor of Lincoln's Inn Square, and his daughter Elizabeth Burley, lived in Bloomsbury Place and both died of tuberculosis.

What is striking in the above sample is how few individuals met their end through trauma or through infection (with the exception of consumption). According to a memorial within the church, the 26 year old James Kirkup (coffin 1051) drowned whilst bathing, whilst one suicide is recorded (Robert Trower, coffin 5059).

Interestingly for this period, acute infection was the recorded cause of death in only seven individuals: two from smallpox, one from croup, two from 'fever' (cause not specified), one from measles, one from scarlet fever and one from typhus fever. One fatality from smallpox was 24 year old Thomas Bland (coffin 1506). His obituary in the *Gentleman's Magazine* (August 1825, 187) indicated that he died of smallpox, despite being inoculated against the disease in his first year of life. Surprisingly, death from cholera, the dreaded 'black one', which raged through Britain's cities and towns periodically throughout the 1830s and 1840s, was not recorded in the sample.

Conclusion

The *depositum* plate inscriptions and historical documentation both indicate that mortality rates and patterns of longevity in St George's crypt population were consistent with other 'middling sort' assemblages of London. The marked differences in child mortality and longevity between these groups and the wider London population may be explained in terms of the highly stratified society of the Metropolis, in which the vast disparity in wealth of the 'haves' and 'have nots' dictated the living conditions and occupations that had such a marked effect on health and survival. Individuals interred within the crypt of St George's Church were amongst the more fortunate members of London's population.

Chapter 6: The human bone assemblage

by Ceridwen Boston, Annsofie Witkin, Angela Boyle and Jennifer Kitch

INTRODUCTION

The skeletal remains of 111 individuals contained within decayed lead coffins were collected for osteological analysis. These were divided into two groups: the named sample, which was the larger group and comprised 72 individuals, and the unnamed sample of 39 individuals. As noted in Chapter 1, the named sample was subject of full osteological analysis, whilst the unnamed underwent less detailed analysis that was primarily aimed at understanding the social demography of the group. Due to these different methodologies, the results of the osteological analysis of the two samples are presented separately in this chapter, but combined where relevant and for discussion.

THE NAMED SAMPLE

Methodology

Preservation and completeness

Skeletal preservation may vary considerably between burials as a result of differences within the immediate micro-environment surrounding each skeleton. Preservation is influenced by a wide range of environmental factors (such as the pH of the surrounding soil, the type and presence of a coffin and materials placed within the coffin itself), and complex interactions between these factors often occurs making preservation within and between assemblages highly variable. Indeed, each burial may be seen as existing within its own niche environment (Henderson 1987, 43). The principal factors that affected preservation within the St George's assemblages were the degree of compression, the type of coffin, the use of absorbent material (such as sawdust and bran within the coffin) and the inclusion of lime, all of which may accelerate or retard diagenesis. The age and sex of the skeleton and some pathological conditions (such as osteoporosis) may also influence bone preservation.

Preservation was scored on a scale from: **1** (Poor) to **4** (Excellent). Preservation categories were defined as follows:

1   **Poor** – cortical bone soft, leached, flaking or eroded – not possible to identify most pathologies, poor preservation of trabecular bone, especially diaphyses and less dense bone, such as vertebrae, ribs and pelves.

2   **Fair** – cortical bone displaying some damage (such as demineralisation, flaking and erosion) but some areas of well preserved bone present – limited potential for observing pathology.

3   **Good** – some damage to cortical bone present, but large areas sufficiently well preserved to identify pathology and non-metric traits and undertake metrical analysis; trabecular bone preservation good with most epiphyses and joint surfaces intact, and good representation of ribs, vertebrae and pelves.

4   **Excellent** – cortical bone pristine not having undergone the above destructive changes to either the cortical or trabecular bone, possible to undertake full osteological analysis.

Completeness was also scored on a four point scale, based on the percentage of the total skeleton present. These categories were defined as follows: 1 (5% – 25% complete), 2 (26% – 50%), 3 (51% – 75%), 4 (76% – near complete).

Skeletal inventory

A pictoral and tabular inventory was created for each skeleton. This recording formed the basis of true prevalence calculations of pathological conditions described below.

Dental inventories were made following the Zsigmondy system (as cited in Hillson 1996, 8-9). Dental notations were recorded by using universally accepted recording standards and terminology (after Brothwell 1981).

Determination of sex

Sexually dimorphic traits emerge after the onset of puberty, and hence, can only be ascribed with any degree of accuracy in skeletons aged greater than 16-18 years. The pelvis is the most sexually dimorphic element, exhibiting features that directly relate to functional evolutionary differences between the sexes (Mays 1998; Mays and Cox 2000), most significantly childbirth in females. Blind studies of individuals of known sex reveal that ascribing sex using this element alone had a reported accuracy as high as 96 % (Meindl *et al.* 1985; Sutherland and Suchey 1991).

The skull is the next most sexually dimorphic element, from which sex may be correctly inferred in up to 92 % of cases (Mays 1998, 38). It has been claimed that sex estimation from the cranium alone has an accuracy of 88 %, (St Hoyme and Iscan 1989, 69), whilst there is a 90% accuracy when the mandible is also present (Krogman and Iscan 1986, 112). This observed sexual dimorphism arises as the result of the action of testicular hormones on the bones of the male skull (ibid., 38), which is characterised by a general increase in robusticity and enlargement of muscle attachment sites. Blind studies of sex estimation undertaken on the named assemblage from Spitalfields revealed that in skeletons where complete skulls and pelves were present accuracy was as high as 98% (Molleson and Cox 1993).

Six cranial features and a maximum of ten pelvic features were used for sexing adults. On the cranium, the features used were selected from Ferembach *et al.* (1980) and Buikstra and Ubelaker (1994). Sexually diagnostic features of the pelvis included the greater sciatic notch and preauricular sulcus (Ferembach *et al.*1980), as well several features of the pubic bone described by Phenice (1969).

Measurements used for sexing were the diameters of the femoral, humeral and radial heads, as well as the length of the clavicles and the width of the glenoid fossae (Chamberlain 1994). Cranial and post-cranial metrics may also be used to ascribe sex, but their potential is limited by the considerable variation between individuals and between populations. A substantial zone of intermediate values exists between the two sexes, rendering sexing using metrical analysis alone very unhelpful in these cases. Post-cranial measurements rely on the generalisation that males (under the influence of male hormones) tend to be taller and more robust than their female counterparts. Considerable variation in such sexual dimorphism has been noted between populations. In the St George's assemblage, a large number of males were gracile, thereby increasing the probability of erroneously ascribing female sex to these individuals. As a result, metrics were treated as being of secondary importance in ascribing sex to individuals of the St George's assemblages.

Osteologically, sex may be ascribed with differing levels of certainty, depending on the extent of sexual dimorphism present and the number of sexually dimorphic sites available for study. Sex categories used in this study reflect this uncertainty: possible male or female (??male or ??female) was used where there is marked uncertainty but where there are sufficient traits to tentatively suggest the sex of the skeleton; probable male (?male) or female (?female) was used where some ambivalence or uncertainty exists, but where the sex of the individual could be ascribed with more confidence than those in the previous category; and male or female was used where there is considerable certainty in the sex of an individual. In order to increase numbers for the present analysis, the female, ?female and ??female categories, and male, ?male and ??male categories were conflated to produce single female and male groups.

Estimation of osteological age

Osteological age reflects the biological age of the skeleton and not the chronological age of the individual. The difference between osteological and chronological age, in part, is due to genetic influences, but largely is the result of external factors, such as nutrition and lifestyle, that impact on skeletal growth and subsequent degeneration (Schwartz 1995, 185). Subadults may be aged more precisely than adults, as the growth and maturation sequence of children is fairly predictable and uniform (Scheuer and Black 2000). The development and eruption of both deciduous and permanent dentition are believed to be less affected by environmental factors than skeletal growth (Roberts 1997, 111), and hence, have been used as the most accurate ageing method in this study. Ageing of adults over the age of 18 years was estimated from bony changes at various sites on the skeleton. The age categories employed in this analysis are shown in Table 6.1.

In order to increase the accuracy of age estimations, multiple methods were employed. Age estimation of subadults involved analysis of the following: dental development of deciduous and permanent dentition (Moorees *et al.* 1963 a and b), diaphyseal long bone length (Maresh 1955; Hoppa 1992) and epiphyseal fusion (Ferembach *et al.* 1980; Schwartz 1995). The last was also used on skeletons aged up to 25 years.

Adults were aged using methods relating to the degeneration of the ilial auricular surface (Lovejoy *et al.* 1985), pubic symphysis (Todd 1921a and b; Brooks and Suchey 1990), and sternal ends of the mid-thoracic rib (Iscan *et al.* 1984, 1985). Methods relating to ectocranial suture closure (Meindl and Lovejoy 1985) were also used but were not as rigorously applied as the aforementioned, as the accuracy and precision of this method is not believed to be high (Cox 2003). The dental attrition ageing method of Roden (1997) was also applied to a small number of named individuals. The method was developed on the 19th century burial assemblage of the Newcastle Infirmary, Newcastle-upon-Tyne. Due to the refined diet enjoyed in the 18th and 19th centuries, dental attrition in this time period was greatly reduced when compared to earlier agricultural societies. It was therefore inappropriate to apply methodologies

Table 6.1: Human bone: Age categories

neonate	< 1 year
infant 1	1-5 years
infant 2	6-11 years
adolescent	12-17 years
young adult	18-25 years
prime adult	26-40 years
mature adult	40-50 years
ageing adult	50+ years
subadult	< 18 years
adult	>18 years

devised for prehistoric and medieval populations (e.g. Miles 1962; Brothwell 1981). Roden's method involved ageing of all subadults using the tooth formation standards developed by Smith (1991), and then sequencing them by age. This was used as a reference for sequencing adult dentition in order of increased attrition. The Infirmary population comprised working class individuals but was contemporary with the St George's crypt assemblage. The method has not been widely used and its implementation in this analysis was to test its usefulness in a contemporary but more affluent population.

Certain more recent ageing methods, such as Buckberry and Chamberlain's (2002) revised method using degeneration of the ilial auricular surface, were not available at the time of analysis.

Estimation of stature

The stature of named individuals was calculated by applying measurements of the maximum length of long bones to regression formulae for white males and females devised by Trotter (1970). Measurements of lower limb bones were preferred over those of the upper limb, as these carry less error. In order to reduce the standard error, only calculations using combined femoral and tibial measurements were included in the analysis below.

Comparative assemblages

The results of the osteological analysis of the St George's crypt sample were compared to broadly contemporary skeletal assemblages from England that derived from differing socio-economic backgrounds. This facilitated exploration of the effects of social class on the demographic structure and patterns of health and disease in these populations. The assemblages were from the Newcastle Infirmary (Boulter *et al.* 1997), the Cross Bones burial ground, London (Brickley *et al.* 1999), Christ Church, Spitalfields, London (Molleson and Cox 1993, Cox 1996) and St Luke's Church, Islington

(Boyle *et al.* 2005). This selection was determined by the availability of data at the time of writing.

The Cross Bones burial ground is believed to have been in use from the middle of the 19th century, within a 10 to 30 year time span. Around 18% of those buried there died in the workhouse. Overall, the individuals buried at the cemetery were the poorest members of an underprivileged community (Brickley *et al.* 1999, 48).

The human remains from Newcastle Infirmary, Newcastle-upon-Tyne, Northumbria, dated between 1745 and 1845, and represented those who died in the hospital. The more affluent classes of the day were treated privately at home, and medical treatment in public hospitals was reserved for the poor who were eligible for medical care under the Poor Law (Nolan 1997). Hence, the assemblage comprises the city's poor, but is also thought to include a large number of sailors.

The named sample from Christ Church, Spitalfields, was interred within the crypt between 1729 and 1852. Trade directories and burial records indicated that most individuals were artisans and master craftsmen (Cox 1996, 69), many of whom had achieved considerable affluence in the silk trade, but remained resolutely middle class. Very few were professionals or were independently wealthy.

The named sample from St Luke's, Islington, derived primarily those interred within the church crypt, and from extramural family vaults. The crypt was in use between 1740 and 1853. Burials in the cemetery commenced slightly earlier in 1734 (Boyle *et al.* 2005, 34). The place of burial and the elaborate lead-lined coffins were characteristic of middle class interments of the period.

Results

Quantification

A total of 781 coffins was removed from the crypt. Of these, 111 coffins were so poorly preserved that the human remains were removed and analysed prior to

Table 6.2: Quantification of coffins by vault, showing numbers of coffins in the named and unnamed samples

	No. of Coffins	No. of Named sample	%age of vault total	%age of sample total (N=72)	No. of Unnamed sample	%age of vault total	Total Studied	%age of vault total
Vault 1	225	11	4.89	15.28	4	1.78	15	6.67
Vault 2	69	4	5.80	5.55	1	1.45	5	7.25
Vault 3	94	10	10.64	13.89	7	7.45	17	18.09
	388	**25**	**6.44**	**34.72**	**12**	**3.09**	**37**	**9.54**
Vault 4	85	24	28.24	33.34	7	8.24	31	36.47
Vault 5	80	11	13.75	15.28	3	3.75	14	17.50
Vault 6	139	6	4.32	8.33	5	3.60	11	7.91
	304	**41**	**13.49**	**56.94**	**15**	**4.93**	**56**	**18.42**
Vault 7	89	6	6.74	8.33	12	13.48	18	20.22
	781	**72**	**9.22**		**39**	**4.99**	**111**	**14.21**

reburial. The assemblage of named individuals that underwent osteological analysis comprised 72 individuals. A skeleton was classified as a named individual if the associated *depositum* plate was legible or partly legible, such that the name and/or the age at death could be discerned. These data are discussed more fully in Chapter 5 above.

The skeletons that comprised the named sample were retrieved from all seven vaults (Table 6.2). All the skeletal remains were recovered from lead-lined coffins. In Vaults 1 to 6, the coffins were neatly stacked and subsequently covered by a layer of sand, which in turn was overlaid by a substantial layer of charcoal. Vault 7 contained redeposited coffins, which had been stacked in a random manner, and some had been upended and folded in two. These had suffered considerably more damage than coffins from the other six vaults (See Chapter 3), resulting in separation of the skeletal remains from their associated *depositum* plate.

Preservation and completeness

The principal factor affecting coffin preservation was compression by overlying coffins in the coffin stacks. More skeletons were retained from the vaults located on the western side of the crypt (41 skeletons from Vaults 4 to 6) than the eastern side (25 skeletons from Vaults 1 to 3). Another factor affecting preservation of the lead shells was damp. Watermarks were clearly visible on the brickwork sealing the western vaults, indicating that these vaults had been much wetter than those on the eastern side. This is likely to account for greater erosion of the lead shells in these vaults, and hence, the greater number of retained skeletons. Moreover, as work progressed, removal methods were refined, with the result that fewer skeletons were retained from those vaults that were emptied last (namely Vaults 2 and 6).

The low retrieval rate of named individuals from Vault 7 (Table 6.2) was due to the destruction of

Table 6.3: Named sample: Completeness and preservation (N = 72)

Completeness	Percentage of sample (n/N)	Preservation	Percentage of sample (n/N)
1 (poor)	1.39% (1/72)	1 (poor)	0% (0/72)
2	12.50% (9/72)	2	27.78% (20/72)
3	30.55% (22/72)	3	59.72% (43/72)
4 (excellent)	55.56% (40/72)	4 (excellent)	12.50% (9/72)

Table 6.4: Named sample: Preservation and location within the crypt

Location	1 (Poor) (n/N)	2 (n/N)	3 (n/N)	4 (excellent) (n/N)	Total percentage of individuals (n/N)
Vault1	0	2.78% (2/72)	11.11% (8/72)	1.39% (1/72)	15.28% (11/72)
Vault 2	0	1.39% (1/72)	2.78% (2/72)	1.39% (1/72)	5.56% (4/72)
Vault 3	0	4.17% (3/72)	9.72% (7/72)	0	13.89% (10/72)
Vault 4	0	9.72% (7/72)	20.83% (15/72)	2.78% (2/72)	33.33% (24/72)
Vault 5	0	2.78% (2/72)	9.72% (7/72)	2.78% (2/72)	15.28% (11/72)
Vault 6	0	6.94% (5/72)	0	1.39% (1/72)	8.33% (6/72)
Vault 7	0	0	5.55% (4/72)	2.78% (2/72)	8.33% (6/72)
Percentage of total sample	0	27.78% (20/72)	59.71% (43/72)	12.51% (9/72)	100% (72/72)

most coffins during their re-deposition in the vault (see Chapter 3 above); many *depositum* plates became detached during this process. Furthermore, the human remains in many coffins had previously been removed and collected as charnel in fertiliser bags. The result was that it was not possible to identify some individuals from Vault 7 with any certainty.

Overall, 86.11% of the skeletons were more than 50% complete, and 72.22% were well or excellently preserved (Table 6.3). There appeared to be no significant difference in skeletal preservation between the vaults (Table 6.4), nor does there appear to have been a correlation between skeletal completeness and their location in the crypt (Table 6.5). The most poorly preserved remains within

Table 6.5 Named sample: Completeness and location within the crypt

Location	1 (Poor) (n/N)	2 (n/N)	3 (n/N)	4 (excellent) (n/N)	Total percentage of individuals (n/N)
Vault 1	0	0	1.39% (1/72)	13.89% (10/72)	15.28% (11/72)
Vault 2	0	0	1.39% (1/72)	4.17% (3/72)	5.56% (4/72)
Vault 3	0	2.78% (2/72)	2.78% (2/72)	8.33% (6/72)	13.89% (10/72)
Vault 4	1.39% (1/72)	2.78% (2/72)	12.50% (9/72)	16.66% (12/72)	33.33% (24/72)
Vault 5	0	1.39% (1/72)	2.78% (2/72)	11.11% (8/72)	15.28% (11/72)
Vault 6	0	5.55% (4/72)	1.39% (1/72)	1.39% (1/72)	8.33% (6/72)
Vault 7	0	0	8.33% (6/72)	0	8.33% (6/72)
Percentage of total sample	1.39% (1/72)	12.50% (9/72)	30.56% (22/72)	55.55% (40/72)	100% (72/72)

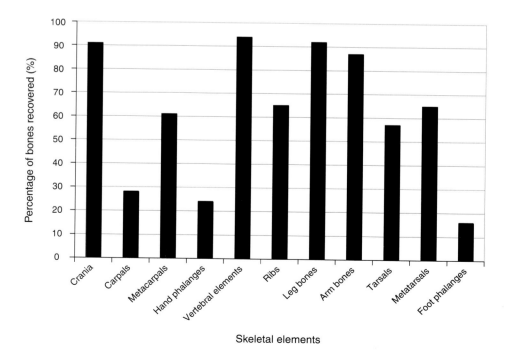

Fig. 6.1   Recovery of skeletal elements (percentage of total bones of each element)

each vault were situated towards the base of the coffin stacks where compression was greatest.

Poorer preservation was noted in skeletons interred within coffins where the base of the inner wooden coffin had been overlaid with a layer of sawdust or bran. Considerable leaching of the bone mineral was observed, leaving the bone soft and easily damaged by handling. White crystals, or brushite, were clearly observed on the cortical bone surfaces. Similar deleterious effects of sawdust on skeletal preservation was observed in another post-medieval assemblage from Bathford, near Bath (Nawrocki 1995, 54).

The skeletal inventories revealed that most bones were represented, except for the small bones of the wrist, fingers and toes, which were under-represented (Fig. 6.1). The best represented elements were crania and the long bones of the lower limbs. Poor recovery by archaeologists was probably the principal factor underlying the under-representation of small bones – not surprising given the cramped conditions and poor lighting within the vaults during the coffin clearance. Moreover, the removal of the lead coffins sometimes opened up wider gaps in the decaying lead and small bones were lost within the general backfill. When they were located it was not possible to associate them with the correct skeleton.

Demography

Demographic analysis of living populations involves the comparison of statistics of fertility, mortality and migration patterns. The demographic analysis of past populations based on skeletal samples normally concentrates on mortality since, in the absence of historical records, fertility and migrations can only be inferred from the osteological data. Documentary sources add another dimension to the study of population structure of the St George's assemblage and are discussed in Chapter 5 above.

Osteological age and sex

Three adults (skeletons 4047, 4075 and 7006) could not be sexed osteologically, and were redistributed according to the sex given on the coffin inscription, which had them recorded as male, male and unknown. The sex distribution within the total sample 52.77% males (n/N=38/72) and 40.28% females (including one older adolescent) (n/N=29/72). Four younger subadults were not sexed in accordance with accepted practice.

The assemblage of 72 skeletons comprised five subadults (6.94 %) and 67 adults (93.06 %) (Table 6.6). There were no young adults (18-25 years) and only five subadults (< 18 years) (Table 6.6; Fig. 6.2). A total of 51 individuals (70.83 %) lived to an age greater than 40 years, and of these, 25 (34.72 %) were aged over 50 years. Mortality increased with age, becoming more pronounced in the mature male adult category (39.5 %; n/N=15/38), and with 50 % of adult males (n/N=19/38) living beyond 50 + years of age. By contrast, there was considerably lower longevity in the female population, with mortality rising steeply to 37.93 % amongst the prime adult (n/N=11/29) and mature adults (n/N=11/29), and falling away to 20.69% in the 50+ category (n/N=6/29). Hence, there was a considerable difference in mortality pattern between the sexes, with 79.31 % of females dying before reaching the age of 50 years, compared to only 50% of their male counterparts. No women died in young adulthood (the prime childbearing age); all, bar one adolescent, were aged greater than 25 years. This may suggest later marriage in this group, but this was not verified by parish or government marriage records.

The London Bills of Mortality of the first four decades of the 19th century reveal that 50 % of the population died before the age of 21 years, and that of these, 40% died before their fifth birthday (Roberts and Cox 2003, 303). Most adults lived to between 30 and 50 years of age (ibid.). A small

Table 6.6 Named sample: Osteological age and sex (includes two adults who have been assigned sex based on biographical and not osteological data)

	Neonate (0-11 months)	Young child (1-5 years)	Older child (6-11 years)	Adolescent (12-17 years)	Young adult (18-25 years)	Prime adult (26-40 years)	Mature adult (40+ years)	Ageing adult (50+ years)	Total
Male	-	-	-	-	-	5.55% (4/72)	20.83% (15/72)	26.39% (19/72)	52.77% (38/72)
Female	-	-	-	1.39% (1/72)	-	15.28% (11/72)	15.28% (11/72)	8.33% (6/72)	40.28% (29/72)
Unknown	2.78% (2/72)	-	4.17% (3/72)	-	-	-	-	-	6.95% (5/72)
Total	2.78% (2/72)	-	4.17% (3/72)	1.39% (1/72)	-	20.83% (15/72)	36.11% (26/72)	34.72% (25/72)	100% (72)

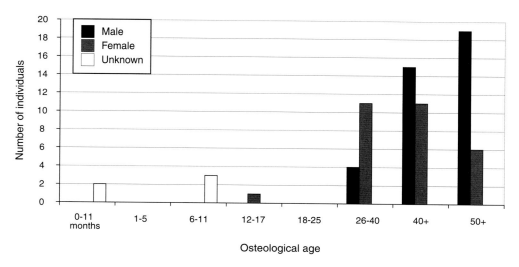

Fig. 6.2   Named sample: Mortality profile based on osteological age (N=72)

proportion (6% in the beginning of the period and 11% at the end) did survive into their 70s and beyond (Roberts and Cox 2003, 304). Osteological analysis of the named sample from St George's crypt reveals a different picture. It shows that 2.8% of the sample had died before they had reached their fifth birthday, 8.34% before they were 21 years old, and 29% of the individuals lived to an age greater than 70 years. The London Bills of Mortality and documented ages are compared in more detail in Chapter 5.

Chronological age and sex

The demography discussed above was undertaken using osteological methodology. It is interesting to contrast the results above with those obtained using the biographical data obtained from the *depositum* plates.

The ages of 14 of the named sample of 72 were not recorded from their coffin plate inscriptions and, for comparative reasons, were redistributed proportionately. The inscriptions revealed that the assemblage comprised five subadults (6.9%; N=72) and 67 adults (93.1%; N=72) (Table 6.7, Fig. 6.3). Forty-four individuals (61.1%; N=72) lived beyond 50 years of age.

Three adults could not be sexed and were redistributed proportionally. Of the total population (N = 72), 56.9 % were male (n=41) and 43.1% were females (n=31). The assemblage therefore comprised more males than females. In the age groups greater than 26 years, there was little difference in mortality rates between the sexes: 83.81% (n/N=26/31) for women and 92.68% (n/N=38/41) for men. It appears that in the mature adult category mortality amongst the females at 19.5 % (n/N=6/31) was greater than that for men, since only one man of the named sample died in that age band. Male mortality in the older age category (70.73%, n/N=29/41) was much higher than that of females (48.39%, (n/N=15/31). Nonetheless, there was a marked increase in females in the 50+ age category when compared to the osteological age and sex data (Fig. 6.4).

Table 6.7 Named sample: Chronological age and sex (redistributed totals) taken from departum plate inscriptions

	Neonate (0-11 months)	Young child (1-5 years)	Older child (6-11 years)	Adolescent (12-17 years)	Young adult (18-25 years)	Prime adult (26-40 years)	Mature adult (40+ years)	Ageing adult (50+ years)	Total
Male	1.39% (1/72)	1.39% (1/72)	1.39% (1/72)	-	-	11.11% (8/72)	1.39% (1/72)	40.28% (29/72)	56.95% (41/72)
Female	-	-	1.39% (1/72)	1.39% (1/72)	4.17% (3/72)	6.94% (5/72)	8.33% (6/72)	20.83% (15/72)	43.05% (31/72)
Total	1.39% (1/72)	1.39% (1/72)	2.78% (2/72)	1.39% (1/72)	4.17% (3/72)	18.05% (13/72)	9.72% (7/72)	61.1% (44/72)	100% (72)(72)

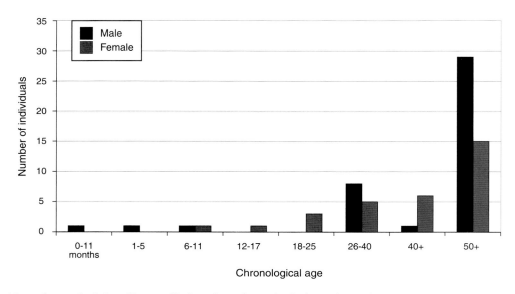

Fig. 6.3   Named sample: Mortality profile based on chronological age (N=72)

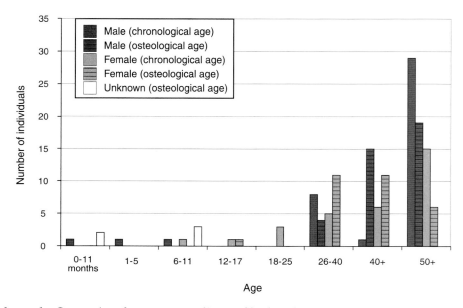

Fig. 6.4   Named sample: Comparison between mortality profiles based on osteological and chronological age (N=72)

Table 6.8: Stature at St George's and in four contemporary skeletal assemblages

	Male (Mean)	Male (Range)	Female (Mean)	Female (Range)
St George's Church, Bloomsbury	1.72	1.52 m-1.85 m	1.60 m	1.49 m-1.72 m
St Luke's Church, Islington	1.70 m	1.55 m-1.93 m	1.58 m	1.49 m-1.72 m
Newcastle Infirmary	1.71 m	1.60 m-1.83 m	1.60 m	1.50 m-1.76 m
Christ Church, Spitalfields	-	1.68 m-1.70 m	-	1.54 m-1.59 m
Cross Bones, Southwark	1.69 m	1.53 m-1.80 m	1.58 m	1.42 m-1.72 m

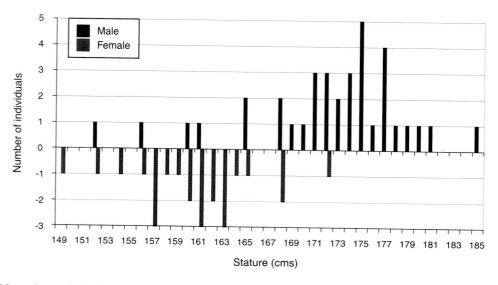

Fig. 6.5   Named sample: Mean stature of males and females (N=15 and 20 respectively)

Stature

Estimated adult female stature (n=20) ranged between 1.48 m and 1.79 m, with a mean stature of 1.60 m. Adult male stature (n=15) ranged between 1.52 m to 1.85 m, with a mean stature of 1.72 m. The wide stature ranges for each sex, and the considerable overlap in individual male and female statures revealed marked height variation within this population (Fig. 6.5). There was a difference of 0.12 m in the mean stature estimation of males and females (Table 6.8).

These means and ranges are broadly comparable with contemporary skeletal assemblages. As might be expected, the mean stature of the St George's crypt sample, which largely comprised fairly affluent members of the artisan and middle classes, was similar to middle class assemblages of Christ Church, Spitalfields, and St Luke's Church, Islington.

Less expected was the fact that mean statures of the predominantly working class burials at the Cross Bones burial ground and the Newcastle Infirmary were also similar (Table 6.8), albeit slightly lower in the former. It might have been expected that there would been a greater difference, reflecting differences in poorer nutrition, living conditions and access to medical care. This, however, does not appear to have been the case. Other factors, such as regional differences in genetic composition of populations may also play a role, particularly when comparing the Newcastle Infirmary population to the London assemblages.

Dental pathology

Dental pathology, such as periodontal disease, caries and ante-mortem tooth loss (AMTL), is most commonly caused by the consumption of carbohydrates (particularly simple sugars) and poor oral hygiene practices. Food residues left on the teeth following consumption of carbohydrates rapidly become colonised by bacteria, and are broken down to form a corrosive acidic plaque. It is this plaque that is responsible for the development of carious lesions on the teeth (Hillson 1996, 269). Plaque may also mineralise, forming a hard unmoveable coating of calculus on the tooth surface, colloquially known as tartar. Periodontal disease is the inflammation of the soft tissues of the mouth, namely the gums, and/or the periodontal ligament and alveolar bone (Levin 2003, 245). Retraction of the gums exposes the vulnerable root of the tooth to attack by acidic plaques, commonly resulting in caries, abscesses and ante-mortem tooth loss.

In the post-medieval period, the consumption of cane sugar gradually increased. In the 16th and 17th centuries, sugar was an expensive and high status luxury available only to the most affluent (Musgrave and Musgrave 2000, 60). However, the development of sugar plantations in the West Indies in the 18th century generated a more readily available and more affordable supply of the commodity to markets in Europe. Sugar consumption gradually spread down the social classes, until by the latter half of the 19th century it was available to all but the most indigent (ibid.). By the early 19th century, sugar was regularly consumed by the middle classes, but was not yet cheap enough to be readily available to the lower classes. However, the St George's population certainly could afford such a luxury, and paid for their pleasure with widespread dental decay.

A wide array of implements used for keeping teeth clean was available in the 18th and 19th

Table 6.9: Comparison of prevalence of dental disease (per tooth) in five contemporary osteological assemblages

Post-medieval assemblages	Ante-mortem tooth loss (n/N)	Abscesses (n/N)	Calculus (n/N)	Caries (n/N)	Enamel hypoplasia (n/N)	Dental fillings (n/N)
St George's Church, Bloomsbury	40.99% (669/1632)	2.82% (46/1632)	70.85% (592/844)	13.39% (110/844)	16.35% (138/844)	0.83% (7/844)
St Luke's Church, Islington	36.10% (1762/4883)	1.78% (87/4883)	46.33% (1042/2249)	9.74% (219/2249)	2.18% (49/2249)	0.27% (6/2249)
Newcastle Infirmary, Newcastle	19.3% (604/3123)	0.9% (29/3123)	55.85% (718/1287)	11% (146/1327)	17% (219/1287)	0.0%
Christ Church, Spitalfields	19.91% (324/1627)	Data not available	Data not available	19.11% (311/1627)	Data not available	0.24% (4/1627)
Cross Bones burial ground, Southwark	17.30% (211/1216)	2.30% 28/1216	Data not available	25.93% (161/621)	Data not available	Data not available

centuries, including toothbrushes with handles made of ornate gold or silver, and ivory toothpicks carried in small, decorated cases (Picard 2000, 154). Tooth powders became increasingly available in the later 18th century. These were made of a wide array of ingredients, many being innocuous, but some included abrasive materials (such as brick dust) and/or caustic substances (including tartaric acid) (Hillam 1990, 5-7; Roberts and Cox 2003, 324). These substances may well have whitened the teeth and striped away calculus, but often also severely damaged the dental enamel beneath. However, habitual cleaning of teeth appears to have been very uncommon in this period, and it is improbable that many people maintained good oral hygiene.

For the purposes of this section, the oral health of the individuals with permanent dentition only is discussed. Subadults with mixed or deciduous dentition were omitted due to the low number of individuals. Of the 68 skeletons with permanent dentition, 62 (91.18%) had jaws present (including permanent *in situ* dentition, loose teeth and maxillae and/or mandibulae with empty or resorbed sockets). In total, 844 teeth were present, 669 teeth had been lost ante-mortem and 119 teeth had been lost post-mortem. Table 6.9 below presents comparative prevalences of major categories of dental pathology of the St George's named sample and other contemporary assemblages. These data are discussed below.

Dental caries

Dental caries involves the destruction of the enamel surface, the dentine (internal part of the tooth) and/or the cementum (outer layer of the roots), and is caused by acid in dental plaque (Hillson 1996, 269). The association of acidogenic bacteria and sugar in the diet is a well established cause of cavitations (Lukacs 1989, 265).

In this study, the size of each carious lesion was classified according to the universally used grading system of Lukacs (1989). However, due to

constraints of the project, a more detailed analysis of lesion's location on the crown, its severity and the identity of the affected tooth are not discussed here.

The prevalence of caries was calculated by dividing the total number of caries (including those with fillings but excluding lesions removed by filing) by the total number of permanent teeth present. The results are therefore an approximation, as it is not known how many of the teeth lost post-mortem had carious lesions. The prevalence rate does provide a general indication of the caries rate within the population. A total of 113 caries was recorded in the 844 permanent teeth analysed – a true prevalence of 13.39%. Thirty-nine of the total 62 skeletons (CPR 62.9%) had lesions with a mean prevalence of 2.9 caries per skeleton.

The caries rate in the St George's assemblage was higher than other contemporary assemblages (Table 6.9), such as St Luke's, Islington, and possibly may reflect a greater intake of simple sugars or the greater longevity of this population. It is unlikely, however, that the trend reflects a status difference between the two populations, as conversely, the caries rate in the Cross Bones assemblage (predominantly comprised of paupers) was the highest of all – almost twice the rate of the St George's population.

Ante mortem tooth loss

The loss of permanent dentition before death is the end result of several disease processes. Calculus deposits can irritate the soft tissue and the underlying bone, which can lead to the reduction of the bone (periodontal disease) and ante mortem tooth loss (AMTL) (Roberts and Manchester, 1995, 45). Teeth may also be lost from peri-apical abscesses, which form through the exposure of the pulp cavity as a result of caries or excessive attrition coupled with localised resorption of the alveolar margin. AMTL is regarded as a degenerative disease where the main contributory factors are old age and poor oral hygiene.

112

The prevalence of ante mortem tooth loss was calculated by dividing the total number of teeth lost ante mortem by the combined total of the permanent dentition, teeth lost ante mortem and post mortem (empty sockets) (n=1632). A total of 669 teeth were lost ante mortem (40.99%). Fifty-three individuals with dentition and/or dental sockets (85.48%; n=53/62) had suffered from ante mortem tooth loss. Of these, three individuals (4.84%) had lost all of their dentition. The mean AMTL per individual was 10.79.

AMTL was more prevalent in this sample than other contemporary assemblages (Table 6.9). Dental decay was probably the most common reason for tooth loss, but another was the deliberate extraction of teeth, either to alleviate toothache, or as a prophylactic elective measure against the pain to come. A third factor was the high proportion of aged individuals within the assemblage.

Dental calculus

Calculus consists of mineralised plaque composed of microorganisms that accumulate in the mouth and become imbedded in a matrix of protein and saliva. Sugar in the diet accelerates this process (Hillson 1996, 254-55). There are two types of calculus: supragingival calculus situated above the gum line and subgingival calculus found below the gum line on exposed roots. More heavy calculus deposits are commonly seen on teeth nearest to the saliva glands (Roberts and Manchester 1995, 55). Regular tooth brushing removes plaque deposits, thereby preventing the formation of calculus.

Calculus deposits were recorded by tooth and by location on the tooth. The size of the deposit was also recorded according to the universal standards set out by Brothwell (1981), in which the deposits were scored as slight, medium or heavy. However, such a detailed data are beyond the scope of this report. The prevalence of calculus was calculated by dividing the number of teeth affected by the total number of teeth present.

A total of 592 teeth of the observed 844 teeth (70.14%) had calculus deposits. Forty-nine individuals displayed calculus (79.03%, n=49/62), with an average of 12.08 affected teeth per person.

Calculus was much more prevalent in this sample than in comparative assemblages (Table 6.9). As regular brushing of the teeth may have prevented calculus formation, it is highly unlikely that these individuals brushed their teeth regularly.

Periodontal disease

The principal predisposing factor in periodontal disease is the accumulation of calculus in dental pockets. The disease begins as gingivitis (an inflammation of the soft tissues), which is transmitted to the jaw itself. Resorption of the bone commences, followed by tooth loss. There are two different ways in which this disease expresses itself. These are horizontal and vertical bone loss. In horizontal bone loss more than one tooth is involved and often the

whole of the dental arcade. All walls surrounding the teeth are lost uniformly. In vertical bone loss, the lesion is localised around one tooth or possibly two. The bone loss around the tooth is irregular and generally without horizontal bone loss (Hillson 1996, 263-65). There is a strong link between the increase of age and the increase of the prevalence of periodontal disease in modern populations, which is also the case with archaeological populations. However, the aetiology is multifactoral with genetic predisposition, environment, diet and hygiene all being predisposing factors in the development of the disease.

Periodontal disease was recorded by subdividing the jaws into four quadrants, which were scored independently. The severity of the disease was scored using the grades set out by Brothwell (1981), namely slight, medium and considerable. However, the calculation of prevalence rates in this detail is beyond the scope of this report and only the crude prevalence rates of periodontal disease are presented: 31 of the 62 individuals (50%) had periodontal disease ranging from slight to considerable.

Periodontal disease was observed on 20% of the named individuals of St Luke's Church, Islington (Boyle *et al.* 2005, 210). Again there is a very high prevalence of the disease amongst the St George's named assemblage, which given the relationship between the disease and oral hygiene, is hardly surprising.

Peri-apical abscesses

The development of an abscess may have many starting points. Bacteria may enter the pulp cavity through dental caries, excessive attrition or trauma to the crown, as well as through dental surgery (see Dentistry below). An abscess may also develop when a periodontal pocket forms by the accumulation of bacteria within pulp cavity, and the infection tracks down to the root apex. As pus accumulates within the dental socket and surrounding alveolar bone, local pressure builds, and eventually precipitates the formation of a hole or sinus in the jaw, through which the pus drains into the overlying soft tissue of the gums (Roberts and Manchester 1995, 50). In this advanced stage, the abscess is visible as a small hole on the surface of the maxilla or mandible.

The prevalence of dental abscesses was calculated by dividing the total number of abscesses by the combined total of teeth lost ante mortem, teeth lost post mortem and permanent dentition. In total, 46 (2.82%) abscesses were recorded out of a possible 1632 sockets observed. Twenty-three individuals (37.10%; n=23/62) had abscesses giving an average of two abscesses per person.

The prevalence of abscesses was slightly higher amongst St George's named assemblage than in contemporary assemblages (Table 6.9). Poor oral hygiene probably played a significant role, but as many abscesses were associated with dental work, such as crowns and transplants, it is unclear the extent to which the high prevalence at St George's can be explained by the greater quantity of dentistry observed in this sample compared to other sites of the period.

Dental enamel hypoplasia

Dental enamel hypoplasia (DEH) manifests on the buccal surface of the crowns of teeth as pits, horizontal lines or lines of pits. These defects are caused by thinning of the enamel, and reflect an interruption or slowing of the normal deposition of enamel during crown formation in the first six or seven years of life (Goodman and Rose 1990; Hillson 1996, 165-66). DEH is thought to result from prolonged episodes of illness or malnutrition lasting at least three weeks (ibid.), but food adulterations, used widely in 18th and 19th century London, may also have played a role in the interruption of normal tooth development. Such defects are most apparent when normal dental development recommences following such an insult. Unlike bone, enamel does not remodel throughout life and so remains as a permanent indicator of such stress episodes in the early years of life.

In the named sample the type of defect (groove, line or pit) and the numbers of lines or grooves were recorded on each tooth. This level of detail has not been quantified here. The prevalence of DEH was calculated per crown visible, excluding crowns where the buccal surface was obscured by calculus, or where the tooth had suffered marked attrition or dental work (eg. filing). Of the total number of teeth observed (N=844) 138 displayed DEH (16.35%). DEH was observed in 40 individuals (64.5%; n=40/62), an average of 5.52 teeth per individual. [138/40=3.45 teeth per individual.

The prevalence of DEH within this group was surprisingly high, given their socio-economic status. In comparison, the rate of DEH from the St Luke's, Islington, assemblage was very low (Table 6.9). The average 'per tooth' prevalence in post-medieval British assemblages collated by Roberts and Cox (2003, 327) was 0.6%. The high rate suggested that the St George's named sample suffered more stress in childhood, but as DEH is only evident in those that had recovered from such episodes, it may be argued that the higher preva-lence of this defect indicates better survival following such an insult. This would be in keeping with the higher social status of this assemblage.

Dental overcrowding

Overcrowding of the dentition, most commonly involving the incisors and canines, is believed to have a multifactoral aetiology, including both genetic predisposition and environmental factors (Hillson 1996). The degree of overcrowding (slight, moderate and severe) was recorded in the named sample, as well as rotation of the individual teeth. The dentition of five individuals (8.06%; n=5/62) showed overcrowding. In all cases this was slight.

Dental anomalies

A range of dental anomalies may be observed in the human dental arcade, including impacted teeth, congenitally absent teeth (agenesis), supernu-merary teeth and the retention of deciduous teeth in adulthood (Hillson 1996). Within the named sample, neither supernumerary teeth nor retained deciduous teeth were present, but a number of individuals displayed impacted and congenitally missing teeth. The prevalence of congenitally missing teeth cannot be established absolutely, as it is not always possible to distinguish between long-standing ante mortem tooth loss and agenesis. Moreover, without radiography, it is not possible to rule out impaction. In edentulous individuals, the absence of the third molar may also be mistaken for ante mortem tooth loss, when in fact the tooth had never developed. It is therefore likely that the total number of congenitally absent teeth has been underestimated.

The teeth recorded as impacted were those that could be observed without radiography. Teeth that were not fully erupted in older individuals were also recorded as impacted. Again, the prevalence of impacted teeth is likely to be underestimated as some may have been recorded as congenitally missing. The location of impacted or congenitally absent teeth was recorded, but this level of detail is beyond the limit of this study. Crude prevalence was calculated for the dental anomalies observed.

Seven individuals (11.29%; n=7/62) had impacted teeth, which, on average affected one or two teeth per person. Sixteen individuals (25.86%; n=16/62) had congenitally absent teeth, the largest number per person being five (skeleton 1052). Third molars were the most commonly missing teeth.

Dental interventions

Until the mid 19th century there was no formal training or qualification for dentists (Gelbier 2005, 446; see also Richards 1968). As part of the pressure from dental practitioners for recognition and improved professional standing the Odontological Society of London and the rival College of Dentists were established in November 1856. The aim was to establish a recognised qualification in dentistry. To this end the College of Dentists founded the Metropolitan School of Dental Science, and the Odontologists founded the Dental Hospital of London in 1858, and the School of Dental Surgery within the Hospital in October 1859 (Gelbier 2005, 447). The first professional qualification in dentistry – the Licence in Dental Surgery (LDS) of the Royal College of Surgeons – dates from 1860.

It was only in the later 18th century that the term 'dentist' came into use (Lindsay 1927, 359). Early dental 'care' was provided by toothdrawers, and by apothecaries and surgeons, for who drawing teeth was just one part of their service (see Bishop, Gelbier and Gibbons 2001a, passim). During the 18th century, dentistry as a distinct profession practiced by itself began to appear, with the emergence of 'operators of the teeth', men such as John Watts of Racquet Court, on the North side of Fleet Street. In 1709 he advertised in Rider's British Almanac:

> Artificial teeth set in so well as to Eat with them, and not to be discovered from Natural, not to be taken out at Night, as is by some falsely suggested, but may be worn years together – also teeth cleaned and Drawn by John Watts, Operator, who applies himself wholly to the said business (quoted in Lindsay 1927, 357)

Watts was later joined by Samuel Rutter. Rutter subsequently worked in partnership with William Green, who in 1756 was appointed 'Operator for the Teeth to King George II'. Thomas Berdmore later worked out of Racquet Court where he was apprentice, then partner, to Green. In 1768 he published *A Treatise on the Disorders and Deformities of the Teeth and Gums*, in which he wrote of

> when first I resolved to devote my whole time and attention to that part of surgery which concerns the dentist's art . . . (quoted in Lindsay 1927, 359)

In 1766 Berdmore became operator for the teeth to George III.

It is estimated 40 dentists operated in London by 1800, and another 20 outside the capital. In 1837 John Gray a surgeon-dentist and member of the Royal College of Surgeons wrote that

> The London Directory contains the names of upwards of one hundred and twenty individuals . . . calling themselves Surgeon-Dentists, while the list of members of the Royal College of Surgeons, published in August, 1836, reduces the number to seven (Gray 1837, 9 footnote)

The *Post Office London Directory, 1841* lists 153 dentists including John Gray himself.

For the privileged, there was an array of treatments on offer. These included fillings, removal of carious lesions, dental implants and various types of dentures using human or artificial teeth. The treatment was expensive, as is clear from an advertisement from 1777 for the services of the eccentric Martin van Butchell (Porter, 2001, 199):

> Van Butchell, Surgeon-Dentist, attends at his House, the upper part of Mount-Street, Grosvenor Square, every day in the Year, from Nine to One o'clock, Sundays excepted.
>
> Name in Marble on the Door. Advice, £2.2s. Taking out a Tooth or Stump, £1.1s. each. Putting in artificial Teeth, £5.5s. each. A whole under Row £42. Upper Row £63. An entire set £105. Natural Teeth £10.10s each. The Money

paid first. (*St James's Chronicle*, 1 March 1777, quoted in Haslam 1996, 245-46)

Fillings and filings

During the 18th and 19th centuries, the cheapest material used in fillings was tin or lead. From the early 19th century, various forms of amalgams became available. These were based on heavy metals (such as mercury mixed with copper) or silver filed from coins (Hillam 1990, 23). Gold fillings were the most suitable material (being chemically inert) but also the most expensive (ibid.). Pellets of amalgam were placed in the tooth cavity and tamped down with a hot instrument. Four (6.45%; n=4/62) named individuals from St George's had fillings. In total, there were seven fillings, of which all but one was gold. The exception was of grey coloured metal (probably lead, tin or amalgam).

The prevalence of fillings was much higher than in the Christ Church, Spitalfields, and St Luke's church, Islington, assemblages (Table 6.9), although overall only a small number of individuals had undergone this treatment in all three assemblages.

Carious lesions that were not filled were sometimes filed or scraped away using scalpels and files, leaving a smooth surface (Hillam 1991, 23; Picard 2000, 154). This treatment was identified in the dentition of four individuals (6.45%; n=4/62). Seven teeth had been treated in this way.

Dentures

From the early to middle 18th century onwards, dentures were available to those who could afford them. These were made from walrus or hippopotamus ivory plates in which real human teeth were riveted. These were commonly known as 'Waterloo teeth', as originally, it was believed that the teeth had been removed from the mouths of healthy young soldiers killed on the famous battlefield. In reality, most human teeth used in dentures came from the poor, who sold their teeth for a pittance (Porter 2001, 198; Bishop, Gelbier and Gibbons 2001b, 576), and from cadavers obtained from grave robbing (Porter 2001, 198). Indeed, there was a roaring trade in human teeth at this time in history.

Dentures could either be partial or full. There were three main types:

1. Full upper or lower swagged gold dentures with ivory molar blocks

2. Two tooth partial upper or lower dentures (made of walrus ivory)

3. Small swagged partial dentures

The upper and lower plates of a full set of swagged (horseshoe-shaped) dentures were kept in place by springs between the lower and upper plates. The plates were metal, often gold, and hence, were extremely expensive. Human teeth were set into these plates by the means of gold pins.

Manufacturers often took considerable pains to achieve a realistic effect with the anterior dentition, but molars were often constructed of roughly carved ivory blocks. Towards the end of the 18th century, human teeth were replaced by models of teeth made of porcelain, which were riveted to the denture plate by means of gold pins. It was not until the latter half of the 19th century that the ivory molar blocks were replaced by porcelain. Once an individual had invested in a gold spring-loaded set, the same denture could be retained for up to forty years. Unlike ivory they did not decay nor did they need replacement because of gum shrinkage (Woodforde 1968).

The springs between the upper and lower plates of swagged dentures were designed to force the plates apart, thereby preventing the upper plate from falling from position when the mouth was opened (Hillam 1990, 16). The springs were often so strong, however, that the wearer had to clench his/her muscles forcefully to shut the mouth again (Picard 2000, 155). Another more alarming effect was the tendency of such dentures to leap involuntarily from the mouth at inopportune moments, much to the hilarity of onlookers. Correct insertion of dentures took dexterity, and poor technique sometimes caused the springs to fail, with unflattering consequences. The vagaries of wearing dentures were mercilessly lampooned by caricaturists of the period, such as Rowlandson (Donald 1996).

The necessity of owning a second pair was explained by John Tomes, surgeon-dentist of the Middlesex Hospital in his book *The Management of Artificial Teeth* (1851) (cited in Woodforde 1968, 65-67). Two whole pages are devoted to the correct way of inserting such a set so as not to damage the springs. Spring failure as a result of incorrect insertion was a fairly common problem and could happen suddenly and without warning, causing the top set to fall out even in conversation. As a result, many people possessed a second pair of dentures, which they carried with them in case of this eventuality. This may explain why the two individuals of the St George's population (one named and one unnamed) who were buried wearing such dentures were interred with a second set.

Another unattractive feature of early dentures was that many were too difficult to fit or to remove easily, and so were worn constantly (Cox 1996, 92; Picard 2000, 155). Oral hygiene was thus not a priority. A dentist to Queen Victoria described a particularly extreme case of a woman whom he fitted with a partial denture. When he saw her again four years later the new teeth were cemented into the mouth with tartar. In her extreme anxiety not to be discovered wearing false teeth, she had not removed them in all that time. The dentist's shock, however, illustrates that her behaviour was not the norm. Nevertheless, it does seem that oral hygiene was not a priority in denture wearers. Moreover, ivory molar blocks began to rot after a short time, causing incredible halitosis (Hillam

1991, 16). Writers of the day describe the 'miasma' issuing from the mouths of wearers. It is thought that fans were used as much to hide bad teeth and dispel bad breath, as to cool the heated brow, or as aids to flirtation (Tomes, 1851, quoted in Woodforde 1968, 51).

A small swagged partial denture was used when only one to three anterior teeth were missing. This comprised a small golden plate to which porcelain or real human teeth were riveted. The denture was held in place by silk ties or metal strips wrapped around adjacent teeth. Partial dentures comprised of ivory blocks were used to replace missing molars, and were designed to serve a masticatory rather than aesthetic function. These blocks were held in place by silk thread tied to remaining teeth.

Only one individual (skeleton 3044) of the named sample was buried with dentures (see Plate 6.7). This older male had two sets, of which one was in a slightly better condition. The dentures were full upper and lower swagged gold dentures with ivory molar blocks and porcelain teeth. Although only one named individual had been buried with his dentures, two more skeletons showed osteological evidence suggesting that they had worn dentures in life. The morphological changes in the alveolar bone can be seen on both the maxilla and the mandible, but were more obvious in the more robust mandible. In each individual the alveolar margin of the bone was more flattened and 'squared', which may be accompanied with a sharp alveolar margin. Most importantly, there is no significant reduction of the symphyseal height at the mental protuberance. Indeed, since the individual still uses the jaws for mastication, the bone does not atrophy through disuse as occurs in edentulous individuals. The total number of individuals who wore dentures in the named sample was therefore three (4.84%; n=3/62). Dentures were also recovered from unnamed burials at St George's (see below), and in other contemporary assemblages, including Christ Church Spitalfields, St Pancras Euston (pers. comm.), and St Luke's Islington.

Dental implants

Towards the end of the 18th century, transplantation of teeth as an alternative to dentures was widely practice (Bishop, Gelbier and Gibbons 2001b, 576 & fig.1 – Thomas Rowlandson, 'Transplanting of teeth'). Incisors and canines were pulled from the mouths of indigent young people with healthy teeth, and immediately transplanted into the mouths of richer and older patients. Transplantation was rarely successful in the long term. Moreover, there was the danger of the spread of disease (such as syphilis) associated with the practice. Finally the increasing availability of porcelain teeth soon made this type of dental intervention redundant (Noble 2002).

Amongst the named sample, transplantation of the crown was also observed in several individuals. This method is not that dissimilar to modern dental implants. The original tooth crown was removed,

Plate 6.1   Skeleton 3027: real tooth crown on a gold peg

leaving the root of the tooth *in situ*. The exposed surface of the root was then filed to a shallow concave U-shape. The new crown transplant was shaped to fit neatly into the root concavity. The new crown transplant was mounted on a metal post (usually gold), and hammered into the root cavity. The root thus served to anchor for the new tooth crown. In an age before anaesthetic, when pain control was limited largely to laudanum and alcohol (Hillam 1991), this must have been an extremely painful procedure.

Three named individuals (4.48%; n=3/62) had transplanted crowns. Only the incisors and the canines were subjected to this treatment, probably because the insertion of the post was only possible on single rooted teeth. The largest number of teeth subjected to the treatment in any one individual (skeleton 3054) was four. Skeleton 3027 had three implants (Plate 6.1). One individual (skeleton 4011) had the shaped root and a central hole but no crown was present. It is possible that instead of a metal post, the crown may have been mounted on a hickory wood post, which had subsequently rotted away. Wooden posts are known from historical records of the period, but do not survive well archaeologically. Not surprisingly, this type of intrusive dental surgery was often caused infection. In the named assemblage from St George's, 50% of implants were associated with apical abscesses.

Skeletal pathology

A wide range of pathologies was observed in the named assemblage, many of them age-related. They fall into the following broad categories: congenital disorders, joint disease, trauma, infectious disease, metabolic disease and neoplastic disease. Also observed were post-mortem surgical interventions and modifications arising from corsetry.

Congenital anomalies

Congenital malformations are pathological changes that occur during foetal development, and abnormalities may be observed shortly after birth or many years later (Roberts and Manchester 1995, 30, 51). Approximately 40% of all abnormalities in live births affect the skeleton. Most of these (90%) are due to genetic anomalies that may be hereditary. Environmental influences, such as maternal rubella, may also cause foetal malformations, such as cleft palate, spina bifida and microcephaly (Roberts and Manchester 1995, 32).

Spina bifida – *Spina bifida occulta* is a mild congenital defect, which consists of non-union of the neural arches of the sacrum. As the name suggests, this defect is usually asymptomatic, as the area of non-union is bridged by membrane, thus protecting the *cauda equina* of the spinal cord. *Spina bifida occulta* is very common, affecting between 5% and 25% of modern populations (Aufderheide and Rodríguez-Martín 1998, 61), and, like other neural tube defects, has been associated with a deficiency in maternal folic acid, zinc and selenium in early pregnancy (Roberts and Manchester 1995). Five individuals in the named sample (6.94%; n=5/72) displayed this defect. The lesions were slight in most individuals, but all five segments of the sacrum of skeletons 4002 and 5056 were affected.

Cleft neural arch: Skeleton 7045 also displayed non-union of the neural arch, leaving open the neural canal. In this case, the affected element was the 7th cervical vertebra.

Sacralisation – Transitional vertebrae are most common in the lumbo-sacral region, occurring in 3-5% of modern populations (Aufderheide and Rodríguez-Martín 1998, 65). Most commonly affected is the fifth lumbar vertebra, which fuses to the first sacral segment below (ibid.). Six individuals of the St George's assemblage (8.3 %; n=6/72) displayed this condition. In keeping with modern populations, females were more commonly affected than males- four females (1059, 4007, 5046 and 7016) and two males (3085 and 4049). Complete sacralisation of the fifth lumbar vertebra was present in all but one individual (skeleton 4007).

Scoliosis – Scoliosis is a lateral curvature of the spine. Often there are two curves, enabling the cranium to be maintained in the mid-sagittal plane. The aetiology of this condition is multi-factoral and may accompany other spinal malformations, such as hemi-vertebrae and transitional vertebrae (Aufderheide and Rodríguez-Martín 1998, 66). Two adult females (2.77%, n=2/72) had slight scoliosis. Skeleton 7016 also had sacralisation, which may have been a contributing factor in the development of the scoliosis.

Fused vertebrae – One individual displayed fusion of the articular processes of the second and the third thoracic vertebrae. The condition was clearly not due to degenerative changes and is more likely to be developmental rather than caused by trauma. The defect is unlikely to have caused discomfort.

Congenital acetabular dysplasia – Congenital acetabular dysplasia or congenital dislocation of the hip is caused by the partial or complete displacement of the femoral head from its normal position within the acetabulum. The condition is bilateral in 25-50% of the cases (Aufderheide and Rodríguez-Martín 1998, 69-70). In unilateral cases, the left hip joint is more often involved. Females are more commonly affected than males, modern frequency being between 1 and 20 per 1000 live births (ibid.). The condition is often not discovered until the child starts to walk. A swaying gait is characteristic of this condition (Roberts and Manchester 1995, 38). Congenital dislocation of the left hip was present in one adult female (skeleton 3027). The acetabulum was malformed, being small, flat and triangular in shape. The dislocation was complete, with formation of a neo-acetabulum superior to the true acetabulum on the lateral surface of the iliac blade. This new joint surface was considerably eburnated (Plate 6.2), as was the left femoral head. These degenerative changes indicated that the individual had been mobile, but she was likely to have been in considerable and constant pain.

Other slight developmental abnormalities – Two individuals had very slight developmental defects. In skeleton 1013, fusion of the right lateral and intermediate cuneiforms was recorded, and in skeleton 6048, a malformed sternum. The anomalous sternum of skeleton 6048 involved non-union of the first and second segment, and the presence of an additional segment. Neither defect would have caused any discomfort.

Joint disease

Osteoarthritis and degenerative joint disease – The most common joint disease in both modern and archaeological populations is osteoarthritis (OA), a disease that affects any synovial joint in the skeleton. In this disease the cartilage within the joint wears away and

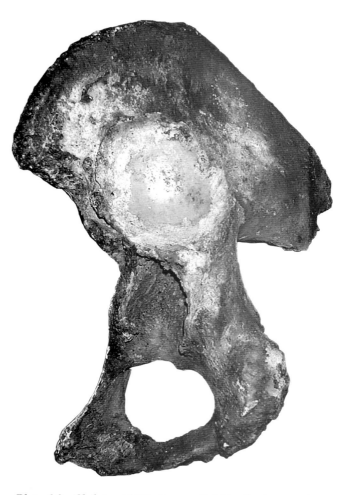

Plate 6.2   Skeleton 3027: Congenital hip displacement

bone on bone friction causes the joint surface to be dense and polished or eburnated. The aetiology of OA is multifactoral but increasing age, genetic predisposition, lifestyle and environmental factors

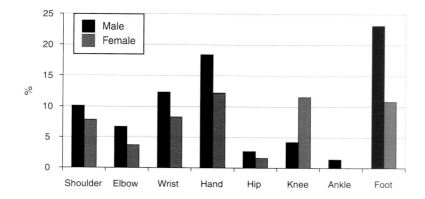

Notes:
Left and right sides combined; Shoulder=gleno-humeral and acromio-clavicular; elbow = distal humerus, and proximal radius and ulna; wrist=distal ulna and radius, scaphoid, lunate; hand=multiple joints except those relating to wrist; Knee=any compartment; ankle=distal tibia and fibula and talus; foot=multiple joints except those relating to ankle.

Fig. 6.6   Named sample: True prevalence of osteoarthritis

all play a role in the development of the disease. Osteoarthritis may be diagnosed on dry bone if eburnation is present. It may also be diagnosed if a combination of at least two of the following is present: pitting, bony contour change, and/or marginal osteophyte (new bone on and/or around the joint surface) (Rogers and Waldron 1995). With the exception of eburnation, these changes are not diagnostic of OA if they occur on their own. This is because they may arise in relation to other disease processes, trauma and/or age related wear and tear of the joint. For the present analysis, osteoarthritis was diagnosed based on the presence of eburnation alone following Rogers and Waldron (1995). Porosity and/or osteophytosis were recorded separately and broadly classified as 'degenerative joint disease' (DJD) or 'spinal degenerative joint disease' (SDJD).

A total of 44 adults (61% of the total named assemblage) displayed one or a combination of these changes involving extra-spinal joints. Mild to severe DJD in the form of joint surface pitting and/or marginal osteophytosis was observed joints of 43 adults (64%; n=43/67), which comprised 30 males (79% of adult males; n=30/38) and 13 females (45% of adult females; n=13/29). Extra-spinal joints that displayed eburnation alone involved 26 individuals (39% of all adults; n=26/67), of whom 20 were male (53% of adult males; n=20/38), and 6 were female (21% of adult females; n=6/29).

There was a difference in the distribution of OA between the sexes (Fig. 6.6; Table 6.10). Males displayed far more lesions of the hands, arms and feet whereas females showed higher rates of osteoarthritis of the knee joints. This may be due differences in occupation, but other variables such as genetic predisposition, build, body mass, age and sex are all significant factors in disease development and the location of lesions on the skeleton. See results for OA in the unnamed individuals below.

Spinal degenerative joint disease (SDJD) – SDJD affected 60 individuals (83% of total population, or 89.5% of adults). These comprised 36 males (95% of adult males; n=36/38) and 24 females (83% of adult females; n=24/29). Only two males and five females did not have spinal lesions. Porosity and/or osteophytosis were recorded as slight, moderate and considerable. In the majority of cases the changes were slight (Table 6.11). OA was recorded in 11% of all observed vertebrae.

The crude prevalence of extra-spinal and spinal OA in the post-medieval period was 25% and 13% respectively (Roberts and Cox 2003 352-353). This was comparable with the crude prevalence calculated for the named individuals from St George's crypt. This contrasted with the crude prevalence of both extra spinal and spinal DJD (11%) in post-medieval populations cited in Roberts and Cox (2003, 352), far lower than those of the St George's assemblage. The average age of the adults in this assemblage was 57 years, with 35 of the 52 aged individuals being over 50 years old. The high prevalence of joint disease within this assemblage is therefore probably age-related, rather than reflective of a lifestyle involving strenuous repetitive activities.

Schmorl's nodes – Schmorl's nodes are identified as indentations on the superior and inferior surfaces of the vertebral bodies. These are caused by the herniation of the intervertebral disc through the end plates and are therefore, in effect, pressure defects. Associated with degenerative disease, Schmorl's nodes have also been linked to activity and trauma, especially in adolescence, or metabolic disorders (Jurmain 1999). Twenty-three named adults, all of them male, displayed Schmorl's nodes. The distribution pattern of these defects in the spinal column revealed that all lesions were located in the lower thoracic and lumbar spine (Fig. 6.7)- the most common location of these lesions.

Rheumatoid arthritis – Rheumatoid arthritis is an autoimmune disease that affects approximately 1% of modern populations (Roberts and Manchester 1995, 116). It is three times more common in females

Table 6.10: Named sample: True prevalence of osteoarthritis in different joints

	Males	%	Females	%
Shoulder	7 / 69	10.1	4 / 51	7.8
Elbow	5 / 74	6.7	2 / 54	3.7
Wrist	8 / 65	12.3	4 / 48	8.3
Hand	12 / 65	18.4	6 / 49	12.2
Hip	2 / 73	2.7	1 / 61	1.6
Knee	3 / 70	4.2	6 / 52	11.5
Ankle	1 / 69	1.4	0 / 50	0
Foot	16 / 69	23.1	5 / 46	10.8

Lefts and right sides combined; Shoulder=gleno-humeral and acromio-clavicular; elbow=distal humerus, and proximal radius and ulna; wrist=distal ulna and radius, scaphoid, lunate; hand=multiple joints except those relating to wrist; Knee=any compartment; ankle=distal tibia and fibula and talus; foot=multiple joints except those relating to ankle.

Table 6.11: Named sample: True prevalence of affected vertebrae

Skeletal change		Percentage of vertebrae affected
SDJD (Porosity and/ or osteophytosis)	Slight	38% (495/1288)
	Moderate	12% (155/1288)
	Considerable	8% (98/1288)
Osteoarthritis		11% (139/1288)

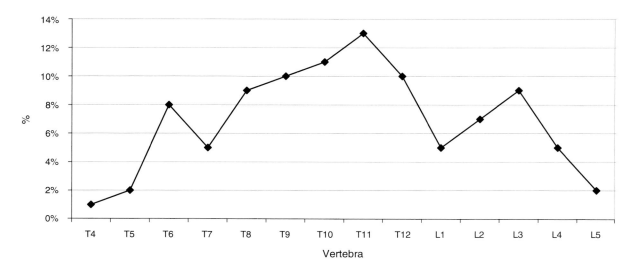

Fig. 6.7   Named sample: True prevalence of Schmorl's nodes on the thoracic and lumber spines.

than in males, with an age of onset in the fourth or fifth decades of life (Rogers and Waldron, 1995, 55-56). Rheumatoid arthritis is a chronic inflammatory disease that affects multiple synovial joints bilaterally, most commonly the hands, feet, wrists and elbows (Roberts and Manchester 1995, 116). The synovial membranes of the joints are initially affected, becoming thickened and granulated. The disease then spreads to the joint cartilage, eventually destroying it. The underlying bone is also eroded and ankylosis (fusion of joints) may occur. The joints become swollen, stiff and very painful. Additional physical symptoms include anaemia, weight loss and fever (Roberts and Manchester 1995, 116; Aufderheide and Rodríguez-Martín 1998, 100). A famous sufferer, who was a contemporary of the St George's population, is thought to have been Samuel Taylor Coleridge. His liberal use of laudanum to contain the led to his opium addiction, and to the penning of such memorable poems as *Kubla Khan – a fragment in a dream* and *The Rime of the Ancient Mariner*. One ageing female (skeleton 5041)

in the named assemblage displayed lesions consistent with rheumatoid arthritis of her feet. The tarsals had fused (Plate 6.3). The right hand was also affected. Radiography is necessary to confirm this diagnosis, however.

Diffuse Idiopathic Skeletal Hyperostosis (DISH) – DISH is characterised by the ossification of the anterior longitudinal spinal ligaments causing a flowing candle wax- like new bone formation, which is usually located on the right side of the vertebral bodies (Rogers and Waldron 1995, 48-49). Enthesophytes (new bone formation at major ligament insertion points) and ossified cartilage are also a feature of this disease (Roberts and Manchester 1995, 120). Symptoms are generally mild but include stiffness and aching. Modern prevalence of the disease ranges between 6 and 12%. It affects more males than females, and 85% of cases are aged over 50 years. There appears to be an association between DISH and Late Onset or Type 2 Diabetes Mellitus and obesity (Rogers and Waldron 1995, 48).

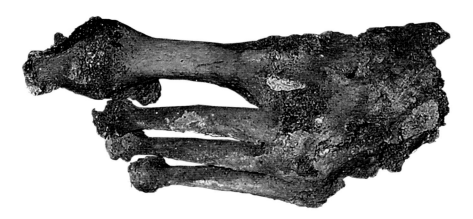

Plate 6.3   Skeleton 5041: rheumatoid arthritis of the left foot

Plate 6.4   Skeleton 1041: DISH

Three individuals in the named sample displayed DISH (4.17%, n=3/72). They were all ageing males (8% of all adult males). DISH involving the spine of skeleton 1041 is shown in Plate 6.4. Although this prevalence was lower than in modern populations, the age and sex of the affected individuals of the St George's assemblage was consistent with modern epidemiology of the disorder. It was comparable with contemporary assemblages of similar socio-economic background, however. The prevalence at Christ Church, Spitalfields, and St Luke's, Islington, was 5.79% and 2.28% respectively (Roberts and Cox 2003, 311; Boyle *et al.* 2005, 239).

Trauma

Fractures – Fractures are either caused by an acute injury to the bone, an underlying disease or repetitive stress (Roberts and Manchester 1995, 68). Fractures were identified on 17 individuals (23.6%; n=17/72), of whom 16 were adult and one was adolescent. Of these 13 were male. A total of 21 fractures were observed, the majority (38%) comprising rib fractures (Table 6.12). Feet suffered the lowest fracture rate of all elements. Most of the fractures were well healed and evidently of long standing. Only one individual (skeleton 5049) displayed perimortem lesions. These consisted of two depressed cranial fractures with no evidence of healing.

The crude prevalence rate in the named sample was comparable to the St Luke's, Islington, assemblage, where fractures were present in 16% of the named individuals (Boyle *et al.* 2005, 230). Overall, the fracture rates were low, consistent with other assemblages in the post-medieval period (Table 6.12).

Table 6. 12: Named sample: Summary of fractures by element

Fracture location	Number of males	Number of females	Total number of fractures	True prevalence of fractures	True prevalence of fractures in post-medieval Britain[1]
Cranium	5.26% (2/38)	3.45% (1/29)	19.06% (4/21)	6.45% (4/62)	0.39% (5/1291)
Radius	2.63% (1/38)	0	4.76% (1/21)	0.81% (1/123)	0.64% (8/1249)
Spine	5.26% (2/38)	0	14.28% (3/21)	0.43% (3/678)[2]	-
Ribs	10.52% (4/38)	6.90% (2/29)	38.10% (8/21)	0.75% (8/1060)	4.23% (88/2081)
Sacrum	2.63% (1/38)	0	4.76% (1/21)	1.61% (1/62)	0.63% (1/160)
Fibula	5.26% (2/38)	3.45% (1/29)	14.28% (3/21)	2.8% (3/107)	0.76% (12/1582)
Foot bones	2.63% (1/38)	0	4.76% (1/21)	0.1% (1/983)	0%
Total number	34.21% (13/38)	13.79% (4/29)	100% (21/21)	-	-

[1] After Roberts and Cox 2003, 302, [2] Thoracic vertebral elements only

Osteochondritis dissecans – Osteochondritis dissecans is a fairly common skeletal disorder of the joint surfaces of the major long bones. Physically active young males (such as athletes) are most often affected in the first two decades of life. This disease is due to a significant localised obliteration of the blood supply, causing necrosis of small areas of joint tissue (Roberts and Manchester 1995, 87). Repeated, low-grade, chronic trauma or micro-trauma is thought to play a role in this injury to the blood vessels (Aufderheide and Rodriguez-Martin 1998). The necrotic bone plaque breaks-off from the joint surface and may remain loose in the joint, causing chronic pain and often precipitating osteoarthritis. Alternatively, the fragment may re-attach in its original position or be resorbed, and no further symptoms will be experienced.

Two male skeletons (1037 and 1057) displayed one such lesion, one located on the navicular bone and on the distal humerus respectively. These represented 5.26% of the males and 2.78% of the named assemblage (N = 72).

Infectious disease

Non-specific infection

Periostitis – Periostitis is an inflammation of the periosteum, the lining of bones. This involvement is often secondary to an infection of the overlying soft tissue, but micro-organisms causing the infection may also be blood-borne (in systemic infection), or more unusually, may originate from the compact or trabecular bone beneath. Periostitis may also be associated with local haemorrhage (due to trauma, scurvy or excess vitamin A intake), chronic skin ulcers or varicose veins (Aufderheide and Rodríguez-Martín 1998, 179).

In the post-medieval period, the crude prevalence rate of periostitis has been reported as 26% (Roberts and Cox 2003, 344). The condition was observed in 27 named individuals from St George's (37.5%; n=27/72), of whom 26 were adult and one was adolescent. They comprised 14 males and 13 females. The lesions were active at the time of death in 10 skeletons (13.8%; n=10/72)- six males and four females. The most common location of the lesions was the tibial shaft, was found in 15 individuals (55.55%; n=15/27), and 16% (22/137) of all tibiae (Table 6.13; Fig. 6.8). This may be due in part to the proximity of the bone to the skin and its susceptibility to recurrent minor trauma (Roberts and Manchester 1995, 130). Peripheral vascular disease (sometimes associated with Diabetes mellitus) may also lead to venous or arterial ulcers. Due to poor blood supply, these are slow to heal and may become infected. If the soft tissue damage reaches

Table 6.13: Named sample: True prevalence of periostitis by element (lefts and right sides combined)

	Males	%	Females	%	Subadults	%	Total	%
Humerus	2 / 77	2.5	0 / 51	0	0 / 6	0	2 / 134	1.5
Radius	1 / 73	1.3	0 / 50	0	0 / 7	0	1 / 130	0.8
Ulna	1 / 74	1.3	0 / 47	0	0 / 7	0	1 / 128	0.8
Femur	6 / 77	7.7	4 / 58	6.8	0 / 7	0	10 / 142	7.0
Tibia	14 / 76	18.4	8 / 55	14.5	0 / 6	0	22 / 137	16.1
Fibula	6 / 67	8.9	6 / 40	15	0 / 6	0	12 / 113	10.6
Ribs	15 / 663	2.2	20 / 397	5	3 / 46	6.5	38 / 1106	3.4

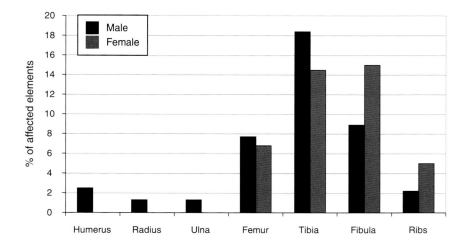

Fig. 6.8 Named sample: True prevalence of periostitis according to element

the underlying bone, an inflammatory reaction of the periosteum may occur. Considering the older age of this sample, this aetiology is probable for some of the lesions present.

Periostitis involved a wider distribution of elements in males than in females (Fig. 6.8). Lesions were identified on upper limb bones of males, but not females. Few were obviously associated with trauma, as very few fractures were observed on these bones (see Table 6.12 above). This may imply systemic disease in the aetiology of periostitis in these individuals, which may include such diverse conditions as syphilis, scurvy, excessive Vitamin A and chronic pulmonary conditions. Further investigation lay beyond the scope of this report.

Males also had more affected tibiae and femora than females. Females showed greater involvement of ribs (all visceral surfaces) and fibulae compared with males. Rib lesions are discussed separately in the following section.

Chronic respiratory disease – The vast majority of respiratory disease leaves no trace on the bones. However, where a lesion (such as a bulla or abscess) approximates the ribs, resorption or new bone proliferation on the visceral surface of the bone may occur (Roberts *et al.* 1998, 56). Traditionally, such lesions were associated with tuberculosis but Roberts *et al.* (1998) concluded that no differential diagnosis was possible without the presence of tubercular lesions in other parts of the skeleton. Acute lobar pneumonia, brochiolec-tasis (eg in chronic obstructive pulmonary disease, such as asthma, chronic bronchitis and emphysaema), and less likely, metastatic carcinoma, non-specific osteomyelitis and syphilis, are all possible causes.

In the St George's named sample, seven individuals (CPR 10%, n=7/72) displayed new bone formation on the visceral surface of the ribs. These included one older adolescent female (5049), three adult females (3022, 3027 and 7081) and three males (1057, 1077 and 1527), whilst female skeleton 7011 showed similar lesions on the neck of the right ribs. These bony changes to the rib shafts were more common among females (13%; n=4/31) than males (7%; n=3/41). Lesions were active in three individuals (1057, 5049 and 7081).

Maxillary sinusitis – The aetiology of maxillary sinusitis is multifactoral and may be caused by allergies, smoke and upper respiratory tract infections (Roberts and Manchester 1995, 131). In the smoky, polluted air of 18th century London, it's presence is thus to be expected. The observation of the lesions is dependent on access to the maxillary sinus cavities. The vast majority of crania from the named assemblage were intact, and hence, the sinuses could not be examined. Maxillary sinusitis is therefore likely to have been considerably under-recorded in this sample. New bone formation within the sinuses was observed in two adult males

(1057 and 3002) and one female (4007), or 4.2% of the total assemblage. This crude prevalence is lower than figure of 6.88% reported for post-medieval British assemblages by Roberts and Cox (2003, 299), possibly reflecting better air quality in Bloomsbury, that made it 'esteemed the most healthful [place] of any in London' (Strype 1720, Bk 4 chap IV, 85).

Ear infection – Ear infections were observed in two individuals, one female (skeleton 4035) and an ageing male (skeleton 1041). The former had otitis externa (infection of the ear canal or external ear). The latter had mastoiditis. This condition was probably the end result of a middle ear infection (otitis media), suffered in the early years of his life. In untreated otitis media, accumulated pus in the middle ear perforates the eardrum and drains from the ear canal. However, in his case, the accumulated pus burst through the bone of the middle ear and settled in the air cells of the mastoid process, where it eventually formed a draining sinus in the external surface of the bone. This is a relatively rare occurrence and is potentially very dangerous, as had the infection drained internally, it may have spread to the brain and surrounding tissue causing encephalitis or meningitis.

Specific infection

Syphilis – Venereal syphilis was long the most serious and dreaded of the sexually transmitted diseases. The disease was first encountered in the western world in the 15th century AD, and rapidly spread across Europe (Roberts and Cox 2003, 340). By the post-medieval period, the 'great pox', or the 'French pox' as syphilis was known in England, had become a significant health problem. Prevention of contagion using early forms of condoms, and treatments using mercury and guaiacum were largely unsuccessful (ibid.). It was really only with the invention of penicillin in the 1930s that any serious inroad was made in the control of this disease. Venereal syphilis is a sexually transmitted infection caused by the bacterium *Trepanima pallidum,* and is the only one of the treponematoses (a group of diseases that includes yaws, pinta and endemic syphilis) that may be fatal. Syphilis is transmitted by sexual contact or may be passed from an infected mother to her foetus. The latter is known as congenital syphilis.

Venereal syphilis acquired in adulthood is a chronic infection characterised by three clinical stages separated by latent stages with no visible symptoms (Arrizabalaga 2003, 316). In primary syphilis, a small painless ulcer or chancre appears on the genitals (and less commonly elsewhere) within 2 – 6 weeks of infection. In most cases, after a brief latent period, there is a secondary stage characterised by widespread lesions on the skin and in the internal organs, a painless rash, fever, malaise and bone ache. These symptoms disappear after a few weeks, but in 25% of sufferers they recur during the first two years (ibid.). The tertiary stage only develops in a third of untreated cases, and only following a latent phase that may vary in length from one year to more than 20 years. It is this tertiary stage that causes profound systemic damage and results in insanity and death. The bacterium causes progressive destruction of a number of systems of the body, including the skin, the mucous membranes, the bones, the heart and blood vessels and the nervous system. Nervous system involvement causes a loss of positional sense and sensation that manifests as locomotor ataxia (a stumbling, high stepping gait), and bouts of insanity, generally known as general paralysis of the insane (ibid.; Roberts and Manchester 1995, 153). Fatality from tertiary syphilis occurs through cardiovascular involvement, such as a ruptured aneurysm, or cardiac valve failure.

Congenital syphilis – syphilis transmitted to the unborn child of a mother suffering from venereal syphilis – occurs in 80% of pregnancies where the mother is infected (Aufderheide and Rodríguez-Martín 1998, 164). The spirochete bacteria are transmitted across the placenta to the foetus after the first 16 – 18 weeks *in utero*. Spontaneous abortion and stillbirth are commonly associated with the condition. Surviving infants frequently manifest with developmental anomalies, such as deafness, cusp malformations of the permanent dentition (Hutchinson's incisors and mulberry molars), interstitial keratitis, impaired cognitive development, periostitis, osteochondritis and osteomyelitis. Syphilitic infection of the scalp, historically described as 'scald head', was a very visual, unsightly manifestation of congenital syphilis.

The London Bills of Mortality attributed between one and 30 deaths per year to 'scald head' in the period between 1740-1810 (Roberts and Cox 2003, 341-2). The true mortality rate of congenital syphilis was probably much higher. Nevertheless, many sufferers of congenital syphilis did survive into mature adulthood. One young adult male (skeleton 6071) had irregular lobulations on the cusps of the first molars, characteristic of mulberry molars, a feature consistent with congenital syphilis.

Lesions consistent with venereal syphilis were present in two adult male individuals from the named sample at St George's (skeletons 3085 and 4069), representing 2.99% of the total adult population (N= 67). This prevalence was higher than most other assemblages of this period. Only Newcastle Infirmary had a higher rate at 3.7%, perhaps not surprising in an assemblage that included a high proportion of sailors. Other middle class assemblages (such as Christ Church, Spitalfields, and Kingston-upon-Thames reported rates of 0.21% and 0.28%, respectively (Roberts and Cox 2003, 341). It is a problem to explain why prevalence of venereal syphilis seen at St George's is higher than in the assemblages of similar socio-economic background. It may be that these individuals chose to spend more money on extra-curricular activities, such as whoring.

Indeed, Bloomsbury was not far distant from the notorious red light district of the West End, which centred on Covent Garden and Piccadilly (Picard 2000). *Harris's List of Covent Garden Ladies*, first compiled by Samuel Derrick in 1757, was an indispensible guide for the well-heeled sexual tourist to the Metropolis in the late Georgian period (Rubenhold 2005). It gives considerable insights into the sex trade of the time, and lists amongst others a Miss Sh-rd of 46 Googe Street,

> a very desirable companion . . . of middle size, inclined to be fat [with] . . . a posterior inclined to be luscious (ibid.).

This 'most pleasing pupil of pleasure' had several City 'friends' and lawyers from Gray's Inn and the Temple. One wonders if these included any of the many lawyers interred in St George's crypt. Derrick's flattering descriptions of the many ladies of pleasure in various updated editions of his list is in stark contrast to his attitude to a Miss Young of No. 6 Cumberland Court, Bridge Street, who

> has very lately had the folly and wickedness to leave a certain hospital, before the cure of a certain distemper which she had was completed, and has thrown her contaminated carcass on the town again, for which we hold her inexcusable (ibid, 158).

The 'certain distemper' is likely to have been syphilis.

Tuberculosis – Tuberculosis may be spread to humans by the ingestion of infected meat and milk. The strain responsible is *Mycobacterium bovis*. Alternatively, the disease may be spread from person to person by inhalation of airborne bacilli present in expectorated phlegm. The seat of the primary lesion in this form of tuberculosis is most commonly the lungs, and is caused by the strain *Mycobacterium tuberculosis*. The latter route was the more common in the 18th and 19th centuries, the spread of infection being facilitated by high population density, poor nutrition and housing, and the lack of hygiene so prevalent amongst the urban poor. The more privileged and renowned of society were not immune to this terrible scourge, however, famous sufferers including Keats, Anne and Emily Brontë and Chopin (Dormandy 1991), all contemporaries of the St George's population. Since potential sufferers are at their most vulnerable in adolescence, the disease was given a romantic sheen- of young people tragically cut down before their time. The physical symptoms of gently wasting away added to this notion (ibid.). Yet the reality of the disease for the majority of sufferers was far from romantic, and tuberculosis hit the working classes hardest. Amongst the poor, it was the leading cause of death in the 19th century (Humphreys 1997, 137). Bills of Mortality from the late 18th and early 19th century show a mortality rate due to consumption at around 25% (Roberts and Cox 2003, 338).

Bony lesions are not present in the majority of tuberculosis cases. Recent clinical studies have shown that skeletal involvement is found in only 1% of patients, and before the availability of antibiotics, this figure averaged 5% – 7% (Aufderheide and Rodríguez-Martín 1998, 133). Most cases of tuberculosis therefore go unrecognised in palaeopathology. Lesions involving the spine have been reported in 25-50% of cases of skeletal tuberculosis (Roberts and Manchester 1995, 138). These lytic lesions in the vertebral bodies caused by tubercular abscesses eventually cause the spine to collapse, through compression fractures of the vertebral bodies. Where profound hunchback or kyphosis results, these changes are known as Pott's disease.

In addition to the rib lesions discussed above, one prime adult female (skeleton 7011) of the St George's assemblage (1.39%, n=1/72), showed spinal lesions consistent with tuberculosis. The average prevalence calculated from four post-medieval sites by Roberts and Cox (2003, 339) was 0.62%, whilst a higher rate of 1.6% was reported from Newcastle Infirmary, not unexpected in this working class assemblage.

Metabolic disease

Cribra orbitalia and porotic hyperostosis – Cribra orbitalia is widely thought to occur in response to a deficiency of iron during childhood, most commonly the result of inadequate dietary intake of iron, and/or as a result of severe intestinal parasite infestation (Stuart-Macadam 1991, 101). Iron is a central component of haemoglobin, the molecule necessary for the transportation of oxygen in the red blood cells of the blood. Red blood cells are produced within the red bone marrow of a number of bones of the body, which include the diploë of the cranial vault, the sternum and the pelvis. In childhood, the diploë are particularly important, but become a secondary site of red blood cell production later in life. In iron deficiency anaemia, the body attempts to compensate for low serum iron levels by hypertrophy of these bones. In children, this manifests osteologically as an increased porosity and thickening of the diploë of the cranial vault (known as porotic hyperostosis) and of the orbital sockets (Cribra orbitalia). Cribra orbitalia is often used as a generic indicator of physical stress in childhood. The physical symptoms of anaemia are shortness of breath, fatigue, pallor and palpitations (Roberts and Manchester 1995, 167).

The orbits of seven individuals (CPR 9.7%; n=7/72) displayed cribra orbitalia, of which three had active lesions at the time of death (3064, 4039 and 7053). Given the childhood nature of the disease, it is unsurprising that these active lesions were found in subadults- two infants and one adolescent. The true prevalence of the assemblage was 10.5% (n =13/124 orbits). Using Stuart-Macadam's (1991) scoring system, the severity of

the lesions were rated as Type 1 in skeletons 4030 and 7043, Type 2 in skeletons 3064, 4013 and 4039, Type 3 in skeletons 6085 and 7053, whilst skeleton 2029 displayed a Type 4 lesion in the left orbit and a much less developed Type 1 lesion in the right.

The crania of one adult male (6048) and one female (2008) displayed porotic hyperostosis- a crude prevalence of 2.8 % (n=2/72) and a true prevalence of 3.2% (N=2/62 crania). The total number of skeletons with lesions that were consistent with iron deficiency was 10 (13.89%, n=10/72). The crude rate of cribra orbitalia in the Christ Church, Spitalfields, assemblage was 34% (Molleson and Cox 1993) and in the named assemblage of St Luke's, Islington it was 9.5% (Boyle *et al.* 2005, 235). Interestingly, the lowest prevalence was noted in the paupers of the Cross Bones assemblage (4.05%). The association between cribra orbitalia and higher social class may reflect infant feeding practices of the day, in which pap or panada was substituted for breast milk early in infancy. This gruel essentially comprised flour and water, and was very deficient in nutrients, including iron. It was also associated with an increased risk of gastric infections from poor quality water (Roberts and Cox 2003, 307). The poor, who through economic necessity were forced to breastfeed longer than their more affluent counterparts, appear to have spared their children some of the illnesses afflicting children of the middling sort.

Rickets – Vitamin D is mainly synthesised by the skin when it is exposed to sunlight, but may also be obtained from foods such as eggs and oily fish. Rickets is caused by a childhood deficiency of this vitamin. Vitamin D is needed for the uptake of calcium, and hence, normal mineralisation of bone. In rickets the bone becomes softened, allowing the bones to distort. Most common is bowing of the weight bearing bones of the legs, but if rickets develops when an infant is crawling, the long bones of the arms may be affected also (Roberts and Manchester 1995, 173). In severe cases, the individual may become markedly knock-kneed, making locomotion difficult and painful. Large nodules of bone may also grow on the end of the ribs producing a concave or pigeon chest. The pelvic bone may also deform, making childbirth impossible later in life. Other symptoms include muscle and joint pain, abdominal pain and muscle spasm (Beck 1997a, 130).

The industrialisation of Britain caused a substantial increase of this condition in urban areas, due to the persistent pall of smoke and smog overhanging the cities. In the overcrowded slums with their overhanging buildings, sunlight was largely blotted out. Children of the poor also had to work indoors for most of the daylight hours and were therefore even more susceptible to developing rickets. To less industrialised people on the Continent, rickets become known as the English disease (Geber pers.comm.). The children of the more privilege

Plate 6.5 Skeleton 5068: rickets and fracture of the fibular shaft

classes were also at risk from the pervasive air pollution, and were not helped by the fashionable infant feeding practices described above (Roberts and Cox 2003, 308).

One ageing adult female (skeleton 5068) had characteristic bowing of the femora and tibiae indicative of childhood rickets (Plate 6.5). The prevalence of 1.8% in the named sample from St George's, compares favourably with rates from the pauper burial ground of Cross Bones, Southwark, and the middle class crypt of Christ Church, Spitalfields, which produce rates of 6.8% and 3.6%, respectively.

Neoplastic disease

Benign neoplasm – The only benign neoplasm present within the assemblage was a button osteoma on the skull of an ageing adult female (skeleton 4007). This type of lesion consists of a small round projection of dense bone commonly situated on the frontal bone. It would have been asymptomatic (Roberts and Manchester 1995, 188). *Malignant neoplasm* – In modern studies, 20% of all cancer fatalities spread to bone. This is one of the reasons why malignant neoplasms are rare in archaeological assemblages. In addition, most cancers become more common with increasing age. It is thus reasonable to assume that in archaeological populations, where the mean lifespan was much shorter, cancers would be less prevalent (Roberts and Manchester 1995, 192-193).

Metastatic carcinoma is secondary cancer that has spread from a primary tumour. The primary site in bone metastases is the breast in females and the prostate in males. These cancer spread throughout the body through the blood stream, and secondary sites are therefore most commonly located in trabecular bone of the cranium, vertebrae, ribs, sternum, pelvis and major long bones (Aufderheide and Rodríguez-Martín 1998, 388).

Two individuals (2.8%, n/N=2/72) within the named assemblage displayed lesions consistent with metastatic carcinoma. They were both ageing adult females (skeletons 5043 and 5061), and given their age and sex it is probable they both had suffered from breast cancer. The prevalence from St George's Church is rather high compared to similar assemblages, and probably reflects an ageing population. Only one individual (0.10%) had metastatic carcinoma in the Christ Church, Spitalfields, assemblage (Roberts and Cox 2003, 352).

Post-mortem medical interventions

Craniotomies had been performed on two adult male individuals (skeleton 1077 and 3090) (2.8%, n/N=2/72). This procedure involved the removal of the top of the skull in the horizontal plane in order to examine the brain. There were no skeletal clues as to why the procedure had been carried out.

In the Georgian and Victorian periods, post-mortem dissection was an uncommon procedure, and usually one over which the deceased and their relatives exercised little control. In the 18th century there was a growing need in medical institutions for cadavers on which students might learn anatomy and practice dissection. In 1752, the Company of Surgeons was granted the corpses of all executed felons. However, demand far outstripped supply, and many additional cadavers were supplied to anatomy halls by 'resurrectionists', who raided graveyards, exhuming recently buried corpses and selling them on for a handsome profit (Porter 1997, 318). Public outrage at this practice reached a height in 1829 with the notorious case of Burke and Hare in Edinburgh. The outcome of this outrage was the passing of the Anatomy Act (1832), which permitted the medical profession to take for dissection all 'unclaimed bodies' of those dying without family, or those dying in the workhouse or hospital. As a result of the act, there was a reduction in body-snatching, but the act also served to deepen the fear and shame amongst the poor of dying on the parish (Rugg 1999, 222).

The antipathy to the notion of being dissected was based around religious and social perceptions. The Christian belief in the resurrection of the whole body on Judgement Day led to fears that dissection would damage the spiritual state of the dissected person. A deep-seated solicitude for the corpse causes reactions of revulsion at the indignities imposed on the body during exhumation and dissection. In particular, with regards to female corpses, the physical exposure of the naked body to the gaze of young men was perceived as harrowing, a process tantamount to sexual assault (ibid.).

In view of these almost universal sentiments regarding dissection, it is perhaps puzzling that these two skeletons from St George's crypt had undergone a craniotomy, when clearly they were neither felons nor had died friendless on the parish. It is possible that both men had consented to the procedure, perhaps because of unusually progressive views on medicine and the academic necessity for dissection. Memorial plaques within the church, and documentary sources record the interment of at least five medical doctors within the crypt. However, skeleton 1077 is that of Edward Littledale, Esq., bibliophile (d. 1837), and brother of Right Honourable Sir Joseph Littledale (coffin 1511), judge of the Court of Queen's Bench (*The Gentleman's Magazine* 1842, 319-20). Edward Littledale's address was given as Gray's Inn Square, and his age as 57 years (sic) in the death notice in *The Gentleman's Magazine* (1837, 667). Skeleton 3090 is that of Charles Thomson (b. 1758, d. 1821), Master in Chancery, appointed February 1809 (Hadyn 1851, 241).

Alternatively, some craniotomies may have been the result of autopsy rather than dissection. There is an important distinction to make between dissection and autopsies, the former being very intrusive and destructive to the point of there being no remains left for burial, whereas the latter was minimally intrusive insofar as only the lesion or part of the body which needed to be examined was investigated. Autopsy was carried out to primarily establish cause of death, but also in order to further knowledge of a particular ailment or lesion. Indeed, forensic medicine emerged in medical journals as a separate field in the early part of the 19th century (Crawford 1991, 203). As such, it may very well be possible that the legislation that covered dissection of unclaimed paupers did not cover autopsies, as they were distinctly different interventions. Indeed, the two individuals with craniotomies from St George's crypt died in 1821 and 1837, respectively before and after the passing of the Anatomy Act.

The craniotomy performed on Charles Thomson may well have been part of an autopsy. The *Gentleman's Magazine* of July 1821 recorded how 'suddenly at his house in Portland Place, Charles Thomson, esq, ... had had a paralytic stroke, and had been in a declining state for some time past...'. It is probable that the craniotomy was performed to investigate his stroke.

A less probable alternative explanation is that these craniotomies were performed on the sly without the consent of the deceased or their relatives. Such craniotomies are fairly easy to hide from the incurious if the dissection of the skin is concealed beneath the hair. It is possible that their families may have interred them remaining none the wiser of these interventions. The presence of this type of post-mortem intervention in post-medieval assemblages is not unusual with a national prevalence of 1.62% (Roberts and Cox 2003, 315).

Social modification – the effects of corsetry

The right and left ribs of one ageing adult female, Catherine Warren (skeleton 7016), displayed a deformity of the rib shafts, such that the angle of each of the lower ribs was very exaggerated or acute, presenting as squaring and flattening anterior-posteriorly. The lower part of the rib cage was affected bilaterally. The abnormally acute angulation of the ribs may have been caused by the habitual wearing of a tight-laced corset.

Corsets of the latter half of the 18th century were known as stays. Amongst the less affluent, stays were often of leather and were frequently worn without an overlying fabric covering. These stays, made malleable by sweat and oil from the skin, did not prove an impediment to household duties, allowing considerable movement (Picard 2000, 216). More expensive stays were of different construction and were very much more restrictive. The more expensive corsets were usually highly decorated and worn as an outer garment with or without shoulder straps. In the 18th century, stays or corsets were worn by aristocratic men and women and increasingly by the growing middle classes.

More expensive adult female stays consisted of panels that were reinforced by thin whalebone to make the garment very stiff. Stays moulded the upper body to resemble an inverted cone with the purpose to achieve a thin waist and a flattened anterior-posterior profile. Some women undertook tight-lacing in order to achieve this fashionable shape. Although a moderately laced corset was unlikely to have caused any physical harm, a tightly laced corset would have compressed the lower ribs, narrowing the ribcage. This would have compressed the inner organs, often leading to physical discomforts, such as dizziness, nausea, breathing difficulties, heart palpitations and indigestion. When a corset was laced this tightly, fainting was not uncommon (Werner *et al.* 1998, 94).

There appeared to be conflicting opinions in 18th century medicine about the effects of tightly laced corsets on women's health. For example Nicholas Andry, paediatrician and Professor of Medicine in the College Royal, and Dean of the Faculty of Physick, Paris, suggested that every child should wear a corset from the age of five years (Andry 1743, quoted in Schwarz 1979, 553). Other practitioners were much more critical of corsetry on health. A late 18th-century publication by von Sömmerring (1793) included an engraving depicting constriction of the abdomen and the lower ribs by tight lacing (reproduced by Fee *et al* 2002; see also Schwarz 1979, fig. 3) as an aid in demonstrating the deleterious health effects of this fashion.

Constrictive fashions that emphasised a narrow waist changed with the advent of the French Revolution, and were replaced by long loose fitting dresses with waistlines just beneath the bust (the so-called Empire line), reminiscent of the dress of Classical Greece and Rome. It is however unlikely that everybody in this interim period stopped wearing stays. Some women may have been physically unable to go without them due to atrophied back muscles. Many older men and women in the Regency period chose to retain outdated fashions of their youth, including wearing stays, wigs, hair powder and patches long after they had gone out of vogue.

Classically inspired loosely draped dresses and less restrictive underwear, however, lasted only *c.* 20 years, but by 1815 corsets were very much back fashion. Corsets of the early 19th century became so rigid and constrictive that they alarmed medical professionals of the day. This was in part due to invention of the metallic eyelet by a French army doctor during the Napoleonic Wars, which allowed the corsets to be clinched even tighter without damaging the fabric.

Skeleton 7016, the ageing adult female with rib deformations, died aged 78 years in 1834. She probably started wearing stays in her youth in the early 1770s. Although all females were expected to wear corsets from an early age, this individual was the only one in the assemblage displaying these rib deformities. It may have been that she was particularly fashion conscious, lacing her stays tightly from an early age. Strict mothers often compelled their daughters into tight lacing from late childhood or early adolescence, and Catherine Warren may well have been one of these unfortunate girls. Tight lacing would explain why not all females show the characteristic rib deformations and explain the rarity of the lesions. Similar changes in rib morphology were noted in one female from St Luke's, Islington (Boyle *et al.* 2005) and one from the late Georgian Quaker burial ground in Kings Lynn, Norfolk (skeleton 30547) (Mahoney 2004).

THE UNNAMED SAMPLE

Introduction

The unnamed sample comprised 37 individuals whose age and sex could not be identified from *depositum* plate inscriptions. In addition, the named skeletons of John Rigge (6055) and Benjamin Wood (4032) were erroneously included in the unnamed sample (Table 6.14). These 39 skeletons underwent low-resolution osteological analysis using methodologies described below.

The lack of legible *depositum* plate inscriptions in these burials, and hence the anonymity of these 39

skeletons, is entirely a factor of taphonomy and did not indicate different treatment of the dead in the named and unnamed assemblages. Crushing and tearing of the lead shells occurred as a result of compression by overlying coffins in the coffin stacks, and during later spatial re-organisation within the vaults, the latter being most evident in Vault 7. Corrosion of the lead due to water seepage was present in the lower stacks of Vaults 4 and 5, and contributed to the weakness and collapse of the lead shells on lifting.

No true difference existed either in the richness of the coffin furniture or in the social and economic standing of the individuals comprising the two groups. In many respects, such as palaeodemography and some pathology rates, they may be regarded as a single population. The difference between the two lies in the osteological methodology employed in their osteological examination, which limited the comparisons of prevalences of skeletal pathology and non-metric traits.

Methodology

Unlike the named sample, which was fully analysed, the unnamed skeletons only underwent low-resolution osteological analysis. As with the named sample, age, sex and stature were fully estimated. An inventory of each skeleton was created to allow the calculation of true prevalence of pathological conditions. Bone preservation and completeness were recorded, as was dentition. Dental pathology prevalences were calculated per tooth in accordance with accepted practice. The skeletons were not formally examined for pathology or for non-metric traits, but those pathologies or traits noted in the course of osteological examination were recorded. Any non-metric traits noted are not reported here, but this information has been retained in the archive. Skeletal pathology is presented here, but the true prevalence may be under-reported as a result of this methodology. Bone measurements (with the exception of maximum long bone length used in stature estimation) were not undertaken on this sample.

Age, sex and stature were estimated using the same osteological methodology as the named assemblage, described above. Recording of preservation and completeness, dentition and dental pathology were likewise undertaken in the same manner.

Results

Preservation and completeness

Bone preservation within the unnamed sample varied considerably from poor to excellent. Preservation was rated on a four-point scale, from 1 (poor) to 4 (excellent) as described above for the named sample. Thirteen skeletons were poorly preserved, the bone having demineralised and becoming soft and crumbly to touch. In a number of

Table 6.14: Unnamed sample: Summary of the age, sex, stature, completeness and preservation (N = 39)

Coffin No.	Osteological Age	Age category	Osteological Sex	Stature	Preservation	Completeness
1084	40-44 y	mature adult	male	168.07	1	3
1097	35-50 y	prime adult	male	167.08	1	3
1129	14-15 y	Adolescent	subadult		3	3
1142	50+ y	ageing adult	possible male	164.06	1	4
2042	30-40 y	prime adult	female		1	3
3007	20-24 y	young adult	female	171.49	4	4
3013	30-40 y	adult	male	174.83	2	2
3017	12-13 y	Adolescent	subadult		3	2
3044	45-51 y	mature adult	male	179.51	3	4
3083	37-44 y	prime adult	female	164.68	1	4
3087	44-48 y	mature adult	male		1	3
3093	44-54 y	mature adult	male	181.33	1	4
4029	24-31 y	prime adult	female	154.53	2	3
4032	35-42 y	prime adult	male	167.68	3	4
4052	adult	adult	female	166.20	1	2
4054	33-46 y	prime adult	male		1	2
4061	59-71 y	ageing adult	male	163.52	3	4
4068	63-71 y	ageing adult	female	157.87	3	4
4077	35-44 y	prime adult	male	167.03	3	4
5028	40-50 y	mature adult	female	155.64	4	4
5042	60+ y	ageing adult	possible male		1	3
5051	adult	adult	female	162.04	1	3
6055	50+ y	ageing adult	male	171.45	3	3
6059	40-49 y	mature adult	female		1	1
6060	40-44 y	mature adult	male	171.71	3	3
6111	14-15 y	Adolescent	subadult		3	4
6129	50+ y	ageing adult	male		1	2
7001	50+ y	ageing adult	female	161.87	1	2
7003	24-27 y	prime adult	female	166.83	2	2
7004	60+ y	ageing adult	female		2	2
7005	65-78 y	ageing adult	male	159.62	2	4
7007	20-24 y	young adult	female	164.30	3	3
7008	65-78 y	ageing adult	male	170.67	3	2
7009	65-78 y	ageing adult	male	162.85	2	2
7010	25-50 y	mature adult	female	146.19	3	4
7017	50+ y	ageing adult	male	172.79	1	1
7049	45-54 y	ageing adult	male	168.33	4	3
7053	11-13 y	Adolescent	subadult		4	3
7062	35-45 y	mature adult	male	167.03	4	3

cases, crystal formation (brushite) was observed on the bone surface, giving it a shimmering appearance. These changes were most noticeable in skeletons where the coffin had been filled with large amounts of sawdust or bran, and where the coffin had been exposed to prolonged wet conditions. Of the remainder of the sample, the preservation of six skeletons was rated as fair (2), 13 as good (3) and five as excellent (4).

All attempts were made to recover the elements of each skeleton from both within the coffin and the vault. For many skeletons, small bones, such as carpals and phalanges, were missing. This is probably due to a combination of poor retrieval of these elements in the sub-optimal lighting of the vaults, and the poorer preservation of these small,

less robust bones. Completeness of the skeleton was scored on a four-point scale, 4 representing 76-95% completeness; 3 representing 50-75%; 2 representing 25-49% completeness, and 1 representing less than 25%. Preservation and completeness of each skeleton is summarised in Table 6.14 above. Most skeletons were grade 3 (50-75% complete).

Composition of the sample

Distribution of sex and age

Thirty-nine skeletons were analysed, of which 35 were adult (Table 6.15; Fig. 6.9). All adults in the sample could be sexed. Fourteen females (40%), 19 males (54.29%) and two possible males (5.71%) were identified. The predominance of males is not well understood, but may be an artefact of the fairly small sample size, but is consistent with the sex distribution recorded from *depositum* plates.

There were no infants or young children in the assemblage, but four subadults were aged between 12 and 14 years. The absence of the very young, may be explained by better preservation of the smaller infant and child coffins, which could be lifted intact from the vaults. A large proportion of these small coffins were positioned in the upper layers of the coffin stacks and hence, suffered less crushing and distorting than many of the adult coffins. As a result, no infant or child coffins were breached and hence, no skeletons were available for analysis.

There were only two young adults (5.56% of the total sample), both of whom were female. A number of infant bones were discovered in the adult coffin of one of the young woman (skeleton 7003), suggesting that she and the infant may have died as a result of the complications of pregnancy or child-birth. Unfortunately, due to the disturbed nature of the bones, it could not be established if the infant

bones had still been *in utero*, or if the deaths of mother and child had occurred peri-natally or post-natally. Childbirth was a leading cause of mortality amongst women of childbearing age (women in the young and prime adult age categories). Labour was a hazardous undertaking for both mother and child, but complications following childbirth also accounted for many fatalities. By the early 19th century, pueperal fever, or streptococcal septa-caemia following childbirth, was responsible for the death of 5-20% of maternity patients in most major European hospitals (Carter 2003, 266). Medical doctors were found to be the most important vectors in the spread of the infection between patients, often transmitting the bacteria from decaying cadavers examined during anatomy sessions to their maternity patients (ibid.).

The number of individuals in each age category increased with increasing age, peaking in the ageing adult category (50+ years). This age group comprised 33.33% of the total unnamed sample. Due to the limitations of ageing methodology available to osteologists, there are few reliable means of ageing

Table 6.15: Unnamed sample: Osteological age and sex (N = 39)

	Neonate (0-11 months)	Young child (1-5 years)	Older child (6-11 years)	Adolescent (12-17 years)	Young adult (18-25 years)	Prime adult (26-40 years)	Mature adult (40+ years)	Ageing adult (50+ years)	Adult >18 years	Total
Male	-	-	-	-	-	10.26 (4/39)	15.38 (6/39)	25.64 (10/39)	2.56 (1/39)	53.87 (21/39)
Female	-	-	-	-	5.13 (2/39)	10.26 (4/39)	7.69 (3/39)	7.69 (3/39)	5.13 (2/39)	35.90 (14/39)
Unknown	-	-	-	10.26 (4/39)	-	-	-	-	-	10.26 (4/39)
Total	-	-	-	10.26 (4/39)	5.13 (2/39)	20.51 (8/39)	23.08 (9/39)	33.33 (13/39)	7.69 (3/39)	100 (39)

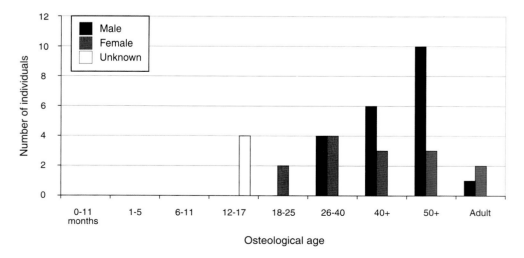

Fig. 6.9   Unnamed sample: Mortality profile (N = 39)

older individuals precisely. Under-ageing of skeletons is a well-recognised methodological problem in osteology (Mays 1998, 50). Sternal rib end degeneration is the only macroscopic method for estimating ages greater than 60 years. Using this method, five individuals (skeletons 4061, 4068, 7005, 7008 and 7009) were aged to greater than 60 years, and three were older than 70 years when they died.

The overall age profile of the unnamed sample was that of an ageing population. This correlates with the osteological age distribution of the named sample and is also consistent with biographical data (see Chapter 4).

Stature

It was possible to estimate stature in 28 of the 35 adults of the unnamed assemblage. The mean stature of males (N = 16) was estimated at 1.715 m

Table 6.16: Unnamed sample: Summary of the skeletal pathology (N = 39)

Skeleton No	Age category	Sex	Infection	Joint disease	Congenital	Trauma	Metabolic	Interventions
1084	40-44 y	male		OA, SDJD				
1097	35-50 y	male						
1129	14-15 y	subadult						
1142	50+ y	possible male		OA, SDJD, DJD				
2042	30-40 y	female		OA, SDJD				
3007	20-24 y	female						
3013	30-40 y	male						
3017	12-13 y	subadult						
3044	45-51 y	male	partly healed periostitis femoral shafts	SDJD		Right 4th meta-tarsal haematoma		
3083	37-44 y	female						
3087	44-48 y	male						
3093	44-54 y	male		OA; SDJD				
4029	24-31 y	female						
4032	35-42 y	male						
4052	adult	female						
4054	33-46 y	male		SDJD				
4061	59-71 y	male	active periostitis R tibial shaft	OA; SDJD				
4068	63-71 y	female		OA; DJD				
4077	35-44 y	male						craniotomy
5028	40-50 y	female		SDJD				
5042	60+ y	possible male		OA; SDJD				
5051	adult	female		DJD; SDJD				
6055	50+ y	male		DJD				
6059	40-49 y	female		OA				
6060	40-44 y	male						
6111	14-15 y	subadult					Cribra orbitalia	
6129	50+ y	male		OA;DJD;SDJD		3 fractured right ribs		
7001	50+ y	female		DJD; SDJD				
7003	24-27 y	female	possible childbirth complications					
7004	60+ y	female		SDJD				
7005	65-78 y	male		SDJD				
7007	20-24 y	female						
7008	65-78 y	male		OA		crush fracture L3; scoloisis		
7009	65-78 y	male		SDJD; DJD				
7010	25-50 y	female		OA; DJD; SDJD				
7017	50+ y	male						
7049	45-54 y	male		SDJD, DISH				craniotomy
7053	11-13 y	subadult						
7062	35-45 y	male						

or 5ft 6in. Average adult female stature (N = 12) was estimated at 1.658 m or 5ft 3in. Skeleton 1142, the only possible male with measurable long bones, had an estimated stature of 1.641 m or 5ft 4in. Average male stature of the unnamed sample was equivalent to the mean male stature (1.71 m) of the crypt and lower churchyard of St Bride's, London (Roberts and Cox 2003, 308), and two centimetres taller than the Christ Church, Spitalfields, population (Molleson and Cox 1993, 24; *ibid.*). It was the same as the average stature for men from 12 post-medieval sites cited by Roberts and Cox (2003).

The mean female stature of the unnamed group was approximately 10 centimetres taller than their Christ Church, Spitalfields, counterparts (Molleson and Cox 1993, 24), and five centimetres taller than the average female stature of 12 post-medieval populations cited in Roberts and Cox (2003, 308).

Skeletal pathology

Although the skeletons of the unnamed sample were not formally examined for pathology, evidence of trauma, infection, joint disease and metabolic disorders were noted on cursory inspection. Table 6.16 summarises these data. Explanations of the pathology described below may be found in the named assemblage report.

It is important to reiterate that because the skeletons were not formally examined for pathology, a number of more subtle bone modifications may have been overlooked, and hence, disease prevalences may be erroneously low. This is especially true for periostitis and well-healed, well aligned fractures. Thorough examination of vertebrae for pathological conditions was undertaken, however, and hence it is unlikely that the prevalence of SDJD and spinal OA were underestimated.

Infection

Periostitis was observed on two elements only, one femur (TPR 6%) and one tibia (TPR 3). The lesions involved male skeletons 3044 and 4061. On skeleton 3044, a considerable area of partly healed new bone was present on the anterior cortical surface of the distal two-thirds of the left and right femoral diaphyses. This was probably due to the presence of a non-specific infection. Healed new bone formation was also observed on the lateral diaphysis of the right fourth metatarsal of the same skeleton. The underlying cause may have been localised trauma or the ossification of a small haematoma, but the presence of periostitis may suggest a more systemic aetiology for these lesions.

Skeleton 4061 also had experienced localised and non-specific periostitis. A small area of healed new bone growth was present on the anterio-medial aspect of the mid-shaft of the right tibia.

Joint disease

Osteoarthritis and degenerative joint disease (DJD) – Twenty-one individuals (53.85%), twelve males and nine females, showed degenerative joint changes, (identified by the presence of porosity and osteophytosis on the joint surface).

DJD affected the spine in 17 adults of the unnamed assemblage (CPR 48.6 % of adults). Most commonly affected extra-spinal joints were the clavicle (particularly the sterno-clavicular joint) and the carpals and metacarpals of the hands. The last two affected more males than females. Porosity and/or osteophytosis were observed on the extra spinal joints of eight individuals (four males and four females) and the spinal joints of 17 individuals (11 males and six females).

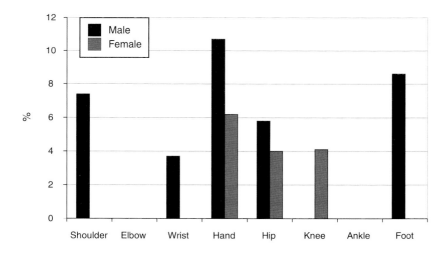

Notes:
Left and right sides combined; Shoulder=gleno-humeral and acromio-clavicular; elbow = distal humerus, and proximal radius and ulna; wrist=distal ulna and radius, scaphoid, lunate; hand=multiple joints except those relating to wrist; Knee=any compartment; ankle=distal tibia and fibula and talus; foot=multiple joints except those relating to ankle.

Fig. 6.10   Unnamed sample: True prevalence of osteoarthritis

Table 6.17: Unnamed sample: True prevalence of osteoarthritis in different joints

	Males	%	Females	%
Shoulder	2 / 27	7.4	0 / 24	0
Elbow	0 / 35	0	0 /25	0
Wrist	1 / 27	3.7	0 / 22	0
Hand	3 / 28	10.7	1 / 16	6.2
Hip	2 / 34	5.8	1 / 25	4
Knee	0 / 35	0	1 / 24	4.1
Ankle	0 / 28	0	0 / 20	0
Foot	2 / 23	8.6	0 / 19	0

Lefts and right sides combined; Shoulder=gleno-humeral and acromio-clavicular; elbow=distal humerus, and proximal radius and ulna; wrist=distal ulna and radius, scaphoid, lunate; hand=multiple joints except those relating to wrist; Knee=any compartment; ankle=distal tibia and fibula and talus; foot=multiple joints except those relating to ankle.

Osteoarthritis (OA) was identified from eburnation only OA was present in 11 individuals (CPR 31%; 11/35 adults)- seven males (33.3%, 4/21 males) and four females (28.6%, 4/14 females). In common with the named sample, it is most probable that the high prevalence of these bony changes was associated with the older age distribution within the sample. All but one individual (skeleton 2042), who only manifested with DJD, had an average osteological age above 40 years.

Distribution of osteoarthritis across the skeleton indicated that in the unnamed Sample, the hands (TPR 9.1%) were most commonly affected, followed by the feet (TPR 4.8%), the hip (TPR 5.1%), the shoulder (TPR 3.9%), the wrist (TPR 2%), and the knee (TPR 1.7%). Males suffered more from OA in all the above joints, with the exception of the knee, which affected one female. (Fig. 6.10; Table 6.17). This pattern broadly echoes the distribution of lesions in the named sample. The predominance of OA in males at St George's differs from modern western populations where OA occurs with more frequency and severity in females (Denko 2003, 235). This difference, in part, may be explained by the greater longevity of males in this assemblage. It should be borne in mind, however, that the assemblages of St George's were fairly small.

Diffuse idiopathic skeletal hyperostosis (DISH) – DISH was observed in one individual from the unnamed sample (skeleton 7049). Thoracic vertebrae 4 to 12 were fused together along the right side, displaying the dripping candle wax appearance characteristic of this disease (Rogers and Waldron 1995). Vertebrocostal joints of the right ribs 7, 8, 10 and 12, and left ribs 7, 8, 9 and 12 showed pronounced ossification of the costal cartilage, resulting in the fusion of these joints. The sterno-clavicular joints were likewise fused. No other osteoblastic changes, such as enthesopathies, were noted on other parts of the skeleton.

The age of male skeleton 7049 (45-54 years) is typical of most DISH sufferers, where age of onset of the disease usually occurs from 50 years onwards.

Trauma

There was relatively little evidence for trauma. The fourth right metatarsal of skeleton 3044, an adult male, displayed new bone formation, probably secondary to localised trauma or an ossified haematoma. Without radiography, a differential diagnosis cannot be made. Adult male skeleton 6129 had fractured three mid-thoracic ribs on the right side, whilst one fracture of the right rib was found in skeleton 3087. This gives a true prevalence of 3.96% of right ribs, or 2.1% of all ribs present. Slight thickening of the shafts was evident adjacent to the necks of the three ribs of skeleton 6129, and on a shaft fragment in skeleton 3087. The lesions were well healed and evidently of long standing. Rib fractures are usually the result of a direct blow to the ribcage, or a direct fall onto the affected side (Roberts and Manchester 1995, 77). Interestingly, skeleton 3087 appeared accident prone, as his left clavicle and left humerus displayed healed fractures, also.

Skeleton 7008 had suffered a crush fracture of the body of the third lumbar vertebra. Crush or compression fractures result when a sudden excessive force is applied to the bone in the vertical plane and the bone is compressed along the plane of impact (Ortner and Putchar 1981, 56, forming a wedge shaped vertebral body. In many cases, this condition occurs in individuals where the bone is already weakened by underlying osteoporosis of the spinal column (ibid.). It was not possible to determine, through macroscopic analysis alone, whether skeleton 7008 had osteoporosis. Widespread osteophytosis of vertebral bodies C4 to L1 was, however, present. The body of L3 was compressed on the left side. This wedging resulted in a left sided displacement of the spinal column, or scoloisis.

Metabolic disorders

The bone of the upper lateral right eye socket of adolescent skeleton 6111 displayed a mixture of small and large foramina, characteristic of Type 3 cribra orbitalia (Stuart-Macadam 1991, 109). In skeleton 6111, another symptom of childhood stress, dental enamel hypoplasia, was also present. Marked lines of thinned enamel were evident on 27 out of 28 tooth crowns. The number of lines per tooth varied between one and five, indicating at least five prolonged episodes of illness or malnutrition in the first six to seven years of life. Adolescent 6111 appeared to have suffered chronic or recurrent and prolonged episodes of ill health for much of his or her short life.

Craniotomy

The skulls of two male skeletons (4077 and 7049) had undergone post-mortem craniotomies. In both cases, the skull had been opened in the horizontal plane with the incision through the frontal, parietal and occipital bones. Skeleton 7049 had further skeletal evidence of dissection: seven ribs and the manubrium of the sternum had been sawn through in order to open up the thoracic cavity to reveal the heart and lungs.

The number of craniotomies in the St George's assemblages was unexpected (see discussion above), but, given the number of medical doctors buried in the crypt, it is possible that at least some volunteered their bodies to science. The breast-plate (8122) of a John Scott M.D., who died on the 30th of July 1849, aged 66 years, was found loose in one of the northern vaults. Although it is highly speculative to tie this name to the skeleton of the older of the two unnamed dissected skeletons, it nevertheless interesting to note that at least one unnamed male skeleton in the crypt was that of a medical practitioner. It seems probable that skeletons 4077 and 7049 were either medical doctors or individuals who placed a very high value on the advancement of medical knowledge.

Dental pathology

The results and prevalence of dental diseases are summarised in Table 6.18 below.

Caries and abscesses

Thirty-eight carious lesions were recorded in the 470 teeth present (8.09%). This prevalence is comparable with caries rates from the broadly contemporary burial group from St Bartholomew's church, Wolverhampton (8.10%), but is lower than those cited from contemporary middle class crypt populations of St Nicholas', Sevenoaks (14.07%) and Christ Church, Spitalfields (17.99 %) (cited in Roberts and Cox 2003, 326).

The rate of abscess formation was 4 out of a total of 865 sockets present (0.462%). This prevalence is broadly comparable to those found at St Bartholomew's church, Wolverhampton (0.35%), and at St Nicholas' church, Sevenoaks (0.4%) (ibid.).

Periodontal disease

Bony changes as a result of periodontal disease were observed in 14 individuals with existing jaws (38.8%, N=36). The severity of the retraction of the alveolar bone was graded as slight, moderate or considerable (Brothwell 1981). Three individuals manifested with slight retraction, one with slight to moderate, seven with moderate, one with moderate to considerable, and two with considerable periodontal disease.

Ante mortem tooth loss (AMTL)

Thirty of the 36 individuals with extant maxillae and/or mandibles had suffered the loss of least one tooth before death (83.3%). Total AMTL was observed in five skeletons (3044, 4068, 7001, 7004 and 7005). The prevalence of AMTL per socket was 32.83% (284/865). The high rate of tooth loss probably reflects poor oral hygiene and the aged nature of the unnamed population, since dental disease is accumulative with age. It was impossible to distinguish between those teeth lost as a result of caries, and those deliberately extracted by a tooth-puller or dentist. The rate of AMTL amongst the unnamed sample was broadly comparable with St Nicholas's Church, Sevenoaks (37.95 %) and the Quaker cemetery of Kingston-upon-Thames (34.61%), but considerably higher than the rate from Christ Church, Spitalfields (12.5%) (ibid.). This discrepancy may be due to the larger proportion of subadults in the last population, compared to the St George's crypt sample.

Calculus

Calculus was observed in 17 of the 20 individuals examined in the unnamed sample (85%). The prevalence per tooth was 60.08% (162/266). This is higher than the mixed class population of St Luke's church, Islington (Boyle *et al* 2005) (46.33%) and the working class population of the Newcastle Infirmary (55.85%) (ibid.).

Dental enamel hypoplasia

Dental enamel hypoplasia (DEH) was recorded on 12 individuals in the unnamed sample. Seventy-eight of a total of 216 tooth crowns with clearly visible buccal surfaces displayed DEH (36.11%). The number of lines varied between one and five lines per tooth. In the majority of cases, the lines were clearly visible but not marked. An exception was adolescent skeleton 6111, where the DEH lines were very numerous and very marked, suggesting at least five episodes of prolonged ill health in childhood.

Dental interventions

The wealthy upper-middle class assemblage within St George's crypt displayed a considerable amount of dental work, including the filing of carious teeth, the filling of caries with various metals (such as gold, mercury amalgam and lead), and the use of prostheses, such as crowns, bridges and dentures. Dental treatment is discussed more fully in the named sample report above.

In the unnamed sample, two full sets of dentures, and three partial dentures were discovered buried with their owners. Of these, three had gold plates onto which human or porcelain tooth crowns were riveted (skeletons 3044, 4032 and 7010) (Plate 6.6, skeleton 4032). One partial denture was formed from a block of carved ivory (skeleton 7008).

Table 6.18: Unnamed sample: Summary of the dental pathology and dental interventions

Coffin No	Abscesses	Calculus	Caries	DEH	Crowding	Peridontal disease	AMTL	Teeth present	PMTL	Not present	Total sockets	Dental interventions
1084	0									32	0	
1097	0	10	3	6	present		7	22	3	0	32	V-shaped notches
1129	0	4	3				0	27	1	4	28	
1142	0		0			slight	8	7	2	15	17	
2042	0	9	5	4			8	11	2	11	21	
3007	0		0				3	22	7	0	32	
3013								0		32	0	
3017	0		0				0	20	1	11	21	
3044	0						32	0	0	0	32	2 full gold sets
3083	0	11	1		present	moderate	3	16	0	13	19	
3087	1	15	2	5		moderate	3	20	0	9	23	U-shaped notches
3093	2	6	1	6		moderate to considerable	7	22	2	1	31	
4029	0	4	4	3			1	7	0	24	8	
4032	1	14	2	8	present	slight to moderate	1	27	4	0	32	
4052					present			0		32	0	partial gold denture
4054	0	14	0	7	present	moderate	7	21	1	3	29	
4061	0	4	3			considerable	21	8	3	0	32	
4068	0						27	0	0	5	27	
4077	0	18	0	6	present	slight	3	20	0	9	23	
5028	0	21	3	1		moderate	6	21	5	2	32	
5042	0	1	0			moderate	16	1	7	8	24	
5051	0	23	0	5		slight	4	23	0	5	27	
6055	0	2	0	1		moderate	6	6	0	20	12	
6059	0	0	0				9	3	2	18	14	
6060								0		32	0	
6111	0	0	1	26			0	28	0	4	28	Pb or Hg amalgam filling
6129	0						32	0	0	0	32	
7001	0						16	0	0	16	16	
7003	0	0	0			moderate	1	13	0	18	14	
7004	0						32	0	0	0	32	
7005	0						29	0	0	3	29	
7007	0				present		0	5	10	17	15	anterior ivory block
7008	0	0	0				12	3	1	16	16	
7009	0		2			considerable	5	18	4	5	27	
7010	0	3	4				15	8	6	3	29	
7017	0	3	1		present		0	20	2	10	22	partial gold denture
7049	0						6	22	4	0	32	
7053	0	3	0				0	26	0	6	26	
7062	0		3				2	23	4	1	31	
Prevalence	4/865	162/266	38/470	78/216	7	14/35	284/865					
Percentage	0.462%	60.09%	8.09%	36.11%		40%	32.83%					

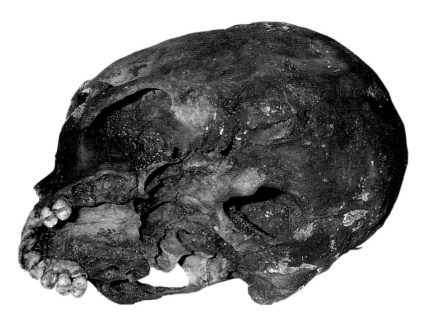

Plate 6.6   Skeleton 4032 wearing a gold partial denture

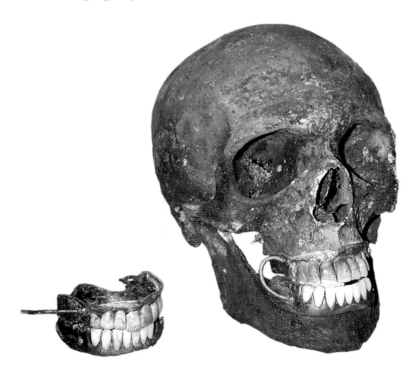

Plate 6.7   Skeleton 3044 wearing one set of swagged dentures. A second pair was found within his coffin

Skeleton 3044 was buried wearing a full set of dentures (Plate 6.7). An extra pair of dentures had been placed within his coffin. Both pairs of dentures were constructed of a gold plate onto which porcelain teeth had been riveted by means of gold pins. The upper and lower dentures were joined by gold springs.

U- and V-shaped notches cut into the enamel and underlying dentine at the cemento-enamel junction were observed on the teeth of skeletons 1097 and 3093 respectively. They appear to have been cut in order to facilitate the attachment of ligatures to hold partial dentures in place.

One individual (skeleton 6111) had a single filling of grey metal (probably lead or mercury amalgam) in his right first mandibular molar.

DISCUSSION OF THE NAMED AND UNNAMED SAMPLES

Demography

The mortality profile for the entire assemblage (111 individuals) reflects an ageing population consisting largely of adults (Fig. 6.11). Subadults are under-represented (Tables 6.6 and 6.15). The longevity of the population probably reflects the affluence, and hence, the better health and living conditions enjoyed by this population. These results are comparable with the age at death distribution established using *depositum* plates (see Table 6.7 and discussion above), bearing in mind the under representation of infants in the osteological sample as a result of preservation.

A large proportion of the assemblage comprised males, 53% (n = 59/111) compared to 39% (n = 43/111), which were female. There is an observed tendency for female skeletons, particularly the skull, to become more masculine in appearance following the menopause, and this may lead to bias in sex estimation in favour of males in skeletal assemblages (Mays and Cox 2000). However, for the present assemblage, this result would seem to reflect a reality because the sex distribution given by *depositum* plates also reflects a bias towards males (see Table 6.7).

Interestingly, greater longevity is reflected among males than females, and these differences do not immediately appear due to death during childbirth, as only two females in the osteological sample were attributed to the young adult category. There is a sharp rise in female mortality, however, in the prime adult age category. It is interesting to consider the extent that this may reflect a social practice of pregnancies and childbirth among females of prime adult ages in this community. A memorial plaque

within the church commemorates Mary Madden, who died in childbirth, and the death of her newborn son five days later. She was only 26 years old. However, the absence of young females in the osteological sample is not borne out by the total population (N=621) whose sexes are known from the coffin plate inscriptions. Here, 19 young females (2.81%) were identified. Differences in the number of young females according to osteological data and biographical data probably reflect inadvertent bias implicit in the small sample size.

Health status

Overall, the demographic structure, oral and skeletal health, and evidence of expensive dentistry within the entire assemblage are consistent with an affluent population. These individuals enjoyed a comparatively low childhood mortality rate, and a large proportion of the adult population lived into old age, many dying beyond their 70s. They were nevertheless susceptible to many illnesses. Some experienced diseases associated with fine living and expensive taste. One such disease was DISH, another was dental decay. Dental disease was widespread in this population, and a number had taken recourse to painful and expensive dental treatments of the day, such as fillings, implants, dentures and filings, despite their many inadequacies. Implants often invited new problems, such as dental abscesses. The emphasis on slender waists in women appears also have created new health problems for a few women, with tight-lacing causing deformation of the ribs in one female.

Fashionable infant feeding practices may underlie the higher prevalence of iron deficiency anaemia in this population than that found amongst the poor of the city. Again, the affluence of this

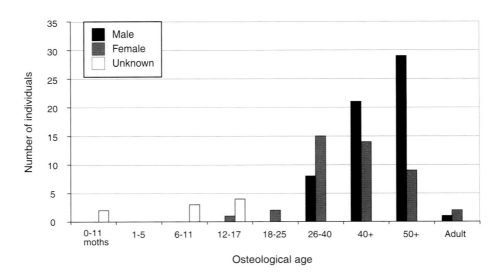

Fig. 6.11   *Named and unnamed samples combined: Mortality profile based on osteological age (N=111)*

Bloomsbury set would have enabled them to pay for a nursemaid to care for the child, replacing breastmilk with gruel at a very tender age, to the detriment of the child's health.

Although Bloomsbury was famed as one of the more genteel and healthier parts of the city, its residents could not entirely escape the health effects of living in the overcrowded, polluted and poorly planned and regulated city that was late Georgian London. Evidence for infectious diseases, such as tuberculosis, was present in the assemblage, as well as the much feared French Pox. Indeed, a gentleman did not have to stray far from the church in his search for vice, both in less salubrious areas, such as the Rookery (Plate 4.3), or in more elegant establishments in Bloomsbury itself. Some paid for these pleasures dearly.

Many of those interred within St George's crypt survived to old age, and suffered the many the aches and pains that flesh is heir to, with high levels of age-related pathologies, such as degenerative joint disease, osteoarthritis, dental decay and tooth loss. This ageing population also displayed another disease common to older populations – cancer – a disease rarely seen elsewhere in the palaeopathological record.

Chapter 7: Examination of methods used to estimate osteological age and sex

by Ceridwen Boston and Louise Loe

AGE AT DEATH METHODS

Adults

The ages of 52 adults that were studied osteologically were known from the biographical data. This presented a rare opportunity to examine the performance of a number of the osteological ageing techniques described in Chapter 6. Osteological analysis was undertaken without knowing the identity or age of the skeleton beforehand. Osteological age was then compared with chronological age, in order to assess the accuracy and precision of the ageing methods used.

A maximum of six methods was used on skeletons aged over 28 years. Two additional methods (dental development and epiphyseal fusion) were used in adults aged younger than 28 years. The results of these two methods are discussed in the subadult ageing section below. The number of ageing methods used on each skeleton was limited by the bone preservation and completeness of the individual. Table 7.1 summarises the number of ageing methods employed on this assemblage.

The most commonly used adult ageing method was the auricular surface degeneration scoring system published by Lovejoy *et al* (1985), which was applied to 47 (90.38%) skeletons (Table 7.2). This high number reflects the good survival rate because of the relatively high bone density of the articular surface. The next most common ageing method involved observations relating to cranial suture obliteration, which was applied to 41 (78.84%)

skeletons. Unlike many skeletons in less protected burial environments, the sternal end of 4th rib was often well preserved in the named sample from St George's, and was used to age 27 (51.92%) individuals. The Suchey-Brooks system was used on the pubic symphyses of 28 (53.85%) skeletons, and the Todd method on 26 (50%) individuals. Roden's (1997) dental attrition scoring was used to age 14 individuals (26.92%).

Some interesting observations were made when the results of these ageing methods were compared to the chronological ages of the individuals (known from the coffin plate inscriptions). The accuracy and precision of each ageing method is discussed individually below. The osteological age at death obtained by each method and the actual age of the individual is presented in Table 7.3

Auricular surface

When comparing the osteological age ranges provided by the auricular surface with the chronological age at death, 21 (44.68%) individuals were aged correctly; 18 (38.30%) were osteologically under-aged by an average of 13 years, and eight individuals (17.02%) were over-aged by an average of 5.5 years. All the young adults (n = 2), and a 22.22% (n = 2) of the prime adults were correctly aged. Five prime adults (62.5%) were over-aged, and one (11.11%) was under-aged. Of those individuals aged between 40 and 50 years, 60% (n = 3) were aged correctly and 40% (n = 2) were over-aged. Of the individuals aged over 50, 44.16% (n =

Table 7.1: Quantification of age assessment methods used per skeleton (N= 52)

Number of methods used	6	5	4	3	2	1	Total
Number of individuals	3	13	8	13	13	2	52
% of individuals	5.77%	25%	15.38%	25%	25%	3.85%	100%

Table 7.2 Quantification of ageing methods used (N= 52)

Auricular surface (n/N)	Suture closure (n/N)	Sternal rib end (n/N)	Pubic symphysis (Suchey-Brooks) (n/N)	Pubic symphysis (Todd) (n/N)	Dental attrition (n/N)
90.38% (47/52)	78.84% (41/52)	51.92% (27/52)	53.85% (28/52)	50% (26/52)	26.92% (14/52)

Table 7.3 Chronological age of adults compared with biological age (N = 52). All ages are given in years.

Skeleton Number	Chronological age at death	Auricular surface age	Cranial suture closure age	Dental attrition age	Pubic symphysis age (Suchey and Brooks)	Pubic symphysis age (Todd)	Sternal rib end age
1041	83	>60	35-56		34-86	>50years	43-55
1052	56	50-55		25-31	23-57	40-45	54-64
1055	85	50-55	45-55		27-66	45-49	
1057	57	40-50	43-46		27-86	45-49	34-42
1059	23	20-25					24-32
1068	71	50-59	35-60				
1077	58	50-59	>40	36	27-86	45-49	
1527	70	50-55	>50				
1564	81	>60	>40		27-66	45-49	65-78
2006	57	40-44	45-52	31-36	25-83	>45	43-71
2008	27	31-44	45-53	24-25	21-53	27-35	34-46
2020	38	30-34	39	30-31			
3002	77	54	40-49	42			
3022	57	>60	40-50				43-58
3085	77	45-50	45-51	45			
3090	63	45-55	40-52	38-44	27-66		54-64
4002	86	50-55	45-55				
4003	78		35-57				70-82
4007	80	>60	22-40		21-46	30-39	
4011	64	>60	34-57		27-66	45-49	65-78
4013	43	45-50			27-66	40-45	34-42
4017	75	50-54	>40				
4019	44	40-44	35-52				
4024	28	40-49	45-58				33-46
4035	41	40-44	32-51				
4036	55	45-49	35-57				
4047	49	55-60	45-51				
4049	57	50-55	40-50		27-66	45-49	
4065	81	54-63			42-87		59-71
4069	82	>60	41-52		27-66	>50	26-32
4070	56	50-54	43-52				34-54
4073	68	50-54	>50		27-66	45-49	
4074	65	40-44	30-45				24-32
4075	69	>60	35-58	42-51	34-86	>50	43-55
5007	36	35-39		25	21-57	27-35	26-32
5012	53		45-52	31-38	27-66	45-49	
5039	84	>60			34-86	>50	65-78
5041	67	>63					38-52
5043	52	40-44	45-56		27-66	30-35	32-46
5056	86		40-52		34-86	>50	
5070	62	45-50	43-53		27-66	45-49	55-64
5071	55	45-60	34-58				
6048	39	45-55	40-52		23-57	40-45	43-55
6071	27	30-34			19-40	22-24	
6085	21	20-25					
6110	26				21-53	22-26	
6121	35	30-35	40-50	25-30			
7006	33	35-39			26-70	30-39	
7016	78	>55	>50				
7043	62		>50	30			54-64
7045	60	50-59	40-50	24-30			33-46
7081	41	35-44	35-45		26-70	35-39	33-46

14) were correctly aged and 54.84% (n = 17) were under-aged.

It therefore appears that the method worked well for young adults, but greater inaccuracy was noted in the prime, mature and ageing adult categories. The general tendency was to over-age prime and mature adults and to under-age individuals older than 50 years.

Cranial suture closure

Ageing by cranial suture closure was undertaken on 41 individuals. The accuracy of this method was poor, however, and only 15 (36.58%) individuals were correctly aged. Twenty-one (51.22%) skeletons were under-aged by an average of 17.52 years, and five (12.19%) individuals were over-aged by a mean of 10.4 years. All skeletons that were under-aged were in the 50+ age category. Those that were under-aged were all prime adults.

This method is based on the assumption that the cranial sutures fuse in a predictable sequence from about age 30 to 50 years. The poor correlation between osteological and chronological age indicates considerable individual variation in the timing of suture closure.

Dental attrition

None of the 14 individuals were correctly aged by this method, on average being under-aged by 19 years. The prime adults were under-aged by 6.25 years and the individuals in the 50+ category by an average of 26.78 years. This clearly shows that the method became more inaccurate with increasing age. It is therefore clear that this method cannot be used for this type of post-medieval population, but further research is required to establish its usefulness in skeletal assemblages composed of working class individuals.

Pubic symphysis

Ageing methods based on degeneration of the pubic symphysis developed by Brooks and Suchey (1990) and Todd (1921a and 1921b) were incorporated and contrasted. The Suchey-Brooks method correctly aged 23 of the 28 skeletons examined (82.14%). Five (17.86%) individuals were under-aged by an average of 17.2 years. All individuals that were under-aged were in the 50+ years age category. The lack of precision of the Suchey-Brooks system (evidenced in large age ranges using a 95% confidence interval) does however limit its usefulness.

The Todd method was applied to 26 individuals, of whom 10 (38.46%) were correctly aged. The method under-aged 14 (53.84%) individuals by a mean of 14.64 years. Two individuals (7.69%) were over-aged by an average of seven years.

Sternal rib ends

Ageing from degenerative changes to the sternal rib end is a method that is not commonly available to osteoarchaeologists, due to the poor survival of this fragile element, but at St George's preservation of this element was fairly good. The method specifies that the fourth rib is used, but in this study a rib from the mid-chest region (not necessarily the fourth rib) was chosen. This was necessary due to the fragmentation of rib shafts that made specific identification of the fourth rib problematic. The advantage with this method is that individuals that may be osteologically aged up to 78 years. Theoretically, this enables ageing of older individuals beyond the 50-60 years limit of other ageing methods.

Of the 27 skeletons aged using this method, 10 (37.04%) were aged correctly; thirteen (48.15%) were over-aged by an average of 13.61 years, and four (14.81%) were under-aged by an average of 5.5 years.

Statistical analysis

Statistical analysis was undertaken to examine the correlation between known age at death and osteological age at death, as described above. Two types of analysis were performed: multiple linear regression and curve fitting on the scattergrams of the individual age indicators. The results of these analyses are detailed and discussed in Appendix 2 and summarised here.

Multiple linear regression

This analysis examined the correlation between known age at death and all age indicators combined. The incompleteness of data meant that only a combination of four of the six ageing methods could be used on a total of 13 skeletons. The methods incorporated were those that relate to the pubic symphysis (Brooks and Suchey 1990), the sternal rib end, cranial suture closure and the auricular surface. For the 13 individuals, the results showed a high degree of correlation between known age at death and osteological age ($R=0.836$; $P=0.031$), with the auricular surface making the greatest contribution to this result (Appendix 2). The results also showed systematic under estimation of the ages of older adults, a result that is consistent with those reported by Molleson and Cox (1993, 171) who tested osteological ageing methods against known age at death in a sample from Spitalfields. However, unlike Spitalfields, the present sample showed no systematic over estimation of the age of young adults. This difference may be because the auricular surface ageing method was not employed in Molleson and Cox's study.

Regression of the individual age indicators

This analysis examined the correlation between each individual age indicator with known age at death. All six ageing methods were examined for all

52 individuals using different numbers and combinations of individuals, depending on the availability of data (see Table 7.3). Lines of best fit were computed using graphs as visual summaries. Results showed that the auricular surface has the highest correlation with known age at death (coefficient of correlation=0.454; N=47), followed by dental attrition (coefficient of correlation=0.418; N=15), then the pubic symphysis (Suchey-Brooks: coefficient of correlation=0.175; N=28; Todd: coefficient of correlation=0.378; N=26), with the sternal rib end in fourth place (coefficient of correlation=0.191; N=28). Virtually no correlation with age was shown by the results for cranial suture closure (coefficient of correlation=0.002; N=41).

Discussion of ageing methods

All ageing methods contain a degree of error due to variability in ageing processes between individuals, which is dependent on a complex interplay of genetic and activity related factors (Mays and Cox 2000). It is therefore impossible to assign an age with 100% accuracy. Moreover, inter-observer error in age estimation also may also be responsible for discrepancies in ageing, particularly among less experienced osteologists. However, by using multiple methods and broad age categories it was hoped that a high degree of accuracy was obtained (ibid.).

Overall, all ageing methods, except dental attrition, were found to be very accurate when applied to adults younger than 30 years of age. This trend was also reflected when statistical analyses were performed. Poorer correlation between osteological and chronological age was found in the 30 and 50 years age categories, with some methods underageing, and others over-ageing individuals by as much as 10-15 years. This variability is illustrated in three individuals (skeletons 2008, 7045 and 7081) that were chosen at random (Figs 7.1-7.3).

Overall, ageing methods tend to under-age skeletons by approximately 15 years. This trend is particularly apparent in the ageing population of St George's, as under-ageing became more pronounced with increasing age. It also highlighted the paucity of osteological ageing methods for skeletons older than 40 years. These findings are also supported by statistical curve fitting.

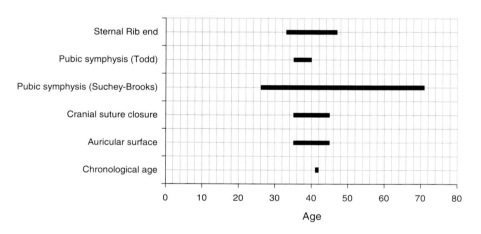

Fig. 7.1   Skeleton 7081: comparison of age determinations using different ageing methods

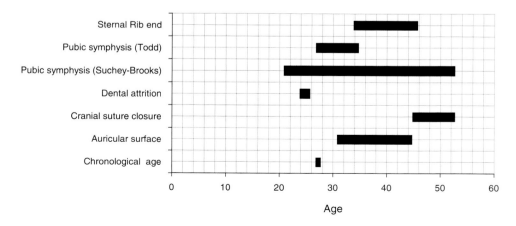

Fig. 7.2   Skeleton 2008: comparison of age determinations using different ageing methods

To conclude, more ages estimated with the Suchey-Brooks system correlated with known age at death than those using other indicators did (Fig. 7.4). However, statistical analysis indicated that the auricular surface was the most accurate method. Further, although the wide age ranges in each phase ensure a high accuracy, they render the Suchey Brookes method all but meaningless. The sternal rib end method appears useful for ageing older adults as this is the only method with age categories that continued into the ninth decade of life. The indicator with the lowest percentage of accuracy was dental attrition (Figure 4.5), but multiple linear regression and regression analysis showed cranial suture closure to be the least reliable method.

Subadults

The chronological ages of four subadults were known from coffin plate inscriptions. These individuals were aged osteologically using a maximum of three methods (Table 4.11). Due to the small sample size, this section will only contain a general discussion of the results since any attempt to quantify accuracy of these methods is meaningless.

Discussion of ageing methods

Observations on dental development were employed to age three subadults. The results were correlated with chronological age (Table 7.4).

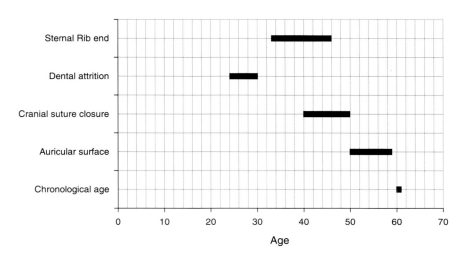

Fig. 7.3   Skeleton 7045: comparison of age determinations using different ageing methods

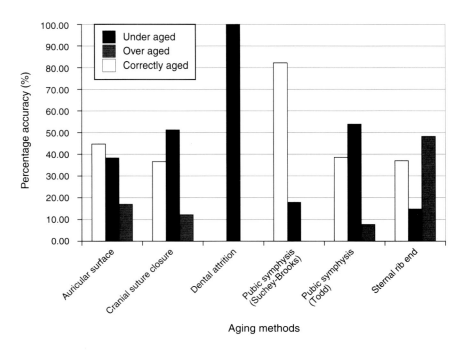

Fig. 7.4   Bar graph showing percentage accuracy in ageing methods (N=52)

Table 7.4 Chronological age of subadults compared with biological age

Skeleton Number	Age at Death (years)	Age at Death (months)	Age at Death (days)	Dental development	Epiphyseal fusion	Long bone length
3041			17	0 – 5 months		40 – 40 weeks
3064	6			6 – 8 years	4 – 6 years	5 – 5 years
4039		19			0 – 1 years	1 – 1.1 years
5049	15			12 – 16 years	16 – 17 years	

Ageing by epiphyseal fusion provided a more random result, with two of the three children under-aged, and one over-aged by a year. Similar results were obtained using diaphyseal long bone measurements, in which two of the three were under-aged.

The methods used to age the subadults provided impressive results with a high level of accuracy and narrow age ranges. Dental development was more accurate than skeletal development. There was a greater tendency to under-age than over-age subadults. Saunders and Hoppa (1993), using the known aged assemblage from St Thomas' church, Belleville, Ontario, found little or no discrepancy between modern growth curves for long bones and this 19th-century Canadian population. They concluded that most subadults in archaeological populations died of acute illness, and hence, did not suffer retarded skeletal development before death. This was not the case with the two children from St George's, who did display delayed epiphyseal fusion and stunting before death. This argues for a more chronic pattern of ill health, possibly due to a single specific chronic disease or disorder (e.g. tuberculosis), or from a repeated onslaught of different environmental stressors from which the children never recovered. No such pattern was observed in the adolescent (5049), where dental and epiphyseal fusion ages broadly concurred.

Sexing methods

All subadults and any adult individual with an unknown real and/or osteological sex were omitted from the analysis. The sex of 65 adults recorded osteologically was known from coffin plate inscriptions, and 68 adults could be sexed osteologically. Of the former, 36 (55.39%) were male and 29 (44.62%) were female. Of the latter, 36 (52.94%) were male, 30 (44.12%) were female and the sex of two (2.94%) could not be determined. Only one individual (a female) had been sexed incorrectly- an accuracy of 98.46%.

It was clear that some features of the cranium and pelvis were more representative of the documented sex of the individuals than others, and that the pelvis was markedly more reliable in determining sex than the cranium (Table 7.5). Sex estimation from pelvic morphology was found to be the most

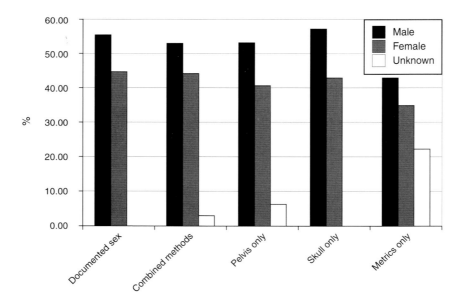

Fig. 7.5 Percentages of adult males and females estimated using different methodologies (N = 63)

144

accurate method (Fig. 7.5). This was not unexpected (see discussion in methodology section above). Sex estimation from pelvic morphology also produced the lowest intermediate values, as well as probable males and females.

Considerably more males were diagnosed from skull morphology alone. In addition, a high proportion of probable males and females was also estimated using these features. During the analysis it was noted that many female crania displayed several masculine traits, particularly those in the older age categories.

By contrast, skeletons sexed from metrics resulted in a preponderance of females. There was also a large number whose sex could not be determined (Table 7.5 and Fig. 4.6). Of all the methods employed, this one was the least reliable.

Table 7.5 Sex determination per method used (N=63)

Sex	Pelvic sex (n/N)	Cranial sex (n/N)	Metric sex (n/N)
Female?	4.69% (3/64)	20.63% (13/63)	6.35% (4/63)
Female	35.94%	22.22%	28.57%
Male?	3.12% (2/64)	7.94% (5/63)	14.29% (9/63)
Male	50.0% (32/64)	49.21% (31/63)	28.57% (18/63)
Indeterminate	6.25% (4/64)	0.0% (0/63)	22.22% (14/63)

Chapter 8: Burial practice and material culture

by Ceridwen Boston

BURYING THE DEAD OF THE PARISH

The burial ground

One of the general principles adopted by the Commissioners and embodied in the supplementary Act of 1712 relates to the burial grounds of new churches. It was determined that these should be sited some distance from the churches. The architect Vanburgh had demanded churches should be

> free'd from that Inhuman custom of being made Burial Places for the Dead. A Custome in which there is something so very barbarous in itself besides the many ill consequences that attend it. . . . There is now a sort of happy necessity on this occasion of breaking through it, since there can be no thought of purchasing ground for church yards, where the churches will probably be placed . . . there must therefore be cemeteries provided in the skirts of the Towne . . .

The restricted area of the churchyard of St George did not allow for extramural burial on anything but a minor scale. As a result, the Commissioners had little choice but to purchase a separate piece of land to serve as the parish burial ground. In 1713 a three acre site costing £300 was purchased for the purpose. It was situated to the north-east of Brunswick Square in the parish of St Pancras, immediately to the north of the Foundling Hospital (see Fig. 4.3 above). The north half of the site was for the use of St George's church, while the south was used by the neighbouring parish church of St George the Martyr.

By 1845, several tombs were falling down, and the ground had a wild and desolate appearance. By 1855, the burial ground was full and had to be closed. It was subsequently developed into a public recreation ground. The gravestones were moved to the surrounding walls, and only a few large tombs remain *in situ*. Today most of the inscriptions are illegible. However, Frederick Teague Cansick recorded and published an illustrated record of the 981 inscriptions that were still decipherable (Cansick 1869). As one would expect of a prosperous parish like Bloomsbury, the names included a large number of professional men and several who had settled or made their fortunes in the colonies. Curtiss Brett, who died in 1784, is commemorated thus:

Twelve times the Great Atlantic crossed | To Fortune paying court | In many a terrible Tempest toss'd | But now I'm safe in Port.

It is likely that the memorials to the more prosperous residents buried in the cemetery are comparable to the affluent residents who chose to be buried in the vaults. It is likely that many of the graves in the cemetery without memorials were the burials of the less affluent residents of the parish.

The crypt

For the first 90 years, the vaults beneath Hawksmoor's church were not used. Proposals to lease them to a wine merchant in 1788 had been considered but rejected, and an alternative proposal to lease them to a brewer was considered totally unsuitable.

The 1801 census shows that the population of Bloomsbury had increased to nearly 8000. The Vestry met in May 1803 to consider

> adopting measures for depositing dead bodies in the vaults under the church as they foresaw the burial ground would otherwise be full within 30 years. It was resolved that an opening be made in the floor of the church and an apparatus constructed from thence into the vaults.

The fee for this privilege was 10 guineas if buried under the church and 14 guineas if buried under the chancel. It was a condition that all bodies be encased within lead coffins. Clearly the expense both of the interment and the cost of a lead shell precluded all but the more affluent of the parish – a factor that has considerable ramifications when interpreting the social demography and palaeopathology of the skeletal sample from the crypt. Interments in the crypt in lead coffins began in 1803 and continued until 1856.

The earliest interment in the crypt is that of Mrs Mary Ann Watts (coffin 3025) who died in January 1804. She is the only certain interment in 1804. There are 7 burials known from 1805. Over the 53 years that the crypt was in use as a place of burial, the rate of interment varied between 2 and 34 burials per annum, with an average of 12 per year. Throughout its use as a place of burial, the crypt accommodated only a fraction of the total population buried in the parish of St George's, Bloomsbury. Between 1801-1840, parish burial records (including crypt and churchyard burials) list the burials of 8656 individuals, an average of 216.4 per year. Initially crypt burials formed a very small percentage of total burials for the parish. From 1803 to the end of 1810 only 57 crypt burials are known (see above Table 5.1). This is less than 2% of all burials in the parish in the period. In the decade to 1820 there were 152 certain burials (7.78%). Burial in the crypt was most popular in the two decades from 1821 to 1840, with a peak between 1825 and 1833 (see above Fig. 5.1). In these two decides crypt burials formed more than 10% of total burials in the Parish. The single year with most known crypt burials was 1825 with 32. From 1833 the number of burials in the crypt slowly declined. From 1851 to 1856 there are only 11 known burials.

By 1844 the Vestry minutes records that many coffins were by now in so decayed and in such an 'offensive' state that it was decided they should be placed in a side vault and bricked up. From the distribution of post-1844 coffins within Vaults 1 to 7, it is unclear to which side vault the Vestry minutes refer. From the description of the decayed state of some coffins within the crypt in 1844 is not surprising that from the early 1840s onwards only a few interments were still being made in the crypt. There were 64 known burials from 1841 to 1850, and 11 between 1851 and 1856.

The crypt was closed for burial in 1856. The closures of both burial ground and crypt were in part a response to the Burial Act of 1852, which had prohibited further burial within crypts and churchyards in London, in favour of the new garden cemeteries, such as Kensal Green and Highgate (Curl 2002; Friar 2003, 69). In 1856 the St George's vestry finally resolved 'hermetically to seal the entrance to the vaults.' It was made clear that

> parties whose connections lie in the vaults take the necessary steps for the removal of the remains of their connections.

It is unclear to what extent the latter directive was followed. One memorial in the church, however, records the removal of the remains of Sophia (surname illegible) to the family vault in the newly fashionable cemetery of Kensal Green.

There is no record in the Vestry minutes that the churchyard surrounding the church was ever used as a place of burial, and there was no evidence from test pits 1-4 excavated in the churchyard to indicate that there were any burials (Chapter 2). The problem of burial space in the parish was finally resolved by obtaining an allotment in the Woking Cemetery owned by the London Necropolis Company, 'a bad though the best substitute available'.

MATERIAL CULTURE

Historical background

In Britain from the late 17th century onwards, it became customary to cover the coffin with upholstery of baize or velvet, and to decorate the lid and side panels of coffins with studs and metal coffin fittings. By 1700-20 the funeral furnishing trade was a firmly established business, providing fittings for all classes of people and at various costs, depending on the status and wealth of the deceased (Litten 1991). The financial investment in funerary panoply grew over the course of the 18th century, reaching its zenith in the 1840s. Even amongst the poor the importance of providing a decent burial was keenly felt (May 1996). However, for those that could afford it, the coffin itself was just one aspect of the elaborate mourning and funerary practices surrounding the death of a loved one in this period. Funerals of the wealthy frequently involved processions of black draped hearses, black plumed horses, mutes and chief mourners, a complex symbolism involving appropriate mourning dress, grand memorials and, of course, the heavily decorated coffin itself.

However, after the 1840s, public sentiment changed yet again. Increasingly, such effusive displays of mourning were seen as excessive and undesirable. In particular, elaborate expensive funerals began to be regarded as vulgar, ostentatious displays of wealth and status and were increasingly considered to be in poor taste. In this period many caricatures stigmatise undertakers as avaricious vultures, preying on the vulnerability of families in grief, exploiting other peoples' misfortunes and their desire to be seen to 'do the right thing' by the dead. During the middle and later Victorian period a taste for simpler funerals became the norm, and persists with us today. Interestingly, in the further reaches of the old British Empire elements of the earlier burial traditions persist. Coffin fittings very much in the elaborate early Victorian mode were being manufactured in Birmingham and shipped out to the Caribbean, and in particular to Jamaica, as recently as the 1960s. The coffins from St George's church date to the heyday of the late Georgian/early Victorian funerary tradition at its most extravagant.

Early 19th-century perceptions of death

Social historians have often accused the Victorians of a morbid and unhealthy obsession with death. What is clear is that they celebrated this rite of passage more than any other, in terms of preparation for death, funeral ritual, and the long period of mourning that followed it. Victorian deathbed scenes, as depicted in the literature and art of the day, may seem to modern eyes morbid or mawkishly sentimental, but they represent a genuine attempt to confront the awful reality of death, so that when one's time came Death could met with serenity and calm resignation. In a society where the infant mortality rate varied between 20-50% (Rugg 1999), where epidemic infections could sweep through cities with terrifying ease and where medical interventions were still rudimentary and powerless to halt the advance of many diseases, such as tuberculosis, death was a familiar part of life. Rather than deny the very real presence of death in everyday life, the Victorians chose to accept and celebrate it, to give it centre stage. This response may be seen as a very human, understandable and therapeutic confrontation of humanity's deepest fear, rather than being regarded as a morbid fixation.

Rugg (1999) writes that this Victorian concept of a 'good death', death faced with equanimity, came about through a number of ideological and medical developments in the early years of the 19th century. Advances in medical knowledge and a more widespread trust placed in the medical profession lead to a transformation of the deathbed experience, with the doctor's presence being as central to the proceedings as that of the cleric. A heavy reliance on opiates to ease the pain of the dying served to disarm death of much of its terror. Instead of the emphasis on the physical torments of death and the spiritual torments of hell that had so dominated the thinking of earlier generations, the later Georgians and early Victorians were now more able to perceive death as a gentle slipping away, a falling asleep. Christian teaching also changed emphasis in this period. God became much more a God of Love than a God of Vengeance, and instead of hellfire and eternal damnation a gentler concept of the afterlife as heavenly and as an eternal rest developed. Considerable emphasis was placed on heavenly reunion with loved ones in the afterlife, and was a great source of comfort to the bereaved. The ideas of the Romantic movement also had a profound effect on attitudes to death and grieving. The movement's emphasis on individualism and the expression of sentiment made the outward displays of grief more socially acceptable, even desirable, both in an emotional and in a material sense (ibid).

The material culture surrounding death and mourning was particularly rich in the 19th century. Memorials to the dead abounded in many forms. For example, it was common practice to draw or paint the dead or dying, and later in the period, to photograph the corpse. Death masks were sometimes taken of the face or hands of the dead. An example of such effigies was found in the coffin of six year old Anna Stringfield (3064) at St George's church, and will be discussed more fully below. Locks of hair were often collected as keepsakes, or converted into jewellery.

Correct mourning dress was rigidly prescribed, and individuals failing to adhere to social conventions risked social ostracism. The period of mourning varied with the closeness of the relationship. Widows were expected to be in deep mourning for a year and a day following the death of their husband, and to wear only dull lustreless fabrics such as crepe or bombazine. After this they might wear more lustrous fabrics, such as black silk. After two years the widow might go into half-mourning when she was permitted to wear purple or mauve. In addition to prescriptions on dress, the social behaviour of the bereaved was rigidly laid out. For example, a widow might not attend public functions, and was prohibited from re-marriage for a year following the death of her husband. By contrast, a widower could remarry as soon as he pleased, but his new wife was expected to go into mourning for her predecessor (May 1996).

Social display of mourning manifested strongly in funerary ritual, and proved an admirable medium through which the social prominence of the deceased and family could be displayed. The necessity of giving a good 'send-off' to a loved one was felt by all classes of society. Failure to provide an appropriate funeral reflected on an individual's respectability (Richmond 1999), and many poorer individuals beggared themselves in the attempt to put on a decent funerary spectacle (May 1996). This opportunity for social display was not missed by the professional class interred in the crypt of St George's church. May (1996) estimates that the average sum spent on a funeral of this social class was in the region of £100. In addition, the cost of interment within the crypt at St George's was 10 guineas, or 14 guineas-. if, like Dame Caroline Biscoe (coffin 3078), one specifically wished to be buried beneath the chancel (Meller 1975). The richness of the coffins found within the crypt is eloquent testimony of the social ambitions of this class (see Plate 8.8).

Coffins

Coffin materials and construction

Coffins used in the later post-medieval period were of the flat lidded single-break type, and those found at St George's church were no exception. During the Georgian/Victorian period, coffins varied considerably in construction and material, ranging from the simplest unadorned wooden coffins of pauper funerals, to triple layered affairs, heavily adorned with velvet and encrusted with elaborate metal fittings, for the burial of the wealthier classes. The most inexpensive coffins were a simple construction of a single layer of wooden planks, fixed together with iron nails at the corners and along the coffin length. More elaborate wooden coffin constructions were double layered, or possessed a double lid. Some lids were especially designed to foil attempts by 'resurrectionists', or body snatchers, to open the coffin and steal the corpse for later sale to anatomy schools for dissection (Litten 1991). The wooden coffin may or may not have been upholstered and decorated with metal coffin fittings, depending on the wealth and inclination of the mourners.

More expensive coffins possessed a lead shell. Such coffins are most commonly used for interments in the crypts of churches and within intra- and extra-mural vaults and brick-lined shaft graves. The lead coffins or shells served to slow, and sometimes arrest the decay of the corpse. Georgian and Victorian belief in the importance of the integrity of the physical body on the Day of Judgement underlay some of the motivations to halt the natural corruption of the corpse. It also fed into the gentle, romantic metaphor of death as eternal rest, de-emphasising and sometimes denying the processes of physical decay that had so pre-occupied people of the later medieval and earlier post-medieval periods (Tarlow and West 1998; Rugg 1999). On a practical level, the containment of body liquor within a water- and air-proof container was of particular importance when interring individuals within the church vaults or beneath the floor of the church itself. In many churches, as in St George's, encasement within a lead shell was a basic requirement of interment in the church crypt. At St George's church this directive was carried through in practice in all but one case.

Lead-lined coffins were either double or triple layered. Double-layered coffins were composed of a lead shell either enclosed by, or enclosing a wooden coffin. Triple shelled coffins had a wooden inner coffin within a lead shell, the lead itself being enclosed within an ornately decorated and upholstered outer wooden case.

Triple coffins represent a great investment in time, materials and money and, as such, indicated the wealth and social prominence of the deceased and his or her surviving family. The inner wooden coffin was usually constructed of elm, which was particularly favoured for being more impermeable to water than many other available woods. Planed elm planks were glued and screwed together, and the seams caulked with Swedish pitch. The interior of the coffin was usually lined with fabric, most commonly cambric, a fine linen originally from Cambray, Flanders (Litten 1991). Often a decorative frill of punched 'lace' covered the coffin sides. Aesthetically this was most important where the corpse was to be viewed prior to burial. Fragments of coffin lining were found adhering to the internal wood of many open coffins at St George's church. Punched 'lace' frills were found in two coffins, but were poorly preserved.

Traditionally, the base of the inner coffin was covered with a shallow calico-covered layer of sawdust or bran, which helped to absorb some of the body fluids released during putrefaction. It was noted at St George's church, and also at St Luke's church, Islington (Boyle *et al.* 2005) and at St Nicholas' church, Sevenoaks (Boyle *et al.* 2002), that plentiful sawdust or bran within the coffin correlated closely with poorer preservation of the skeleton. This is probably the result of the leaching of the inorganic bone minerals due to the more acidic environment created by the decaying bran or

sawdust (Janaway 1996). As an alternative to this sawdust or bran layer, the corpse was sometimes laid out on a mattress, with a pillow beneath the head (Litten 1991). This practice reflects the strong symbolic association between death and sleep that developed in the later Georgian/Victorian period (Rugg 1999). No evidence for mattresses was found in coffins in St George's crypt.

The inner wooden coffin was sealed and encased within a lead shell. The fashioning of the lead shell was beyond the capabilities of most coffin makers, and was usually undertaken by a local plumber (Litten 1991). Unlike the inner or outer wooden coffins, the lead shell had to be bespoke. Lead sheets were cut and shaped around the inner wooden coffin. The pieces of lead were then soldered together to created a water- and airtight container. Then, either an inscription was engraved directly onto the lead shell, or a fairly plain inner coffin breastplate was soldered or riveted on. The inner breastplate of Anne Porral (Plate 8.1) shows an error in the inscription, erroneously naming her Mary rather than Ann. The mistake was crossed through and corrected. This

Plate 8.1   Inner breastplate of Ann Porral (coffin 2013) showing the error in her Christian name. Mary has been deleted and Ann inserted

error would not have been observed by mourners since it was concealed by the outer wooden case. The outer breastplate correctly named her Ann.

The outer wooden case of triple layered coffins was prepared and covered with upholstery and decorated with iron or brass studs, escutcheons and lid motifs in advance of the placement of the lead shell within it. A breastplate was also riveted onto the coffin. Lowering the lead coffin into the outer wooden coffin or case was a difficult and delicate business, considerable care being necessary not to pierce the lead shell. The shell was also very heavy, usually requiring six men to lift it by means of lengths of webbing. The shell was lowered into the outer wooden case, and the webbing was then cut and removed. The lid of the outer wooden coffin was then screwed or bolted into place (Litten 1991).

The middle and upper classes in this period invested considerable sums on the funeral and in particular on the coffin, The coffins at St George's church are typically elaborate examples of the period. Almost all were of the triple wood-lead-wood variety described above. Coffin 3095, was unusual because it was a simple single unnamed wooden coffin, upholstered in baize. Another coffin (2058; David Edwards a dressing case manufacturer of King Street) was unique at St George's church because it had two outer wooden cases, in addition to a lead shell and an inner wooden coffin. Coffin 5071 was a double coffin and lacked the outer wooden case. On this coffin the *depositum* inscription was formed from large individual letters of lead soldered individually and directly onto the lead shell. It read 'Catherine relict of Robert Morris of Brunswick Square Died 6th August 1825 Aged 55 years'. Litten (1991) writes that this type of lettering was designed to be viewed, and hence, would not originally have been covered by an outer wooden case. This is the only definite double coffin found on site. The rest of the coffins appear originally to have been of the triple wood-lead-wood type.

Lime in the coffin

One coffin (4054) was found to have a layer of lime filling the space between the lead shell and the outer wooden case. It is not clear why the coffin of this 17 year old woman, who died on 10th June 1818, was treated in this way. In Victorian England it was common practice to cover the bodies of cholera victims with lime as a public health measure to contain the contagion. However, cholera only spread to England in 1831-32 (Roberts and Cox 2003), 13 years after the death of this individual, and hence, could not have been the disease that had caused her death. It is probable that the use of lime in burials before this date was less disease-specific and was a more general response to a raft of different acute infectious diseases. A similar treatment with lime was seen in one coffin from St Luke's church, Islington (Boyle *et al.* 2005).

Preservation of the coffins

The general condition of the coffins at St George's church varied greatly. Coffins towards the bottom of the stacks were least well preserved, having suffered considerable vertical crushing from the weight of overlying lead coffins. For this reason, the side panels of the outer wooden case seldom survived. The wood of the lid was in better condition. Lead shells were frequently crushed vertically and many were breached along the seams. The lead shells of infant coffins were most likely to be found intact. The coffins in Vault 7 were particularly poorly preserved. The majority of these appeared to have been redeposited in 1991, and many coffins had been severely compressed, folded, twisted and torn apart in order to fit them into the limited space of the small vault.

The general condition of each coffin at St George's church was estimated on a scale of one to four, 1 being poorly preserved and 4 being very good. The proportion of triple coffins in each category is listed in Table 8.1.

Table 8.1: Overall level of preservation of triple coffins (N = 775)

Preservation Rating	Preservation	Number of coffins (n = 775)	Percentage of total coffins
1	poor	398	51.35
2	fair	228	29.42
3	good	90	11.6
4	very good	59	7.60

Coffin fittings

Introduction

From the early 18th century, the upholstery of outer wooden coffin cases was decorated with a suite of metal coffin fittings or furnishings. The number and materials used for the fittings was testimony to the wealth and hence, status, of the deceased and their family. Considerable variation may be observed across the classes of Georgian and Victorian society. However, it is important to note that even the less well-off went to considerable pains to bury their loved one with as many accoutrements as they could afford. With the exception of the fairly plain wooden coffin 3095, all other coffins at St George's church reflect the wealth of this predominantly upper-middle class population.

A full suite of fittings comprised from one to four *depositum* plates (an inner and outer breastplate, a headplate and a footplate), lid motifs, escutcheons, and grips and grip plates. In addition, the brass or iron studs, originally used to secure the upholstery to the wooden case, were arranged to create complex patterns on the lid and side panels of the coffin, thus becoming decorative device. An illustration of the elaborate coffin of the Duke of Wellington shows one example of a full suite of coffin fittings (Fig. 8.1).

Grips were produced by casting, but the rest of coffin fittings were stamped using dies (May 1996). Between 1720 and 1730 these were produced by hand-operated die stamping machines, but after later power-assisted machines were used. Coffin fittings could then be produced *en masse* and by the mid- to late-Georgian period were financially accessible to a wider public (ibid.).

Excavations of the 18th- and 19th-century churchyard and crypt of Christ Church, Spitalfields, London, undertaken in the 1980s, revealed a large number of coffin fittings. The taxonomy compiled from these fittings (Reeves and Adams 1993) forms the basis for identification of the styles in vogue throughout this period. The coffin fittings at St George's church were compared to this catalogue and a large number of matches were found (n= 465). However an additional 77 hitherto unknown styles were identified. These were drawn on site and are illustrated in Appendix 3 (Figs A3.1-A3.40).

Comparisons between coffin fittings from St George's church and those from other contemporary sites has proved valuable in refining the dating of the fittings. In addition to Christ Church, Spitalfields, the fittings from St George's church's were compared to those from St Luke's, Islington (Boyle *et al.* 2005) and St Bartholomew, Penn, Wolverhampton (Boyle *et al.* 2002), two sites recently excavated by Oxford Archaeology. Table 8.2 summarises the results of these comparisons. In the following discussion, styles first recognised and catalogued at Christ Church, Spitalfields are prefixed by the abbreviation CCS; those first recognised at St Luke's church, Islington, are prefixed by OLR, and, finally, new styles from St George's church, Bloomsbury, are prefixed BBM.

Symbolism of motifs used on coffin fittings

The motifs displayed on coffin fittings were not merely decorative, but were deeply imbued with symbolism. Many represented Christian symbols of death, eternal life and resurrection, whilst others owe more to secular symbolism. Classical symbolism abounded, the urn, an Ancient Greek symbol of mourning, being a very popular motif well into the 1850s (Plate 8.2). Some motifs refer to the age of an individual, others to unexpected or premature deaths. For example, the broken column denotes untimely or unexpected death, a life cut short prematurely. Cherubim were particularly favoured for the coffins of infants and children. Angels and cherubim are very popular motifs on all types of coffin fittings at St George's church, for example on the ubiquitous grip plate CCS 3 (Plate 8.3), and the new style of lid motif BBM 4 (Fig. A3.28). Angels obviously denote heaven and the afterlife (Plate 8.4), but a cherub's head without a body symbolises the soul (Plates 8.3 and 8.5). Angels blowing trumpets represent God's glory and victory over death, or alternatively the Day of Judgement.

Composite symbolism was often used. One example, found on several coffins at St George's church, is lid motif CCS 4 (Plate 8.6), which depicts a snake biting its tail, intersected by an inverted flaming torch. The circle formed by the snake, and the snake consuming its tail symbolises eternity, life without end. The flaming torch symbolises life. By being inverted, however, it represents death instead of life. The snake motif recurs on the apex of lid motif BBM 8 (Plate 8.2; Fig. A3.30) whilst the inverted torches may be seen again on breastplate BBM 16 (Fig. A3.16).

A few of the more common motifs and their symbolism in a Victorian burial context are listed below:

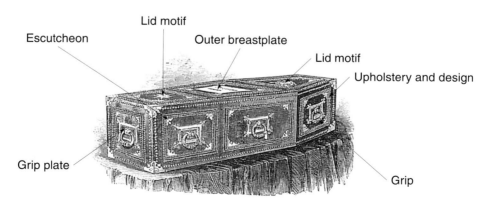

Taken from May 1996, 28

Fig. 8.1   The elaborate coffin of the Duke of Wellington, displaying a full suite of coffin fittings (after May, 1996, 28)

Table 8.2: Summary of coffin fittings from the 18th and 19th century churches in England, based on typologies from Christ Church, Spitalfields

Types Outer Breastplates	Christ Church, Spitalfields N = 325	n	St Luke's, Islington N = 100	n	St. Bartholomew's, Penn, Wolverhampton N = 47	n	St. George's, Bloomsbury N = 182	n	Overall date range from the four sites N = 655	n
CCS 1	1729-1807	15	1775	1	1811-1855	40	1848	1	1729-1855	57
CCS 2	1839-1845	2	1814	1	undated	1	1830	1	1814-1845	5
CCS 3	1810-1821	11							1810-1821	11
CCS 4	1783-1822	5	undated	1			1819	1	1783-1822	7
CCS 5	1827-1847	3							1827-1847	3
CCS 6	1783-1852	25	1802-22	10			1805-1824	16	1783-1852	51
CCS 7	1779-1794	2			undated	2	1827	1	1779-1827	5
CCS 8	1767-1825	34	1785-1880	9			1805-1832	18	1767-1880	61
CCS 9	1773-1797	12	1773-1814	7			1825-1834	4	1773-1834	23
CCS 10	undated	1							undated	1
CCS 11	undated	1							undated	1
CCS 12	undated	2							undated	2
CCS 13	1799	1							1799	1
CCS 14	1743-1818	4					1818	1	1743-1818	5
CCS 15	1824	2							1824	2
CCS 16	1835	1							1835	1
CCS 17	1828	1							1828	1
CCS 18	1765	10							1765	10
CCS 19	1761	1							1761	1
CCS 20	1813-1847	3	1790-1853	18			1814- 1852	19	1790-1853	40
CCS 21	1824-1847	21	1828-1850	27			1812- 1846	29	1812-1850	77
CCS 22	1821	1					1818-1819	2	1818-1821	3
CCS 23	1831	1					1830-1843	2	1830-1843	3
CCS 24	1782-1819	4					1809-1826	3	1782-1826	7
CCS 25	1832	1					1845	1	1832-1845	2
CCS 26	1832-1849	3					1835	1	1832-1849	4
CCS 27	1788-1839	3			undated	2	1814	1	1788-1839	6
CCS 28	1829-1842	4	1844	1			1822-1823	2	1822-1844	7
CCS 29	undated	2							undated	2
CCS 30	1809-1832	3					1819-1826	3	1809-1832	6
CCS 31	1759-1821	3							1759-1821	3
CCS 32	1830	1					1833	1	1830-1833	2
CCS 33	1802	1							1802	1
CCS 34	1820	1							1820	1
CCS 35	1806-1825	6							1806-1825	6

Table 8.2 (continued): Summary of coffin fittings from the 18th and 19th century churches in England, based on typologies from Christ Church, Spitalfields

Types	Christ Church, Spitalfields		St Luke's, Islington		St. Bartholomew's, Penn, Wolverhampton		St. George's, Bloomsbury		Overall date range from the four sites	
CCS 36	1821	1							1821	1
CCS 37	1796	1	1795	1					1795-1796	2
CCS 38	1779-1825	6							1779-1825	6
CCS 39	1794	2							1794	2
CCS 40	1788	1							1788	1
CCS 41	1764-1767	3							1764-1767	3
CCS 42	1777	1							1777	1
CCS 43	1793-1797	2							1793-1797	2
CCS 44	1828-1829	2							1828-1829	2
CCS 45	undated	1							undated	1
CCS 46	1771-1821	6					1806-1846	7	1771-1846	13
CCS 47	undated	1					1810-1840	2	1810-1840	3
CCS 48	1835	1							1835	1
CCS 49	undated	1			undated	2			undated	3
CCS 50	1780-1821	6							1780-1821	6
CCS 51	1795	1							1795	1
CCS 52	1778-1794	4							1778-1794	4
CCS 53	1834	1					1825-1833	2	1825-1834	3
CCS 54	1827	1							1827	1
CCS 55	1820-1826	3							1820-1826	3
CCS 56	1825	2							1825	2
CCS 57	1812-1824	2							1812-1824	2
CCS 58	1823	1							1823	1
CCS 59	1793	1							1793	1
CCS 60	undated	1							undated	1
CCS 61	1765-1786	3	1808	1			1811	1	1765-1811	5
CCS 62	1811	1							1811	1
CCS 63	1775	1							1775	1
CCS 64	1777-1794	4	1783	1					1777-1794	5
CCS 65	1778	1							1778	1
CCS 66	1761-1770	6							1761-1770	6
CCS 67	1769-1777	3	1802	1			1807-1826	8	1769-1826	12
CCS 68	1768	1							1768	1
CCS 69	1765-1803	3							1765-1803	3
CCS 70	1777-1778	2							1777-1778	2
CCS 71	1765	1							1765	1
CCS 72	1765	1							1765	1
CCS 73	1776	1							1776	1

Table 8.2 (continued): Summary of coffin fittings from the 18th and 19th century churches in Engand, based on typologies from Christ Church, Spitalfields

Types	Christ Church, Spitalfields		St Luke's, Islington		St. Bartholomew's, Penn, Wolverhampton		St. George's, Bloomsbury		Overall date range from the four sites	
CCS 74	1777	1							1777	1
CCS 75	1782	2							1782	2
CCS 76	1785-1793	2							1785-1793	2
CCS 77	1823	1							1823	1
CCS 78	1827	1							1827	1
CCS 79	1790	1							1790	1
CCS 80	1777-1786	2							1777-1786	2
CCS 81	1836	1							1836	1
CCS 82	1820-1829	5	1800-1830	17			1806-1848	47	1800-1848	69
CCS 83	1747	1							1747	1
CCS 84	1833-1836	2	1828-1835	4			1810-1842	15	1828-1842	21
CCS 85	1835	1					1810	1	1810-1835	2
CCS 86	1795-1811	2					1805	1	1795-1811	3
CCS 87	1827	1							1827	1
CCS 88	1770	1							1770	1
CCS 89	1758	2							1758	2
CCS 90	1827	1							1827	1
CCS 91	1824	1							1824	1
CCS 92	1832	1	1848	1					1832	2
CCS 93	1852	1							1852	1
CCS 94	1829	1							1829	1
CCS 95	1737-1746	2							1737-1746	2
CCS 96	1732	1							1732	1
CCS 97	1793	1					1823	1	1793-1823	2
CCS 98	1776	1							1776	1
CCS 99	1772	1							1772	1
CCS 100	1775	1							1775	1
CCS 101	1768	1							1768	1
CCS 102	1739	1							1739	1
CCS 103	1806-1809	2							1806-1809	2
CCS 104	1784-1789	2							1784-1789	2
CCS 105	1753	1							1753	1
CCS 106	undated	1							undated	1
CCS 107	1794	1							1749	1
CCS 108	1806	1							1806	1
CCS 109	undated	1							undated	1
CCS 110	1827	1							1827	1
CCS 111	1788	1							1788	1

Table 8.2 (continued): Summary of coffin fittings from the 18th and 19th century churches in England, based on typologies from Christ Church, Spitalfields

Types	Christ Church, Spitalfields		St Luke's, Islington		St. Bartholomew's, Penn, Wolverhampton		St. George's, Bloomsbury		Overall date range from the four sites	
	N = 216	n	N = 59	n	N = 10	n	N = 54	n	N = 339	
CCS 112	1757	2							1757	2
CCS 113	1811	1							1811	1
CCS 114	undated	1							undated	1
Grip Plates									*Overall date range*	
CCS 1	1812-1825	9	1816-1840	2					1812-1840	11
CCS 2	undated	1					1821	1	1821	2
CCS 3	1768-1842	100	1787-1880	30	1837	8	1807-1841	33	1768-1880	171
CCS 4	undated	2	1807-1850	5			1827-1843	3	1807-1850	10
CCS 5	1729-1815	15	1807	6			1829	1	1729-1829	22
CCS 6	undated	1	1820-1848	7					1820-1848	8
CCS 7	1791-1813	5							1791-1813	5
CCS 8	undated	2							undated	2
CCS 9	1784-1827	22					1826	1	1784-1827	23
CCS 10	undated	1							undated	1
CCS 11	1795-1849	2					1842	1	1795-1849	3
CCS 12	1761	1							1761	1
CCS 13	1798	1							1798	1
CCS 14	1843-1845	4	1844-1847	2			1824-1843	4	1824-1847	10
CCS 15	undated	1							undated	1
CCS 16	undated	2					1836	1	1836	3
CCS 17	1765-1793	2	1826	1			1817-1828	2	1765-1828	5
CCS 18	undated	1							undated	1
CCS 19	1763	2							1763	2
CCS 20	undated	4							undated	4
CCS 21	undated	1							undated	1
CCS 22	undated	1							undated	1
CCS 23	undated	1							undated	1
CCS 24	1794-1806	4			undated	1			1794-1806	5
CCS 25	1833-1847	10	1841	1	undated	1	1840	1	1833-1847	13
CCS 26	1819	2							1819	2
CCS 27	1779	2	undated	1					1779	3
CCS 28	undated	1							undated	1
CCS 29	1776	1	undated	1					1776	2
CCS 30	1747	1							1747	1
CCS 31	1823	3	1810-1830	3			1810-1846	6	1810-1846	12

Table 8.2 (continued): Summary of coffin fittings from the 18th and 19th century churches in England, based on typologies from Christ Church, Spitalfields

Types	Christ Church, Spitalfields	n	St Luke's, Islington	n	St. Bartholomew's, Penn, Wolverhampton	n	St. George's, Bloomsbury	n	Overall date range from the four sites	
CCS 32	undated	1							undated	1
CCS 33	1806-1828	8							1806-1828	8
CCS 34	1799	1							1799	1
CCS 35	undated	1							undated	1
Grips	*N=514*	*n*	*N= 135*	*n*	*N= 101*	*n*	*N= 90*		*Overall date range N = 840*	
CCS 1	1747-1847	29	1762-1853	12	1811-1849	13			1747-1853	54
CCS 2	1763-1837	88			2- 1813	5	1828	1	2- 1763-1837	94
			2a – 1811	29	2a- 1830s	33			2a- 1811-1830s	62
			2b-undated	1	2b- undated	5			2b- undated	6
CCS 3	1729-1827	121	3-1820-1850	3	1836-1837	3	1807-1836	3	3-1729-1850	130
			3a-17.9-1830	11					3a- 17..9-1830	11
			3b-1835-1840	49					3b- 1835-1840	49
CCS 4	1743-1847	176	1761-1880	12	1811-1836	40	1805-1847	71	1743-1880	299
CCS 5	1744-1835	72	1796- 1822	8			1809-1830	7	1744-1835	87
CCS 6	1839-1849	19	1777-1844	10	undated	1	1835-1848	5	1777-1849	35
CCS 7	1821-1849	2					1842	1	1821-1849	3
CCS 8	undated	1							undated	1
CCS 9	1770	2					1844	1	1770-1844	3
CCS 10	1837	2			undated	1	1825	1	1825-1837	4
CCS 11	undated	1			undated	1			undated	1
CCS 12	undated	1							undated	1
Lid motifs	*N =124*	*n*	*N= 13*		*N = 2*		*N = 67*		*Overall date range N = 206*	
CCS 1	1839	5	1820	1	1829	1	1821-1850	4	1821-1850	11
CCS 2	1795-1847	39	1797-1838	2			1809-1847	15	1795-1847	56
CCS 3	1821-1824	10	1831	1					1821-1831	11
CCS 4	undated	6	1835-1847	3			1835-1847		1835-1847	9
CCS 5	1798	2							1798	2
CCS 6	1779-1847	30	1797-1844	2	undated	1	1810-1852	19	1779-1852	52
CCS 7	1849	1					1842	1	1842-1849	2
CCS 8	1832-1849	3					1816	1	1816-1849	4
CCS 9	1849	1					1842	1	1842-1849	2
CCS 10	1793-1820	3	undated	1					1793-1820	4
CCS 11	1822-1843	5							1822-1843	5
CCS 12	undated	1					1835	2	1835	3

Table 8.2 (continued): Summary of coffin fittings from the 18th and 19th century churches in England, based on typologies from Christ Church, Spitalfields

Types	Christ Church, Spitalfields		St Luke's, Islington		St. Bartholomew's, Penn, Wolverhampton		St. George's, Bloomsbury		Overall date range from the four sites	
		n								
CCS 13	undated	3					1836-1852	4	1836-1852	7
CCS 14	undated	1	1822	2			1813-1841	17	1813-1841	20
CCS 15	undated	1							undated	1
CCS 16	1789	1							1789	1
CCS 17	1821-1824	2							1821-1824	2
CCS 18	undated	1							undated	1
CCS 19	undated	1	1840	1					1840	2
CCS 20	undated	1							undated	1
CCS 21	undated	1							undated	1
CCS 22	1794	1							1794	1
CCS 23	undated	2							undated	2
CCS 24	1798	1							1798	1
CCS 25	undated	1					1825-1833	3	1825-1833	4
CCS 26	undated	1							undated	1
	N =174		N = 20		N = 0		N = 72		Overall date range N = 266	

Escutcheons	Christ Church, Spitalfields		St Luke's, Islington		St. Bartholomew's, Penn, Wolverhampton		St. George's, Bloomsbury		Overall date range	
		n								
CCS 1	1776-1827	45	1797-1836	5			1804-1847	27	1776-1847	77
CCS 2	1839	2	1822	1			1822-1839	3	1822-1839	3
CCS 3	1815	6	1822	1			1837	1	1815-1837	8
CCS 4	1779-1839	24	1787-1831	3			1818-1824	2	1779-1839	29
CCS 5	undated	3					1833-1836	2	1833-1836	5
CCS 6	1823-1835	10	1826-1838	3			1806-1846	14	1806-1846	27
CCS 7	undated	1					1817	1	1817	2
CCS 8	undated	1							undated	1
CCS 9	1779	5					1779	1	1779	6
CCS 10	1779-1839	17					1835-1852	3	1779-1852	20
CCS 11	1832-1845	4	1841	1			1835-1852	3	1832-1852	8
CCS 12	1779-1847	30	1799-1807	4			1813-1831	6	1779-1847	40
CCS 13	1833-1835	11	1847	1			1821-1843	11	1821-1847	23
CCS 14	1811-1822	7							1811-1822	7
CCS 15	undated	1							undated	1
CCS 16	1842	2	undated	1			1829	1	1829-1842	4
CCS 17	undated	1							undated	1
CCS 18	undated	1							undated	1
CCS 19	undated	2							undated	2
CCS 20	undated	1							undated	1

Table 8.2 (continued): Summary of coffin fittings from the 18th and 19th century churches in Engand, based on typologies from Christ Church, Spitalfields

Types	Christ Church, Spitalfields		St Luke's, Islington	St. Bartholomew's, Penn, Wolverhampton	St. George's, Bloomsbury	Overall date range from the four sites	
Upholstery stud-work	N = 382	n	N = 2	N = 0	N = 47	Overall date ranges	N = 431
CCS 1	1739-1843	104			1829-1830 — 2	1739-1843	106
CCS 2	1747-1839	35				1747-1839	35
CCS 3	1744-1833	47	1831 — 1			1744-1833	48
CCS 4	1743-1821	17				1743-1821	17
CCS 5	undated	2				undated	2
CCS 6	1821	6				1821	6
CCS 7	undated	4				undated	4
CCS 8	1792	3				1792	3
CCS 9	1760-1825	23			1806-1827 — 4	1760-1827	27
CCS 10	1761-1849	3				1761-1849	3
CCS 11	1746-1811	21			1827 — 1	1746-1827	22
CCS 12	1781	2				1781	2
CCS 13	undated	1				undated	1
CCS 14	1759-1825	10				1759-1825	10
CCS 15	1822	2				1822	2
CCS 16	1754	2			1807 — 1	1754-1807	3
CCS 17	undated	1				undated	1
CCS 18	1809	2				1809	2
CCS 19	undated	1				undated	1
CCS 20	1752-1757	2				1752-1757	2
CCS 21	undated	1				undated	1
CCS 22	1808	1				1808	1
CCS 23	1813	1				1813	1
CCS 24	1812-1852	19			1826-1856 — 6	1812-1852	25
CCS 25	1847	5				1847	5
CCS 26	1815-1817	2				1815-1817	2
CCS 27	1750-1816	2				1750-1816	2
CCS 28	undated	1				undated	1
CCS 29	undated	1				undated	1
CCS 30	1813	1				1813	1
CCS 31	1757	2				1757	1
CCS 32	undated	2				undated	2
CCS 33	undated	1				undated	1
CCS 34	1823	3				1823	1
CCS 35	1825	4			1826-1836 — 8	1825-1836	12

Table 8.2 (continued): Summary of coffin fittings from the 18th and 19th century churches in England, based on typologies from Christ Church, Spitalfields

Types	Christ Church, Spitalfields		St Luke's, Islington		St. Bartholomew's, Penn, Wolverhampton	St. George's, Bloomsbury		Overall date range from the four sites	
CCS 36	1842	4	1847	1		undated	1	1842-1847	6
CCS 37	1799	1						1799	1
CCS 38	1802-1821	2						1802-1821	2
CCS 39	undated	1						undated	1
CCS 40	1825-1839	7				1828-1845	4	1825-1845	11
CCS 41	undated	1				1812-1831	4	1812-1831	5
CCS 42	undated	1						undated	1
CCS 43	undated	1						undated	1
CCS 44	1819	2						1819	2
CCS 45	1809-1826	2						1809-1826	2
CCS 46	undated	2				1806-1846	15	1806-1846	17
CCS 47	1820	2						1820	2
CCS 48	1821-1839	2						1821-1839	2
CCS 49	undated	1						undated	1
CCS 50	undated	1						undated	1
CCS 51	undated	1				1812	1	1812	2
CCS 52	1770-1782	4						1770-1782	4
CCS 53	1794	1						1794	1
CCS 54	undated	1						undated	1
CCS 55	undated	1						undated	1
CCS 56	undated	4						undated	4
CCS 57	undated	1						undated	1
CCS 58	undated	4						undated	4

Bible	denotes a cleric or religious layman (Plate 8.7; Fig. A3.27)
Book	faith, learning, a scholar, memory (especially where it has a dog-eared page)
Shells	fertility, resurrection and pilgrimage (particularly the scallop shell)
Sunbursts	renewed life after death (Fig.A3.38)
Crown	the crown of Jesus, immortality, righteousness, glory of eternal life;

	social prominence (Plate 8.4)
Flame	eternal life
Scroll	life and the passing of time
Skull	death and mortality
Winged face	the departing soul (Plates 8.3 and 8.5; Fig.A3.38)

Flowers have long played a symbolic role in funerals, the colour and species conveying complex ideas about life, death and rebirth. In the early

Plate 8.2 Lid motifs BBM 13 (left) and BBM 8 (right)

0 ___ 5 cm

Plate 8.3 Grip plates CCS 3 (left) and BBM 3 (right)

Plate 8.4   Lid motifs CCS 13 (left) and CCS 6 (right)

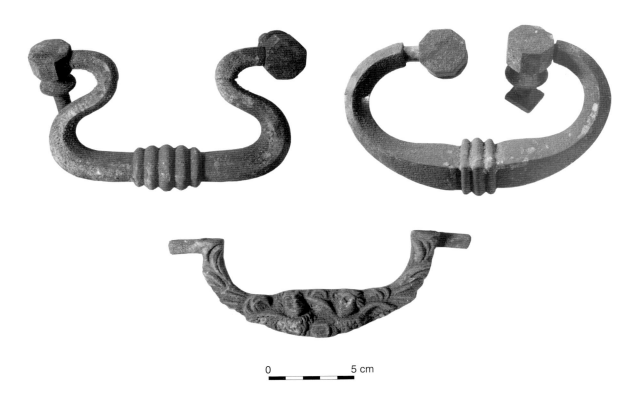

Plate 8.5   Grips BBM 1 (top left), BBM 2 (top right), and CCS 4 (bottom)

Victorian period the placement of wreaths of flowers on the coffin was largely confined to the funerals of girls and young maidens. Evergreens and white flowers, such as roses or lilies, were acceptable. Bright colours were frowned upon, and even the stamens of white lilies were cut off lest the golden pollen diminish the impression of purity (May 1996). Over the course of the 19th century, the laying of wreathes on the coffin and on the grave became more widespread through society (ibid.).

Breastplates and grip plates are particularly rich in foliage and floral motifs. Whilst the majority are stylised or generic plants, occasionally it is possible to recognise the species. Lilies and chrysanthemums have long been associated with death. Lilies are particularly associated with the Virgin Mary, and were most commonly found with women's burials. The lily was taken to represent purity, resurrection and the restoration of innocence of the soul at death. Roses are frequently depicted on breastplates and represent beauty, hope and unfailing love. Depending on the stage of their opening, the rose may represent the age of the person at the time of their death, a bud denoting a child, a partial bloom a teenager, and a rose in full bloom, an adult. Other plant motifs depicted on the fittings from St George's church are listed below:

Acanthus leaves	heavenly garden
Daisy	childhood innocence, youth, Jesus the Infant
Fleur-de-lis	flame, passion, love of a mother
Laurel	distinction in life, victory over death
Oak	stability, strength, honour,

	eternity, the cross of Jesus, liberty
Palm	spiritual victory over evil, success, eternal peace, Jesus' victory over death
Poppy	peace, sleep (and hence, death), consolation
Thistle	earthly sorrow, Christ's crown of thorns, Scotland as country of origin

Upholstery and stud-work

The outer wooden coffin was usually upholstered in either velvet or baize (Plate 8.8), although the coffins of a number of infants at St George's church appear to have been covered with a loosely woven shiny blue fabric that was probably raw silk. Although the charcoal that had overlaid the coffin stacks had blackened the upholstery of many of the coffins, a number of coloured velvets were observed on both adult and child coffins. Black was overwhelmingly the most common colour, but upholstery of mustard yellow, dark blue, dark green, red and brown was also observed. Several infant coffins were upholstered in turquoise a colour particularly popular for baby burials in the early 19th century (Litten 1991).

Due to vertical crushing of many of the lower coffins, few of the side panels of the outer wooden cases were preserved. The lids fared better, with large numbers being preserved sufficiently well to identify the upholstery stud decoration. In addition to the 47 matches made with the Christ Church, Spitalfields taxonomy, 29 new upholstery stud

0   5 cm

Plate 8.6   Lid motifs BBM 11 (left) and CCS 4 (right)

0   5 cm

Plate 8.7 Lid motif BBM 1 (top) and BBM 12 (bottom)

styles were identified, in most cases from the lid pattern alone (Appendix 3: Figures A3.41-48).

At St George's church, upholstery studs were made exclusively of brass or iron. Of the 395 coffins with extant stud-work, recording of the metals used were made on 325 coffins (82.28 %). Copper alloy was the more popular metal, recovered from 173 coffins (53.56 %), and iron from 152 coffins (47.06 %). Of the latter, the nails on five coffins had been painted, or enamelled, black, and on two had been dipped in tin to create a silvered effect (see Table 8.3).

Depositum *plates*

Depositum plates – breast, head and footplates – were riveted onto the upholstered coffin in the positions that their names suggest. All legible breastplates at St George's church bore inscriptions giving the title, name, age and date of death of the deceased. Occasionally, additional information was included, such as their place of birth or residence,

their profession in the case of a man, or the profession of their father or husband in the case of a woman, and relationships to other family members. Inner breastplates usually bore similar information to the outer breastplate, but sometimes contained less detail. The information from the head and footplate inscriptions was largely restricted to the name, title and year of death of the deceased. From the 781 coffins and 146 detached *depositum* plates, found within the crypt at St George's church, 673 individuals could be identified. Such information is a rich source of biographical and palaeodemographic data on the population interred here (see above Chapters 4 and 5 respectively).

Small differences in detail in the central panel motifs and frequent variations in the border designs were noted on many breastplates. Inner and outer border motifs are found in different combinations and the same border motifs are found on breastplates with different central panels. This suggests that composite designs were

164

Plate 8.8   Examples of wooden coffin cases showing coffin fittings and upholstery

produced by using separate dies for the central panels and the inner and outer borders, in a manner not dissimilar to that used in printing. In this way, by combining different combinations of borders and central panels, a diverse range of breastplate motifs could be offered to the discerning customer.

The majority of the outer breastplates (N = 403) was made of lead or brass, the former being heavily decorated with a stamped central motif and borders. The material of nine breastplates was not recorded. Of the assemblage of known material, lead composed 61.93 % (n = 244) of the metal used for breastplates, whilst brass composed 31.73% (n = 125); iron 2.79 % (n = 11); silvered tin 2.03 % (n = 8), and tin pewter 1.52 % (n = 6) (Table 8.3). Lead breastplates were occasionally enamelled or painted black. Brass breastplates tended to be plainer, but four bore inscribed coats-of-arms. These were difficult to discern due to the fineness of the inscription and the oxidation of the brass.

The inner breastplate, foot and head plates are generally far less decorative than the outer breastplate. Many were completely plain, bearing nothing but the inscription, but a number were bordered with simple lines of punched circles or stylised leaf or flower motifs. These *depositum* plates were almost exclusively of lead. Of the 427 inner breastplates recovered from St George's church, only three were

not of lead (0.70%). These were composed of iron. The material for the endplates (n = 176), likewise, was overwhelmingly of lead (98.30%). Three exceptions were composed of iron. Whilst the shape of the inner breastplates varied between rectangular, tapered or lozenge-shaped (often mimicking the shape of the outer breastplates), the endplates were uniformly rectangular.

Grips and grip plates

Once solely functional, the grips with which mourners carried the coffin became stylistically more elaborate during this period, as did the grip plates which attached the grips to the coffin. Eight of the grip types identified at St George's church (N = 71) matched with examples from the Christ Church, Spitalfields. The most ubiquitous of these was CCS 4 (Plate 8.5), found on 71 coffins (78.89%), followed by CCS 5 (9.86%). Frequently, but certainly not in all cases, grip plate CCS 3 (Plate 8.3) and grip CCS 4 (Plate 8.5) were found together as a set. Grip plate CCS 3 was overwhelmingly the most popular at St George's church, found on 33 of the 54 coffins that could be matched to the Christ Church, Spitalfields catalogue. This ubiquity is echoed in the assemblages from Christ Church, Spitalfields; St Luke's, Islington; and St Bartholomew's, Penn (see Table 8.5). Of the total numbers of these grip plates

Table 8.3: Summary of known metals used for coffin fittings (N = 1623)

Fitting type	N	Iron	Lead	Brass	Silvered tin	Tin pewter	Ormolou
Outer breastplate	394	11 (2.79%)	244 (61.93 %)	125 (31.73%)	8 (2.03%)	6 (1.52%)	0
Inner breastplate	427	3 (0.70%)	424 (99.30%)	0	0	0	0
Endplate	176	3 (1.71%)	173 (98.30%)	0	0	0	0
Coffin grips	134	108 (80.60%)	0	25 (18.66 %)	0	0	1 (0.74 %)
Grip plates	67	21 (31.34%)	3 (4.47%)	30 (44.78%)	8 (11.94%)	5 (7.46%)	0
Lid motifs	49	19 (38.78%)	4 (8.16%)	21 (42.86%)	2 (4.08%)	3 (6.12%)	0
Escutcheons	53	16 (30.19%)	4 (7.55%)	32 (60.37%)	0	1 (1.89%)	0
Upholstery studs	323	152 (47.06%)	0	173 (53.56%)	0	0	0

from the four sites, grip plate CCS 3 accounts for 50.44% of the total assemblage; and grip CCS 4 for 35.6% of the grips. In addition to the styles that could be matched to Christ Church, Spitalfields, four new styles of grips (BBM 1- 4; Figs. A3.39-40) and three new grip plate types (BBM 1- 3; Figs. A3.37-38) were identified. These are discussed more fully below.

Because grips needed to be strong, the metals used were restricted to iron and brass, whereas a greater variety of materials could be used for the grip plates. At St George's church, 108 of the 134 coffins with grips of recognised metal (80.6%) were of iron. Of the remainder, 25 were of brass (18.66%), and one was of ormolou (0.746%). Of the 67 coffins with grip plates of known material, 43.28% were of brass; 31.34% were of iron; 11.9% were of silvered tin; 8.96% were of tin pewter; and 4.48% were of lead (see Table 8.3).

Lid motifs and escutcheons

Lid motifs and escutcheons are stamped pieces of metal decorating the upholstery of the outer wooden case. Lid motifs are larger than escutcheons and tend to be located centrally in the chest and knee areas of the coffin lid. Escutcheons are most commonly found in the corners and along the margins of the stud-work panels on the lid and side panels of the upholstered outer wooden case.

Two hundred and twenty-one lid motifs were recovered at St George's church. Being composed of thin stamped sheets of metal, lid motifs are more prone to corrosion than some of the thicker, more robust coffin fittings. The worst preserved lid motifs

were those made of iron; the details of the decoration often being indiscernible due to rusting. The metal composition of 49 lid motifs was recorded. Brass constituted the most popular material (60.37 %); followed by iron (30.19 %); lead (8.16 %); tin pewter (6.12 %) and silvered tin (4.08 %). Sufficiently well preserved lid motifs were compared with the Christ Church, Spitalfields taxonomy. Sixty-seven could be matched to styles found in this catalogue. The most popular motif was CCS 6 (Plate 8.4), two angels holding aloft a crown (n = 19), followed by CCS 14 (essentially the same design as grip plate CCS 3), a design of a cartouche encircled by scrolls and leaves and surmounted by two cherubim (n = 17). Four hitherto undated lid motifs (CCS 12, 13, 14 and 25) from Christ Church, Spitalfields, can now be dated using the St George's assemblage. In addition, thirteen new lid motif types were recognised (BBM 1- 13; Figures A3.27-35). BBM 6, 7, 9 and 10 were composite motifs composed of three or more separate elements (Figs. A3.29, 31-32).

Escutcheons were recovered from 123 coffins at St George's church. Like lid motifs, these metal fittings were made of very thin sheets of stamped metal, and hence, were more prone to corrosion than more robust fittings, such as breastplates and grips. It is probable that originally there were more escutcheons than the examples which have survived. Variation in the metal used in escutcheons was similar to that found in lid motifs. In 70 cases, the metal used was not recorded. From the 53 coffins for which the metal is known, 32 were of brass (60.37%); 16 of iron (30.19%); four of lead (7.55%) and one of tin pewter (1.89 %).

Escutcheons from 72 coffins were sufficiently well preserved to be compared with the Christ Church, Spitalfields taxonomy (see Table 8.5). CCS 1 was the most common style (a cartouche motif surrounded by swirling foliage), forming 37.5 % of the total assemblage. This was followed by CCS 6, a stylised flower motif (19.44 %). The eight new types that were identified at St George's (BBM 1-8; Fig. A3.36; Plate 8.9) will be discussed below.

New coffin fitting types from St George's church
(Tables 8.4-8.5)

In addition to the many coffin fitting styles that matched the Christ Church Spitalfields taxonomy, there were 82 unrecorded styles from St George's church (Appendix 3, Figs A3.1–A3.48). Some could be matched to new types identified at the St. Luke's, Islington assemblage (identified by the prefix of OLR) (Boyle *et al.* 2005). The new types from these

0 _____ 5 cm

Plate 8.9   Escutcheons CCS 13 (top left), CCS 12 (top right), BBM 8 (bottom left) and BBM 1 (bottom right)

two sites and from St Bartholemew's, Penn, Wolverhampton, recently excavated by Oxford Archaeology (Boyle 2002), can be added to the catalogue from Christ Church, Spitalfields, to create a more comprehensive taxonomy of coffin fittings with more accurate dating than hitherto has been available.

Upholstery stud work

Compared to Christ Church, Spitalfields, considerably more diversity in upholstery stud patterns was noted at St George's church. Twenty-nine new styles were identified on 132 coffins (BBM 1–BBM 29; Figures A3.41-48). Unfortunately, as a result of the vertical crushing of the coffins, many of the side panels of the outer wooden cases had been destroyed. For this reason, many of the new styles of patterns of the upholstery studs are derived from coffin lids alone. Where the side panels were extant, these have been recorded. Upholstery stud-work BBM 1 (dated 1804–1845) was by far the most common style with 62 examples. There were 26 examples of BBM 2 (dated 1814–1852). Most of the other upholstery stud patterns were found as single examples. The number of examples and the date ranges of these new types are summarised in Table 8.4.

Breastplates

Many of the breastplates at St George's church were variations on the styles recorded at Christ Church, Spitalfields. Where the style differences were minor the breastplate was not regarded as a new type. However, where three or more differences were remarked, a new style was declared. At St George's church, 26 new breastplate types were identified on 34 coffins. Some of these matched new types found at churchyard and crypt site of St. Luke's, Islington, London (Table 8.4).

Grips and grip plates

Most of the grips and grip plates at St George's church could be identified with types found in the Christ Church, Spitalfields taxonomy. Four new grip designs (BBM 1-4; Figs A3.39-40) were found on seven coffins. One of these (BBM 2, dated 1813-1842) was found to match OLR 7 from St. Luke's, Islington. Three new grip plates were identified on three coffins at St George's (BBM 1-3; Figs. A3.37-38). No matches were found between these new types and those from St Luke's, Islington.

Lid motifs

Thirteen new lid motifs were identified on 16 coffins from St George's church. Four were composite motifs involving between three and five pieces of decorative moulded metal placed together to create a motif (BBM 6, 7, and 9-10; Figs A3.29, 31-2). Some of the smaller elements were used elsewhere singly as escutcheons. For example, BBM 9 is composed of four corner escutcheons placed together to form a star (Fig. A3.31), and BB7 is made of escutcheon BBM 5 (a flower motif) and a stylised foliage motif (Fig. A3.29). BBM 10 (Fig. A3.32) is composed of two BBM 4 escutcheons and a CCS 9 escutcheon. The other lid motifs were single pieces of lead, tin or copper. They depict a crown, a bible, an angel, the crucifixion of a very Herculean Christ, and tombs and flaming urns (Figs. A3.27, 30, 35). Lid motif BBM 11 (Fig. A3.33) is the same style as grip plate CCS 16, but was found attached to the coffin lid in the position of a lid motif, and hence, has been included here as a new type. A single match was found between lid motifs from St George's and St Luke's, Islington: BBM 9 (dated 1830) very closely resembles OLR 5 (see Table 8.4).

Table 8.4: *New types of coffin fittings from St. George's church, Bloomsbury, and St. Luke's church, Islington, that could be matched stylistically (N = 9). N represents the number of examples found, with the number of dated examples shown in brackets.*

St George's	Date	N	St Luke's	Date	N	Overall date	N
Breastplates							
BBM 5	1820-1834	2 (2)	OLR 17	1830	1 (1)	1820-1834	3 (3)
BBM 23	undated	2 (0)	OLR 4	1823	1 (1)	1823	3 (1)
BBM 8	1813-1818	4 (4)	OLR 16	undated	2 (0)	1813-1818	6 (4)
BBM 9	1823- 1825	2 (2)	OLR 9	undated	1 (0)	1823-1825	3 (2)
BBM 16	1852	1 (1)	OLR 8	1812	1 (1)	1812-1852	2 (2)
BBM 26	1835	1 (1)	OLR 32	1838	2 (1)	1835-1838	3 (2)
BBM 1	1834	1 (1)	OLR 21	1823	1 (1)	1823-1834	2 (2)
Grips							
BBM 2	1813-1842	4 (4)	OLR 7	undated	1 (0)	1813-1842	5 (4)
Lid motifs							
BBM 9	1830	2 (1)	OLR 5	1852	1 (1)	1830-1852	3 (2)

Table 8.5: *Date ranges of the new types of coffin fittings identified at St George's.*
N *refers to total numbers found, with the number of dated examples in brackets*

Type	Breastplates	N	Upholstery studs	N	Grips	N	Grip plates	N	Lid motifs	N	Escutcheons	N
BBM1	1834	1 (1)	1804 – 1845	62 (50)	1836	1 (1)	1836	1 (1)	1836 – 1840	2 (2)	1827 – 1836	3 (2)
BBM2	1832	1 (1)	1814 – 1852	26 (22)	1813 – 1842	4 (4)	1852	1 (1)	1832 – 1836	2 (2)	1838	1 (1)
BBM3	1830	1 (1)	Undated	1 (0)	1850	1 (1)	Undated	1(1)	Undated	1 (0)	1838	1 (1)
BBM4	1815	1 (1)	1805	1 (1)	1836	1 (1)			1837	1 (1)	1826	1 (1)
BBM5	1820 – 1834	2 (2)	1832	1 (1)					1814	1 (1)	Undated	1 (0)
BBM6	1805	1 (1)	1830	1 (1)					1826	1 (1)	1817	1 (1)
BBM7	1834 – 1841	2 (2)	1825 – 1831	5 (4)					Undated	1 (0)	1852	1 (1)
BBM8	1813 – 1818	4 (4)	1827	2 (1)					1852	1 (1)		
BBM9	1823 – 1825	2 (2)	Undated	1 (0)					1830	2 (1)		
BBM10	1815	1 (1)	Undated	1 (0)					Undated			
BBM11	1831	1 (1)	1809 – 1839	3 (3)					Undated			
BBM12	1812	1 (1)	1816 – 1818	4 (4)					Undated			
BBM13	1813	1 (1)	1825 – 1830	3 (2)								
BBM14	1835	1(1)	1821	1 (1)								
BBM15	Undated	1 (1)	1825	1 (1)								
BBM16	1852	1 (1)	1811 – 1813	3 (2)								
BBM17	1806	1 (1)	1814 – 1820	2 (2)								
BBM18	1815	1 (1)	1810	1 (1)								
BBM19	1824	1(1)	1826	1 (1)								
BBM20	1854	1 (1)	Undated	1 (0)								
BBM21	1827	1 (1)	1815	1 (1)								
BBM22	1836	2 (1)	1821	1 (1)								
BBM23	Undated	2 (0)	1842	1 (1)								
BBM24	1837	1 (1)	1815 – 1821	2 (2)								
BBM25	1845	1 (1)	Undated	1 (0)								
BBM26	1835	1 (1)	1831	1 (1)								
BBM27			1830	1 (1)								
BBM28			1810	1 (1)								
BBM29			1824	1 (1)								

Escutcheons

At St George's church, eight new styles of escutcheons were found on eight coffins. Three depict stars in different stylistic forms (BBM 1, 2 and 6, Fig. A3.36; Plate 8.9), one depicts an angel (BBM 3), another a flower (BBM5) and three are abstract designs of foliage of classical inspiration (BBM 4, 7 and 8; Plate 8.9). All but BBM 7 were made of brass. BBM 7 was made of of black painted tin that matched the other coffin fittings on coffin 2007.

Grave clothes and grave goods

Textiles: shrouds and coffin linings

Janaway (1998) comments on the great variation in dressing corpses in the 18th and 19th centuries. A loose sheet or winding cloth was often placed under the corpse and used to line the open coffin, and later was folded over to cover the corpse, often being pinned in place. A rouched or punched lace ruffle often adorned the coffin sides as discussed above.

The corpse itself was often clothed in a crudely-made shroud. Nightdress-like shrouds, often with a ruffle round the neck and down the front, began to replace the earlier practice of dressing the dead in everyday personal clothing in this period (ibid.). At St George's church, the preservation of textiles within the inner wooden coffin was generally poor. From the lack of fastenings, such as buttons or hooks-and-eyes, it is assumed that most individuals buried at St George's church were dressed in shrouds. In a number of lead coffins, shroud fragments were found adhering to the bone. The fabric could seldom be identified, but those that were appeared to have been made of linen. No woollen shrouds were recorded. One shroud found in the waterlogged coffin of a Mrs Catherine Morris, died 1825, aged 55 years (5071) was exceedingly well preserved. This linen shroud was in the style of a nightdress. The sleeves were raglan, and all the seams of the shroud had been hand sewn. The bottom of the shroud was decorated with a thick border of punched 'lace', bearing foliage and sun motifs.

Grave goods

There were mo grave goods or even personal affects. No jewellery or hair or clothing adornments were found within the coffins at St George's church. One exception is the coffin of an older man was a small round box, interpreted as a snuffbox. Unfortunately the box had corroded too much to be opened and the contents examined. Several individuals had been buried wearing bridges and dentures, and two were buried with an additional set (see above Chapter 6).

Plate 8.10   Discovery of the death masks in the coffin of Anna Stringfield (coffin 3064)

Death masks

One highly unusual burial was that of a six-year old girl, Anna Stringfield (died 6 December 1835). Her coffin (3064) was found to contain three plaster effigies: two death masks of an older woman, and one of a right hand (Plates 8.10-8.11). In addition, a folded silk shawl was recovered from within the coffin, together with a short length of folded patterned velvet ribbon. The death masks are clearly of the same elderly woman. The face from which the mask had been moulded had been very wrinkled. Depression of the contours around the mouth indicates that the individual had lost most, if not all her teeth. The cast of the right hand also suggests that of an elderly woman. The hand is small and very narrow, and the skin was evidently very wrinkled when the cast was made. Impression of the veins on the back of the hand could clearly be seen. The nails were well manicured, and the fingers were in a loosely flexed position. Green staining of the palm of the hand cast suggests that something of copper alloy (possibly a coin) had originally been placed there.

Why these casts were included in the coffin is not entirely clear. It is assumed that they represent a relative of the young girl, Anna Stringfield, probably a grandmother. There were eight members of the Stringfield family interred in the crypt of St George's church. Anna she was baptised on 22 March 1829. Anna's parents were John and Anna Stringfield (née Frickelton) and they lived in Duke Street, and her father was a butcher. A memorial plaque within the church itself also commemorates this family. (See Chapter 4 above for more discussion of the Stringfield family). Three generations of the family died within one decade between 1827 to 1836: her grandfather Thomas Stringfield (consumption, 15 Nov 1827, aged 67), her father, John (dropsy, 2 Sep 1832, aged 37), her mother, Anna (consumption, 12 July 1833, aged 25 years), and her paternal grandmother, Mary ('inflammation', 4 Nov 1833, aged 71 years), and finally Ann herself (6 Dec 1835). Anna was found in Vault 3, but the rest of her family were interred in Vault 6. The daughter, Anna, had outlived them only by a couple of years. Although it can never be proven, it is very possible that the child Anna had been cared for by her grandmother Mary in the few months between the death of her mother, and Mary's own death. It is very possible that the death-masks are of Mary Stringfield, and were placed within the coffin on the instructions of their sole surviving member of the family, her son and Anna's uncle, William Stringfield.

CONCLUSION

The interments within the crypt of St George's church date to the heyday of the late Georgian/early Victorian funeral at its most extravagant. The wealth and social aspirations of the professional classes buried here are reflected in the richness of the coffins. The clearance of the crypt has provided valuable opportunity to investigate both the biographies of individuals, and to develop our

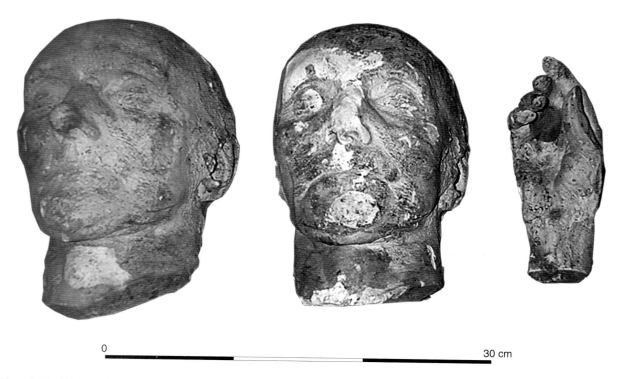

0   30 cm

Plate 8.11   Plaster death masks and the cast of a hand found within the coffin of Anna Stringfield (coffin 3064)

understanding of the material culture of late post-medieval funerary ritual. Although much is known historically about Victorian responses to death, the examination of the coffins and coffin fittings of the period is a relatively new field of enquiry. The excellent groundwork laid by Reeves and Adams (1993) from excavations at Christ Church, Spitalfields, in the 1980s requires considerable refinement and development. In comparing the Spitalfields taxonomy with contemporaneous sites, such as St Luke's church, Islington, St Bartholomew church, Penn, and St George's church, Bloomsbury, it has been possible to refine the dating of different fitting styles, and to identify many hitherto unrecognised designs. Already it is becoming apparent that some styles, such as grip plate CCS 3; grips CCS 2, CCS 3 and CCS 4, and breastplates CCS 6, CCS 8, and CCS 21, enjoyed extensive and prolonged popularity, often spanning as long as a century, whilst other styles are much more unusual. An accurate time-scale for the latter is more difficult to establish, given the small number of the samples. It is also apparent that certain styles were popular on some sites and not others. Breastplate designe CCS 82 was found in large numbers at St George's church (n = 47) and at St Luke's church, Islington (n = 17), but in the much larger assemblage of Christ Church, Spitalfields, it numbered just five.

From this growing body of data a more accurate and comprehensive corpus of coffin fitting styles of the period is being developed. The coffin fitting assemblage from St George's church has been particularly valuable in this process. The excellence of preservation of the coffins, the quantity and richness of the fittings has provided valuable new dating of known fittings, and the identification of 76 new styles.

Today, growing secularisation, an overwhelming modern preference for cremation over burial, and an ever-increasing demand for real estate has precipitated an acceleration in the clearance of church crypts, churchyards and cemeteries within urban contexts. There is no reason to believe that this trend will reverse in the near future. It is thus particularly imperative that accurate and comprehensive recording of coffins and their furniture is undertaken. It is hoped that the existence of a more comprehensive and updated catalogue of fittings will facilitate this recording, and will expand our knowledge of this hitherto under-researched field.

Chapter 9: Discussion and conclusions

by Angela Boyle and Ceridwen Boston

INTRODUCTION

The archaeological proposals for mitigating the impact of the proposed works on the surviving archaeology at St George's church, Bloomsbury, were outlined in a Written Scheme of Investigation. Due to the acknowledged historical and archaeological potential of this burial assemblage it was decided that Oxford Archaeology should be in attendance on the exhumation company BGS, in order to record the material culture of late Georgian/early Victorian funerals and osteological data from the skeletal assemblage. The work also included limited structural recording of areas of Hawksmoor's church, such as the crypt, the western stairwells, an early well and a possible undercroft on the eastern side of the churchyard, and below-ground structures in areas flanking the steps at the front of the building.

RESEARCH ISSUES IN POST-MEDIEVAL BURIAL

Research issues in post-medieval archaeology were recently defined in some detail (Reeve 1998, 222). It is clear that the relationship between the historical documentation and the condition of the archaeological material (both skeletal and artefactual) is critical. Areas of particular concern include:

- *Funerary archaeology.* Including charnel pits, mass graves, artefact developments, taxonomies, social and gender archaeology, the English funeral, ownership and choice of vaults, burials as entities, graveyard methodology, location of interments in relation to memorials

- *Osteoarchaeology.* Including palaeodemography and demography, biological anthropology, pathology, epidemiology, osteological methodology (pathology, age and sex, stature), forensic science, clinical medicine, genealogy

- *Archaeological methodology.* Theory and practice, curation procedures and environments

- *Evidence for known historical events,* such as epidemics

Although the clearance of burials from churchyards and crypts has accelerated in recent years, there is still no recognised research agenda for post-medieval burial within London. This is an omission which is currently being addressed by the Archaeological Advisor for the London Diocese (John Schofield pers. comm.).

Although slow in starting, the archaeological and documentary potential of post-medieval burial is now recognised. Whilst Christ Church, Spitalfields, remains the type-site for this period, a growing number of burial clearances in London have undergone detailed osteoarchaeological and/or historical investigation. These include excavations at St Marylebone, Westminster, the Crossbones cemetery, Southwark, the Davenant Centre in White Chapel Road, and St George-the-Martyr, Southwark, (all MoLAS); St Pancras, Clerkenwell, (Giffords, PCA and MoLAS); St Bride's, and the Devonport buildings, Greenwich, and St Luke's , Islington (OA). Many of the above sites are still in progress or exist as grey literature.

In this report, an attempt has been made to compare data from a number of these sites. It is hoped that a wider synthesis will be undertaken in the future, in particular, making comparisons between assemblages of different social class. Considerably more research into working class burials of this period is required, their importance having been somewhat eclipsed by burials of the 'middling sort'. This may in part be redressed by the White Chapel Road and Southwark burial excavations, when this data becomes available.

THE ARCHAEOLOGICAL AND HISTORICAL VALUE OF THE ST GEORGE'S ASSEMBLAGE

The archaeological resource at St George's was assessed according to a series of criteria prior to commencement of work. The criteria were: completeness, condition, rarity, historical documentation and group value. These are summarised below:

Completeness

The completeness and integrity of the human skeletal assemblage from St George's crypt was considerable, with the majority of elements of the skeletons retrieved from the open coffins.

Condition

Conditions within the crypt were largely dry, with the exception of the lower courses in Vaults 4 and 5, where considerable mould had developed. Accumulation of water in the lowest stacks of coffin in these vaults had preserved textiles, such as shrouds and inner coffin linings in a small number of coffins.

Unlike other church sites, such as St Luke's church, Islington, there had been no illicit interference with the dead. The coffins in Vaults 1-6 do not appear to have been disturbed since their relocation in the mid-19th century. The most severe destruction of coffins was as a result of the vertical stacking of coffins which had led to crushing of coffins in the lower levels of stacks. This did limit identification of upholstery stud patterns on the side panels of a large proportion of the coffins, but as the lids were frequently well preserved, recovery of upholstery stud patterns, lid motifs, escutcheons and breastplates was generally very good.

The condition of the coffins in Vault 7 was very different from the condition of coffins Vaults 1 – 6. These coffins had been moved in recent times and had suffered considerable modern damage and interference, resulting in the destruction of many and disturbance of their skeletal remains.

Nevertheless, considerable new information on coffin fittings typologies was retrieved from the overall assemblage.

The preservation of the skeletal material was generally good, although the presence of bran and sawdust in many coffins had had a deleterious effect on the bone, with demineralisation apparent on many skeletons. Nevertheless, preservation was sufficiently good to provide valuable demographic data.

Rarity

Although it is clear that other similar post-medieval assemblages survive in London, many have been excavated by exhumation companies, with little or no recording of the material culture of these burials or depositional sequences. Consequently, they have limited archaeological and historical value.

The size of the St George's assemblage and the good state of preservation both of the coffins and human remains, combined with the documentary evidence, does enhance the rarity and research potential of the group. The unprecedented number of named individuals allowed for valuable blind testing of osteological methods (Chapter 7 above, and Appendix 2), that has considerable value in refining such methodologies in the future.

The *depositum* plate inscriptions complement other sources of information, such as parish records, for the burials in the parish in the period 1803-1856. Surviving parish burial records were particularly valuable in contrasting the structure of the crypt sample with the wider Bloomsbury population, and comparisons with London Bills of Mortality have highlighted the differences between the crypt population, which is predominantly middle and upper class, with the wider populous of the city.

The biographical data collected from coffin plate inscriptions is of great historical value, representing as it does 90.5% of the burials within the crypt. The crypt interments predate in large measure the introduction of civil registration of births, marriages and deaths. The considerable documentary evidence collected during the crypt clearance has greatly enhanced and complemented the archaeological information. There remains a considerable potential for more detailed historical analysis of families and individuals, beyond was has been possible in this report.

Group value

The value of the group is high due to the good state of preservation of the human bone assemblage and the high proportion of named individuals. More detailed comparisons with the growing number of contemporary assemblages does warrant considerably more research.

Research potential

With this in mind it was argued that the resource would have the potential to address a limited number of research objectives as follows:

- Development of the crypt and graveyard through time by discussion of stratigraphy and formation processes on site

- Enhancement of our understanding of post-medieval funerary contexts and the archaeological techniques employed

- Enhancement of osteological techniques through the study of individuals of known age and sex

- Development of our knowledge of funerary rites and the treatment of the dead

- Analysis of the construction, use and modification of the crypt structure.

The aim of the archaeological work was to record and interpret as much detail as was possible within the parameters of a relatively rapid exhumation and re-interment exercise. It was expected that the archaeological data collected would contribute to the study of the history and development of funeral trends and the demography of the population of the crypt.

The objectives of the archaeological work were to record the preservation conditions within the crypt and churchyard, the inscriptions on coffin plates, the human remains and undertake limited sampling of human skeletal remains with biographical data.

THE REBURIAL DEBATE

The crypt clearance at St George's required a Faculty, one of the conditions of which was that all burials (including both skeleton *and* coffin) would be sleeved and reburied within a very limited period by BGS. Reburial was ongoing during the crypt clearance, and coffins and their contents were reinterred as soon as osteological analysis was completed. St George's church is not alone in having a requirement for relatively rapid reburial of human remains. This has considerable implication fieldwork approaches and for the further research potential of assemblages of this period.

Recent relevant developments

Guidelines relating to crypt clearance were recently produced by the IFA (Cox 2001). Although the IFA had previously produced guidelines for the excavation of human remains (McKinley and Roberts 1993), these related primarily to the excavation of skeletons from earth-cut graves. Prior to the publication in 2001 no guidelines or protocols existed for the excavation of burials in crypts or where soft tissue survived. The aim of Cox's paper (ibid, 14) was to 'set out a protocol that seems appropriate in light of the Spitalfields experience and that experienced by archaeologists involved with the recent dead elsewhere (e.g. Boyle and Keevill 1998; Bashford and Pollard 1998).'

The most recent version of the Archaeology Policy of the London DAC was issued in January 2005 and took account of the report produced by the Human Remains Working Group and published by English Heritage (Mays 2005). Archaeological contractors are now required to frame their WSIs within this policy. In its executive summary the Working Group states 'If burial grounds, or areas within burial grounds, which may contain interments more than 100 years old have to be disturbed – whether for minor building work or larger scale development – to a depth that is likely to disturb burials, the relevant areas should be archaeologically evaluated. Any subsequent exhumations should be monitored, and if necessary carried out, by archaeologists' (Mays 2005, 4). In the DAC view, there should be archaeological recording in a crypt clearance. A crypt often contains hundreds, if not thousands, of coffins and skeletons. The health and safety issues are significant and affect the nature and extent of archaeological work. National guidelines are available and continue to be developed. The archaeological project which excavated 18th-and 19th-century coffins in the crypt of Christ Church, Spitalfields in the 1980s has become a national standard of what can be achieved (Reeve and Adams 1993). Early consultation with the DAC, English Heritage and the local planning authority is recommended if crypt clearance is contemplated.

The following recommendations made by the Working Party are particularly significant:

- If living close family members are known and request it, excavated human remains should be reburied

- Excavated human remains shown after due assessment to have limited research potential should be studied and then reburied

- Reburial should normally be by inhumation rather than by cremation

- When excavated human remains are more than 100 years old and have significant future research potential, deposition in a suitable holding institution should be arranged. Redundant churches or crypts provide an acceptable compromise between the desirability of deposition in a consecrated place and the desirability of continued research access. This has already done in some instances. A working party, to succeed the Human Remains Working Group, should be set up to pursue this, looking in particular at funding and at establishing proper working practices.

At the annual conference of the Institute of Field Archaeologists in Winchester in 2005 a session entitled 'The excavation of post-medieval cemeteries: why, when and how? (but not necessarily in that order)' was organised by Jacqueline McKinley of Wessex Archaeology and Simon Mays of English Heritage. The writers were asked to contribute because of their involvement in the St Luke's project, as well as a number of other similar jobs in London and elsewhere (for example Boyle 2004).

Archaeological excavation of post-medieval cemeteries is a relatively new phenomenon. Until *c* 20 years ago most burials of this date were subject to removal by cemetery clearance companies with no archaeological involvement. This changed with the work at Christ Church, Spitalfields in the 1980s as archaeologists and osteologists demonstrated the immense wealth of information, relating to all aspects of the burials, which could be recovered, particularly where the archaeological data could be linked to written records.

There are a large number of post-medieval cemeteries containing an immense number of burials and with ever increasing pressure on land and the need to update church buildings to the needs of the 21st century, growing numbers of such cemeteries (and crypts) are being totally or partially cleared. Archaeologists are commonly being asked to undertake such work, but the levels of recording and analysis required may vary from cemetery to cemetery and archaeologists need to ensure that they are not simply a more 'politically correct' method of clearance. Archaeologists who took part in the session considered what types of information might be obtained and what constitutes an appropriate level of investigation and recording. It was recognised that is necessary to ensure that methodologies for on-site archaeological recording not only accommodate the practical demands imposed by exhumation works but also generate data sets of real analytical value.

CONCLUSION

The St George's crypt clearance was extremely challenging, both for the archaeologists who took part and indeed for BGS the exhumation company. The logistics were complex, given the unexpected number of coffins, and it took effort from both parties to achieve an acceptable method of working together. The approach to the archaeology had previously been employed with success at St Nicholas, Sevenoaks, (Boyle and Keevill 1998), the Quaker cemetery at London Road, Kingston-upon-Thames (Bashford and Pollard 1998; Start and Kirk 1998), St Bartholomew's church, Penn (Boyle 2004) and subsequently at St Luke's church, Islington (Boyle *et al.* 2005). The osteological and artefactual analysis of the material from St George's has yielded an enormous amount of valuable information on both burial practice and the population who were interred in the church.

Appendix 1: Alphabetical list of named individuals known from coffin plates

APPENDIX 1 begins overleaf

ABBREVIATIONS USED IN APPENDIX 1

Manuscript sources

LMA P82/GEO1/63	London Metropolitan Archives, Searchers' Reports for Saint George's Bloomsbury Jan 1771-Apr 1834
TNA PROB 11	The National Archives, Prerogative Court of Canterbury wills,
SUN MS11936	Guildhall Library MS 11936/444-560 Sun Assurance policy registers, 1808-1839.

Printed sources

Annals of Philosophy =	*The Annals of Philosophy* (ed Thomas Thomson), Vol 1 (Jan-Jun 1813) – vol 16 (July-Dec 1820), London
Annual Register =	*The Annual Register, or view of the history, politics, and literature for the Year . . . ,* (1758 – present) London
Blackwood's =	*Blackwood's Edinburgh Magazine,* 1817-1905, Edinburgh and London
Gazette =	*The London Gazette,* 'published by authority'
GM =	*Gentleman's Magazine,* 1736-1868, London
London Magazine =	*The London Magazine* (ed. John Scott), 1820-1829, London
Holden's 1811 =	*Holden's Annual London and Country Directory . . for the Year 1811, First Volume, London Part.* London 1811
Kent's Directory 1794 =	*Kent's Directory for the Year 1794. Cities of London and Westminster, & Borough of Southwark.*
List of Names 1815 =	*A List of the Names of the Members of the United Company of Merchants of England, Trading to the East Indies, 1815*
Pigot's Glos 1830 =	*Pigot's Directory of Gloucestershire, 1830*
PO London 1808 =	*Post Office annual directory for 1808*
PO London 1829 =	*Post Office London Directory for 1829.*
PO London 1841 =	*Post Office London Directory for 1841, Part 1: Street, Commercial & Trades; Part 2: Law, Court & Parliamentary*
PO London 1852 =	*Post Office Directory of London, with Essex, Hertfordshire, Kent, Middlesex, Surrey and Sussex*

Online sources

IGI	International Genealogical Index, Church of the Latter Day Saints, accessible online at www.familysearch.org/eng/default.asp
Old Bailey Proceedings	accessible online at www.oldbaileyonline.org
Pallot's Marriage Index	Pallot's Marriage Index 1780-1837, accessible at www.ancestry.co.uk
Pallot's Baptism Index	Pallot's Baptism Index 1780-1837, accessible at www.ancestry.co.uk
1841 Census, 1851 Census	accessible at www.ancestry.co.uk

Coffin	Plate	Forename	Surname	M/F/Y/U	Age at Death	Inscription Text
6027		Francis	Abbott	M	76y	Francis Abbott | Esqr | Died 19th Nov | 1842 | in his 77th Year
1139		Elizabeth	Adams	F	33y	Mrs | Elizabeth | Adams | Died 4th Feby | 1814 | aged 33 years
1563		Jane	Addison	F	56y	Jane Relict | of | Ralph Addison | Esqre | Died 14th Feby | 1850 | aged 56 Yrs
1565		Ralph	Addison	M	69y	Ralph Addison | Died August 6th | 1840 | aged 69 years
1567		Harriet	Agnew	F	53y	Mrs | Harriet Agnew | Died 11th <u>May</u> | 1815 | aged 53 years
1566		Mary	Agnew	F	45y	Miss | Mary Agnew | Died 6 Novr | 1831 | in her 45th year
1564		William	Agnew	M	81y	William Agnew | Esqr | Died 18th April | 1828 | aged 81 years
	8024	William	Alexander	M	64y	William Alexander | Esquire | Died 18th Jany | 1814 | Aged 64 Years
	8114	William	Alexander	-	-	William Alexander | Esqr | Died 18th Jany | 1814 | Aged 64 Years
4034		Jane	Allcock	F	83y	Mrs | Jane Allcock | Died 15th Jany | 1831 | Aged 83 Years
	8019	Mary Ann	Allcock	Y	20y	Miss Mary | Ann Allcock | 1830
	8097	Mary Ann	Allcock	-	-	Miss | Mary Ann | Allcock | Died 26th Feby | 1830 | In her 21st Year
1119		William Plaxton	Allcock	M	62y	Willm Pla . . . . . | Allcock Esq. | Died 7 Jany | 1840 | aged 62 years
3057		Elizabeth	Anderson	F	39y	Mrs | Elizth Anderson | Died 9th February | 1817 | aged 39 years
1059		Jane	Anderson	F	23y	Miss | Jane Anderson | of Udoll North Britain | Died 5th April | 1814 | aged 23 years
1027		Mary	Anderson	F	86y	Mrs | Mary Anderson | Died 17th March | 1820 | aged 86 Years
5005		George	Andrews	Y	9m	Master | Geoe Andrews | Died Marh 6th | 1819 | Aged 9 months
5014		George	Anstey	M	64y	George A<u>nst</u>ley | Esq | Died 22nd Septr | 1826 | Aged 64 years [outer plate]]. George A<u>st</u>ley | Esq | Died 22nd Septr | 1826 \ Aged 64 years [inner plate]]
1085		John	Armstrong	M	39y	John Armstrong | M.D. | Born 8th May | 1784 | Died 12th Decr | 1829
1148		Spearman	Armstrong	Y	1y	Spearman Armstrong | Born 27th Septr | 1828 | Died 21st Octr | 1829
6057		Elizabeth Ann	Ashmore	Y	15y	Elizabeth Ann | Ashmore | Died 27th July | 1844 | Aged 15 Yrs
5053		Mathias	Aspden	M	75y	Mathias Aspden | Esqr | from the City of Philadelphia | Merchant | Died 9th August | 1824 | Aged about 75 Years
1573		John	Atkinson	M	69y	John Atkinson | Esqr | Died 29th Sept | 1828 | in his 70th year
1575		Margaret	Atkinson	F	66y	Mrs | Margt Atkinson | Died 30th Septr | 1825 | aged 66 years
1553		Martha	Atkinson	F	79y	Mrs | Martha | Atkinson | Died 17th Jun | 1837 | aged 79 yrs
1574		Thomas	Atkinson	M	80y	Thomas Atkinson | Esqr | of Lincoln's Inn Fields | & of Bedford Place | Died 4th Augst | 1836 | aged 80 years
4038		Peter	Aube	Y	4d	Master | Peter Aube | Died 15th June | 1828 | Aged 4 Days
1512		Alexander	Auldjo	M	63y	Alex Auldjo | Esq | Died 21st May | 1821 | Aged 63 Yrs
6126		Elizabeth	Awe	F	-	Elizabeth Awe | Died 10th September | 1837 | ......
2018		*G . . .*	*Ba . . . . . a . . x*	Y	*6½ m*	*Mast G . . . Ba . . . . . a . . x Died Feb 12 18 . 2 | Aged 6½ mon*
4082		Edward	Baiton	M	-	Captn | Edward Baiton | Died 7th April | 1838 | Aged . . . .
6014		Robert	Balmanno	M	24y	Mr | Robt Balmanno | Obt 11th March | 1818 | Aetat 24 Years
6030		James Langley	Bankes	M	42y	Ja Langley Bankes | Esqr | Died 4th May | 1839 | Aged 42 Years
3094		*Dr . . . . . . lill*	*Bardo*	U	-	*M . r Dr . . . . | . . . lill Bardo | 1831*
5022		Arthur Henry	Barker	Y	9y	Arthur Henry | the Son of | George Barker | Esqr | Born 2nd March 1839 | Died 1st July 1848

Notes/Sources	will	MI	Year
of Rolls Yard, Chancery Lane (will TNA PROB 11/1971); of 24 Brunswick Sq (*PO London 1841*)	Y	Y	1842
spinster, Southampton St (*List of Names 1815*)			1814
widow, Montague St, Russell Sq (*GM* April 1850, 447; Will TNA PROB 11/2109); wife of Ralph Addison (1565)	Y	Y	1850
of Temple Bar (Will TNA PROB 11/1932); Montague St, Russell Sq, and Esher Lodge, Surrey (*GM* Sept 1840, 329); husband of Jane Addison (1563)	Y	Y	1840
?wife of William Agnew (1564); of Russell Sq, died of consumption, aged 53, 15 Aug 1815 (LMA P82/GEO1/63); Mrs Agnew, wife of Capt. Agnew, Russell-square' (*GM* Aug 1815, 279)			1815
?dau of William Agnew (1564) and Harriet Agnew (1567)			1831
of Russell Sq (Will TNA PROB 11/1739); Gower St (*List of Names 1815*); ?husband of Harriet Agnew (1567); of Russell Sq, died of old age, aged 81, 14 Apr 1828 (LMA P82/GEO1/63); died in Russell Sq (*GM* May 1828, 475)	Y		1828
of the Island of Saint Vincent , West Indies (Will TNA PROB 11/1892); Provost Marshal General of the Mainland of St. Vincent, brother Elizabeth Rose (6050) (MI)	Y	Y	1814
mother of Mr Allcock of Woburn Pl (*GM* Feb 1831, 187) (1119); of Woburn Pl, died of old age, aged 83, 18 Jan 1831 (LMA P82/GEO1/63)			-
?dau of William Allcock (1119)			1831
			1830
of St George (Will TNA PROB 11/1921); of No 48 Woburn PL (*PO London 1829*); director of the Imperial Brazilan Mining Association (English 1825, 10); governor of Christ's Hospital 1833 (Trollope, 1834, 335)			-
of Walworth, Surrey (Will TNA PROB 11/1589)	Y		1840
of Marchmont St, died of consumption, aged 23, 3 Apr 1814 (LMA P82/GEO1/63)	Y		1817
			1814
widow, St George Bloomsbury (Will TNA PROB 11/1621); No 23 Southampton Row, Bloomsbury (SUN MS 11936/475/927775 24 Feb 1817); of Southampton Row, died of old age, aged 86, 21 Mar 1820 (LMA P82/GEO1/63)	Y		1820
of Upper Bedford Pl, died of convulsions, aged 9 months, 7 Mar 1819 (LMA P82/GEO1/63)			1819
of Montague St, N Russell Sq (Will TNA PROB 11/1827); No 1 Russell Sq (SUN MS11936/501/1026736 27 Jan 1825); of Guilford St, died of spasms, aged 65, 23 Sep 1826 (LMA P82/GEO1/63)	Y		1826
doctor of medicine, Bloomsbury (Will TNA PROB 11/1763)	Y		1829
of Russell Sq, died of consumption, aged 1, 25 Oct 1829 (LMA P82/GEO1/63)			1829
dau of James Ashmore, barrister at law (1841 Census),			1844
merchant, Philadelphia, United States (Will TNA PROB 11/1701); Richmond Surrey (*List of Names 1815*); of King St, died of consumption, aged 76, 10 Aug 1824 (LMA P82/GEO1/63)	Y		1824
husband of Martha Atkinson (1553); John Atkinson married Martha Edwards, 29 July 1780 at St George's, Hanover Sq (IGI)			1828
wife of Thomas Atkinson, of Bedford Place (1574) (*GM* Oct 1825, 380); Margaret Borough married Thomas Atkinson, 28 Nov 1783 at St Clement Danes, Westminster (IGI); of Bedford Pl, died of consumption, aged 66, 5 Oct 1825 (LMA P82/GEO1/63)			1825
widow, Liverpool St, Middx (Will TNA PROB 11/1872); wife of John Atkinson (1573); John Atkinson married Martha Edwards, 29 July 1780 at St George's, Hanover Sq (IGI)	Y		1837
gentleman, Lincoln's Inn Field (Will TNA PROB 11/1868); Thomas Atkinson, esq. of Lincoln's Inn Fields died in Bedford Place (*GM* Sept 1836, 332); Thomas Atkinson married Margaret Borough, 28 Nov 1783 at St Clement Danes, Westminster (IGI)	Y		1836
			1828
merchant; Berners St, Middx (Will TNA PROB 11/1644); 'Business man, militia officer, JP and politician' (Tulchinsky 1966)	Y		1821
			1837
			-
			1838
son of Alexander Balmanno and Ann Anderson (m. 1790, St Marylebone, Pallot's Marriage Index); b. 17 Jun 1793, chr. 21 Jul 1793, St Olave, Hart St (IGI; Pallot's Baptism Index); Alexander Balmanna, mechant, 75 Queen St, Chaepside (*PO London 1808*)			1818
silk merchant (Will TNA PROB 11/1913); No 8 Upper Bedford Pl, Russell Sq (SUN MS 11936/548/1211871, 20 Jan 1836); chr 15 Nov 1796 at All Saints, Loughborough, son of Langley and Lydia Bankes (IGI)	Y	Y	1839
			1831
father probably George Barker of No 1 Gray's Inn Sq (SUN MS 11936/523/1105496 17 Mar 1830) and No 26 Montague Pl, Russell Sq (SUN MS 11936/531/1141249, 8 May 1830)			1848

Coffin	Plate	Forename	Surname	M/F/Y/U	Age at Death	Inscription Text
3031		Edward Fisher	Barker 1843	Y	1y	Edward Fisher	the infant son of	George Barker	Esqr	Died 17th March	1843	age of 18 months [outer plate] Edw Fisher	infant son of	Geoe Barker Esqr	Died 17th March	1843	age of 12 month [inner plate]
3081		Frank	Barker	Y	3y	Frank Barker	Died 25th June	1843	aged 3 years
3030		George William	Barker	Y	3w	George Willm	Barker	Died 16th July 1830	aged 3 weeks
2005		Joseph	Barker	Y	8y	Master	Joseph Barker	Died 7th June	1807	aged 8 years
2003		Joseph Huggins	Barker	M	32y	Joseph Huggins	Barker Esqr	Died 22nd Novr	1805	aged 32 years
2024		William	Barker	M	45y	Willm Barker	Esqr	Died 8 Septr	1814	Aged 45
6104		John	Barnes	M	34y	John Barnes	Esq	Of the Inner Temple	Died 21th (sic) April	1833	Aged 34 Years
1042		Emily Matilda	Barry	F	34y	Emily Matilda	Wife of	Chas Upham Barry	Esqr	Died 24th November	1835	aged 34 years
4069		Edwin	Barton	M	82y	Edwin Barton	Esq	Died 12th Jan	1828	Aged 82 Yrs
4001		David	Bateson	M	63y	Mr	David Bateson	Died 19th Marh	1821	In his 63rd Year
5080		*David*	*Baxendale*	M	-	*Mr	David Bax . . . dale	Died 31st	1813	. . . . . . Years	Baxendale	. . . 3 [foot plate]*
3062		Ellen Renica	Baxendale	Y	13w	Miss Ellen	Renica Baxendale	Died 30th April	1827	aged 13 weeks
1080		Ann	Bayley	F	59y	Ann Bayley	Born 21st day of December	1771	Died 16th day of August	1831
1554		Catherine Howell	Beaumont	F	61y	Catherine E̲lwell	Bea̲umont	1826
1571		Daniel	Beaumont	M	83y	Daniel Beaumont	Esqr	Died 15th March	1821	in the 84th year of his life
1572		John Percival	Beaumont	M	74y	John	Percival Beaumont	Esqr	Late Captain	in the 30th Regiment	Died 25th Feby	1844	aged 74 years
1514		Elizabeth	Beckwith	F	76y	Mrs Elizth	Beckwith	Died 2 Jan	1814	aged 76 years
1531		Letitia	Beetson	F	64y	Mrs	Letitia	Beetson	Died 27 Aug	1830	in her 65th year
1018		William	Beetson	M	78y	William	Beetson Esq.	Died 11th Septr	aged 78 years
6029		Robert	Bell	M	85y	Genl. Robert Bell	of the Honble	E.I. Compy Servce	Madras Artillery	Died 26th March	1844	in the 86 Year of his Age
1114		Jane	Benson	F	-	Miss	Jane Benson	1839 [head plate]
6132		Georgina Emily	Berkeley	Y	7y	Georgina	Emily Berkeley	Died 27th March	1839	Aged 7 Years
1052		Jesse	Biggs	M	56y	Mr	Jesse Biggs	Died 31st Jany	1831	aged 56 Y. .
	8104	William	Biggs	M	70y	Willm Biggs	Esqr	Died Marh 5th	1814	Aged 70 Yrs
	8031	Thomas Chapman	Billing	M	29y	Mr	Thomas Chapman	Billing	1825
5062		William	Bingley	M	48y	The Revd	William Bingley	Died . . th March	1823	Aged . . Years
6064		Sarah	Birch	F	70y	Mrs	Sarah Birch	Died 8 March	1832	Aged 70 Years
4024		Joseph William Edwin	Biscoe	M	28y	Captn Joseph	Willm Edwin	Biscoe	Died 24 Marh	1827	Aged 28 yrs
1506		Thomas	Bland	M	22y	Mr	Thomas Bland	Died 8th Augst	1825	Aged 22 Years
5078		Henrietta	Blundell	Y	4y	Henrietta Blundell	Died 21st Feby	1829	Aged 4 Year
4075			Booth	M	69y	Mr	. . . . Booth	. . . . May	1831	Aged 69 Years
1503		Miles	Booty	M	52y	Miles Booty	Esq.	Died 30th Nov	1815	aged 52 years

Notes/Sources	*will*	*MI*	*Year*
father probably George Barker of No 1 Gray's Inn Sq (see 5022)			
			1843
of Montague Pl, died of convulsions, aged 3, 17 Jul 1830 (LMA P82/GEO1/63); father probably George Barker of No 1 Gray's Inn Sq (see 5022)			
			1830
			1807
			1805
of Bloomsbury (Will TNA PROB 11/1560); probably William Barker of No 19 Woburn Place (*Holden's* 1811)	Y		1814
gentleman, No. 2 Torrington St (Will TNA PROB 11/1818); of Torrington St, died of 'inflammation', aged 33, 25 Apr 1833 (LMA P82/GEO1/63)	Y		1833
wife of Charles Upham Barry, born Emily Matilda Dodd, married 1829, St George's Bloomsbury (Pallot's Marriage Index); No 41 Torrington Sq (SUN MS 11936/519/1092858, 25 Jun 1829; MS 11936/534/1153599, 28 Mar 1833); death notice *GM* Jan 1836, 98			1835
			1828
upholder & cabinet maker, Bloomsbury (Will TNA PROB 11/1642); of Holborn, died of stoppage in the stomach, aged 62, 21 Mar 1821 (LMA P82/GEO1/63)	Y		1821
			1813
dau of Lloyd Salisbury Baxendale , solicitor (*PO London 1841*, 896) and Ellen Baxendale, formerly Ellen Salisbury (*GM* Dec 1825, 560)			1827
of No 26 Upper Chapman St (SUN MS 11936/497/1006521, 30 July 1823); of Southampton St, died of consumption, aged 59, 26 Aug 1831 (LMA P82/GEO1/63)			1831
spinster, Bloomsbury (Will TNA PROB 11/1713); Catherine Howell Beaumont, of Bloomsbury Sq, died of cancer, aged 61, 18 May 1826 (LMA P82/GEO1/63)	Y		1826
gentleman, Bloomsbury (Will TNA PROB 11/1641); of Hart St, died of old age, aged 84, 18 Mar 1821 (LMA P82/GEO1/63)	Y		1821
captain on half pay, 30th Regt of Foot, Bloomsbury (Will TNA PROB 11/1994); Bernard St, Russell Sq (*GM* April 1844, 439)	Y		1844
widow, Bloomsbury (Will TNA PROB 11/1551); late of the City of York	Y	Y	1814
late Letitia Waring, wife, St George Bloomsbury (Will TNA PROB 11/1775); wife of William Beetson (1018)	Y		1830
of Woburn Pl, Russell Sq (Will TNA PROB 11/2061); husband of Letitia Beetson (1531); No 7 Francis St, Tottenham Court Rd (SUN MS 11936/468/917885, 25 April 1816; MS 11936/480/954226, 29 April 1819), then No 8 Woburn Place, Russell Sq (SUN MS 11936/492/995369, 14 Aug 1822; MS 11936/530/1143131, 18 July 1832)	Y		1847
general, Honorable East India Company service, Russell Sq (Will TNA PROB 11/1996); Madras Artillery (*Dodwell & Miles* 1838, 8-9)	Y	Y	1844
			1839
2nd dau of Charles Berkeley, of Montague Pl (*GM* May 1839, 552-230) and No 53 Lincoln's Inn Field (*Gazette*, Issue 20809, 4371)			1839
gentleman, Montague St (Will TNA PROB 11/1781); of Montague Pl, died of asthma, aged 56, 2 Feb 1831 (LMS P82/GEO1/63)	Y		1831
			1814
of Broad St, died of 'inflammation', aged 29, 20 Sep 1825 (LMA P82/GEO1/63)			1825
clerk, Bloomsbury (Will TNA PROB 11/1668); naturalist and Cof E clergyman; writer on botany, topography and zoology (*DNB*, Rev William Bingley); of Charlotte St, died of 'inflammation', aged 48, 17 Mar 1823 (LMA P82/GEO1/63)	Y		1823
widow, Park St, Camden Town (Will TNA PROB 11/1796)	Y		1832
b. c 1800, in Devon, christened Broad Clyst, Devon 24 Mar 1800 (IGI); of Kenton St, died of 'spasm', aged 28, 28 Mar 1827 (LMA P82/GEO1/63)			1827
son of Michael Bland esq of Montague Pl, Russell Sq, died of smallpox at the Brew house in Chiswell St (*GM* Aug 1825, 187); of Montague Pl, died of smallpox, aged 22, 11 Aug 1825 (LMA P82/GEO1/63)			1825
of Woburn Pl, died of scarlet fever, aged 4, 23 Feb 1829 (LMA P82/GEO1/63)			1829
			1831
of St Sidwell's, Exeter (Will TNA PROB 11/1577); died 'at Mr White's, Hart-street, Bloomsbury' (*GM* vol 85, pt 2, Supplement, 641); related to John Gillam Booty, solicitor, of No 1 Guilford St? (*Survey of London*, vol 24, 'The Foundling Hospital and Doughty Estates'); of Hart St, died of asthma, aged 52, 3 Dec 1815 (LMA P82/GEO1/63)	Y		1812

Coffin	Plate	Forename	Surname	M/F/Y/U	Age at Death	Inscription Text
5040		Robert	Bowles	M	67y	Major Genl | Robert Bowles | Died 6th Sept | 1812 | In his 68th Year [inner plate]
6022		William	Bowyer	M	64y	William Bowyer | Esqre | Died 16 July | 18 . 7 | Aged 64
3078		Caroline Alecia	Brisco	F	67y	Dame | Caroline Alecia | Brisco | Relict of the late | Sir John Brisco Bart | of Crofton Hall Cumberland | Died 27 Dec | 1824 | aged 67 years
3041		George Seley	Broderick	Y	17d	Master | George Seley | Broderick | Died 6th Septr | 1825 | aged 17 Days
2012		Isabella	Brodrick	Y	9y	Miss Isabella Brodrick Died 6th Feby 1829 aged 9 years
7052		Margaret Isabel	Brodrick	Y	16y	Margt Isabel | Brodrick | Born 27th Octr 1812 | Died 19th July | 1829
2051		Ann	Brown	F	59y	Mrs Ann Brown | Died 10 July 1831 | aged . . .
4051		Dorothy	Brown	F	-	Miss | Dorothy Brown | Died 27th Sept | 1826
	4087	Dorothy	Brown	F	-	Miss | Dorothy Brown | Died 27th Sept | 1826
3009		George	Brown	M	70y	George Brown | Esqre | Died 13th April | 1829 | aged 70 years
6012		James	Brown	M	79y	James Brown | Esqre | Died 26th Nov | 1843 | Aged 79 Yrs
6092		Mary	Brown	F	79y	Mrs | Mary Brown | Died 5th June | 1855 | Aged 79 Years
6093		Sarah	Brown	F	-	Sarah Brown | Died 3rd June | 1817
2052		Sarah	Brown	F	-	Mrs Sarah Brown | Died 29th July 1823 | aged . . years
1121		Thomas	Brown	M	62y	Mr | Thomas Brown | Died 25th Septr | 1840 | aged 62 years
	8054	Elizabeth Dundas	Buchanan	Y	15y	Miss Elizabeth | Dundas Buchanan | 1836
	8076	Elizabeth Dundas	Buchanan	-	-	Miss | Elizabeth Dundas | Buchanan | Died 27th June |1836 | Aged 16 Yrs & 4 mons
	8105	Elizabeth Dundas	Buchanan	-	-	Miss | Elizth Dundas | Buchanan | Died 27th June |1836 | Aged 16 yrs & 4 mons
1128		Catharine	Bullock	F	30y	Catharine Bullock | Wife of Edwd Bullock Esqr | of the Inner Temple | Died 11 June 1839 | aged 30 years
1067		Dorothy	Bullock	F	58y	Dorothy Bullock | Relict of the Late | Edward Bullock | Esq | Died 29th April | 1836 | aged 58 years
1016		Edward	Bullock	M	52y	Edward Bullock | Esq | Died 10th Febry | 1824 | in his 53rd year
	1584	Edward	Bullock	-	-	Edwd Bullock | Esqre | Died 10th Feby 1824
1561		Edward	Bullock	Y	11m	Mastr | Edward Bullock | Died 20th Jany | 1835 | aged 11 mons
	8131	Samuel	Burford	M	35y	Samuel Burford | Esqr | Died Jany 3rd | 1815 | In his 36th Year
4064		Mary	Burke	F	75y	Mary Burke | Died 21st Nov | 1833 | Aged 75 Yrs
1054		Elizabeth	Burley	F	31y	Miss | Eliz Burley | Died 7th May | 1827 | aged 31 years
1053		George	Burley	M	73y	George Burley | Esq. | Died 25th Dec | 1823 | aged 73 yrs
1009		Mary	Burley	F	-	Mary | Relict of | George Burley | Esq. | Died 14th July 1836 | aged . . . years
1022		William	Burley	M	37y	William Burley | Esqre | Died 26th March | 1847 | aged 37 years
1068		Henry	Burnet	M	71y	Henry Burnet | Esqre | Died 15th April | 1833 | aged 71 years
1133		Mary	Burnet	F	69y	Mrs | Mary Burnet | Died 9th Feby | 1832 | aged 69 years
5079		Louise	Burnham	Y	13m	Miss Louise | Burnham | Died 21st Jan | 1817 | Aged 15 Months
4076		Elizabeth	Burton	F		Mrs Elizabeth Burton | Died 20th Octr | 182 . | Aged . 7 . . Years
5084		Catherine	Butcher	F	65y	Mrs Cathe Butcher | 1830
6049		John	Bygrave	M	94y	John Bygrave | Died 19th April | 1847 | Aged 94 Years
4084		William Moffat	Burnie	Y	3d	Mastr William | Moffat Burnie | Died 9th April | 1815 | Aged 3 days
5012		John	Campbell	M	53y	John Campbell | Esq | Died 24th Feb | 1834 | Aged 53 Years

Notes/Sources	will	MI	Year
major general in the service of the Honorable the United Company of Merchants of England Trading to the East Indies, Upper Fitzroy Street (Will TNA Prob 11/1542); Bomaby Presidency (Adjutant General's Office, 1798)	Y		1812
of Great Coram St, died of 'inflammation', aged 64, 15 Jul 1827 (LMA P82/GEO1/63)			1827
widow of Sir John Brisco; (Will of Sir John Brisco, TNA PROB 11/1437); born Caroline Alicia Flemming, dau.of Gilbert Fane Fleming and Lady Camilla Bennet, dau. of Charles Bennet, 2nd earl of Tankerville (*Complete Baronetage*).	Y	Y	1824
			1825
			1829
			1829
of Holborn, died of consumption, aged 59, 10 Jul 1831 (LMA P82/GEO1/63)			1831
spinster, Kensington (Will TNA PROB 11/1717)	Y		1826
			-
Bloomsbury (Will TNA PROB 11/1754); of Russell Sq, died of dropsy, aged 70, 16 Apr 1829 (LMA P82/GEO1/63)	Y		1829
merchant, Bloomsbury Sq (Will TNA PROB 11/1991); *GM* Jan 1844, 105	Y		1843
widow, St George Bloomsbury (Will TNA 11/2215); 25 Bloomsbury Sq (1851 Census)	Y		1855
spinster, Bloomsbury (Will TNA PROB 11/1593)	Y		1817
			1823
artist, colourman, High Holborn (Will TNA PROB 11/1934); see National Portrait Gallery website (https://www.npg.org.uk/live/ artistsupp_b.asp)	Y		1840
death 'In Montagu Place, Elizabeth Dundas Buchanan, fourth surviving daughter of the late Lieut.-Colonel Buchanan, Royal Engineers, in her 16th year' (The Court Magazine, vol IX, June-Dec 1836, viii)			1836
			-
wife of Edward Bullock, barrister of the Inner Temple, dau-in-law of Edward Bullock of Jamaica (1016); born Catherine Cripps, youngest dau of Joseph Cripps, MP for Cirencester, married 1832, 5 children (*GM* Feb 1858, 222)			1839
widow of Edward Bullock (1016); born Catherine Harrison dau of Thomas Harrison, attorney general of Jamaica.			1836
Upper Bedford Pl, Russell Sq (Will TNA PROB 11/1681); husband of Dorothy Bullock (1067); Edward Bullock of Jamaica (*GM* Feb 1858, 222); died of 'an apoplectic attack while attending the West India meeting at the city of London Tavern' (*The Connaught Journal*, Galway, Thursday, February 19, 1824); of Upper Bedford Pl, died of apoplexy, aged 52, 15 Feb 1824 (LMA P82/GEO1/63)	Y		1824
			-
?son of Edward and Catherine Bullock			1835
laceman and haberdasher, No. 99 Oxford St (Will TNA PROB 11/1564)	Y		1815
			1833
spinster, Bloomsbury (Will TNA PROB 11/1726); of Bloomsbury Pl, died of consumption, aged 31, 9 May 1827 (LMA P82/GEO1/63)	Y		1827
gentleman, Lincoln's Inn (Will TNA PROB 11/1680); husband of Mary Burley (1009); solicitor in partnership with John Beardsworth and Daniel Moore – Messrs Beardsworth, Burley and Moore, No 8 Lincoln's Inn Square (*Salisbury & Winchester Journal*, Monday Aug 18 1788; *The Reading Mercury*, Monday 3 Feb 1794); of Bloomsbury Pl, died of consumption, aged 73, 26 Dec 1823 (LMA P82/GEO1/63)	Y		1823
widow, Bloomsbury Pl (Will TNA PROB 11/1864); wife of George Burley (1053)	y		1836
died 'in York-pl, Portman-sq (GM May 1847, 560); of York Pl, Portman Sq (Will TNA PROB 11/2053)	Y		1847
of St George Bloomsbury (Will TNA PROB 11/1814); ?husband of Mary Burnet (1133); of Keppel St, died of a liver complaint, aged 71, 19 Apr 1833 (LMA P82/GEO1/63)	Y		1833
?wife of Henry Burnet (1068); of Keppel St, died of a hernia (sic), aged 69, 10 Feb 1832 (LMA P82/GEO1/63)			1832
of Holborn, died of water on the head, aged 13 months, 25 Jan 1817 (LMA P82/GEO1/63)			1817
possibly Elizabeth Burton, widow of Islington (Will TNA PROB 11/1750, 10 Jan 1829)	Y		1828
widow, High Holborn (TNA PROB 11/1769); of Holborn, died of dropsy, aged 65, 23 Mar 1830 (LMA P82/GEO1/63)	Y		1830
attendant, British Museum (1841 Census)			1847
of Russell Sq, died of convulsions, aged 3 days, 9 Apr 1815 (LMA P82/GEO1/63)			1815
possibly John Henry Campbell of Hammersmith (Will TNA PROB 11/1828)	Y		1834

Coffin	Plate	Forename	Surname	M/F/Y/U	Age at Death	Inscription Text
5039		John	Campbell	M	84y	John Campbell | Esq | Died 12th June | 1818 | Aged 84 Years
	8036	Mary	Campbell	F	81y	Mrs | Mary Campbell | 1837
	8085	Mary	Campbell	-	-	Mrs | Mary Campbell | Died 16th July | 1837 | Aged 81 Years
	8106	Mary	Campbell	-	-	Mrs | Mary Campbell | Died 16th July | 1837 | Aged 81 years
1070		*Can....*		U	-	..... | .... Can.... | Died 31st Jan | . 8 .. | .....
1048		John	Capper	M	87y	John Capper | Esquire | Died 26th April | 1835 | in his 88th year
1102		Ann	Cartwright	F	68y	Mrs | Ann Cartright | Died .. Decr | 1824 | aged 68 Yrs
6065		Maria	Cartwright	Y	18y	M— | Maria Cartwright | Died 7th Feby | 1810 | Aged 18 Years
3501		Henry Randle	Case	Y	8y 11m	Henry Randle Case | Died 27th Sepr | 1819 | Aged 8 Years and 11 mons
1062		Helen	Cavendish	F	62y	Mrs | Helen Cavendish | Died 26th July | 1828 | aged 62 years
6121		Mary	Chandler	F	35y	Mrs | Mary Chandler | Died 15th August | 1834 | aged 35 years | .....
6063		Charles	Charlesworth	M	47y	Mr | Chas Charlesworth | Died 23rd Jany | 1805 | in his 48th Year
2021		Jane	Charretie	F	75y	Mrs Jane Charretie | Died 10th Dec | 1835 | aged 75 years
4002		Philip	Charretie	M	86y	Philip Charretie | Esqr | Died 14th Octr | 1827 | Aged 86 years
1507		Eliza	Children	F	74y	Mrs | Eliza Children | Died 1st Septr | 1839 | aged 74 years
1037		John	Children	M	-	John .... e | Child ... Esqre | Died 10th Jany | 1852 | in his . 5 year
3074		Anne	Church	F	36y	Mrs | Anne Church | Died 25 Oct | 1831 | aged 36 years
3079		John	Church	M	62y	John Church | Esq | Died 28th July | 1825 | aged 62 years
2033		Thomas	Churm	M	59y	Mr | Thos Churm | Died 8 July | 1831 | aged <u>3</u>9 yrs
5004		Joseph	Circuit	M	44y	Mr | Joseph Circuit | Died 11 March | 1822 | Aged 44 Years
6124		Isaac Samuel	Clamtree	M	63y	Isaac Samuel Clamtree | Esq | Died 10th ...... | 182. | Aged 63 Years
3053		Esther	Clark	F	83y	Mrs | Esther Clark | Died 3rd Aug | 1836 | aged 83 years
3006		Thomas	Clark	M	68y	Thomas Clark | Esqr | Died 26th July | 1826 | aged 68 Yrs
1056		Elizabeth	Clay	F	51y	Mrs | Elizabeth Clay | Died 9th June | 1811 | aged 51 years
5074		William	Clay	M	76y	William Clay | Esqre | Died 21st March | 1824 | in his 76th Year
3010		Phillip	Conley	Y	5y	Master Phillip Conley | Died 13th Sept | 1825 | aged 5 yrs
5049		Catherine	Conoley	Y	15y	Miss | Cathe Conoley | Died 13th March | 1833 | Aged 15 Years
6078		Sarah	Coombe	F	77y	Mrs Sarah Coombe | Died 5th August | 1838 | Aged 77 Years
	8092	Anna Helena	Correa	Y	-	*? D Anna Helena A Correa Filla Henrici A Correa et | .... Candidae A Correa, Spes Cura, Caricia Amor | .... Parentibus suis erat in Funchalenst, Deocese | .... Madelrae sexto die Kalendr 11 August 11 Anno | Domini 1801 nnata Futi in Dei Fidl Sub Parentium | ... raed.. ata: ab Patri Amicis omnibus qui Parentibus | Admirata Teneraque sicut eios Germinans in nora | inexpectaea per ... in civitae... Apscessa | Full octavo die Kalendrii Decembre Anno Domini 1808 | In cuio que subito ascendi ubi in gloria Angeloriam | Resquiescat in Pace.*
6004		Anne	Cotton	F	62y	Mrs | Anne Cotton | Died 16th March | 1814 | aged 62 years
7045		Jane Dennis	Covell	F	60y	Mrs Jane Dennis ... ell | Died 10th July 1838 | Aged 6 . Years
	8064	Jane Dennis	Covell	-	-	Mrs Jane | Dennis Covell | Died 10th May | 1838 | Aged 60 Yrs
7055		John	Covell	M	74y	Major | John Covell | Died 17th Septr | 1834 | Aged 75 Years
	8081	John	Covell	-	-	John Covell | Esqr | late Major of 76th Reg | Died 17th Septr | 1834 | Aged 74 yrs
3026		Julia	Cowley	Y	13y	Miss | Julia Cowley | Died 21 April | 1825 | aged 13 years
1109		Peter	Coxe	M	90y	Peter Coxe | Esqr | Died 22nd Jany | 1814 | in the 91st year | of his life
5007		Henry Whitfield	Cresswell	M	35y	Henry Whitfield | Cresswell Esqr | died 17th Feby | 1828 | in his 36th year Henry Whitfield | Cresswell Esqre | 1828

Notes/Sources	*will*	*MI*	*Year*
gentleman, Bloomsbury (Will TNA PROB 11/1606); of Hart St, died of dropsy, aged 84, 12 Jun 1818 (LMA P82/GEO1/63)	Y		1818
widow, Bloomsbury; (Will TNA PROB 11/1882)	Y		1837
			-
			-
of Bloomsbury (Will TNA PROB 11/1850)	Y		-
of Hunter St, died of dropsy, aged 68, 17 Dec 1824 (LMA P82/GEO1/63)			1835
			1824
grandson of Randle Ford (3502) and Elizabeth Ford (3503); son of Henry Case and his 2nd wife Elizabeth Ford; b 11 Oct 1810 (IGI)			1810
of Great Coram St, died of cancer, aged 62, 27 Jul 1828 (LMA P82/GEO1/63)			1819
			1828
of Bloomsbury (Will TNA PROB 11/1420)	Y		1834
widow , No 3 Burton Crescent, Middx (Will TNA PROB 11/1856)	Y		1805
of Brunswick Sq (Will TNA PROB 11/1731)	Y		1835
wife , the British Museum, St George Bloomsbury (Will TNA PROB 11/1840); formerly Eliza Towers, widow, 3rd wife of John Children (1037), married 1810 Marylebone (Pallots Marriage Index)	Y		1827
of the British Museum, Russell St (Will TNA PROB 11/2147); husband of Elizabeth Children (1507); *DNB*, John George Children	Y		1839
			1852
of Bedford Pl (Will TNA PROB 11/1702); of Bedford Pl, died of mortification, aged 62, 25 Jul 1825 (LMA P82/GEO1/63)	Y		1831
plumber, No 4 Hyde St, Bloomsbury (SUN MS 11936/465/899498, 23 Nov 1814; *Old Bailey Proceedings*, 17 Feb 1819, Ref. No. f18190217-1); of Hyde St, died of a paralytic [stroke], aged 59, 9 Jul 1831 (LMA P82/GEO1/63)			1825
butcher, Bloomsbury (Will TNA PROB 11/1655); No 5 Bloomsbury Market (SUN MS 11936/490/989828, 11 Mar 1822); of the Market, died of asthma, aged 44, 16 Mar 1822 (LMA P82/GEO1/63)	Y		1831
gentleman, Bloomsbury Sq (Will TNA PROB 11/1666); of Bloomsbury Sq, died of apoplexy, aged 63, 16 Jan 1823 (LMA P82/GEO1/63)	Y		1822
widow, Hendon, Middx (Will TNA PROB 11/1865); ?wife of Thomas Clark (3006)	Y		1823
of Hendon, Middx (Will TNA PROB 11/1715); ?husband of Esther Clark (3053); of Bury Pl, died of consumption, aged 68, 31 Jul 1826 (LMA P82/GEO1/63)	Y		1836
?wife of William Clay (5074)			1826
of Upper Gower St (Will TNA PROB 11/); ?husband of Elizabeth Clay (1056)	Y		1811
			1824
			1825
spinster, Somers Town, Middlesex (Will TNA PROB 11/1899)	Y		1833
			1838
			1814
			1814
widow, Red Lion Sq (Will TNA PROB 11/1895); wife of John Covell (7055) ; widow of Major Covell deceased, died of inflammation of the throat, aged 59, 9 May 1838 (Death certificate)	Y		1838
			-
formerly Major, 76th Regiment of Foot (Will TNA PROB 11/1841; *GM* Nov 1834, 654); husband of Jane Covell (7045)	Y		1834
			-
of Russell Sq, died of convulsions, aged 13, 22 Apr 1825 (LMA P82/GEO1/63)			1825
of Bloomsbury (Will TNA PROB 11/1993); auctioneer, writer and poet, died at his home in Wilmost St, Brunswick Sq (DNB, Peter Coxe)	Y		1814
Supernumerary Proctor excercent in the Ecclesiastical Courts in Doctors' Commons (Will TNA PROB 11/1741; *GM* Feb 1828, 188))	Y	Y	1828

Coffin	Plate	Forename	Surname	M/F/Y/U	Age at Death	Inscription Text
5002		Mary	Cresswell	F	50y	Mary Cresswell I Died 15 April 1809 I aged 50 Mrs I Mary Cresswell I 1809 [footplate]
5013		Richard Cheslyn	Cresswell	M	69y	Richard I Cheslyn Cresswell I Esq I Died 11th Feby I 1824 I in the 70th Year I of his Age
4003		William Henry	Crowder	M	78y	Willm Henry I Crowder I Esqre I Died 29th March I 1830 I Aged 78 Yrs
1066		Elizabeth	Crump	F	60y	Mrs I Elizth Crump I Died 21st July I 1825 I aged 60 years
1036		Joseph	Crump	M	78y	Joseph Crump I Esqr I Died 18th August I 1825 I aged 78 years
1118		Jane	Cundale	F	84y	Mrs I Jane Cundale I Died 30th April I 1840 I aged 84 years
1019		John	Cundale	M	63y	John Cundale I Esq I Died 8th July I 1819 I aged 63 Yrs
	8045	Jane	Curtis	F	37Y	Jane Curtis I Died 22 April I 1811
	8110	Jane	Curtis	-	-	*Julie* Curtis I Departed this life I 22nd Day of April I 1811 I in the 38th year I of her life
2061		Henry	Dampier	M	58y	Henry Dampier I Knight I . . . . I Died 3rd Feb 1816
1017		Sarah	Davies	F	46y	Mrs I Sarah Davies I Died 17 Feby I 1833 I aged 46 yrs
1076		Hannah	Davis	F	68y	Mrs I Hannah Davis I Died 3rd May I 1838 I aged 68 years
	3101	Hannah	Davis	-	-	Mrs I Hannah Davis I Died 3rd May I 1838 I aged 68 years
	8115	Thomas Lewis Owen	Davis	M	71y	Thoas Lewis Owen I Davis Esqre I Died 15th Jany I 1828 I Aged 74 Y
	8117	William	Davis	M	36y	Mr I William Davis I Died 23rd June I 1827 I Aged 36 Years
1570		Ann	Day	F	59y	Miss I Ann Day I Spinster I Died 27th Jany I 1827 I aged 59 years
1541		Ann Catherine	Day	Y	16y	Ann Catherine Day I Died 24th May 1818 I aged 16 years
1519		Ansell	Day	Y	4m	Master I Ansell Day I Died 26 Jan I 1808 I aged 4 mon
1542		Susannah	Day	F	39y	Mrs I Susannah Day I Died 5th Sept I 1810 I aged 39 years
1535		Thomas	Day	Y	12y	Mastr Thos I Day I Died 24th June I 1815 I Aged 12 Years
1536		William	Day	M	42y	Willm Day I Esqr I Died 5th May I 1807 I aged 42 years
	8070	Charles	de Constant	M	73y	Charles de Constant I Esqr I of Geneva I Obit 15th July I 1835 I Aetat 73
	8087	Charles	de Constant	-	-	Charles I de Constant I Esq I of Geneva I Obit 15th July I 1838 I Aetat 73
	vault 2, 11	Lewis Andrew	de la Chaumette	M	72 y	Lewis Andrew . . . . Cha . . . tte Esq. F.R. . I Obit . January 1836 I Aetat 72
5043		Anne Phoebe	Debary	F	52y	Mrs I Anne . . . . I Debary I Died 15th Feb I 1829 I Aged 52 Years
5035		Richard	Debary	M	58y	Richard Debary I Esqr I Died 8th January I 1826 I in his 59th Year
1086		Robert	Dennett	M	77y	Robert Dennett I Esqr I Born 6th Feb 1760 I Died 14th May I 1837
	1582	Robert	Dennett	-	-	Robert Dennett I Esq I Born 6th Feby 1760 I Died 14th May 18[37] I aged 77
6091		Samuel	Denton	M	47y	Samuel Denton I Esqr I Died 27th March I 1806 I Aged 47 Years
6128		Susanna	Deverill	F	76y	Mrs I Susanna D. . . . . I Died 13th S . . . . . I 1823 I Aged 70 Years
3067		Edward	Dew	M	76y	Edward Dew I Esq. I Died 22 Jan I 1834 I in his 77 year
6017		Justin	Dick	M	74y	Justin Dick I Esq I Died 9th August I 1818 I Aged 74 Years
5019		Mary	Dickinson	F	50y	Mrs I Mary Dickinson I Died 21st Decr I 1810 I Aged 50 Years
6086		Elizabeth	Dobson	F	53y	Mrs I Elizabeth Dobson I Died 5 June I 1818 I Aged 53 Yrs
6070		Maria	Dobson	F	-	Maria Dobson I Died May 29 I 1834
6054		Susanna	Dobson	F	72y	Susanna Dobson I Died 1 Dec I 1840 I Aged 72 Years
1106		William	Dodd	M	72y	William Dodd I Esq I Died 10th May I 1832 I aged 72 years

Notes/Sources	will	MI	Year
wife of Richard Cheslyn Cresswell (5013); of Bloomsbury Sq, died of cancer, aged 50, 18 Apr 1809 (LMA P82/GEO1/63)		Y	1809
of Queen's Sq (Will TNA PROB 11/1686); 'Proctor of Doctors' Commons and one of the Deputy Registrars of the Prerogative Court, Canterbury' (*London Magazine, March 1824*, 336); husband of Mary Cresswell (5002)	Y	Y	1824
of Clapham Common, Surrey (Will TNA PROB 11/1769); of Montague Pl (*Annual Register 1859*, 419); of Montague Pl, died of consumption, aged 79, 31 Mar 1830 (LMA P82/GEO1/63)	Y		1830
wife of Joseph Crump (1036); of Charlotte St, died of 'inflammation', aged 60, 21 Jul 1825 (LMA P82/GEO1/63)			1825
of Charlotte St, Bedford Sq (Will TNA PROB 11/1702); of Charlotte St, died of consumption, aged 78, 20 Aug 1825 (LMA P82/GEO1/63); husband of Elizabeth Crump (1066)	Y		1825
widow, Tavistock Sq (Will TNA PROB 11/1927); wife of John Cundale (1019)	Y		1840
merchant, Hart Street, Bloomsbury (*GM* July 1819, 92; Will TNA PROB 11/1618); husband of Jane Cundale (1118); of Hart St, died of 'mortification', aged 63, 17 Jul 1819 (LMA P82/GEO1/63)	Y		1819
spinster, Bloomsbury (Will TNA PROB 11/1522); of Hart St, died of consumption, aged 38, 24 Apr 1811 (LMA P82/GEO1/63)	Y		1811
			-
Justice of His Majesty's Court of Kings bench, Montague Pl, Russell Sq (Will TNA PROB 11/15770; of Montague Pl, died of dropsy, aged 58, 8 Feb 1816 (LMA P82/GEO1/63); see *DNB*, Sir Henry Dampier	Y		1816
of King St, died of a tumour, aged 46, 18 Feb 1833 (LMA P82/GEO1/63)			1833
			1838
			-
of Bloomsbury Sq, died of stone, aged 71, 14 Jan 1828 (LMA P82/GEO1/63)			1828
bookseller, Bloomsbury (Will TNA PROB 11/1731); of Southampton Row, died suddenly, aged 36, 28 Jun 1827 (LMA P82/GEO1/63)	Y		1827
of Bloomsbury (Will TNA PROB 11/1721); of Keppel St, died of 'ossification of the heart', aged 59, 1 Feb 1827 (LMA P82/GEO1/63)	Y		1827
of Keppel St, died of consumption, aged 16, 29 May 1818 (LMA P82/GEO1/63)			1818
of Montague St, died of 'inflammation', aged 4 months, 29 Jan 1808 (LMA P82/GEO1/63)			1808
widow, Montague St (Will TNA PROB 11/1515); ?wife of William Day (1536); of Montague St, died of dropsy, aged 39, 5 Sep 1810 (LMA P82/GEO1/63)	Y		1810
of Montague St, died of consumption, aged 12, 26 Jun 1815 (LMA P82/GEO1/63)			1815
of Bloomsbury (Will TNA PROB 11/1461); ?husband of Susannah Day (1542); of Montague ST, died of consumption, aged 42, 8 May 1807 (LMA P82/GEO1/63)	Y		1807
died 'At Russell-square, aged 73, Charles de Constant, esq. of Geneva' (*GM* Aug 1835, 219); Charles de Constant de Rebecque known as 'le Chinois'; married Anne Louise Renee Achard, da of the Swiss banker Jacques Achard Aug 1798 (IGI)			1835
			-
of St George Bloomsbury (TNA PROB 11/1856); Stock Exchange (*List of Names* 1815)	Y		1836
widow, St Giles, Middlesex (Probate inventory or declaration TNA PROB 31/1278/654-794A); second dau of Lt Col Downman (MI); wife of Richard Debary (5035)	Y	Y	1829
of Lincoln's Inn Field (MI); of Bedford Pl, Russell Sq (*Holden's 1811*); husband of Anne Phoebe Debary (5043)		Y	1826
of Bloomsbury (Will TNA PROB 11/1879); No 39 Lincoln's Inn Field (SUN MS 11936/482/962139, 17 Jan 1820)	Y		1837
			-
of Russell Sq now resident at Turnham Green, Middx (Will TNA PROB 11/1446); first husband of Arabella Gascoyne (6073) (*Naval Chronicle* 20, 1808, 493)	Y		1806
possibly Susanna Deverill, of Great Russell St, died of old age, aged 76, 18 Sept 1823 (LMA P82/GEO1/63)			1823
of Guilford St, Russell Sq (Will TNA PROB 11/1828); died in Queen Sq, Bloomsbury, aged 76, late Examiner of King's Dues, and collector of City Dues, at the Custom House (*GM* June 1834, 666)	Y		1834
			1818
			1810
spinster, Bloomsbury (Will TNA PROB 11/1605); of Keppel St, died of dropsy, aged 53, 5 Jun 1818 (LMA P82/GEO1/63)	Y		1818
spinster, Bloomsbury (Will TNA PROB 11/1833)	Y		1834
spinster, Keppel St, Russell Sq (Will TNA PROB 11/1939)	Y		1840
gentleman, No 37 Fleet St, London (TNA PROB 11/1799); of Torrington Sq, died of consumption, aged 72, 15 May 1832 (LMA P82/GEO1/63)	Y		1832

Coffin	Plate	Forename	Surname	M/F/Y/U	Age at Death	Inscription Text
3075		Hannah	Donaldson	F	-	Mrs | Hannah Donaldson | Died 8th Sept | 1811
3080		William	Donaldson	M	70y	Willm Donaldson | Esq | Died 23rd Feb | 1806 | aged 70 years
1518		Emily Charlotte	Donne	U	4y 6m	Emily | Daughter of | H & C Donne | 1823
1107		Sarah	Dove	F	46y	Mrs | Sarah Dove | Died 20th May | 1837 | aged 46 years
	3099	Elizabeth	Draper	F	44y	Elizabeth | Wife of | Thomas Draper Esq | Inspector of Hospitals | in His Majesty's Service | Died 30th Sepr | 1834 | Aged 44 Years
4041		Caroline	Drew	Y	18m	Caroline | Daughter of David L . . . [&] | Lydia Drew | Died 3rd June | Aged 18 months
4028		John	Drew	Y	9m 18d	John | Son of David & Lydia Drew | Died 21st Novr | 1822 | Aged 9 months & 18 days
6125		Ann	Driver	F	40y	Ann Driver | Died 31 January | 1830 | Aged 40 years
4016		John	Duer	M	-	John Duer | Esqr | Captn in His Majesty's | Royal Navy | Died 17th Novr | 1814
1088		Charlotte	Duff	F	88y	Mrs | Charlotte Duff | Died 15th Feby | 1847 | aged 88 years
7068		Mary Anne	Dunbar	F	39y	Mrs Mary | Anne Dunbar | Wife of | William Dunbar Esqr | formerly of Cricklade Wilts | Died 11th April | 1829 | Aged 49 Years
	8041	Mary Anne	Dunbar	-	-	Mrs Mary | Anne Dunbar | 1829
	8127	Mary Anne	Dunbar	-	-	Mrs Mary Anne | Dunbar Wife of | Wiliam Dunbar Esqr | formerly of Cricklade Wilts | Died 11th April | 1829 | Aged 49 Years
	8068	William	Dunbar	M	60y	William Dunbar | Esqr | Died 21st March | 1842 | . . . . . . 60 Years
6053		Jane	Eden	F	82y	Mrs | Jane Eden | Died 3rd July | 1815 | Aged 82 Years
2037		David	Edwards	M	22y	D . . . . . Edwards | son of Thos [and] Elizth Edwards | . . . . . . of Holborn | Born 25th September 1825 | Died 12th May 1848
2058		David	Edwards	M	51y	David Edwards | Esq | Died 3rd April | 1831 | aged 51 years
2053		Elizabeth	Edwards	F	46y	Mrs Elizth Edwards | Died 20th August 1847 | aged 46 years
4019		Hannah	Edwards	F	44y	Mrs | Hannah Edwards | Died 4th March | 1816 | Aged 44 Ys
5001		Honoria	Edwards	Y	5m 15d	Miss Honoria Edwards | Died 17th March | 1808 | Aged 5 months | & 15 Days
6090		John	Elphic	M	51y	Mr | John Elphic | Died 17th May | 1833 | Age 51 Years
6081		Elizabeth	Elphick	F	61y	Mrs | Elizabeth Elphick | Died 17 November | 1838 | Aged 61 Years
1578		Amelia	England	Y	11m	Miss | Amelia England | Died 25 March | . . 17 | aged 11 mons
4073		Joseph	England	M	67y	Mr | Joseph England | Died 14th Oct | 1831 | in his 68th Year
	8077	Robert	Evans	M	55y	Robert Evans | Esq | Died 27th Jany | 1807 | Aged 59
6123		Jean	F . . . . ron	F	85y	Mrs | Jean F. . . . ron | Died 10th Oct. | 1823 | Aged 85 Years
1100		Ann Maria	Fairfax	F	60y	Mrs Ann | Maria Fairfax | . . . . 7th May | 1824 | aged 66 years
1090		William	Fairfax	M	51y	William Fairfax | Esqr | Late Captain of the | Hugh Inglis | Hon[b]le East India | Company's Service | Died 19th March 1817 | aged 51 years
	8056	Joan	Falconer	F	82y	Mrs Joan | Falconer | Died May 8 | 1827 | Aged 82
1123		Emma	Farhill	Y	19y	Miss Emma | Farhill | Died August 2nd | 1806 | aged 19 years
1081		Sarah	Farhill	Y	16y	Sarah | Daughter of | George Farhill Esq. | & Sarah his Wife | Died 27th March | 1815 | aged 16 yrs
4009		Robert	Ferguson	M	84y	Robert Ferguson | Esqr | Died 11th Oc . . | 1830 | Aged 84 Years
2057		Elizabeth	Finch	F	67y	Mrs | Elizabeth Fin . . . | Died 3rd August | 1801 | aged 67 years
1132		John	Fl	M	28y	John Fl . . . . . | Esq. | . . . . . 21st Jany | . 8 . 6 . . . 28 years
3503		Elizabeth	Ford	F	47y	Mrs Elizth Ford | Died 23rd June | 1806 | Aged 47 Y
3502		Randle	Ford	M	59y	Randle Ford | Esq | Died 1st Janry | 1811 | Aged 59 Yrs
2066		John	Forenson	M		John Forenson | Esq | Died 11th January | 1811 | . . . .
3032		George Edward	Forster	Y	10y	Masr | George Edward | Forster | Died 27th Jany | 1819 | aged 10 years

Notes/Sources	*will*	MI	Year
wife of William Donaldson (3080); 'Mrs Hannah Bell', relict of William Donalsdon (MI)		Y	1811
of Temple Bar (Will TNA PROB 11/1439); husband of Hannah Donaldson (3075)	Y	Y	1806
of Montague Pl, died of 'inflammation', aged 4 years 6 months, 9 May 1823 (LMA P82/GEO1/63)			1823
wife of William Richard Dove 'of this parish'		Y	1837
died 29 Sep (sic) 'In Queen-sq., Bloomsbury, the wife of Thos. Draper, esq. Inspector-general of hospitals in Jamaica' (*GM* Nov 1834, 554); Thomas Draper Inspector General of Army Hospitals, Kensington (Will of Thomas Draper, TNA PROB 11/2120)	(Y)		1834
dau of David Drew of Balham Hill, Surrey (Will TNA PROB 11/2179), and Lydia Drew, widow of Peckham, Surrey (TNA PROB 11/2223); of King Street, died of 'teeth', aged 18 months, 5 June 1821 (LMA P82/GEO1/63)	(Y)		1821
son of David & Lydia Drew: see 4041; of King St, died of whooping cough, aged 9 months, 24 Nov 1922 (LMA P82/GEO1/63)	(Y)		1822
			1830
lieutenant in His Majesty's Ship the Albion in His Majesty's Royal Navy, of St Pancras, Middx (Will TNA PROB 11/1963)	Y		1814
widow, No 10 Russell Sq (Will TNA PROB 11/2073)	Y		1847
wife of William Dunbar (8068); of Henrietta St, died of apoplxy, aged 39, 10 Apr 1829 (LMA P82/GEO1/63)			1829
			-
			-
of No 49 Manchester St, Manchester Sq, Middx (Will TNA PROB 11/1963); husband of Mary Anne Dunbar (7068); died in Queen St, Cavendish Sq; formerly Captain 40th Regiment (*GM* May 1842, 561)	Y		1842
of Charlotte Pl, died of old age, aged 82, 7 Jul 1815 (LMA P82/GEO1/63)			1815
son of Thomas and Elizabeth Edwards (2053), 21 King St, High Holborn, Bloomsbury (1841 Census)			1848
dressing case manufacturer, King St, Bloomsbury (Will TNA PROB 11/1785); of King St, died of 'inflammation', aged 51, 7 Apr 1831 (LMA P82/GEO1/63)	Y	Y	1831
wife of Thomas Edwards, mother of David Edwards (2037), 21 King St, High Holborn, Bloomsbury (1841 Census; *PO London 1841*)			1847
			1816
			1808
of Kingsgate St, died of asthma, aged 51, 6 May 1833 (LMA P82/GEO1/63)			1833
			1838
dau of Joseph England (4073); of Wilmot St, died of croup, aged 11 months, 29 Mar 1817, (LMA P82/GEO1/63)			1817
carpenter and builder, St Pancras, Middx (Will TNA PROB 11/1792); ?father of Amelia England (1578); of Wilmot St, died of 'inflammation', aged 67, 19 Oct 1831 (LMA P82/GEO1/63)	Y		1831
of Bloomsbury (Will TNA PROB 11/1455); of Charlotte St, died of 'inflammation', aged 55, 28 Jan 1807 (LMA P82/GEO1/63)	Y		1807
			1823
?wife of William Fairfax (1090); of Southampton Row, died suddenly, aged 60, 12 May 1824 (LMA P82/GEO1/63)			1824
captain of the ship Hugh Inglis in the service of the United Company of Merchants trading to the East Indies (Will TNA PROB 11/1591); ?husband of Ann Maria Fairfax (1100); of Southampton Row, died of an abcess, aged 51, 21 Mar 1817 (LMA P82/GEO1/63)	Y		1817
			1827
			1806
Sarah, only daughter of George Farhill, Esq. (*GM* April 1815, 75)			1815
gentleman, St Pancras (Will TNA PROB 11/1780); possibly Charlotte St, Rathbone Pl (*List of Names 1815*); of Hunter St, died of old age, aged 84, 10 Oct 1830 (LMA P82/GEO1/63)	Y		1830
of Great Russell St, died of inflammation, aged 67, 4 Aug 1807 (LMA P82/GEO1/63); *possibly* widow, Meetinghouse Alley, St George, Middlesex (will TNA PROB 11/1456)	Y		1807
			-
formerly Elizabeth Langford Brooke, married Randle Ford (3502) 13 Dec 1785, Rostherne, Cheshire (IGI)			1806
of Bloomsbury Sq (Will TNA PROB 11/1518); of Wexham, Bucks (IGI); barrister; husband of Elizabeth Ford (3503); of Bloomsbury Sq, died of -, aged -, 5 Jan 1811 (LMA P82/GEO1/63)	Y		1811
			1811
of Southampton St, died of consumption, aged 10, 29 Jan 1819 (LMA P82/GEO1/63)			1819

Coffin	Plate	Forename	Surname	M/F/Y/U	Age at Death	Inscription Text
6116		John	Foulerton	M	63y	Captain ǀ John Foulerton ǀ R N ǀ Died 16th Nov ǀ 1827 ǀ Aged 63 Yrs
1150		Mary	Foulerton	F	27y	Miss ǀ Mary Foulerton ǀ Died 18th Sepr ǀ 1820 ǀ ....
5050		Charlotte	Fraiser	Y	10y	Miss ǀ Charlotte Fraiser ǀ Died 27th May ǀ 1829 ǀ Aged 10 Years
1074		Elizabeth	Francis	F	30y	Mrs ǀ Elizth Francis ǀ Died 24 July ǀ 1826 ǀ in the 31st yr ǀ . . . . . .ge
5033		Marie	Francklin	F	76y	Mrs ǀ Marie ǀ Francklin ǀ Died 25th Dec ǀ 1836 ǀ Aged 76 Yrs
	8075	Alex	Fraser	Y	18y	Alex Fraser ǀ Esqr ǀ Eldest Son of ǀ Thos Fraser Esq ǀ of Lead . .chae ǀ in the County of Inverness ǀ Obit 23rd . . 18 ǀ Aetat 18 Years
5025			Fraser	F	30y	. . . . ǀ Youngest Daughter of Captain Fraser ǀ Died 26th [or 28th] May ǀ 1832 ǀ Aged 30 Years
3073		Hester	French	F	36y	Mrs ǀ Hester French ǀ Died 26 June ǀ 1821 ǀ aged 36 years
1500		Sophia	Fuseli	F		Mrs ǀ Sophia Fuseli ǀ 1832
4021		*G . . . . ia*	*Ga . . ns*	*F*	*64y*	*Mrs ǀ G . . . . ia Ga . . ns ǀ Died 20th Decr ǀ 1835 ǀ Aged 64 Yrs*
5015		Jane	Gamble	F	57y	Jane Gamble ǀ Spinster ǀ Died 24th Augst ǀ 1817 ǀ Aged 57 Years
4074		Fanny	Garthwaite	F	62y	Mrs Fanny ǀ Gaithwaite ǀ Died 2 . . of February ǀ 1813 ǀ Aged 62 Yrs
6073		Arabella	Gascoyne	F		Mrs Colonel ǀ Arabella Gascoyne ǀ Widow ǀ Died 8th April ǀ 1835
6011		Joseph	Gasgoyne	M	71y	Lieut. Colonel ǀ Joseph Gasgoyne ǀ Honble East India ǀ Company's Service ǀ Died 21st March ǀ 1830 ǀ Aged 71 Years
1124		John Broke	Gaunt	M	61y	J[oh[n ǀ Broke Gaunt ǀ Died 3rd Augst ǀ 1834 ǀ aged 61 years
4033		Louisa . . . . . inica	Gavaron	Y	13y 9m	Louisa . . . . . inica Gavaron ǀ Died 25 May ǀ 1826 ǀ Aged 13 Yrs & 9 Mons
	2072	Louisa . . . . . inica	Gavaron	-	-	. . . . Louisa . . . . . inica Gavaron ǀ Died 25th May ǀ 1826 ǀ Aged 15 years & 9 months
6032		Cathrine	Gehot	F	72y	Mrs Cathrine Gehot ǀ Died 23 May ǀ 1824 ǀ Aged 72 Years
7043		Gilbert	Gollan	M	62y	Gilbert Gollan ǀ Esqr ǀ late of the Island ǀ St. Vincent ǀ Died Jany 26th 18[09] ǀ Aged 62 Years
	8071	Gilbert	Gollan	-	-	Here are deposited ǀ the Remains of ǀ GILBERT GOLLAN ǀ late of the ǀ Island of St. Vincent ǀ Esquire ǀ after a most painful and . . . ious illness which he bore with ǀ Christian fortitude and r esignation ǀ . . . . . . Life on the 26th Jany ǀ 1809 ǀ . . . . 62 Years
2026		Louisa	Gore	Y	12y	Miss ǀ Louisa Gore ǀ Died 5th Novr ǀ 1814 ǀ in her 12th Year
	2073	Louisa	Gore	-	-	Miss Louisa Gore ǀ Daughter of John & Mary Gore of Boston, New England ǀ . . . . ǀ Aged . . years & 7 months
3045		Aaron John	Graham	M	65y	Aaron Graham ǀ Esq ǀ Died 21st Decr ǀ 1818 ǀ aged 65 Years Aaron Graham ǀ Esq ǀDied 24th Dec ǀ 1818 ǀ aged 65 years
3070		Edward Lloyd	Graham	M	38y	Captain ǀ Edwd Lloyd Graham ǀ R.N. ǀ Died 27th May ǀ 1820 aged 38 years
3002		Charles	Grant	M	77y	Charles Gran[t] ǀ Esqr M.P. ǀ Died 31st Oct ǀ 1823 ǀ aged 77 Yr
3014		Charles	Grant	M	52y	Charles Grant ǀ Esqr ǀ Died 23rd April ǀ 1823 ǀ aged 52 years
3049		Elizabeth	Grant	Y	23d	Miss ǀ Elizh Grant ǀ . . . . . ǀ Died 6th January . . . . ǀ aged 23 days
3003		Jane	Grant	F	70y	Mrs ǀ Jane Grant ǀ Died 23rd Jany ǀ 1827 ǀ Aged 70
3021		Joseph	Grant	Y	19m	Mast ǀ Joseph Grant ǀ Died 15th Septemr ǀ 1807 ǀ aged 19 mons
3027		Maria Jane	Grant	U	-	Miss ǀ Maria Jane ǀ Grant ǀ Died 23rd May ǀ 1828 [Second plate appears to read: '1823']
3037		Robert	Grant	Y	3y 11m	Robert ǀ Son of Robert & Sophia Grant ǀ . . . .
	3105	Robert	Grant	-	-	Robert ǀ Son of ǀ Patrick and Sophia Grant ǀ Died . . . May ǀ . . . . ǀ Aged 3 Years ǀ & 11 months
6048		William	Grant	M	39y	Mr ǀ William Grant ǀ Died 31st July ǀ 1824 ǀ Aged 34 Years
3024		William Thomas	Grant	M	54y	William ǀ Thomas Grant ǀ Esqre ǀ Died 15th May ǀ 1848 ǀ in the 55th year of his life
1524		Barbara	Gray	F	55y	Mrs ǀ Barbara Gray ǀ 1831
4008		Julianna	Gray	F		Julianna Gray ǀ Died 31st . . . . . ǀ 1837 ǀ . . . . . . Years
1548		Mary	Gray	F	52y	Mrs ǀ Mary Gray ǀ Died 16th Feby ǀ 1825 ǀ aged 52 years

Notes/Sources	will	MI	Year
of Upper Bedford Pl, Russell Sq, merchant (*Annals of Philosophy*, July-Dec 1816, 398); one of the elder bretheren of Trinity House (Cotton, 1818, 244)			1827
dau of John Foulerton (6116); of Bedford Pl, died of consumption, aged 27, 19 Sept 1820 (LMA P82/GEO1/63)			1820
			1829
of Bernard St, died of consumption, aged 30, 26 Aug 1826 (LMA P82/GEO1/63)			1826
spinster, Bloomsbury (Will TNA PROB 11/1871)	Y		1836
			1818
			1832
			1821
widow of Charlotte St, Fitzroy Sq (Will TNA PROB 11/1798); Sophia (née Rawlins) wife of Henry Fuseli (Will TNA PROB 11/1703), artist, keeper of the Royal Academy London (*DNB* Henry Fuseli)	Y		1832
			1835
			1817
possibly Fanny Garthwaite, of Bernard St, died of 'inflammation', aged 65, 26 Feb 1817 (LMA P82/GEO1/63)			1813
2nd wife of Joseph Gascoyne (6011), married 1808, St George's Hanover Sq (Pallot's Marriage Index); widow of Samuel Denton (6091) (*Naval Chronicle* **20**, 1808, 493)			1835
of Tavistock Sq (Will TNA PROB 11/1768); husband of Arabella Gascoyne (6073)	Y		1830
gentleman, Bloomsbury (Will TNA PROB 11/1835); died in Charlotte St, aged 60 (sic) (*GM* Sept 1834, 331); 'Alathea, relict of John Broke Gaunt esq. of London' died at Ipswich 14 Dec 1852 (*GM* Feb 1853, 217)	Y		1834
dau of Theodore Gavaron (of Tavistock Sq: Will TNA PROB 11/1932) and his wife Maria Magdalena.	(Y)		1826
alternative reading of age: 15y 9m	(Y)		-
of Great Russell St, died of consumption, aged 72, 27 May 1824 (LMA P82/GEO1/63)			1824
of the Island of St Vincent (TNA PROB 11/1492); of Streatham St, died of consumption, aged 62, 28 Jan 1809 (LMA P82/GEO1/63)	Y		1809
			-
			1814
			-
of St Giles and St George, Bloomsbury (Will TNA PROB 11/1612), Secretary to the Governors of the Island of Newfoundland, 1779-1791 (Privy Council 1927, vol. IV, 1919)	Y		1818
Captain in His Majesty's Navy, of Cheltenham, Glos (Will TNA PROB 11/1657)	Y		1820
of St George Bloomsbury (Will TNA PROB 11/1824); director of the East India Company (*DNB*, Charles Grant); of Russell Sq, died of spasms, aged 77, 2 Nov 1823 (LMA P82/GEO1/63)	Y	Y	1823
			1823
			-
widow, St Marylebone (Will TNA PROB 11/1742); wife of Charles Grant (3002), dau of Thomas Fraser of Balnain (*DNB*, Charles Grant)	Y		1827
			1807
spinster, St Pancras (Will TNA PROB 11/1742)	Y		1828
			-
			-
of Plumtree St, died of 'inflammation', aged 39, 3 Aug 1824 (LMA P82/GEO1/63)			1814
son of Charles Grant (3002) and Jane Grant (3003), born 1793 (DNB, Charles Grant)			1848
possibly widow, Clapham, Surrey (Will TNA PROB 11/1828); of Southampton Row, died of consumption, aged 55, 4 Jul 1831 (LMA P82/GEO1/63)	Y		1831
spinster, St George Bloomsbury (Will TNA PROB 11/1889)	Y		1837
of Southampton Row, died of consumption, age 52, 16 Feb 1825 (LMA P82/GEO1/63)			1825

Coffin	Plate	Forename	Surname	M/F/Y/U	Age at Death	Inscription Text
5016		Thomas	Gray	M	66y	Mr | Thos Gray | Died 14th Octr | 1822 | Aged 65 Yrs
1523		William	Gray	M	67y	William Gray | Esqre | Died 9th Jany | 1842 | aged 67 years
1149		Catherine	Green	F	74y	Catherine | Relict of | Edward Green | Esq. | Died 13 March | 1832 | aged 74 years
1072		Arabella	Groom	F	34y	Arabella Groom | Born 27th Septr | 1778 | Died 8th March | 1813
1105		William	Groom	M	54y	William Groom | Esqre | Died 25th . . . | 1830 | aged 54 years
6097		Thomas	Guillod	M	42y	Thomas Guillod | Esq | Died 10th March | 1815 | Aged 42 Years
5083		Sarah	Ha	F	-	Mrs Sarah Ha . . . .
1004		Robert	Halham	M	61y	Robert Halham | Esq. M.D. | Died 24th Nov | 1845 | aged 61 years
5027		James	Hall	M	75y	Mr | James Hall | Died . . . . Novr | 1832 | Aged 70 Years
5031		Jean Robertson	Hamilton	Y	10y	Miss Jean | Robertson Hamilton | Died 2nd Novr | 1817 | Aged 10 Yea
3023		Charles	Hammond	Y	8y 6w	Chas Hammond | Died 21 Oct | 1826 | aged 8 years | & 6 weeks
2048		Sarah Maria	Hammond	F	22y	Sarah Maria Hammond | Born 7th Septr 1818 | Died 13th Septr 1840
2006		Sophia	Hammond	F	57y	Sophia | Wife of | William Hammond | Esqr | Died 14th Novr | 1840 | aged 57 years
3018		Laura Teresa	Hansard	Y	18m	Miss | Laura Teresa | Hansard | Died 4 May | 1826 | Aged 18 mons
4046		Elizabeth	Hanson	F	47y	Mrs | Elizth Hanson | Died 30th March | 1814 | Aged 4 . years
	3102	Elizabeth	Hanson	F	47y	Mrs | Elizabeth Hanson | Died 30th March | 1814 | Aged 47
1117		Thomas	Harison	M	59y	Tho Harison | Esqr | Died 8th Decer | 1830 | in his 60th year
4023		Roger	Harries	M	79y	Roger Harries | Esqr | Died 12th March | 1839 | In the 80th Yr of his Age
2062		Jane	Harris	F	60y	Miss | Jane Harris | Died 9th January | 1836 | aged 60 years
5068			Harris	F	-	Mrs | . . . . . . Harris | . . . . | . . . . . | . . . . | . . . .
	8014	William	Harris	M	-	William Harris | Esquire | Died 21st June | 1826 | aged . . . Years
	8038	William	Harris	-	-	William Harris | Esqr | 1826
	8096	William	Harris	-	-	Willm Harris | Esqr | Died 2. . . June | 1826
5065		John	Harrison	M	80y	John Harrison | Esqre | Died 21st Septr | 1841 | Aged 80 Yrs
4072		Mary	Harrison	F	78y	Mrs | Mary Harrison | Died 7th August | 1831 | Aged 78 Years
	8079	Richard	Harrison	M	74y	Mr | Richd Harrison | Died 28th Jany | 1812 | Aged 74 Years
	8094	Richard	Harrison	-	-	Mr | Richd Harrison | Died 28th Jany | 1812 | Aged 74 Yrs
1513		Charles John	Harrison Batley	M	13y	Charles John | Harrison Batley | Esqre | Died 30 Jany | 1841
2035		Mary	Harrison Batley	Y	16y 67d	Miss Mary Harrison Batley | Daughter of Char[les] Harrison Batley MP] for Beverley in the County of York | . . . . is love | Died [13 Aug] | 1827 | aged 16 . . . and 6Z days
5075		Ann	Hasker	F	49y	Mrs | Ann Hasker | Died 21st Janry | 1815 | Aged 50 Years
1055		Thomas	Hasker	M	84y	Thomas Hasker | Esqr | Died 4th April | 1837 | in his 85th year
6100		Mary	Hattam	F	78y	Mary Hattam | Spinster | Died 26th Sepr | 1828 | Aged 78 years
1045		Thomas	Hattam	M	81y	Thomas Hattam | Esqr | Died 9th May | 1826 | in the 82nd year | of his age
3059		Walter	Hattam	M	65y	Walter Hattam | Esq | Died Jan 27th | 1807 | aged 65
1046		Helen	Hay	F	87y	Mrs | Helen Hay | Died 25th March | 1839 | aged 87 yrs
7070		Mary	Hay	F	36y	Miss | Mary Hay | Died 27th July | 1825 | Aged 36 Years
	8040	Mary	Hay	-	-	Miss | Mary Hay | 1825
	8102	Mary	Hay	-	-	Miss | Mary Hay | Died 27th July | 1825 | Aged 36 Years
1047		William	Hay	M	88y	William Hay | Esqr | Died 11th March | 1830 | aged 88 yrs
2069		*Henrica*	*Hayor*	*F*	*28y*	*Mrs | Henrica Hayor | Died 12th Nov | 1805 | aged 28 years*
5044		Elizabeth	Heisch	Y	19y	Miss | Elizabeth Heisch | Died 24th April | 1832 | Aged 19 Yrs

Notes/Sources	will	MI	Year
gentleman, Bloomsbury (Will TNA PROB 11/1663); of Hart St, died of asthma, aged 66, 18 Oct 1822 (LMA P82/GEO1/63)	Y		1822
gentleman, Hammersmith, Middx (Will TNA PROB 11/1957)	Y		1842
of Bedford Pl, died of apoplexy, aged 74, 15 Mar 1832 (LMA P82/GEO1/63)			1832
wife of William Groom (1105), formerly Arabella Maude (Burk 1836, 87)		Y	1813
of St George Bloomsbury (Will TNA PROB 11/1772); 10 Lincoln's Inn Fields (*Holden's* 1811); solicitor to the Board of Control for the Affairs of India (Elmes 1831, 70); Richard and William Groom, solicitors, Henrietta St, Cavendish Sq (Durham RO, D/Lo/C 317); husband of Arabella Groom (1072); of Russell Sq, died of 'inflammation', aged 54, 28 Apr 1830 (LMA P82/GEO1/63)	Y	Y	1830
wine merchant, St George Bloomsbury (Will TNA PROB 11/1569); wine and brandy merchant No 3 Cockspur St (*PO London 1808*); wine and brandy merchant, No 27 Craven St, Strand (SUN MS 11936/449/844307, 26 April 1810); 7 Hart St (*Holden's* 1811); of Hart St, died of consumption, aged 42, 12 Mar 1815 (LMA P82/GEO1/63)	Y		1815
			-
			1845
of Montague St, Russell Sq (Will TNA PROB 11/1808); of Montague St, died of paralysis, aged 75, 5 Nov 1832 (LMA P82/GEO1/63)	Y		1832
of Keppel St, die of water on the head, aged 10, 14 Nov 1817 (LMA P82/GEO1/63)			1817
of Great Coram St, died of 'water head', aged 8, 20 Oct 1826 (LMA P82/GEO1/63)			1826
			1840
wife of William Hammond (b c 1779) of Russell Sq (1841 census); wife of William Hammond, stockbroker, died of decay of nature, aged 57, 14 Nov 1840 (Death certificate)			1840
4th dau, 9th child of Luke Graves Hansard (1781-1841) and his wife Elizabeth Hobbs (d. 1857); of Bedford Sq (Luke Graves Hansard will TNA PROB 11/1945 image 359/320-321); of Bedford Sq, died of whooping cough, aged 18 months, 5 May 1826 (LMA P82/GEO1/63)	(Y)		1826
of Bloomsbury Sq, died of fever, aged 47, 1 Apr 1814 (LMA P82/GEO1/63)			1814
			-
			1830
merchant, Regent Sq (Will TNA PROB 11/1908)	Y		1839
spinster, No 13 Mabledon Pl, New Rd, Middx (Will TNA PROB 11/1856)	Y		1836
			-
widower and planter, No 17 Gloucester St, Queen Sq (Will TNA PROB 11/1728)	Y		1826
			-
			-
victualler, Browns Lane, Spitalfields (Will TNA PROB 11/1952)	Y		1841
spinster, Bloomsbury (Will TNA PROB 11/1789); possibly Mary Harrison, spinster, Swan St, Minories (*List of Names 1815*)	Y		1831
upholsterer, St George Bloomsbury (Will TNA PROB 11/1530)	Y		1812
			-
son and heir of Charles Harrison Batley, MP for Beverley, brother of Mary Harrison Batley (2035), b. 1827 (*GM* vol 97 Pt 1, Supplement, 640)			1841
dau of Charles Harrison Batley, MP for Beverely, Montague St, Russell Sq; sister of Charles John Harrison Batley (1513) (*GM* Sept 1827, 282)			1827
?wife of Thomas Hasker (1055); of Woburn Pl, died of dropsy, aged 49, 23 Jan 1815 (LMA P82/GEO1/63)			1815
of Tavistock Pl, Russel Sq (Will TNA PROB 11/1876); ?husband of Ann Hasker (5075)	Y		1837
?sister of Thomas Hattam (1045); of Great Russell St, died of old age, aged 80, 28 Sept 1828 (LMA P82/GEO1/63)			1828
of St Pancras, Middx (Will TNA PROB 11/1713); No 16 Percy St (*List of Names 1815*); ?brother of Mary Hattam (6100)	Y		1826
of St George Bloomsbury (Will TNA PROB 11/1456)	Y		1807
widow, Russell Sq (Will TNA PROB 11/1909); ?wife of William Hay (1047)	Y		1839
			1825
			-
			-
of Russell Sq (Will TNA PROB 11/1768); ?husband of Helen Hay (1046); Upper Charlotte St, Rathbone Pl (*List of Names 1815*); of Russell Sq, died of old age, aged 88, 10 Mar 1830 (LMA P82/GEO1/63)	Y		1830
			1805
dau of Frederick and Elizabeth Heisch, b 12 May 1813, chr 12 Jun 1813 at St Botolph without Aldgate (IGI)			1832

Coffin	Plate	Forename	Surname	M/F/Y/U	Age at Death	Inscription Text
4063		Christian	Hely Hutchinson	M	61y	The Honble | Christian Hely | Hutchinson | Died 8th July | 1825 | Aged 61 Years
4070		Christopher	Hely Hutchinson	M	56y	The Honble | Christopher Hely | Hutchinson | M.P. | for the City of London | Died 26th Aug 1826 | Aged 56 Years
4005		Maria Louisa	Hely Hutchinson	Y	1y 5m	Maria Louisa | Hely Hutchinson | Daughter of | the Honle A.A. Hely Hutchinson | and | Catherine Maria Hely Hutchinson | Died on the 7th December | 1825 | Aged 0ne year and Five Months
4083		Richard	Hely Hutchinson	M	68y	The Right Honble | Richard Hely | Hutchinson | Earl of Donoghmore | Died 22nd Augt | Aged 68 Years
4012		Ann	Hewit	F	65y	Mrs | Ann Hewit | Died 23rd June | 1830 | Aged 65 Years
3033		Mary Isabella	Heywood	F	27y	Mary Isabella | Youngest daughter of | Samuel Heywood | Sergeant at Law & | Susanna his Wife | daughter of John Cornwall, Esq.
3012		Susanna	Heywood	F	63y	Susanna | second daughter of the | late John Corn[wall] Esqr | of Portland Place | wife of Sam Heywood | Sergeant at Law | Died 19th January 1822 | aged 63 years
1822						
	8027	Susannah Fotheringham	Hill	F	21y	Mrs Susanh F. Hill | Died Septr 12th 1819 | Aged 21 years
	8130	Susannah Fotheringham	Hill	-	-	Mrs Susannah | Fotheringham Hill | Died Sepr 12th | 1819 | Aged 21 years
3504			Hilton	Y	1m 6d	. . . . H . lton Died . . . . | Aged 1 month and 6 days grand daughter of E & R Ford
6006		John James	Hirtzel	M	64y	John James | Hirtzel Esqre | Died 13th Octr | 1815 | Aged 64 Yrs
6101		Elizabeth	Hitches	F	59y	Mrs | Elizabeth Hitches | Died 7th Oct | 1820 | Aged 59 Years
6113		Julia	Hobson	F	40y	Julia | Wife of Campbell Wright Hobson | Esq | Died 20th Sept | 1840 | Aged 40 Yrs
3042		James John	Hodge	Y	4m 3w	Mastr James | John Hoge | Died 16 Sept | 1806 | aged 4 mons 3 weeks
5061		Elizabeth	Hollam[by]	F	72y	Mrs | Elizth Hollan . . | Died 30th | . . . | 18 . . | Aged . . . .
4079		Mary	Holland	F	38y	Mrs | Mary Holland | Died 9th Sept | 1823 | Aged 38 Years
	8011	Thomas	Holloway	M	60y	Mr | Thomas Holloway | Died 13th November | 1826 | Aged 60 Years
	8037	Thomas	Holloway	-	-	Mr | Thos Holloway | 1826
	8119	Thomas	Holloway	-	-	Mr | Thomas Holloway | Died 13th Novr | 1826 | Aged 60 yrs
1151		Henry	Holmes	M	44y	Mr | Henry Holmes | Died | 28th October 1831 | aged 44 years
1087		John	Holmes	M	64y	John Holmes | Esq. | Died 23rd May | 1840 | aged 64 years
1516		Mary Susan	Holmes	F	34y	Mrs Mary | Susan Holmes | Died 29 Augst | 1829 | in the 35th year of her age
4035		Susannah	Holt	F	41y	Mrs | Susannah Holt | Died 27th April | 1810 | in her 41st Year
7021		Harold Ridley	Hone	Y	18y	Harry Riddley | Hone | Died 31st Jany | 1828 | Aged 18 Yrs
6117		Joseph Terry	Hone	M	65y	Joseph Terry Hone | Died 18th August | 1831 | Aged 65 Yrs
7079		Ann Sophia	Horne	Y	14y	Miss | Ann Sophia | Horne | Died 16th April | 1814 | Aged 14 Yrs
	8048	Ann Sophia	Horne	-	-	Miss | Ann Sophia | Horne | 1814
	8073	Ann Sophia	Horne	-	-	Miss | Anna Sophia | Horne | Died 16th April | Aged 14 years
3035		Catherine T.	Horne	Y	1m 10d	Miss | Cathn. T. Horne | Died 16th Augst 1834 | aged 1 month & 10 days
	3060	Catherine	Horne	-	-	Miss | Cathe Horne | Died 16th Augst 1834 | aged 4 mons | and 16 days
3022		Jane	Howe	F	57y	Mrs | Jane Howe | Died 4th Septr | 1841 | aged 57 years
	8065	Sarah	Hughes	F	61y	Mrs | Sarah Hughes | Died 22nd Jany | 1809 | Aged 61 Yrs
5026		Thomas Low	Hughes	M	86y	Thomas Low | Hughes Esq. | Died 9th Feb | 1829 | Aged 86 Years
	8051	James Watson	Hull	M	-	James Watson Hull | Esqr | 1831
2001		Margaret Redman	Hull	F	32y	Miss Margt | Redman Hull | Died 4th June | 1827 | aged 32 years
3052		Maria	Hulme	F	37y	Mrs Maria Hulme | Died 1 . th March | 1823 | Aged 37 years
1141		John Henry	Hume	M	51y	Revd John | Henry Hume | Died 22nd Jany | 1848 | aged 51 years

Notes/Sources	*will*	*MI*	*Year*
(Will TNA PROB 11/1695)	Y		1825
of Bulstrode St, Middx (Will TNA PROB 11/1723); younger brother of Richard Hely-Hutchinson (4083); see *DNB*, Christopher Hely-Hutchinson	Y		1826
dau of Augustus Abraham Hely Hutchinson (*GM*, Sept 1834, 314); Augustus was the younger brother of Richard Hely-Hutchinson (4083) and older brother of Christopher Hely-Hutchinson (4070); of Hunter St, died of 'water head', aged 1 year 5 months, 10 Dec 1825 (LMA P82/GEO1/63)			1825
Bulstrode St, Manchester Sq (*GM* Oct 1825, 371); elder brother of Christopher Hely Hutchinson (4070); see *DNB*, Richard Hely-Hutchinson			1825
of King St, died of consumption, aged 65, 29 Jun 1830 (LMA P82/GEO1/63)			1830
(Will of Samuel Heywood, TNA PROB 11/1747); Bedford Pl, died of consumption, aged 27, 21 Oct 1822 (LMA P82/GEO1/63)	(Y)		1822
Died ǀ on the 16 day of October ǀ 1822 ǀ aged 27 years			
wife of Samuel Heywood (Will of Samuel Heywood, TNA PROB 11/1747); of Bedford Pl, died of consumption, aged 63, 22 Jan 1822 (LMA P82/GEO1/63)	(Y)		
of Wilmott St, died of consumption, aged 21, 14 Sept 1819 (LMA P82/GEO1/63)			1819
			-
unidentified graddaughter of Elizabeth and Randle Ford			-
merchant, St George Bloomsbury (Will TNA PROB 11/1587); of Great Coram St, suddenly (*GM* Oct, 1815, 382)	Y		1815
			1820
Julia Anstey m Campbell Wright Hobson, at St Pancras, 1829 (Pallot's Marriage Index)			1840
			1806
Mrs Elizabeth Hollamby, d 30 Apr 1829 (MI)		Y	1829
			1823
of Southampton Crt, died of apoplexy, aged 60, 11 Nov 1826 (LMA P82/GEO1/63)			1826
			-
			-
of Whitefriars, City of London (Will TNA PROB 11/1791B)	Y		1831
of Brunswick Sq (Will TNA PROB 11/1929)	Y		1840
			1829
			1810
of Southampton St, died of consumption, aged 18, 1 Jan 1828 (LMA P82/GEO1/63)			1828
barrister at law and bencher of that Honorable Society of Westminster (Will TNA PROB 11/1793)	Y		1831
of Hunter St, died of 'inflammation', aged 14, 18 Apr 1814 (LMA P82/GEO1/63)			1814
			-
			-
			1834
alternative reading of age: 1 m 10d			-
widow, Canton Pl, Limehouse, Middx (Will TNA PROB 11/1851); widow of Mr Howe, gentleman, died of natural decay and effusion of the chest, aged 87, 4 Sept 1841 (Death certificate)	Y		1841
widow, Devonshire St, Queen's Sq (Will TNA PROB 11/1503)	Y		1809
			1829
of Farquhar House, Hornsey Lane, Highgate, Middx (Will TNA PROB 11/1785); Great Beddow, Essex (*List of Names 1815*); 'of County Down, Ireland' (MI); father of Margaret Redman Hull	Y	Y	1831
3rd dau of James Watson Hull (8051)			1827
			1823
vicar, clerk of Figheldean and Hilmartin, Wiltshire (Will TNA PROB 11/2078); vicar of Calne; chaplain to the Earl of Rosslyn (*GM*, June 1834, 663)	Y		1848

Coffin	Plate	Forename	Surname	M/F/Y/U	Age at Death	Inscription Text
6021		Thomas White	Hurst	M	57y	Thos White Hurst ǀ Esqre ǀ . . . . . ǀ Died 27th Febry ǀ 1834 ǀ Aged 57 Years
5030		Amelia	Huson	F	81y	Amelia Huson ǀ Died 9th Decr ǀ 1817 ǀ Aged 81 Years
5017		William	Huson	M	73y	William Huson ǀ Esq ǀ Died 15th August ǀ 1817 ǀ Aged 73 Years
4007		Mary	Huster	F	80y	Mrs ǀ Mary Huster ǀ Died 12th Jany ǀ 1838 ǀ Aged 80 Years
1031		Henry Julius	Hutchinson	M	29y	Henry Julius ǀ Hutchinson Esqr ǀ L.L.B. ǀ Died 19th Nov ǀ 1813 ǀ aged 29 Years
1501		John	Hutchinson	M	-	John ǀ Hutchinson ǀ 1815
1032		Julia	Hutchinson	Y	12y	Miss ǀ Julia Hutchinson ǀ Died 20th December ǀ 1807 ǀ aged 12 years
6005		Charles Earle	Huxley	M	28y	Mr ǀ Charles ǀ Earl Huxley ǀ Died 17th Feby ǀ 1828 ǀ in the 29th Yr ǀ of his Age
4010		Elizabeth	Jackson	F	72y	Elizth Jackson ǀ Died 23d Feby ǀ 1823 ǀ in Her 72d Year
6082		Hanna	James	F	36y	Mrs ǀ Hanna James ǀ Died 4th Nov ǀ 1814 ǀ Aged 36 Years
4011		Robert	James	M	64y	Robert James ǀ . . . . t ǀ Esqr ǀ Died . . . Feb 17th ǀ 1841 ǀ Aged 64 Years
1075		Elizabeth	Jeakes	F	57y	Miss ǀ Elizth Jeakes ǀ Died . . . . . . ǀ . . . . ǀ ag . . .
1079		James	Jeakes	M	64y	James Jeakes ǀ Esq ǀ Died 8th April ǀ 1837 ǀ aged 64 yrs
1013		John	Jeakes	Y	74y	Mr ǀ John Jeakes ǀ Died 18th July ǀ 1818 ǀ aged 74 years
1015		Joseph	Jeakes	M	39y	Mr Joseph Jeakes ǀ Died 16th July ǀ 1818 ǀ aged 39 Yrs
1024		Martha	Jeakes	F	67y	Mrs ǀ Martha ǀ Jeakes ǀ Died 9th July ǀ 1813 ǀ aged 67 yrs
1057		Thomas	Jeakes	M	57y	Mr ǀ Thomas Jeakes ǀ Died 20th . . . . . ǀ 1839 ǀ aged 37 yrs
1025		Elizabeth	Jeffries	F	65y	Elizth Jeffries ǀ Died 16th May ǀ 1841 ǀ aged 65 Yrs
4004		Elizabeth	Johnson	F	85y	Mrs ǀ Elizth Johnson ǀ Died 22nd Decr ǀ 1837 ǀ aged ǀ 85 yrs
	8124	Elizabeth	Johnston	F	65y	Elizth Johnston ǀ Died 13th Decr ǀ 1815 ǀ Aged 65 Years
	8129	Kitty	Jones	F	53y	Mrs Kitty Jones ǀ Died June 17th ǀ 1817 ǀ Aged 53 Years
2004		Richard Charles	Jones	Y	11y 19d	Richd Chrs [or Chas] ǀ Jones ǀ Esqr ǀ Died 19th October ǀ 1807 ǀ aged 11 years 7 & 19 days
1525		John	Jortin	M	69y	John Jortin ǀ Esqr ǀ Died 21st May ǀ 1843 ǀ in his 70th year
1549		John Bearpacker	Jortin	Y	13y	Master John ǀ Bearpacker Jortin ǀ Died 30th Decr ǀ 1827 ǀ aged 13 years
	1583	John Bearpacker	Jortin	-	-	Master John ǀ Bearpacker Jortin ǀ Died 30th Decr ǀ 1827 ǀ aged 13 years
1551		Sarah Bayley	Jortin	F	62y	Sarah Bayley ǀ George Jortin ǀ Died 24th Jany ǀ 1840 ǀ aged 62 years
6028		Edward	Jourdan	M	78y	Major ǀ Edward Jourdan ǀ Died 26th Septr ǀ 1830 ǀ in the 79th Yr of his Age
6120		John	Jourdan	M	64y	John Jo . . . an ǀ Esq ǀ Died 6 Oct ǀ 1811 ǀ Aged 64 Years
7020		Daniel	Julian	M	83y	*Danl Julian Esq ǀ Inocidaler ǀ .Po..he Small .... Baby ǀ Died 3rd Feby ǀ 1819 ǀ Aged 83 Years*
6068		Ann	Kay	F	40y	Mrs ǀ Ann Kay ǀ Died 11th October ǀ 1816 ǀ Aged 40 Yrs
2040		James	Kaye	Y	8m	Master James Kaye ǀ Died 17 Jan ǀ 1831 ǀ aged 8 months
5010		Jacolina	Keith	F	-	Miss Jacolina Keith ǀ Died 3 Feby ǀ 1819
7077		Elizabeth	Kerbey	F	44y	Mrs ǀ Elizabeth Kerbey ǀ Died 19th June ǀ 1824 ǀ Aged 44 Yrs
	8100	Elizabeth	Kerbey	-	-	Mrs ǀ Elizabeth Kerbey ǀ Died 19th June ǀ 1824 ǀ Aged 44 Years
6008		John	Keysall	M	78y	John Keysall ǀ Esq ǀ Died 2 May ǀ 1813 ǀ Aged 78 Years
6085		[Catherine] Eleanor	[Key]sell	F	21y	Miss ǀ . . . . Elear ǀ . . . sell ǀ . . . . 27th July ǀ 1816 ǀ Aged 21 Yrs
6007		Elizabeth Olney	Keysell	F	34y	Mrs ǀ Eliza Olney ǀ Keysell ǀ Died 28th June ǀ 1829 ǀ Aged 34 Years
6138		Ellen	Keysell	Y	4m 19d	Miss ǀ Ellen Keysell ǀ Died 13th Nov ǀ 1830 ǀ Aged 4 Ms 19 Days
6119		Frances	Keysell	F	64y	Mrs ǀ Franl Keysell ǀ Died 10th August ǀ 1819 ǀ in her 64 Year

Notes/Sources	*will*	*MI*	*Year*
			1834
spinster, Southampton Pl, Euston Sq, Middx (TNA PROB 11/2066)	Y		1817
gentleman, Bloomsbury (TNA PROB 11/1595); of Southampton St, died of consumption, aged 73, 19 Aug 1817 (LMA P82/GEO1/63)	Y		1817
servant, decay of nature attended with arthralgia, aged 80, 12 Jan 1838 (Death certificate)			1838
			1813
of Burton St, St Georges (Will TNA PROB 11/1623)	Y		1815
of Montague St, died of consumption, aged 12, 10 Dec 1807 (LMA P82/GEO1/63)			1807
cabinetmaker, upholsterer and upholder, of 16 John St, Oxford St (Sun MS 11936/499/1017765 8 July 1824; MS 11936/504/1033922 17 August 1825) ; son of Joseph and Sophia Huxley, chr at St Saviour's, Southwark 31 Mar 1799 (IGI)			1828
possibly spinster, St Dunstan, Stepney, Middx (Will TNA PROB 11/1687); possibly Elizabeth Jackson, spinster, Kentish Town (*List of Names 1815*); of Great Russell St, died of 'inflammation', aged 72, 25 Feb 1823 (LMA P82/GEO1/63)	Y		1823
			1814
of Bedford Pl (Will TNA PROB 11/1942); surgeon, 9 Bedford Pl (*PO London 1841*); surgeon, died of complcations of disease of the brain, bowel and bladder, aged 64, 17 Feb 1841 (Death certificate)	Y		1841
possibly of Little Russell St, died of apoplexy, aged 57, 11 Feb 1832 (LMA P82/GEO1/63)			1832
retired officerof the Indian Navy, Halliford, Middx (Will TNA PROB 11/1880)	Y		1837
of Little Russell St, died of apoplexy, aged 74, 28 Jul 1818 (LMA P82/GEO1/63)			1818
engraver; of Little Russell St, died of fever, aged 39, 15 Feb 1818 (LMA P82/GEO1/63)			1818
of Little Russel St, died of cancer, aged 67, 13 July 1813 (LMA P82/GEO1/63)			1813
builder, St George, Bloomsbury (Will TNA PROB 11/1921); carpenter, died of inflammation of the liver, aged 57, 20 Dec 1939 (Death certificate)	Y		1839
			1841
widow, St Marylebone (Will TNA PROB 11/1890)	Y		1837
spinster, Bloomsbury (Will TNA PROB 11/1816)	Y		1815
of Bloomsbury (Will TNA PROB 11/1593); of Bedford Pl, died of cancer, aged 53, 21 June 1817 (LMA P82/GEO1/63)	Y		1817
of Montague St, died of convulsions, aged 11, 23 Oct 1807 (LMA P82/GEO1/63)			1807
of Charlotte St, Bedford Sq (Will TNA PROB 11/1981); 'John Jortin Esq. Nible House, Wootton under Edge, Glos (*Pigot's Glos 1830*); husband of Sarah Bayley Jortin (1551); father of John Bearpacker Jortin (1549) (MI St Martin's, North Nibley, Glos)	Y		1843
son of John Jortin (1525) and Sarah Bayley Jortin (1551) (MI St Martin's, North Nibley, Glos)			1827
			-
1st wife of John Jortin (1525); dau of Edward Bearpacker, mother of John Bearpacker Jortin (1549) (MI St Martin's, North Nibley, Glos)			1840
of Devonshire St, Portland Pl (Will TNA PROB 11/1777); No 43 Devonshire Pl (*List of Names 1815*); brother of John Jourdan (6120)	Y	Y	1830
of Bedford Pl (Will TNA PROB 11/1526); brother of Edward Jourdan (6028); of Bedford Pl, died of consumption, aged 64, 9 Oct 1811 (LMA P82/GEO1/63)	Y	Y	1811
			1819
			1831
of Great Russell St, died of 'dropsy in the brain', aged 8 months, 19 Jan 1831 (LMA P82/GEO1/63)			1831
			1819
of Hart St, died of apoplexy, aged 44, 21 Jun 1824 (LMA P82/GEO1/63)			1824
			-
of Queen Sq, Middx (Will TNA PROB 11/1544); banker	Y		1813
spinster, St George Bloomsbury (TNA PROB 11/1583)	Y		1816
wife of of Broad St, died of consumption, aged 34, 1 Jul 1829 (LMA P82/GEO1/63)			1829
of Broad St, died of 'inflammation', aged 4 months, 17 Nov 1830 (LMA P82/GEO1/63)			1830
wife of Francis Keysell (d 1804: LMA P82/GEO1/63)			1819

Coffin	Plate	Forename	Surname	M/F/Y/U	Age at Death	Inscription Text
6069		Henry	Keysell	M	44y	Mr | Henry Keysell | 1833
1092		Richard	Keysell	Y	10m	Masr | Richd Keysell | Died 10th May | 1827 | aged 10 mons
6019		Richard	Keysell	M	37y	Mr Richd Keysell | Died 25 Sep | 1830 | Aged 37 Yrs
6020		Thomas	Keysell	M	37y	Mr | Thos Keysell | Died 8th Sep | 1825 | Aged 37 Yrs
5056		John	King	M	86y	John .. King | Esq | Died 7th July | 1814 | in his 86th Year
1029		Ann	Kirkup	F	66y	Mrs | Ann Kirkup | Died Janry 14th | 1826 | aged 66 years
6015		Georgiana	Kirkup	F	-	Miss | Georgna Kirkup | Died 24th Novr | 1834
1051		James Fenwick	Kirkup	M	25y	Mr | James | Fennick Kirkup | Died 28th June | 1820 | in the 26th year of his age
	8043	Joseph	Kirkup	M	53y	Joseph Kirkup Esqr | 1813
	8099	Joseph	Kirkup	-	-	Joseph Kirkup |Esqr | Died 1st May |1815 | Aged 53 years
2046		Maria	L	F	54y	Maria L . . . . . . | Died . . . . Feb | 1828 | aged 54 Years
	8083	Elizabeth	Laitridge	F	46y	Miss | Elizth Laitridge | Died 4th Feby | 1815 | Aged 46 Years
1559		Richard Brewster	Lake	Y	10m 2w	Mast Richard | Brewster Lake | Died 2 May | 1833 | aged 10 months & 2 weeks
6135		Ellen Augusta	Lambert	Y	3y	Ellen Augusta | the daughter of Richard [and] Jane Lambert | Died 25th Feb | 1844 | in the 3rd Year of her Age
5052		Mary Hannah	Lambert	Y	17y	Mary Hannah | Lambert | Died 13th Decr | 1843 | in her 17th Yr
2055		James Wake	Law	Y	5y	Master James Wake Law | Died 5th March 1825 | In the 6th year of his age
6037		Edward	Lee	M	65y	Ed . . . d Lee | . . . . 15 Feby | 182 . | Aged 65 Yrs
6024		Emily Susan	Lee	F	43y	Emily Susan | Peed | Died 22nd May | 1847 | in her 44th Year
4080		Esther Maria	Lee	F	81y	Esther Marie Lee | Born 16th July | 1767 | Died 16th Feby | 1849
6025		Richard	Lee	M	21y	Mr | Richard Lee | Died 2nd April | 1820 | Aged 21 Years
6023		William	Lee	Y	13y	Master | William Lee | Died 25th Nov | 1817 | Aged 13 Years
7054		Jane	Lee	F	68y	Mrs Jane Lee | Wife of Johnson Lee | of Kings Lynn | County of Norfolk : Gent | Died 16 May | 1818 | Aged 68 Yrs
	8020	Jane	Lee	-	-	Mrs Jane Lee | Died 16 May | 1818 : Aged 68 Years
	8061a	Jane	Lee	-	-	Mrs | Jane Lee | Wife of Johnson Lee | of Kings Lynn | County of Norfolk Gent | Died 16 of May | 18 . . | Aged 68 Years
7048		Johnson	Lee	M	68y	Died 20th August | 1809 | Johnson Lee Esqr | of Kings Lynn | Norfolk | in his 68th Year
	8109	Johnson	Lee	-	-	Died 20th August | 1819 | Johnson Lee Esqr | of Kings Lynn | in the County of | Norfolk | in his . 8th Year
	8116	Harriot	Lent	F	26y	Mrs | Harriot Lent | Died . . th Septr | 1830 | . . . .
6041		Margaret	Lincoln	F	53y	Mrs | Margaret Lincoln | Died Dec 13th | 1832 | Aged 53 Years
6084		James	Lind	M	77y	James Lind | M.D. | F.R.S. | Died 17th Oct | 1812 | Aged 77 Years
1077		Edward	Littledale	M	58y	Edward Littledale | Esqre | Died 20th April | 1837 | in the 59th year of his age
1511		Joseph	Littledale	M	75y	The Right Honble | Sir Josh Littledale | Knt | 1842
6013		Elizabeth	Lloyd	F	40y	Miss | Elizabeth Lloyd | Died 2nd May | 1839 | Aged 40 Years
2031		Jane	Lockhart	Y	9y	Jean Lockhart | Daughter of Charles & Anne Lockhart | both deceased of New Hall | County of Cromarty | North Britain | Died 7 May 1813 | in the 10th year of her age
2019		Edmund	Lodge	M	82y	Edmund Lodge Esq. K.H. Clarenceux King of Arms | Died 15th Jan 1839 Aged 82 Yrs
1108		Mary Charlotte	Lodge	F	94y	Mary | Charlotte Lodge | Died 27 July | 1854 | aged 94
1001		Julia	Longden	F	-	Miss | Julia Longden | 1840 [head plate]

Notes/Sources	will	MI	Year
of Broad St, died of consumption, aged 44, 2 Aug 1833 (LMA P82/GEO1/63); married Sarah Meabry 31 Aug 1822 (*The Times*, 3 Sept 1822)			
			1833
of Broad St, died of convulsions, aged 10 months, 16 May 1827 (LMA P82/GEO1/63)			1827
of Broad St, died of consumption, aged 37, 28 Sep 1830 (LMA P82/GEO1/63); married Martha Meabry 5 Jan 1822 (*The Times*, 7 Jan1822)			
			1830
			1825
of Guilford St, died 'aged', aged 86, 8 Jul 1814 (LMA P82/GEO1/63)			1814
widow, Blackheath, Kent (Will TNA PROB 11/1708); formerly Ann Stocker, married Joseph Kirkup (8043), 1787, Westminster (Pallot's Marriage Index)	Y	Y	1826
spinster, Blackheath, Kent (Will TNA PROB 11/1841)	Y		1834
son of Joseph Kirkup (8043); 'drowned while bathing' (MI)		Y	1820
Joseph Kirkup, auctioneer (1808) and diamond merchant (1811), auctioneer of Harpur Street (MI); married Ann Stocker (1029), 1787, Westminster (Pallot's Marriage Index)			
			1813
			-
			1828
			1815
of Keppel St, died of infl[amed] lungs, aged 10 months, 5 May 1833 (LMA P82/GEO1/63)			1833
dau of Richard Lambert, attorney & solicitor, and Jane Lambert (1841 Census); b. 18 May 1841, Chr 14 Jan 1842, St Andrew Holborn (IGI); sister of Mary Hannah (5052)			
			1844
dau of Richard Lambert, attorney & solicitor, and Jane Lambert (1841 Census); b. 7 July 1828, chr. 7 Nov 1828, St Andrew Holborn (IGI); sister of Ellen Augusta (6135)			
			1843
of Montague Pl, died of whooping cough, aged 5, 9 Mar 1825 (LMA P82/GEO1/63)			1825
of Upper Bedford Pl (Will TNA PROB 11/1728); husband of Maria Esther Lee (4080); father of Emily Susan Lee (6024), William Lee (6023) and probably Richard Lee (6025)	Y		1827
probably Emily Susan Lee, b 26 Sep 1803, chr 21 Nov 1803 St Marylebone, dau of Edward Lee and Esther Maria Lee (IGI) (6037 & 4080)			1847
widow, Bryanston Sq, Middx (Will TNA PROB 11/2091), wife of Edward Lee (6037), mother of Emily Susan Lee (6024), William Lee (6023) and probably Richard Lee (6025)	Y		1849
of Upper Bedford Pl, died of consumption aged 21, 3 Apr 1820 (LMA P82/GEO1/63); son of Edward Lee (6037) and Esther Maria Lee (4080)			1820
of Upper Bedford Pl, died of fever, aged 13, 1 Dec 1817 (LMA P82/GEO1/63); son of Edward Lee (6037) and Esther Maria Lee (4080)			1817
			1818
			-
			-
of Saint George the Martyr, Middlesex (TNA PROB 11/1622)	Y		1819
			-
of King St, died in child birth, aged 26, 13 Sept 1830 (LMA P82/GEO1/63)	(Y)		1830
of Southampton Pl, Euston Sq (Will TNA PROB 11/1810)	Y		1832
of Russell Sq, died of consumption, aged 77, 19 Oct 1812 (LMA P82/GEO1/63); died in the house of his son-in-law William Burnie (*DNB*, James Lind)			1812
of Grays Inn (Will TNA PROB 11/1878)	Y	Y	1837
one of the Justices of Her Majesty's Court of Queen's Bench (Will TNA PROB 11/1965)	Y		1842
sister in law of James Langley Bankes (6030), dau of Robert Lloyd of Ince Hall, Lancashire (MI)		Y	1839
of Russelll Sq, died fo abcess, aged 10, 7 May 1813 (LMA P82/GEO1/63)			1813
of No 2 Bloomsbury Sq (Will TNA PROB 11/1911)	Y		1839
(Will TNA PROB 11/2206)	Y		1854
			1840

Coffin	Plate	Forename	Surname	M/F/Y/U	Age at Death	Inscription Text
	3108	Elizabeth	Longden	Y	17y	Miss | Elizabeth Longden | Died 29th Oct | 1829 | Aged 17 yrs
1005		John	Longden	M	63y	John Longden | Esq. | Died 9 July | 1826 | aged 63 years
	3106	John	Longden	-	-	John Longden | Esqr | Died 9th July | 1826 | Aged 63
	8074	George	Loudan	M	-	Geoe Loudan | Esq | Died Decembr 8th | 1813 | Aged . 6 Yrs
6131		John	Lowe	M	81y	John Lowe | Born 15th Jan | 1769 | Died 21th (sic) September | 1850
6134		Mary Harriet	Lowe	F	75y	Mary Harriet Lowe | Died 16th Oct | 1852 | Aged 75 Years | Relict of John Lowe Esq
6077		William	Lowe	M	79y	William Lowe | Died 21st Dec | 1849 | Aged 79 Yrs
1526		Harry Herman	Luard	Y	14m	Mast Harry | Herman Luard | Died 26th April | 1816 | aged 14 mons
1144		Adam	Lymburner	M	90y	Adam Lymburner | Esq | Died 10th Jany | 1836 | in his 90th year
4081		Hugh	Mackay	M	-	Hugh Mackay | Esq. | Died 23rd Sepr | .... | Aged 8 . Years
1035		Mary	Madden	F	26y	Mary Wife of | Frederick Madden Esq. | of the | British Museum | Born 7th June | 1803 | Died 26th Feby | 1830
3069		Thomas	Main	M	72y	Thos Main | Esq. | Died 28 Nov | 1818 | aged 72
1014		Mary	Major	F	48y	Mrs | Mary Major | Died 10th Jany | 1836 | in her 49th year
1547		Sophia	Manley	F	37y	Sophia Manley | Spinster | Died .... January | 1823 | in her 37th Year
1540		William Henry	Manley	M	20y	William | Henry Manley | Esqr | Died 28th Decr | 1813 | in his 21st year
3029		Charlotte	Mansfield	F	45y	Charlotte | Second daughter | of the Rt Honble | Sir James Mansfield Knight | Susan his Wife | Died 3rd April | 1821 | aged 45 Years
3019		James	Mansfield	M	87y	The Right Honourable | Sir James Mansfield Knight | Late | Lord Chief Justice | of | the Court of Common Pleas | Died 23 November | 1821 | aged 87 years
4049		William Sanders	Marchant	M	57y	Mr | Willm Sanders | Marchant | Died ...... | 1835 | Aged 57 Years
4044		Keziah	Marchant	F	66y	Mrs | Kez... Mar... | Died 19th May | 1823 | Aged 66 Years [inner plate] | Mrs | Keziah M..... | Died 19th March | 1823 | Aged 66 Years [outer plate]
5038		Selina Catherine R	Mark	Y	6m	Miss Selina | Catherine ..... | Marx | Born 17th June 1825 | Died 9th July | 1825 [outer plate] | Miss Selina | Catherine | Ricoh Marx | Born 17th June | 1825 | Died 19th Decr | 1825
2047		James Diggis Chambers	Marr	Y	1y 14d	Master James Digger Chambers Marr | Died 21st July | 1824 | aged 1 year & 14 days
1034		Mary	Marston	F	64y	Mrs Mary Marston | 1819 | in her 64th Year
1033		Thomas	Marston	M	79y	Thomas Marston | Esqr | Died 16th April | 1825 | in his 80th year
6062		Adam	Martin	M	67y	Adam Martin | Esq | Died 13th April | 1829 | Aged 67 Years
1539		Ann	Martin	F	64y	Mrs | Ann Martin | Died 17th Septr | 1810 | Aged 64 Years
1552		Sarah	Martin	F	85y	Mrs | Sarah Martin | Died 3 Sept | 1817 | aged 85 years
1134		Harriet Catherine	Martindale	F	51y	Mrs Harriet | Cathe Martindale | Died ... Feby | 1843 | aged 51 yrs
	3109		Martyn	Y	0y	The still born | twin sons of | Charles and Clari.... | Martyn | Augt 5th ....
6067		Grace	Martyn	Y	16y	Grace Martyn | Daughter of the Late | Nicholas Martyn | of Lincoln's Inn | Departed this life | Oct 7th 1834 | Aged 16 years
1546		Hannah	Martyn	F	76y	Mrs | Hannah Martyn | Died 31st May | 1810 | aged 76 ....
2044		Hannah	Martyn	F	80y	Mrs Hanh Martyn | Died 11th June | 1805 | aged 80 years [outer plate] | Mrs Hannah Martin Died 11 June 1805 Aged 80 years [inner plate]
1538		John Lee	Martyn	M	69y	The Rev. | John Lee Martyn | Died 19th Aug | 1836 | aged 69 Yrs

Notes/Sources	will	MI	Year
			1829
of Queen Sq, formerly 'of Alicant' (*GM*, July 1826, 93); possibly of Charlotte St, Fitzroy Sq (Will TNA PROB 11/1726)	Y		1826
			-
			1813
attorney at law and solicitor, Montague Pl, Russell Sq (Will TNA PROB 11/2120); husband of Mary Harriet Lowe (6134)	Y		1850
wife of John Lowe (6131)			1852
gentleman, Inner Temple (Will TNA PROB 11/2106); of Montague St, Russell Sq (MI); husband of Eliza Lowe, d. 1858, Hove Sussex (MI)	Y	Y	1849
			1816
of Bernard St, Russell Sq (Will TNA PROB 11/1856); died 'in Bernard-st, in his 90th year' (*GM*, Feb 1836, 211)	Y		1836
possibly Hugh Mackay, No 98 St Martin's Lane (*List of Names 1815*)			--
1st wife of Frederick Madden, of the British Museum; fomerly Mary Hayton, dau of Robert Hayton of Sunderland, Co. Durham, b. 7 Jun 1803; of The Museum, died in 'child bed', aged 26, 1 Mar 1830 (LMA P82/GEO1/63)		Y	1830
of Bloomsbury (Will TNA PROB 11/1611); No 94 Gteat Russell St (*List of Names 1815*); of Great Russell St, died of mortification, aged 72, 2 Dec 1818 (LMA P82/GEO1/63)	Y		1818
			1836
spinster, Bartow Cottage, near Mildenhall, Suffolk (Will TNA PROB 11/1666); Montague St, died of cancer, aged 37, 2 Feb 1823 (LMA P82/GEO1/63)	Y		1823
			1813
spinster of Russell Sq, 2nd dau of Sir James Mansfield (3019) (Will TNA PROB 11/1643; death notice: *Blackwood's*, May 1821, 246); of Russell Sq, died suddenly, aged 45, 6 Apr 1821 (LMA P82/GEO1/63)	Y		1821
late Lord Chief Justice of His Majesty's Court of Common Pleas, Westminster (Will TNA PROB 11/1651); see *DNB* Sir James Mansfield; of Russell Sq, died of old age, aged 88, 26 Nov 1821 (LMA P82/GEO1/63)	Y	Y	1821
			1835
of Little Russell St, died of consumption, aged 66, 22 May 1823 (LMA P82/GEO1/63)			1823
Selina C R Mark, of Bedford Pl, died of convulsions, aged 7 months, 11 Dec 1825 (LMA P82/GEO1/63)			1825
of Bedford Pl, died of convulsions, aged 1 year, 21 July 1824 (LMA P82/GEO1/63)			1824
?wife of Thomas Marston (1033); of Montague St, died of consumption, aged 64, 25 Nov 1819 (LMA P82/GEO1/63)			1819
gentleman, St George the Martyr, Middx (Will TNA PROB 11/1699); ?husband of Mary Marston (1034)	Y		1825
of St Martin in the Fields (Will TNA PROB 11/1756); Tavistock Pl, Russell Sq (*List of Names 1815*); of Bernard St, died of 'paralytic [stroke?]', aged 67, 18 Apr 1829 (LMA P82/GEO1/63)	Y		1829
			1810
of Southampton St, died of old age, aged 85, 6 Sept 1817 (LMA P82/GEO1/63)			1817
wife of Charles Montague Martindale, of the Paymaster General's Office, and 4 Montague St (1841 Census); Harriet Lusada (widow) married Charles Montague Martindale at St George's Bloomsbury in 1835; Harriet Catherine Corneck married David Lousada (of St Botolph, Bishopgate) at St Pancras 1814 (Pallot's Marriage Index)		Y	1843
			-
dau of Nicholas Martyn, 'late of Southampton Row of this parish' and Hannah Martyn (1546)		Y	1834
widow, Bloomsbury (Will TNA PROB 11/1512); widow of Nicholas Martyn of Lincoln's Inn, and Southampton Row; mother of Grace Martyn (6067)	Y	Y	1810
widow, St Marylebone (Will TNA PROB 11/1427)	Y		1805
rector, clerk, Doctor of Divinity, St George the Martyr, Middx (Will TNA PROB 11/1867)	Y		1836

Coffin	Plate	Forename	Surname	M/F/Y/U	Age at Death	Inscription Text
1520		Mary	Martyn	F	74y	Mrs	Mary Martyn	Died 12th March	1835	aged 74 years
	8015	John	Mason	M	37y	Mr	John Mason	Died 6th Marh	1807	Aged 37 yrs
	8022	Mary	Mason	F	68y	Mrs	Mary Mason	1833
	3100	Laura	Mayen . . ch	Y	5y 6m	Miss	Laura Mayen . . . ck	Died 12th May	1808	Aged 5 Years & 6 mons
6026		Udall	McCulloh	F	84y	Mrs	Udall McCulloh	Died 17th June	1842	Aged 84 Years
4018		Isabella	McGeoogh	F	27y	Isabella McGeoogh	Second Daughter of	the County of Armagh	Departed this life	Novr 7th 1817	in her 28th Year
1817						
5029		Joseph	McLean	M	58y	Major	Joseph McLean	Obit 25th Feb	1832	 58
5011		Sophia Charlotte	McLean	F	57y	M . . .	Sophia Charlotte	McLean	Died 9th Novr	1837	Aged 57 Years
2014		Elizabeth	Meabry	F	70y	Elizabeth	Wife of Mr	John Meabry	Died 5th Augst	1841	aged 70 yrs
2032		John	Meabry	M	75y	Mr	John Meabry	Died 7th Sept	1841	aged 75 years
2022		Louisa	Meabry	Y	8y	Miss Louisa Meabry	Died Jan 18th	1820	aged 8 years
2007		William	Meabry	M	45y	Mr William	Meabry	Died 10th April	1852	aged 45 years
3028		Anna Wharton	Metcalfe	Y	11m	Miss Anna	Wharton Metcalfe	Died 1 May	1814	aged 11 mons . . . so many days
4053		Mary	Meux	F	69y	Mrs	Mary Meux	Died Decr 8th	1812	Aged 69 Years
	3104	Mary	Meux	-	-	Mrs	Mary Meux	Died Decr 8th	1812	Aged 69 Years
4058		Richard	Meux	M	79y	Richard Meux	Esq	Died July 2	1809	Aged 79 Years
						Richard Meux	Esq	Died July 2nd	1813	in his 80th Year [inner lead plate]
1530		Louisa Margaret	Mitchell	Y	11m	Miss Louisa	Margt Mitchell	Died 15th Feby	1824	aged 11 mons
4013		William	Mitchell	M	43y	Mr	William Mitchel	Died 15th April	1834	Aged 43 Years
1044		Sarah	Moneypenny	F	29y	Mrs	Sarah	Moneypenny	Died 3rd July	1828	in the 30th year	of her life
4065		Elizabeth Anne	Montgomery	F	81y	Mrs	Elizth Anne	Montgomery	Died 10th Novr	1831	Aged 81
	8082	Hannahretter	Moore	F	66y	Mrs	Hannahretter Moore	Died 24th Octr	1818	Aged 66 Years
	8090	Hannahretter	Moore	-	-	Mrs	Hannahretter Moore	Died 24th Octr	1818	Aged 66 Years
3065		Letitia Maria	Moore	Y	7y	Miss Letitia	Maria Moore	Died 2nd May	1824	aged 7 years
2038		Ann	Morgan	F	41y	Miss Ann Morgan	Died 16th Jan	1812	aged 41 years
7042		George Miller	Morgan	Y	6m 19d	Mastr	George	Miller Morgan	Died 26th July	1823	Aged 2 months 19 Days
	8023	George Miller	Morgan	-	-	Mastr George	Miller Morgan	1823
	8091	George Miller	Morgan	-	-	Mastr George	Miller Morgan	Died 26th July	1823	Aged 2 Mons 19 Days
5071		Catherine	Morris	F	55y	Catherine Morris	Relict of	Robt Morris	Died 6 Aug	1825	Aged 55 [inner plate]
						Catherine Morris	Relict of	Robt Morris Esq	of Brunswick Square	Died 6th August	1825	Aged 55 years [outer plate]
1577		John Leslie	Morris	Y	13m	Master John	Leslie Morris	Died 29 May	1814	in his 13 monh
5070		Robert	Morris	M	62y	Robert Morris	Died 6th Feby	1825	Aged 62 Years
4048		William	Moss	M	67y	William Moss	Esq	Died 24th July	1815	Aged 67 years
5006		Frances	Munden	F	83y	Mrs Frances	Munden	Relict of the late	Joseph Shepherd	Munden	Died 20th September	1837	Aged 83 Years
5032		Joseph Shepherd	Munden	M	73y	Joseph Shepard	Munden	Died 6th Feby	1832	in the 74th Year	of his Age
	8012	Ann	Murcott	F	74y	Mrs	Ann Murcott	Died 4th May	1838	Aged 74 Years
	8025	Ann	Murcott	-	-	Mrs	Ann Murcott	Died 4 Novr 1838
	8123	Ann	Murcott	-	-	Mrs	Ann Murcott	Died 4th Novr	1838	Aged 74 Years
5036		John	Murcott	M	61y	John Murcott	Esqr	Died 19th July	1833	Aged 61 years
4017		William	Murdoch	M	75y	William Murdoch	Esq	Died 11th April	1825	Aged 75 Yrs

Notes/Sources	will	MI	Year
			1835
gentleman, St George Bloomsbury (Will TNA PROB 11/1459); of Queen St, died of consumption, aged 37, 9 Mar 1807 (LMA P82/GEO1/63)	Y		1807
of Museum St, died of consumption, aged 68, 27 Jul 1833 (LMA P82/GEO1/63)			1833
			1808
widow, King St, Bloomsbury (Will TNA PROB 11/1965)	Y		1842
major, half pay of the late 3rd West India Regt of Foot, Somers Town, Middx (Will TNA PROB 11/1797)	Y		1832
Widow, No 20 Fitzroy Sq (Will TNA PROB 11/1892)	Y		1837
wife of John Meabry (2032) Broad Street; Eliza Rufforth married John Meabry (2032) of St Giles in the Field at St George's Hanover Sq 1793 (Pallett's Marriage Index)		Y	1841
Grocer, 7 Broad St (Will TNA PROB 11/1954); husband of Elizabeth Meabry (2014); married Eliza Rufforth at St George's Hanover Sq 1793 (Pallett's Marriage Index)	Y	Y	1841
of Museum St, died of consumption, aged 8 years and 10 weeks, 19 Jan 1820 (LMA P82/GEO1/63)			1820
Drummond St, St Pancras (1851 Census)			1852
of Hunter St, died of whooping cough, aged 11 months, 1 May 1814 (LMA P82/GEO1/63)			1814
?wife of Richard Meux (4058); of Bloomsbury Sq, died of consumption, aged 69, 11 Dec 1812 (LMA P82/GEO1/63) .			1812
			-
of Bloomsbury Sq (Will TNA PROB 11/1559); brewer, owner of the Griffin Brewery (ref); husband of Mary Meux (4053); of Bloomsbury Sq, died 'aged', aged 80, 7 Jul 1813 (LMA P82/GEO1/63)	Y		1813
of Southampton Rw, died of convulsions, age 11 months, 17 Feb 1824 (LMA P82/GEO1/63)			1824
			1834
			1828
widow, Gloucester St, Queen Sq (Will TNA PROB 11/1794)	Y		1831
			1818
			-
			1824
of Great Russell St, died of consumption, aged 41, 10 Jan 1812 (LMA P82/GEO1/63)			1812
of Upper Bedford Pl, died of thrush, aged 2 months, 26 Jul 1823 (LMA P82/GEO1/63)			1823
			-
			-
widow, Brunswick Sq (Will TNA PROB 11/1702); wife of Robert Morris (5070)	Y		1825
of Brunswick Sq, died of whooping cough, aged 14 months, 30 May 1814 (LMA P82/GEO1/63)			1814
of Brunswick Sq (Will TNA PROB 11/); husband of Catherine Morris (5071); of Brunswick Sq, died 'inflammation', aged 63, 8 Feb 1825 (LMA P82/GEO1/63)	Y		1825
wine merchant, High Holborn (Will TNA PROB 11/1572); of Holborn, died of dropsy, aged 67, 27 July 1815 (LMA P82/GEO1/63)	Y		1815
widow, St George Bloomsbury (Will TNA PROB 11/1888); wife of John Shepherd Munden (5032)	Y		1837
of St Pancras (Will TNA PROB 11/1796); husband of Frances Munden (5006); of Bernard St, died of consumption, aged 73, 8 Feb 1832 (LMA P82/GEO1/63)	Y		1832
?wife of John Murcott (5036)			1838
			-
			-
gentleman, Warwick Sq, City of London (Will TNA PROB 11/1820); ?husband of Ann Murcott (8012)	Y		1833
merchant, City of London (Will TNA PROB 11/1698); of Upper Bedford Pl, died of consumption, aged 75, 14 Apr 1825 (LMA P82/GEO1/63)	Y		1825

Coffin	Plate	Forename	Surname	M/F/Y/U	Age at Death	Inscription Text
	3103	William	Murdoch	-	-	William Murdock I Esqr I Died 11th April I 1825 I Aged 75 Years
1568		Robert	Nares	M	76y	The Revd I Robert Nares I Died 23rd March I 1829 I aged 76 years
4014		Thomas	Nash	M	61y	Thoms Nash I Esq I Died 30th May I 1814 I Aged 61 years
1030		Elizabeth	Neale	F	66y	Mrs I Elizabeth Neale I Died 28th April I 1833 I in her 67th year
5082		Sarah	Neale	F	32y	Mrs Sarah Neale I 1826
1021		Thomas	Neale	M	70y	Thomas Neale I Esqre I Died 22 April I 1833 I aged 70 years
1532		Mary	Newcombe	F	70y	Mrs I Mary Newcombe I Died 7th Oct I 1836 I aged 70 years
3036		Georgiana Catherine	Nicholl	Y	5y	Georgiana Cathe I Nicholl I Died 1st May 1821 I aged 5 yrs
2023		Isabella Jane	Nicholson	F	30y	Isabella Jane I the Oldest Daughter of I Isaac Nicholson I Esq. I Died 5th Nov I 1845 I aged 30 years
6034		Ann	Nightingale	F	50y	Mrs I Ann Nightingale I Died 15th Jan I 1825 I Aged 50 Yrs
3008		[William]	Noble	M	63y	Mr Noble I Esqre I Died 23rd Jany I 1805 I aged 63 years [outer plate] Mr Noble I Esqre I Died 23rd Jany I 1805 I aged 63 years [inner plate]
6118		Elizabeth	Nokes	F	73y	Elizabeth I Relict of I ... Mr William Nokes I Died 19th June I 1837 I In the 74 year of her age
6036		Naomi	Nokes	F	27y	Naomi I Wife of I John Nokes Esqr I Died 20th Octr I 1831 I Aged 27 Years
1579		Edward	Ogle	M	60y	Edward Ogle I Esqr I Died 26th March I 1819 I in his 60 year
1576		James	Ogle	M	67y	James Ogle I Esqr I Died 24 Novr I 1823 I aged 67 years
1049		Sarah	Ogle	F	77y	Mrs I Sarah Ogle I Died 10th March I 1844 I in her 78th year
7069		Elizabeth	Oldham	F	70y	Mrs I Elizth Oldham I Died 9th Decemr I 1816 I Aged 70 Years
	8126	Elizabeth	Oldham	-	-	Mrs Elizabeth Oldham I Died 9th Decr I 1816 I Aged 70 years
1039		Oliver	Oxley	M	67y	Mr I <u>Oliver</u> Oxley I Died 10th Feby I 1837 I aged 67 yrs
6010		Charlotte	Pace	F	23y	Miss I Charlotte Pace I Died 15th Jany I 1823 I Aged 23 Yrs
5067		Marianne	Paley	Y	15y	Miss I Marianne Pal . . . . I Died 23rd May I 1825 I Aged 15 Yrs
5003		Frances Paula	Palyart	F	50y	Mrs I Frances I Paula Palyart I Died 6th April I 1814 I in the 50th Year I of her Age
5008		Ignatius	Palyart	M	57y	Ignatius Palyart Esqre I Portuguese I Consul General I Died 22 Decemr I 1818 I Aged 57 Years
3082		Reuben	Parke	M	44y	Reuben Par . . . I Esq. I Died 19th Ap . . . I 1842 I Aged . 4 . . [inner plate] . . . . . . Parke I . . . I Died . . . . Apr . . I . . . . I Aged 44 years [outer plate]
1096		Ann	Parkes	F	89y	Ann Parkes I Died 14th March I 1840 I aged 89 y . . .
6052		Richard	Parkes	M	26y	Mr I Richard Parkes I Died 12th August I 1811 I Aged 26 Years
6103		Richard	Parkes	M	63y	Richard Parkes I Esq I Died Dec 1810 I Aged 63 years
6043		William	Parkes	M	59y	William Parkes I Esqr I Died 31st March I 1820 I Aged 59 Yrs
7086		Elizabeth	Partridge	F	46y	Miss I Elizth Partridge I Died 4th Feby I 1815 I Aged 46 years
1502		Jane Maria	Pearce	F	90y	Mrs I Jane Maria I Pearce I Died 21 Nov I 1819 I aged 90 yrs
1094		John	Penfold	Y	7y	Master I John Penfold I Died 23rd Nov I 1832 I in his 7th Year
6107		Mary	Pewert	F	59y	Mrs I Mary Pewert I Died 24th August I 1820 I Aged 59 Years
3091		Adolph Henry	Pfeil	Y	8y	Mast I Adolph . . . . I . . . . I Died 31st Oct I 1830 I . . . . . 8 Years
1101		Adolph Leopold	Pfeil	Y	7m	Mast. Adolph I Leopold Pfiel I Died 16 Mar I 1814 I aged 7 mons

Notes/Sources	will	MI	Year
clerk, Bloomsbury (Will TNA PROB 11/1757); of Hart St, died of 'inflammation', aged 76, 28 Mar 1829, Archdeacon of Stafford (LMA P82/GEO1/63)			-
of Upper Guilford St (Will TNA PROB 11/1559)	Y		1829
?wife of Thomas Neale (1021); of Bedford Pl, died of consumption, aged 68, 29 Apr 1833 (LMA P82/GEO1/63)	Y	Y	1814
of Charlotte St, died of dropsy, died aged 32, 1 Apr 1826 (LMA P82/GEO1/63)			1833
of Upper Bedford Pl, Russell Sq (Will TNA PROB 11/1817); husband of Elizabeth Neale (1030); of Bedford Pl, died of consumption, aged 70, 23 Apr 1833 (LMA P82/GEO1/63)			1826
widow, St George Bloomsbury (Will TNA PROB 11/1869)	Y		1833
of Russell Sq, died of dropsy, aged 5, 3 Mar 1821 (LMA P82/GEO1/63)	Y		1836
			1821
possibly Isabella Jane Nicholson, dau of Isaac and Leonora Nicholson, chr. At Old Jewry Presbyterian Church 22 Feb 1815 (IGI)			
of Museum St, died of apoplexy, aged 50, 22 Jan 1825 (LMA P82/GEO1/63)			1845
of Bloomsbury (Will TNA PROB 11/1422)			1825
	Y		1805
formerly Elizabeth Harris, widow of Rodney Buildings, New Kent Road, Surrey (Will TNA PROB 11/1886); wife of William Nokes (d. 1836, Will TNA PROB 11/1859)			
of Charlotte St, died of 'inflammation', aged 27, 22 Nov 1831 (LMA P82/GEO1/63)	Y		1837
			1831
of Worthing, Sussex (Will TNA PROB 11/1616); of Warwick House in Worthing (W Sussex RO, Add Mss 46125 7 January 1815); of Southampton St, died of palsy, aged 60, 30 Feb 1819 (LMA P82/GEO1/63); brother of James Ogle (1576)	Y		1819
of Bloomsbury (Will TNA PROB 11/1680); of Southampton St, died of dropsy, aged 67, 26 Nov 1823 (LMA P82/GEO1/63); brother of Edward Ogle (1579), husband of Sarah Ogle (1049)	Y		1823
widow, of Worthing, Sussex (Will TNA PROB 11/1997); wife of James Ogle (1576)	Y		1844
widow, St George Bloomsbury (Will TNA PROB 11/1816); of Southampton St, died of mortification, aged 70, 27 Years14 Dec 1816 (LMA P82/GEO1/63)	Y		1816
dealer, St Giles in the Fields (Will TNA PROB 11/1873); dealer in ready made linen,16 Russell Court (SUN MS 11936/448/825859 20 January 1809); dressmaker, 16 Russell Court (SUN MS 11936/476/931307 3 June 1817); picture dealer (*Old Bailey Proceedings* 21 Feb 1828, Ref No. t18280221-18)	Y		1837
			1823
of Southampton, died of 'spasms', aged 15, 24 May 1825 (LMA P82/GEO1/63)			1825
wife of Ignatius Palyart (5008); of Bedford Pl, died of 'spasm', aged 50, 8 Apr 1814 (LMA P82/GEO1/63)			1814
merchant, 9 London St, Fenchurch St (*The European Magazine and London Review, 87, Dec 1824-Jul 1825*, 381; *Holden's* 1811); 26 Nov 1814, alien (TNA C 205/2); 10, Bedford Pl and Strand on the Green, near Kew, Chiswick (*Holden's* 1811); of Woburn Pl, died of 'inflammation', aged 57, 16 Dec 1818 (LMA P82/GEO1/63)			1818
died in Southampton Row, Russell Sq , brother of Samuel Parke of Leatherhead (*GM* June 1842, 672)			1842
widow, Dulwich, Surrey (Will TNA PROB 11/1926); ?related to William Parkes (6043)	Y		1840
of Broad St, died of consumption, aged 26, 14 Aug 1811 (LMA P82/GEO1/63)			1811
			1810
of Bloomsbury (Will TNA PROB 11/1631); ?related to Ann Parkes (1096); of Charles St, died of apoplexy, aged 59, 4 Apr 1820 (LMA P82/GEO1/63)	Y		1820
spinster, Bloomsbury (Will TNA PROB 11/1566); dau of William Partridge of Nottingham (MI); of Hart St, died of cancer, aged 46, 7 Feb 1815 (LMA P82/GEO1/63)	Y	Y	1815
			1819
?related to Rev George Saxby Penfold (Doctor in Divinity, Dorset Sq: Will TNA PROB 11/2047)	(Y)		1832
possibly Mary Pewtner, widow of St Sepulchre, Middlesex (Will TNA PROB 11/1643)	Y		1820
probably Adolph Henry Pfeil, of Broad St, died of 'dropsy brain' (sic), age 8, 25 Oct 1830 (LMA P82/GEO1/63); son of Adolph Leopold Pfeil, ironmonger of Nos 5 & 6 Broad St (*PO London 1841*) and of Grove Edn Rd, St Johns Wood (Adolph Pfeil, Will TNA PROB 11/2248)	(Y)		1830
son of Adolph Leopold Pfeil, ironmonger of Nos 5 & 6 Broad St (*PO London 1841*) and of Grove Edn Rd, St Johns Wood (Adolph Pfeil, Will TNA PROB 11/2248); of Broad St, died of inflammation, aged 7 months, 22 Mar 1814 (LMA P82/GEO1/63)	(Y)		1814

Coffin	Plate	Forename	Surname	M/F/Y/U	Age at Death	Inscription Text
1041		William	Phelps	M	83y	William Phelps | Esq. | Died 23rd Dec | 1831 | in his 83rd year
3054		Charmel Maud	Phillip	F	-	Char.... | Ph.... | Died May 25th | 1806 [outer plate]
						Charmel | Maud Philipp | Died May 25 | 1806 [inner plate]
6047		Ann	Phillip	F	85y	Mrs | Ann Phillip | Died 31 Dec | 1832 | Aged 85 Yrs
1120		Mary	Philpot	F	67y	Mrs | Mary Philpot | Died 16th Jany | 1841 | aged 67 yrs
6137		Horatio Snraine	Pilcher	Y	6m	Master Horacci | Snraime Pilcher | Born 23th (sic) Sep | 1835 | Died 27th March | 1836
1505		Elizabeth	Planta	F	76y	Elizabeth Planta | Wife of | Joseph Planta Esq. | of | the British Museum | Born Sepr 1744 | Died Feby 2nd 1821
1528		Joseph	Planta	M	83y	Joseph Planta | Esquire | F.R.S. | Principal Librarian of | the British Museum | Born 21st February 1744 | Died 9th December | 1827
3066		.... Chapelle	Plath	U		..... *Chapelle* | ...... *Arthur Plath* | *.. ed 20th No .. | aged* ..... [coffin plate]
						.... | *Plath* | *1839* [foot plate]
1543		Emily Angelica	Platt	Y	13m	Miss Emily | Angelica Platt | Died 25th Sept | 1825 | aged 13 mons
1020		Eleanor	Plege	F	83y	Mrs | Eleanor Plege | Died 13th Dec. | 1838 | aged 83 Yrs
1028		John	Plege	M	77y	John Plege | Esqr | Died 13th July | 1830 | aged 77 yrs
7064		Mary	Poignand	F	80y	Mrs Mary | Poignand | Died Octr 31st | 1825 | Aged 80
	8052	Mary	Poignand	-	-	Mary Poignand | 1825
	8107	Mary	Poignand	-	-	Mrs Mary | Poignand | Died 31st October | 1825 | Aged 80 years
1112		Robert	Poore	M	60y	Robert Poore | Esqr | Died 23rd July | 1818 | in his 60th year
1515		Eleanor	Pope	F	31y	Mrs | Eleanor Pope | Died 23 Sept | 1831 | aged 31 years
1012		Stephen Charles	Pope	Y	1y 7m	Mast[er] Stephen | Charles Pope | Died 24th April | 1833 | aged 1 year | and 7 months
	3110	Stephen Charles	Pope	-	-	Master Stephen | Charles Pope | Died 24th April | 1833 | aged 1 year | and 7 months
2013		Ann	Porral	F	47y	Mrs | ~~Mary~~ | Ann Porral | Died 18th Augst | 1826 | Aged 47 Years
6089		Julia	Porter	F	52y 4m 15d	Mrs | Julia Porter | Died 28th April | 1822 | Aged 52 Years | 4 months & 15 days
3051		Andrew Phillip	Poston	M	78y	Rev | Andrew Philip | Poston | Died 13th May | 1832 | aged 78 years
3072		Ann	Poston	F	99y	Mrs | Ann Poston | Died 7th October | 1805 | in the 99th year | of her age
1103		Margaret Craig	Pratt	U	63y	...s | Ma... | .... raig Pratt | Died 5th April | 1826 | aged 63 years
7015		Ann	Price	F	35y	Miss | Anne Price | Died 16th Feb | 1826 | Aged 35 Years
	8049	Jane	Price	-	-	Miss | Jane Price | 1826
3077		Willoughby	Rackham	M	47y	Willoughby Rackham | Esq | Born 25 Oct | 1778 | Died ... Mar | 1825
1050		John	Read	M	40y	Mr | John Read | Died 4th March | 1825 | aged 40 years
7072		Maria Adelida	Read	Y	18y	Maria Adelida | Read | Died 3rd April | 1852 | Aged 18 Years
	8039	Maria Adelida	Read	-	-	Maria | Adelida Read | 1852
	8098	Maria Adelida	Read	-	-	Maria Adelida Read | Died 3rd April | 1852 | Aged 18 Years
6095		Ann	Reeves	F	67y	Ann | Widow of William John Reeves Esq | Died 8th ..... | 1831 | In the 67th year of her age
6122		William John	Reeves	M	63y	William John | Reeves | Died ... Sept | 1827 | in the 64 Year of his Age
4043		Mary Ann	Regal	F	-	Mrs Mary | Ann Regal | Died ... July | 1825 | in her sleep
4060		Richard	Reid	M	31y	Mr | Richard Reid | Died 1st July | 1824 | Aged ... Years
6139		David Robert	Remington	M	71y	David Robert | Remington Esq | Died 26th Oct | 1854 | Aged 71 Years
6141		Mary	Remington	F	55y	Mrs Mary | Remington | Died 23th Nov | 1854 | Aged 55 Years
4030		Susannah	Reynolds	F	65y	.... | Susannah Reynolds | Died 24th July | 1825 | Aged . 4 Years
6046		Mary	Richard	F	60y	Miss | Mary Richard | Died 20th Nov | 1848 | Aged 60 Years
2034		Henry Boynton	Richardson	Y	5m	Master Henry Boynton | Richardson | nata 3 5
2008		Ann	Richardson	F	27y	Mrs | Ann Richardson | Died 1st July | 1809 | Aged 27 Years
2036		John	Richardson	M	31y	John | Richardson | Esq | Died 28 August | 1812 | aged 31 years

Notes/Sources	will	MI	Year
of Montague Pl, died of old age, aged 83, 21 Dec 1831 (LMA P82/GEO1/63)			1831
			1806
			1832
			1841
			1836
of British Museum, died of gout, aged 76, 3 Feb 1821 (LMA P82/GEO1/63)		Y	1821
died 3rd Dec, buried 9th Dec (DNB, Joseph Planta); of British Museum, died of old age, aged 83, 5 Dec 1827 (LMA P82/GEO1/63)		Y	1827
			1839
of Russell Sq, died of convulsions, aged 13 months, 27 Sept 1825 (LMA P82/GEO1/63)			1825
			1838
			1830
			1825
			-
			-
gentleman, Chiswick, Middx (Will TNA PROB 11/1607); possibly of King St, died of palsy, aged 65, 19 Jul 1818 (LMA P82/GEO1/63)	Y		1818
of Russell Sq (Will TNA PROB 11/1828); ?mother of Stephen Charles Pope (1012)	Y		1831
?son of Eleanor Pope (1515)			1833
			-
			1826
of Great Russell St, died of apoplexy, aged 52, 29 Apr 1822 (LMA P82/GEO1/63)			1822
clerk, Bloomsbury (Will TNA PROB 11/1801); of Hyde St, died of 'mortification', aged 78, 19 Sept 1832 (LMA P82/GEO1/63)	Y		1832
			1805
of Russell Sq, died of dropsy, aged 63, 10 Sept 1826 (LMA P82/GEO1/63)			1826
probably plate for Anne Price			1826
gentleman, Lincolns Inn (Will TNA PROB 11/1698); of Russell Sq, died of stone, aged 47, 4 Mar 1825 (LMA P82/GEO1/63)	Y		-
of Bury Pl, died of consumption, aged 40, 3 Mar 1826 (LMA P82/GEO1/63)			1825
			1826
			1852
			-
widow, Woburn Pl, Russell Sq (Will TNA PROB 11/1793); of Woburn Pl, died of consumption, aged 67, 13 Nov 1831 (LMA P82/GEO1/63)	Y		1831
colourman of Holborn Bridge, City of London (Will TNA PROB 11/1732); of Woburn Pl, died of dropsy, aged 63, 21 Sept 1827 (LMA P82/GEO1/63)	Y		1827
			1825
baker, St George Bloomsbury (TNA PROB 11/1688); of Little Russell St, died of 'inflammation', aged 31, 4 Jul 1824 (LMA P82/GEO1/63)	Y		1824
stockbroker, 14 Montague Pl (1851 Census)			1854
widow, No 16 Bolton St, Piccadilly, Middx (Will TNA PROB 11/2203); Martha, wife of David Remington (6139) (1851 Census)	Y		1854
of Bloomsbury Sq, died of consumption, aged 65, 26 Jul 1825 (LMA P82/GEO1/63)			1825
			1848
of Brunswick Sq, died of 'inflammation', aged 5 months, 25 Aug 1815 (LMA P82/GEO1/63)			1815
			1809
			1812

Coffin	Plate	Forename	Surname	M/F/Y/U	Age at Death	Inscription Text
6056		Elizabeth	Rigge	F	72y	Elizabeth ǀ Wife of John Rigge Esq ǀ Died 8 June ǀ 1836 ǀ Aged 72 Yrs
6055		John	Rigge	M	-	John Rigge Esq ǀ 1838
	5081	Elizabeth	Ro	F	-	. . . Elizabeth ǀ Ro . . . . . . ǀ Died . . . . ǀ . . . . ǀ . . . . . .
	8088	Jane Richardson	Roberts	F	48y	Mrs Jane ǀ Richardson Roberts ǀ Died 5th March ǀ 1819 ǀ Aged s 48 Year
	8125	Jane Richardson	Roberts	-	-	Mrs Jane ǀ Richardson Roberts ǀ Died 5th March ǀ 1819 ǀ Aged 48 Years
2017		Elinor Dorothea	Robertson	Y	10m	Miss Elinor Dorothea ǀ Robertson ǀ Died 28th April ǀ 1815 ǀ Aged 10 mon
7056		Francis	Robertson	Y	5y 3 m	Master ǀ Fran. Robertson ǀ Died 18th April ǀ 1814 ǀ Aged 5 years & 3 months
	8128	Francis	Robertson	-	-	Master ǀ Francis Robertson ǀ Died 18th April ǀ 1814 ǀ Aged 5 years and 3 mons
	8016	Mary	Robertson	F	67y	Miss ǀ Mary Robertson ǀ Died 30th April ǀ 1854 ǀ Aged 67 Yrs
	8046	Mary	Robertson	-	-	Miss ǀ Mary Robertson ǀ 1854
	8121	Mary	Robertson	-	-	Miss ǀ Mary Robertson ǀ Died 30th April ǀ 1854 ǀ Aged 67 Yrs
	8089	Mary	Robertson	F	64y	Mrs ǀ Mary Robertson ǀ Died 2nd Sepr ǀ 1822 ǀ Aged 64 Years
	8118	Mary	Robertson	-	-	Mrs ǀ Mary Robertson ǀ Died 2nd Septr ǀ 1822 ǀ Aged 64 Years
6083		Sarah	Robertson	F	58y	Mrs ǀ Sarah Robertson ǀ Died 26th October ǀ 1840 ǀ Aged 58 Yrs
6130		William	Robertson	M	88y	William Robertson ǀ Esq ǀ Died 14th September ǀ 1825 ǀ Aged 88 Years
	8108	Bridget	Robinson	F	21y	Miss Bridget Robinson ǀ Died 9th Sepr ǀ 1810 ǀ Aged 21 Yrs
7085		Elizabeth Ann	Robinson	F	27y	Miss Elizb ǀ Ann Robinson ǀ Died 24 Marh ǀ 1806 ǀ Aged 27 yrs
	8017	Elizabeth Ann	Robinson	-	-	Miss Elizb ǀ Ann Robinson ǀ Died 24th March ǀ 1806 ǀ Aged 27 yrs
7071		Stratford	Robinson	M	51y	Mr Stratford ǀ Robinson ǀ Died 8th April ǀ 1833 ǀ Aged 51 Years (plate 8018 was read as 31 years)
	8018	Stratford	Robinson	-	-	Mr ǀ Stratford Robinson ǀ Died 8th April ǀ 1833
1510		Elizabeth Mary	Roche	F	58y	Mrs Elizth ǀ Mary Roche ǀ 1833 ǀ Aged 58
1145		James	Roche	M	86y	James Roche ǀ Esq. ǀ Died 14th October ǀ 1838 ǀ aged 86 years
6009		Jane	Rocher	F	72y	Mrs ǀ Jane Rocher ǀ Died 21st March ǀ 1835 ǀ Aged 72 Years
	8055	William	Roe	M	-	Mr ǀ Willm Roe ǀ Died 5th July ǀ 1806 ǀ Aged . . . . .
2043		Mary Taylor	Roger	F	37y	Mrs Mary . . . . Roger ǀ Died 12th April ǀ 1833 ǀ in her 38th Year
4037		Julia Anne	Rogers	Y	7y 10m	Julia Anne ǀ Daughter of ǀ Francis Newman and Eleanna Rogers ǀ Died 8 Jany ǀ 1832 ǀ aged 7 yrs & 10 Months
2060		Joseph	Rolley	M	63y	Joseph Rolley ǀ Esq ǀ Died 9th Sep ǀ 1805 ǀ aged 63 Yrs
6050		Elizabeth	Rose	F	78y	Mrs ǀ Elizabeth Rose ǀ Relict of ǀ the Rev. Doctor Charles Rose ǀ of Graffam Sussex ǀ Died Feb 29th ǀ 1824 ǀ Aged 78 Years
1093		Amy	Rougemont	Y	18m	Amy Rougemont ǀ Born 19th Aug ǀ 1842 ǀ Died 29 Feb ǀ 1844
5024		Forbes	Rougemont	Y	5y 8m	Forbes ǀ Son of Francis Fredk ǀ & Marianne Rougemont ǀ Died 17th Novr ǀ 1838 ǀ Aged 5 Yrs 8 ms
6076		Grace Caroline	Rouse	F	-	Grace ǀ Caroline Rouse ǀ Died 20th Sep ǀ 1856
3092		Grace	Rudland	F	89y	Mrs ǀ Grace P . . . dland ǀ Died 21 Sept ǀ 1828 ǀ Aged 89 Years
	Vault 3	Grace	Rudland	-	-	Mrs ǀ Grace ǀ Rudland ǀ 1828
1082		Ann	Sanders	F	64y	Ann Wife of ǀ Francis William Sanders ǀ Esqr ǀ Died 16th Febr ǀ 1831 ǀ in her 64th year
6044		Eleanor	Sanders	F	22y	Miss ǀ Elenor Sanders ǀ Died 15th June ǀ 1825 ǀ in her 22 Year
1137		Elizabeth	Sanders	F	71y	Mrs ǀ Elizth Sanders ǀ Died 27th Dec ǀ 1810 ǀ aged 71 years
1073		Francis William	Sanders	M	62y	Francis William ǀ Sanders Esqr ǀ Died . . . May ǀ 1831 ǀ aged 62 years
6109		Bisse Phillips	Sanderson	M	42y	Mr Bisse ǀ Phillips Sanderson ǀ Died 12th Feb ǀ 1830 ǀ Aged 42 Years
1111		Jane	Scarlett	F	90y	Mrs ǀ Jane Scarlett ǀ Died 18th July ǀ 1830 ǀ aged 90 years
1038		Edward	Scott	Y	14y	Master ǀ Edward Scott ǀ Died 9th Dec ǀ 1825 ǀ in his 14th year
6058		George Guillum	Scott	Y	6y 6m	Master George ǀ Guillum Scott ǀ Died 15th March ǀ 1817 ǀ Aged 6 Years 6 months

Notes/Sources	*will*	*MI*	*Year*
wife of John Rigge (6055)			1836
gentleman, St George Bloomsbury (Will TNA PROB 11/1900); husband of Elizabeth Rigge (6056)	Y		1838
			-
			1819
			-
dau of Francis Robertson of Lincoln's Inn Fields		Y	1815
son of Francis Robertson of Lincoln's Inn Fields		Y	1814
			-
spinster, Keppel St (Will TNA PROB 11/2191); 5 Keppel St, b St Amais, Jamaica (1851 census)	Y		1854
			-
			-
of Keppel St, died of dropsy, aged 64, 3 Sept 1822 (LMA P82/GEO1/63); ?wife of William Robertson (6130)			1822
			-
spinster, Keppel St (Will TNA PROB 11/1938)	Y		1840
of Keppel St, Bedford Sq (Will TNA PROB 11/1704); of Keppel St, died of old age, aged 88, 19 Sept 1825 (LMA P82/GEO1/63); husband of Mary Robertson (8089)	Y		1825
			1810
			1806
			-
of St James, Westminster (Will TNA PROB 11/1819)	Y		1833
			-
of King St, died of diseased liver, aged 58, 19 Jul 1833 (LMA P82/GEO1/63)			1833
gentleman, St George Bloomsbury (Will TNA PROB 11/1902)	Y		1838
possibly wife of James Rocher, painter of St George Bloomsbury (James Rocher will TNA PROB 11/1776); Jane Wilkinson married James Rocher in 1797, St Martin in the Field (Pallot's Marriage Index),	(Y)		1835
schoolmaster, St George Bloomsbury (Will TNA PROB 11/1446)	Y		1806
of Bernard St, died of 'inflammation', aged 37, 12 April 1833 (LMA P82/GEO1/63)			1833
dau of Francis Newman Rogers; of Woburn Pl, died of 'inflammation', aged 7 years 10 months, 9 Jan 1832 (LMA P82/GEO1/63); (Francis Newman Rogers will TNA PROB 11/2139)	(Y)		1832
			1805
sister of William Alexander (8024); widow of Rev Charles Rose		Y	1824
dau of Francis Frederick Rougemont (Will TNA PROB 11/2066)	(Y)		1844
son of Francis Frederick Rougemont (Will TNA PROB 11/2066)	(Y)		1838
gentlewoman, Woburn Pl, Russell Sq (Will TNA PROB 11/2242); b. c 1781 (Census 1851)	Y		1856
[loose plate Vault 3]			1828
			-
wife of Francis William Sanders (1073); of Montague St, died of consumption, aged 64, 17 Feb 1831 (LMA P82/GEO1/63)		Y	1831
dau of Francis William Sanders (1073) and Ann Sanders (1082); of Upper Montague St, died of consumption, aged 22, 18 June 1823 ((LMA P82/GEO1/63)		Y	1825
wife of John William Sanders of the Island of Nevis; mother of Francis William Sanders (1073); of Hunter St, died of asthma, aged 71, 31 Dec 1810 (LMA P82/GEO1/63)		Y	1810
barrister of Lincoln's Inn (TNA PROB 11/1785); 'eminent lawyer and profound and distinguished writer on legal subjects' (MI); wife of Ann Sanders (1082), son of Elizabeth Sanders (1137); of Montague St, died of tumour, aged 62, 2 May 1831 (LMA P82/GEO1/63)	Y	Y	1831
husband of Anna Stringfield (MI)		Y	1830
of Bedford Pl, died of old age, aged 89, 21 July 1830 (LMA P82/GEO1/63)			1830
			1825
of Great Coram St, died of consumptiom, aged 6 years 6 months, 17 Mar 1817 (LMA P82/GEO1/63)			1817

Coffin	Plate	Forename	Surname	M/F/Y/U	Age at Death	Inscription Text
	8010	John	Scott	M	66y	John Scott | Esqr M.D. | Died 30th July | 1849 Aged 66 Years
	8122	John	Scott	-	-	John Scott | Esqr M.D. | Died 30th July | 1849 | Aged 66 yrs
7076		John	Scott	M	74y	John Scott | Esqr | Died 6th January | 1828 | In the 74th Year | of his age
	8063	John	Scott	-	-	John Scott | Esqr | Died 16th Jany | 1820 | In the 74th Year of his age
5057		Robert	Scott	M	63y	Robert Scott | Esquire | Died 5th Septr | 1836 | Aged 63 Years
6112			Scott	F	36y	Mrs | .... Scott | .... 11th June | 1833 | ....d 36 ....
4045		Walter	Shairp	Y	52y	Walter Sha . . . | Esq | Died 11th July | 1813 | Aged 5 . Years
4050		Jane Claire	Shairp	F	59y	Mrs | Jane Claire | Shiarp | Died 28th Feby | 1832 | in her 60th Year
6115		James	Share	M	79y	Capt Jannes Share | R N | Died 11th Feb | 1831 | Aged 79 Years
6088		Hugh	Shaw	Y	18y	Hugh Shaw | esqr | Died 25th June | 1830 | Aged 18 Years
7075		James	Shaw	M	30y	James Shaw | Esqr | Died 11th Jany | 1818 | Aged 30 years
4020		James	Shaw	Y	17m	Mast | James Shaw | Died 3d May | 1818 | Aged 17 Mons
1104		Ann	Sherwood	F	40y	Mrs | Ann Sherwood | Died 17th June | 1808 | aged 42 years
1071		Sophie Ann	Sherwood	F	45y	Mrs | Sophie | Ann Sherwood | Died 23rd April | 1810 | aged 45 yea
	8035	Elizabeth	Shewen	F	49y	Mrs | Elizth Shewen | 1818
	8086	Elizabeth	Shewen	F	49y	Mrs | Elizth Shewen | Died 20th May | 1818 | Aged 49 Yrs
7084		Ann	Shield	F	85y	Mrs | Ann Shield | Died 30 Dec | 1835 | Aged 85 Years
	8029	Ann	Shield	-	-	Mrs Ann Shield | 1835
2025		Bartholemew	Short	M	72y	Bartholemew | Short | Died 5th Feby | 1820 | aged 72 yrs
1078		Frances Haselrigg	Shuttleworth	F	49y	Mrs | Frances Haselrigg | Shuttleworth | Died 12th Aug | 1845 | aged 49 Yrs
	8113	Deborah	Simpson	F	70y	Mrs | Debrah Simpson | Died 12th April | 1810 | Aged 70 Years
6066		Maria	Simpson	F	35y	Maria | Wife of | Thos Simpson Esqr | Died 11th June | 1826 | Aged 35 Years
1003		Jemima	Sims	F	52y	Miss | Jemima Sims | Younger Daughter of | John Sims, Esq | of White Rock | Glamorganshire | and Jemima Sims | his Wife | Died 22nd Jan 1846 | aged 52 years
1006		Jemima	Sims	F	80y	Mrs Jemima Sims | Relict of the late | John Sims Esq | White Rock | Glamorganshire | Died 17th Jan 1837 | in the 81st year of her age
7018		Eliza	Singer	F	29y	Mrs | Eliza Singer | Died 12th Sept | 1826 | Aged 29 Years
	8032	Eliza	Singer	-	-	Mrs | Eliza Singer | 1826
	8028	Charlotte	Skelton	F	46y	Miss | Charlotte Skelton | 1827
	8057	Charlotte	Skelton	-	-	Miss | Charlotte Skelton | Died 10 May | 1827 | Aged 46 Yrs
	8101	Charlotte	Skelton	-	-	Miss | Charlotte Skelton | Died 10th May | 1827 | Aged 46 years
4067		Anne	Slegg	F	21y	Mrs Anne Slegg | Died 17 Feby | 1813 | Aged 21 Years
	1581	John	Slegg	M	77y	John Slegg | Died 15th July | 1830 | aged 77 yrs
2027		Isabell Campbell	Smith	Y	2y	Isabell Campbell | the Daughter of John and Elizabeth Smith | Died 25th April 1835 | in the 3rd year of her age
1509		Richard	Smith	M	67y	Richard Smith | Esqr | Born 10th May | 1762 | Died 8th Feby | 1830
1113		William	Smith	M	57y	.... | Willm Smith | Died 1st May | 1826 | aged 57 y. .
6035		Vyner	Snell	M	57y	Vyner Snell | Esqr | Died 28 Novr | 1822 | Aged 57 Years
6105		Richard	Square	M	56y	Richard Square (or Souare) | Died June 9th | 1811 | Aged 56 Years
1135		Samuel	Stapleton	M	42y	Major | Sam Stapleton | Died 16 Augst | 1806 | aged 42 years
5054		Frances	Steers	F	75y	Mrs | Frances Steers | Died 15th Decr | 1832 | Aged 75 Years
1562		Isabella Sophia	Stevenson	Y	9m	Isabella | Sophia Stevenson | Died 25th April | 1816 | aged 9 mons
3063		Adelaide Sophia Martha	Stevenson	F	-	Miss Adelaide | Sophia Martha | Stevenson | 1832
1043		William John	Stevenson	Y	7y 6m	William | John Stevenson | Died 2nd June | 1813 | aged 7 yrs 6 mons
1138		Mary	Stewart	F	48y	Mary Stewart | Wife of David Stewart | Esq | Died 21st Decr | 1832 | in the 49th year | of her life
6018		Robert	Stewart	M	63y	Robert Stewart | Esq | Died 12 Jany | 1846 | Aged 63 Years
3084		Robert	Still	M	65y	Robert Still | Esq | of | East Knoyle | in the County of Wilts | Died 24 March 1822 | aged 65 years

Notes/Sources	will	MI	Year
doctor of medicine, St Giles in the Fields (Will TNA PROB 11/2108)	Y		1849
possibly John Fallowfield Scott, gentleman, Lincoln's Inn (Will TNA PROB 11/1754)	Y		- 1828
			- 1836
			1833
of Bedford Pl (Will TNA PROB 11/1546); ?husband of Jane Claire Shairp (4050); of Bedford Sq, died of consumption, aged 52, 12 July 1813 (LMA P82/GEO1/63)	Y		1813
? Wife of Walter Shairp (4045); of Great Coram St, died of apoplexy, aged 59, 2 Mar 1832 (LMA P82/GEO1/63)			1832
Commander in His Majesty's Royal Navy (Will TNA PROB 11/1829)	Y		1831
of Torrington St, died of jaundice, aged 18, 25 June 1830 (LMA P82/GEO1/63)			1830
			1818
			1818
of Great Coram St, died of consumptiom, aged 40, 22 June 1808 (LMA P82/GEO1/63)			1808
			1810
			1818
Anne, otherwise Anne Sheild, otherwise Anne Stokes, Bloomsbury (Will TNA PROB 11/1859)	Y		- 1835
youngest and last surviving brother of the late Rev. Wm. Short, D.D, Preb. of Westminster, and rector of King's Worthy' (*GM Mar 1840, 328*)			-
wife of John Bradley Shuttleworth, merchant, 6 Bedford Place (1841 census; *PO London 1841*)			1820
			1845
			1810
			1826
possibly spinster, St Giles in the Fields (Will TNA PROB 11/2095)	Y		1846
possibly widow, Torrington Sq (Will TNA PROB 11/1898)	Y		1837
of Woburn Pl, died of 'inflammation', aged 29, 13 Sept 1826 (LMA P82/GEO1/63)			1826
spinster, Everett St, Russell Sq (Will TNA PROB 11/1726); of Everett St, died of consumption, aged 46, 14 May 1827 (LMA P82/GEO1/63)	Y		-
			1827
			-
			-
			1813
John Slegg, esq, John St, Bedford Row (*GM June 1820, 562*; *List of Names 1815*); merchant, 36, John St, Bedford Row (*PO London 1826*); director, Royal Exchange Assurance Office (*Devizes and Wilts Gazette, Thursday 23 Mar 1826*)			1830
			1835
of The Museum, died suddenly, aged 68, 14 Feb 1830 (LMA P82/GEO1/63)			1830
of Bloomsbury (Will TNA PROB 11/1713); possibly William Smith esq, Gower St (*List of Names 1815*); of Southampton Row, died of palsy, aged 57, 16 May 1826 (LMA P82/GEO1/63)	Y		1826
of Woburn St, died of consumption, aged 57, 3 Dec 1822 (LMA P82/GEO1/63)			1822
			1811
			1806
widow, Bernard Street, Russell Square (TNA PROB 11/1810)	Y		1832
			1816
			1832
of Great Russell St, died of consumption, aged 7 years 6 months, 7 June 1813 (LMA P82/GEO1/63)			1813
wife of David Stewart (not identified)			1832
of St George Bloomsbury (Will TNA PROB 11/2038)	Y		1846
No 26 South Milton St,near Grosvenor Sq (Will TNA PROB 11/1657)	Y		1822

Coffin	Plate	Forename	Surname	M/F/Y/U	Age at Death	Inscription Text
1545		Phoebe Eliza	Stooks	Y	13m	Phoebe Eliza | the Infant Daughter of Thos & Eliza Stooks | Died (d. 1853, 11th of May 1830 | aged 13 mons
	vault 2, 10	Ely	Stott	M	72y	Ely Stott | Esq | Died 18th <u>Nov</u> 1821 | in his 73rd year
3064		Anna	Stringfield	Y	6y	Miss Anna | Stringfield | Died 6th Dec | 1835 | in her 7th year
6110		Anna	Stringfield	F	26y	Mrs | Anna Stringfield | Died [1]2th July | 1833 | Aged 26 Years
6071		James	Stringfield	M	27y	Mr | James Stringfield | Died 9th May | 1821 | in his 27th Year
6039		John	Stringfield	M	37y	Mr | John Stringfield | Died 2nd Septemr | 1832 | Aged 37 Yrs
6033		Mary	Stringfield	F	70y	M<u>rs</u> | Mary Stringfield | Died 7 Nov | 1833 | Aged 70 Years
6040		Thomas	Stringfield	M	67y	Mr | Thos Stringfield | Died 15th Nov | 1827 | Aged 63 Years
2067			Stringfield	U	28y	. . . . | . . . . Stringfield | Died 8 June | 1807 | aged 28 years
5076		Robert	Stuart	M	65y	Mr | Robert Stuart | Died 31st October | 1810 | Aged 65 Years
5034		John	Tapscott	M	66y	Mr | John Tapscot | Died 18th April | 1829 | Aged 60 years
1058		Martha	Tapscott	F	66y	Mrs | Martha Tapscott | Died 10th Jany | 1839 | aged 66 yrs
1140		Ann	Tatham	F	-	Mrs | Ann Tatham | Died 25th Novr | 1830
1544		Sarah	Tatham	F	68y	M. . . | Sarah Tatham | Died 14th July | 1847 | aged 68 yrs [outer chest plate] M . . . | Sarah Tat[ham] | Died . . . . y | 1847 | aged . . years [inner chest plate]
1527		Thomas James	Tatham	M	70y	Thomas James | Tatham | Esqre | Died 17th Decr | 1850 | aged 70 years
1558		Harriet	Tatischeff	F	66y	Miss | Harriet Tatischeff | Died 9th March | 1843 | in her 67th year
1099		William Elias	Taunton	M	62y	Sir William | Elias Taunton | Kn[ight] | one of His Majesty's Judges | of the Court of King's Bench | Died 11th Jany | 1835 | aged 62 year
4025		Francis Henry	Taylor	M	60y	Frans Henry | Taylor Esq. | Died 9 April | 1815 | Aged 60 Years
2029		Charles	Thesiger	M	69y	Charles Thesiger | Esqr | Died 18th February | 1831 | aged . . years
6042		Albertina Elizabeth	Thierens	F	21y	Miss Albertina | Elizabeth Thierens | Died 31st May | 1844 | Aged 21 Years
6051		John Cornelius	Thierens	M	40y	John Cornelius | Thierens Esqre | of the Colony of | Demerara & Esquibo | Died 14th Augst | 1829 | Aged 40 Years
7044		Amelia	Thomas	F	36y	Amelia | the Wife of | M. | Ligonier Thomas | Died 16th April | 1827 | Aged 36 Years
	8132	Amelia	Thomas	F	36y	Amelia | the Wife of | Mr | Ligonier Thomas | Died 16th April | 1827 | Aged 36 Years
7002		Evan	Thomas	M	67y	Mr | Eva<u>ns</u> Thomas | Died 12th Novr | 1814 | Aged 67 Years
2064		James	Thompson	M	58y	Mr | Jam<u>es</u> Thompson | Died 3d Feb | 1814 | aged 58 years
2063		Mary	Thompson	F	72y	Mrs | Mary Thompson | Died 13th December | 1817 | aged 72 years
3085		Robert	Thompson	M	77y	Robert Thompson | Esq. | Died . . . March | 1816 | Aged 77
3089		Anne Dalzell	Thomson	F	72y	Anne Dalzell | The relict of | Charles Thomson | Esq | Died 9th Jany | 1841 | Aged 72 Years
3090		Charles	Thomson	M	63y	Chas Thomson | Esqr | Master in Chancery | Born 12th April 1758 | Died 5th July 1821
3043		Edward Woodley	Thomson	Y	8y	Mast Edward | Woodley Thomson | Died 6 Aug | 1809 | Aged 8 Years
5041		Hannah	Thompson	F	67y	Mrs Hanh Thomson | Wife of | Mr James Thomson | carpenter | Kings Street Hollow | Died 29th January | 1813 | Aged 61 Years
	8061b	Sarah	Thornton	F	38y	Mrs | . . . . . Thornton | . . . . 31st Augst | 1821 | Aged 68 Yrs
	8033	Sarah	Thornton	-	-	Mrs Sarah | Thornton | 1821
2039		Sarah	Thorpe	F	69y	Mrs | Sarah Thorpe | Died 14th April | 1807 | aged 69 years

Notes/Sources	*will*	MI	Year
dau of Thomas Stooks (d. 1848, Will TNA PROB 11/2082), and Eliza Stooks, widow, No 8 Lower Bedford Pl Will TNA PROB 11/2174); of Bedford Pl, died of 'water on the head', aged 13 months, 15 May 1830 (LMA P82/GEO1/63)	(Y)		1830
Surgeon of Bloomsbury , Middlesex (TNA PROB 11/1651); of Hart St, died of 'apoplexy', aged 72, 26 Nov 1821 (LMA P82/GEO1/63)	Y		1821
dau of John Stringfield (6039) and Anna Stringfield (6110)		Y	1835
widow, St George Bloomsbury (Will TNA PROB 11/1819); wife of John Stringfield (6039); of Duke St, died of consumption, aged 25, 12 July 1833 (LMA P82/GEO1/63)	Y		1833
son of Thomas Stringfield (6040) and Mary Stringfield (6033); brother of John Stringfield (6039); OF Duke St, died of cosumption, aged 21, 14 May 1821 (LMA P82/GEO1/63)			1821
butcher, Bloomsbury (Will TNA PROB 11/1806); son of Thomas Stringfield (6040) and Mary Stringfield (6033); brother of James Stringfield (6071); of Duke St, died of dropsy, aged 37, 4 Sept 1832 (LMA P82/GEO1/63)	Y		1832
wife of Thomas Stringfield (6040), mother of John and James Stringfield (6039 & 6071); of Hart St, died of 'inflammation', aged 70, 7 Nov 1833 (LMA P82/GEO1/63)			1833
butcher, St George Bloomsbury (Will TNA PROB 11/1734); husband of Mary Stringfield (6033), father of John and James Stringfield (6039 & 6070): of Hart St, died of consumption, aged 67, 17 Nov 1827 (LMA P82/GEO1/63)	Y		1827
possibly William Stringfield, died 23 Jul 1837, aged 38 (MI)			1807
stone mason, St George Bloomsbury (Will TNA PROB 11/1517); of Hyde St, died of 'inflammation', aged 65, 10 Nov 1810 (LMA P82/GEO1/630	Y		1810
of Little Russell St, died of 'inflammation', aged 66, 24 Ape 1829 (LMA P82/GEO1/63)			1829
widow, Bloomsbury (Will TNA PROB 11/1907)	Y		1839
spinster, St George Bloomsbury (Will TNA PROB 11/1780)	Y		1830
dau of Thomas James Tatham (1527) , Bedford Pl (1841 Census)			1847
land surveyor, Bedford Pl, Russell Sq (Will TNA PROB 11/2126); Land agent and surveyor, died of asthma, disease of the heart and dropsy many months certified, aged 70, 12 Dec 1850 (Death certificate)	Y		1850
spinster, St George Bloomsbury (Will TNA PROB 11/1980)	Y		1843
judge of His Majesty's Court of Kings Bench, Minster Lovell, Oxfordshire (Will TNA PROB 11/1843)	Y		1835
			1815
collector of His Majesty's Customs of the Island of St Vincent (Will TNA PROB 11/1784); of Montague Pl, died of 'inflammation', aged 69, 17 Feb 1831 (LMA P82/GEO1/63)	Y		1831
dau of John Cornelius Thierens (6051; 'On Friday, the 31st. ult., at Russell-place, Albertina Elizabeth, aged 21, daughter of the late J.C. Thierens, Esq., of Demerara', *The Times* , 4 Jun 1844)			1844
of Woburn Pl, died of 'inflammation', aged 40, 17 Aug 1829 (LMA P82/GEO1/63); 'In London, on the 4th inst., John Cornelius Thierens, Esq., of the colony of Demerara and Essequibo, in the 40th year of his age, after an illness of three days.' *The Times* 24 Aug 1829); father of Albertina Thierens (6042)			1829
			1827
			-
of Thorney St, died of consumption, aged 67, 14 Nov 1814 (LMA P82/GEO1/63)			1814
carpenter of King St, husband of Hannah Thom(p)son (5041); of King St, died of dropsy, aged 58, 5 Feb 1814 (LMA P82/GEO1/63)			1814
			1817
			1816
widow, Albourne Place , Sussex (Will TNA PROB 11/1958); death registered at Cuckfield, Sussex (GRO Index Jan-Mar 1841, Cuckfield Vol 7, p. 237)	Y		1841
Master of Chancery, 10 Feb 1809 (Hadyn 1851, 241); died 'suddenly. at his house in Portland-place. . .He had a paralytic stroke, and had been in a declining state for some time past' (*GM* July 1821, 93)			1821
			1809
wife of James Thom(p)son (2064); Hannah Thompson, of King St, died of gout, aged 67, 1 Feb 1813 (LMA P82/GEO1/63)			1813
of Bury St, died of 'spasm', aged 38, 1 Sept 1821 (LMA P82/GEO1/63)			1821
			-
spinster, St Marylebone (Will TNA PROB 11/1462)	Y		1807

Coffin	Plate	Forename	Surname	M/F/Y/U	Age at Death	Inscription Text
1069		Francis	Thwaites	M	81y	Francis Thwaites | Esqr | Died 24th May | 1837 | in his 81st year
	8013	Susanna	Thwaites	F	83y	Mrs | Susanna Thwaites | Died 16th July | 1845 | Aged 83 Years
	8047	Susanna	Thwaites	-	-	Mrs | Susanna Thwaites | Died 16 July | 1845 | Aged 83 Years
5023		Catherine	Toogood	F	55y	Mrs | Cathe Toogood | Died 5th Jany | 1830 | Aged 55 Years
1127		Isaac	Tooke	M	65y	Mr | Isaac Tooke | Died 7th Nov | 1832 | aged 65 yrs
3039		Alfred	Toulmin	Y	2m	Masr | Alfred Toulmin | Died 10 April | 1809 | aged 2 mons
2011		Mary Anne	Townes	Y	3y 6m	Miss Mary | Anne Townes | Born Novr 15th 1807 | Died May 30th | 1811
2015		Frederick	Townshend	Y	15y	Lord Frederick Townshend Died 27th March 1832 | in the 16th year of age
5021		Mary Ann	Treslove	Y	7m	Miss | Mary Ann | Treslove | Died 4th Augst | 1819 | Aged 7 mons
4039		Edward	Trower	Y	19m	Mastr | Edwd Trower | Died 30th May | 1829 | Aged 19 months
1529		Emily	Trower	Y	11m	Miss | Emily Trower | Died 14th July | 1834 | aged 11 mons
5009		Isabella	Trower	Y	16y	Miss | Isabella Trower | Died 22nd April | 1828 | Aged 16 Years
5059		Robert	Trower	M	43y	Rob Trower | Esq | Died 29th Jany | 1826 | in his 44th Year
7081		Charlotte	Turner	F	41y	Miss Charlotte Turner | Died 11th Augst | 1837 | Died 41 Years
	8111	Charlotte	Turner	-	-	Miss | Charte Turner | Died 11th Augt | 1837 | Died 41 yrs
7083		Henry	Turner	M	65y	Henry Turner | Esqr | Died 9th Feby | 1846 | Aged 65 Yrs
	8021	Henry	Turner	-	-	Henry Turner | Esqre | 1846
7073		John	Turner	M	48y	John Turner | Esqr | Died 1st March | 1846 | Aged 48 years
	8053	John	Turner	-	-	John Turner | Esqre | 1846
	8044	Sarah Elizabeth	Turner	Y	13y	Miss Sarah | Elizth Turner | 1829
	8062	Sarah Elizabeth	Turner	Y	15y	Miss Sarah | Elizabeth Turner | Died 7th Decemr | 1829 | Aged 15 Years
	8112	Sarah Elizabeth	Turner	-	-	Miss Sarah | Elizabeth T . . . . . . | Died 7th Decr | 1829 | Aged 13 Years
6075		Andrew	Tweeddale	M	23y	Mr Andrew Tweeddale | Died 10th Jany | 1827 | Aged 23 Years
5064		Edward	Vandergucht	Y	-	Edward | Son of | Thomas George & Ellen | Vandergacht | Died 15th June | 1821 | Aged . . .
1122		Louisa Maria Frances	Vieusseux	F	38y	Mrs | Louisa Maria Frans | Vieufieux | Died 26th June | 1828 | aged 38 Yrs
1143		Elizabeth	Vigors	F	80y	Mrs Elizth Vigors | Relict of | Lie[u]t . . . . General | . . . . . Vigors | Born 15th Feby 1737 & | Died 22nd July 1817
2009		[Augustus] Algernon	Villiers	M	25y	The Honble | Algernon Villier[s] | Died 13th July | 1843 | aged 25 years
3038		Wilbraham Edward	Villiers	Y	3_m	Wilbraham | Edward Villiers | Died 21st Nov | 1845 | aged $3^{1}/_{2}$ mons
	8026	Thomas	Vinton	M		Mr | Thomas Vinton | 1833
5055		Mary	Virgoe	F	94y	Mrs | Mary Virgoe | Died 9th Decr | 1815 | Aged 94 Years
	8078	Thomas Trower	Virgoe	M		Thomas Trower | Virgoe Esqr | Died 20th Jany | 1830 | In his 78th Yea
1136		Elizabeth	Walker	F	74y	Mrs | Elizabeth Walker | Died 10th Jany | 1829 | aged 74 years
1147		Thomas	Walker	M	72y	Thomas Walker | Esqr | Died 10th Jany | 1820 | in the 72nd year | of his age
	8042	Mary Ann	Wall	F	78y	Mrs | Mary Ann Wall | 1833
	8084	Mary Ann	Wall	F	78y	Mrs Mary | Ann Wall | Died . . . . | 1833 | Aged 7 . Years
	8095	Mary Ann	Wall	F	78y	. . . | Mary Ann Wall | Died 27th Jany | 1833 | Aged 78 Years
4015		Ca . . . . . . al Wignal	Walni	U	50y	. . . . | Wignal Walni . . . . | . . . . | Died 7th . . . | 1818 | Aged 50 Years [outer plate]
						Miss | C . . al Wal . ryn | spinster | Died 7 Dec | 1818 | Aged 50] Years [lead plate

Notes/Sources	will	MI	Year
of Woburn Pl (Will TNA PROB 11/1883); ?husband of Susanna Thwaites (8013)	Y		1837
widow, Woburn Pl (Will TNA PROB 11/2023); independent means, 32 Woburn Pl (1841 census); ?wife of Frances Thwaites (1069)	Y		1845
			-
			1830
wine merchant, No 44 Southampton Row, Russell Sq (Will TNA PROB 11/1808); of Southampton Row, died of disease of the heart, aged 65, 9 Nov 1832 (LMA P82/GEO1/63)	Y		1832
of Hart St, died of smallpox, aged 2 months, 15 Apr 1809 (LMA P82/GEO1/63)			1809
			1811
of Hunter St, died of 'enlargement of the heart', aged 15, 30 Mar 1832 (LMA P82/GEO1/63)			1832
of Charlotte St, died of consumption, aged 7 months, 7 Aug 1819 (LMA P82/GEO1/63); ?dau of Thomas Crosby Treslove of Lincoln's Inn (will TNA PROB 11/ 1946)	(Y)		1819
of Russell Sq, died of 'teething', aged 19 months, 3 Jun 1829 (LMA P82/GEO1/63); b. Nov 1828, Montague Pl, Russell Sq, youngest son of George Trower (d. 1840, will TNA PROB 11/1935) and Isabella Kemble (IGI)	(Y)		1829
b. 27 Aug 1833, Montague Pl, Russell Sq, youngest dau of George Trower (d. 1840, will TNA PROB 11/1935) and Isabella Kemble (IGI)			1834
of Russell Sq, died of consumption, aged 16, 23 Apr 1828 (LMA P82/GEO1/63); b. 1 Feb 1812, Montague Pl, Russell Sq, eldest dau of George Trower (d. 1840, will TNA PROB 11/1935) and Isabella Kemble (IGI)			1828
of Woburn Pl, Russell Sq (Will TNA PROB 11/1712); of Woburn Pl, suicide, aged 43, 2 Feb 1826 (LMA P82/GEO1/63)	Y		1826
spinster, died of fever, aged 41, 11 Aug 1837 (Death certificate)			1837
			-
of Bedford Pl (Will TNA PROB 11/2033); = ?Henry Turner, surgeon, King St, and ?brother of John Turner (7073) (1841 census; *PO London 1841*, 138)	Y		1846
			-
surgeon, Bloomsbury (Will TNA PROB 11/2033); = John Turner surgeon, King St, and ?brother of Henry Turner (7083) (1841 census; *PO London 1841*, 138)	Y		1846
			-
			1829
of King Street, died of consumption, aged 15, 13 Dec 1829 (LMA P82/GEO1/63)			-
			-
of Plumtree St, died of typhus fever, aged 24, 11 Jan 1827 (LMA P82/GEO1/63)			1827
son of Thomas George Vandergucht, gentleman, Strand, Middx (d. 1828, Will TNA PROB 11/1738)	(Y)		1821
			1828
wife (sic) of St Marylebone (TNA PROB 11/1596); wife of Lt Gen Urban Vigors, East India Company service (d. 1815, Will PROB 11/1569).	Y		1817
Hon. Augustus Algernon Villiers, brother of the 4th Earl of Clarendon and of Henry Montague Villiers, Bishop of Durham; Lieut RN 1838 (*GM Sept 1843*, 327); Kt of Isabella the Catholic (Sp) (*New Navy List Aug 1842*, 205)			1843
son of Henry Montague Villiers, Bishop of Durham			1845
gentleman, St Pancras (Will TNA PROB 11/1813)	Y		1833
of Little Russell St, died of old age, aged 94, 13 Dec 1815 (LMA P82/GEO1/63)			1815
of Holborn (Will TNA PROB 11/1767)	Y		1830
widow, Bloomsbury (Will TNA PROB 11/1752); ?wife of Thomas Walker (1147); of Bloomsbury Sq, died of 'inflammation', aged 74, 15 Jan 1829 (LMA P82/GEO1/63)	Y		1829
(Will TNA PROB 11/1642); ?husband of Elizabeth Walker (1136); of Hart St, died of consumption, aged 72, 10 Nov 1820 (LMA P82/GEO1/63)	Y		1820
widow, St Pancras (Will TNA PROB 11/1812)	Y		1833
			-
			-
			1818

Coffin	Plate	Forename	Surname	M/F/Y/U	Age at Death	Inscription Text
2068		Joseph	Ward	M	75y	Joseph Ward | Esq | Died 13th Feb | 1821 | aged 75 years
3047		Katherine Maria	Ward	Y	2y 10m	Miss | Katherine Maria Ward | Died 5 September | 1841 | aged 2 years | & 10 months
7016		Catherine	Warren	F	78y	Miss | Cathe Warren | Died 1 July | 1834 | 78 Years
5045		George	Waterford ...	Y	11m 22d	Master George | Waterford ... | Died 17th Septr | 1814 | Aged 11 months | & 22 Days
1060		Harriet	Waters	Y	16y	Miss | Harriet Waters | Died 20th June | 1819 | aged 16 years
7065		Millecent	Waters	Y	14y	Millecent Waters | Died 14th Decr | 1818 | Aged 14 Years
	8030	Millecent	Waters	Y		Millecent Waters | Died 1818
	8050	Millecent	Waters	Y		Millecent Waters | Decr 1818
	8067	Millecent	Waters	Y		Millecent Waters | Died 14th Decber | 1818 | Aged 14 years
3025		Mary Ann	Watts	F	33y	Mrs | Mary Ann Watts | Died 11th Jan | 1804 | aged 33 years [Second plate appears to read: '14th Jan']
5063		Phillip	Werner	M	64y	Phillip Werner | Esqr | Died 2nd May | 1819 | Aged 64 Yrs
6114		Sarah	Westwood	F	45y	Mrs | Sarah Westwood | Died 4 August | 1818 | Aged 45 Years
	8093	Sarah	White	F	74y	Mrs | Sarah White | Died 12th Septr | 1819 | Aged 74 Years
6061		Emily Susan	Whitehurst	Y	20y	Miss | Emily Susan Whitehurst | Born 17th Octr | 1810 | Died 21st Augst | 1831
3048		Charles Robert Claude	Wilde	Y	6m 18d	Master | Charles Robert | Claude Wilde | Died 29th Augst | 1814 | aged 6 months | & 18 days
2020		Edmund	Wilkinson	M	38y	Mr | Edmund Wilkinson | Died 4th July | 1831 | aged 38 years
2049		John	Williams	M	70+y	John Williams | Esq. | Died 27 November | 1823 | aged 7 . Years
2059		Alexander	Williams	M	64y	Alexander Williams | late of Chichester | Died 29th Octr | 1810 | aged 64 Years
6016		Anne	Williams	F	33y	Miss | Anne Willyams | Died 27th October | 1835 | Aged 33 Years
6080		Elizabeth	Williams	F	78y	Mrs | Elizth Williams | Died 1st April | 1828 | Aged 78 Yrs
1504		Mary	Williams	F	74y	Mary | Widow of | John Williams Esq | many years Vestry Clerk of | St. Dunstans in the West | whose remains were interred at | Fryern Barnet | Died 9th March 1835 | aged 74 years
1560		Mary Portia	Williams	Y	2m	Mary Portia | Daughter of | Robert & Mary | Williams | Born 5th June | 1828 | Died 27th Augst | 1828
	8103	Reginald	Williams	M	55y	Reginald Williams | Esqr | Died 7th Novr | 1828 | Aged 55 Years
	3107	Robert	Williams	M	61y	Robert Williams | Esqr. M.D. | Died 24th Novr | 1845 | Aged 61 Years
	8034	Sarah	Williams	F		Mrs | Sarah Williams | 1825
2054		Susanna	Williams	F	80y	Mrs | Susanna Williams | Died 20th Nov | 1826 | aged 80
2045		Thomas	Willis	M	74y	Revd Thomas Willis L.L.D. | Rector of St. George Bloomsbury thirty seven years | Died 9th Nov 1827 | aged 74 years
6072		Ann	Wilson	F	76y	Ann Wilson | Relict of | Mathew Wilson | Esq | Died 23rd August | 1836 | Aged 76 Yrs
2016		Henry George	Wilson	M	48y	Henry George Wilson Esqre | Died 14 Oct 1836 | aged 48 years
	8009	Mary Ann	Wilson	F	44y	Miss Mary | Ann Wilson | Died 27th March | 1831 | Aged 44 Years
	8120	Mary Ann	Wilson	F	44y	Miss | Mary Ann Wilson | Died 27th March | 1831 | Aged 44 years
2041		Matthew	Wilson	M	83y	Lieut Colonel Matthew Wilson | Died 15th July | 1836 | in his 83rd Year
6133		Emma Margaret	Winsland	Y	18y	Emma Margaret | Winsland | Died 31th (sic) March | 1848 | Aged 18 Years
6079		Lucy Anne	Winsland	Y	11y	Miss | Lucy Anne | Winsland | Died 15th August | 1833 | Aged 11 Years
6136		Nicholas	Winsland	M	56y	Nicholas Winsland | Esq | Died 27th Jan | 1846 | Aged 56 Years
6140		Nicholas Charles	Winsland	Y	10w	Nicholas Charles | Winsland | Died 27th Oct | 1824 | Aged 10 weeks
3093		..... lip West .. n	Wood	M		..... lip West ... n | Wood Esq. | Died 30th May | 1839 | in his .. Year

Notes/Sources	will	MI	Year
possibly Joseph Ward, attorney, No 44 Bedford Sq (*Holdens's 1811*)			1821
			1841
			1834
			1814
of Russell Sq, died of consumption, aged 16, 21 Jun 1819 (LMA P82/GEO1/63)			1819
Mellecent Waters, of Russell Sq, died of consumption, aged 15, 16 Dec 1818 (LMA P82/GEO1/63)			1818
			-
			-
			-
			1804
of Red Lion Sq (Will TNA PROB 11/1616); Dr Philip Werner, late of Gibraltar, died in Red Lion Sq (*GM*, May 1819, 492)	Y		1819
of King Street, died of dropsy, aged 45, 12 Aug 1818 (LMA P82/GEO1/63)			1818
widow, St George Bloomsbury (Will TNA PROB 11/1620); of Museum St, died of dropsy, aged 74, 14 Sept 1819 (LMA P82/GEO1/63)	Y		1819
			1810
eldest son of Thomas Wilde 1st Baron Truro; of Guilford St, died of convulsions, aged 6 months, 30 Aug 1814 (LMA P82/GEO1/63)			1814
probably Edmund Watkinson, chemist of St Anne, Soho, Middlesex (will TNA PROB 11/1789); chemist & druggist, 10 King St, Soho (*PO London 1829; SUN MS 11936/504/1029303, 20 April 1825 & MS 11936/473/931286, 22 May 1817*)	Y		1831
			1823
merchant, St George Bloomsbury (Will TNA PROB 11/1517); of Charlotte St, died of consumption, aged 64, 5 Nov 1810 (LMA P82/GEO1/63)	Y		1810
			1835
possibly Elizabeth Williams, spinster, St Mary Islington, Middx (Will TNA PROB 11/1763)	Y		1828
(Will TNA PROB 11/1846)	Y		1835
possibly Tertia Mary Williams, of Bedford Pl, died of 'inflammation', aged 3 months, 30 Aug 1828 (LMA P82/GEO1/63)			1828
of Montague St, died of 'inflammation', aged 60, 8 Nov 1828 (LMA P82GEO1/63)			1828
			1845
of Upper Bedford St, died of 'infammation', aged 47, 3 & 4 Sept 1825 (LMA P82/GEO1/63)			1825
of Charlotte St, died of 'mortification', aged 80, 21 Nov 1826 (LMA P82/GEO1/63)			1826
Rector, Dr of Laws, St George Bloomsbury (Will TNA PROB 11/1734); of Rectory House, died of the stone, aged 74, 9 Nov 1827 (LMA P82/GEO1/63)	Y		1827
widow of Col Matthew Wilson (2041)			1836
of St George Bloomsbury (Will TNA PROB 11/1871)	Y		1836
of Guilford St, died of dropsy, aged 44, 31 Mar 1831 (LMA P82/GEO1/63)			1831
			-
possibly Matthew Wilson, St George Bloomsbury (Will TNA PROB 11/1866); husband of Ann Wilson (6072)	Y		1836
?dau of Nicholas Winsland (6136)			1848
?dau of Nicholas Winsland (6136); of Great Russell St, died of 'inflammation', aged 14, 20 Aug 1833 (LMA P82/GEO1/63)			1833
builder, St George Bloomsbury (Will TNA PROB 11/2013); painter and glazier, of 18 Queen St (*Holden's 1811; Old Bailey Proceedings, 28 Oct 1818*, Ref No. t18181028-88); builder, of Duke St (SUN MS 11936/517/1086467, 4 February 1829; *Old Bailey Proceedings, 7 July 1838*, Ref No. t18380709-1740); of 44 Great Russell St (SUN MS 11936/517/1086468, 4 February 1829); of 84 Great Russell St (*PO London 1941*)	Y		1846
son of Nicholas Winsland (6136); of Great Russell St, died of inflammation, aged 10 weeks, 28 Oct 1824 (LMA P82/GEO1/63)			1824
possibly Philip Whittle Wood, late Extra Clerk in the Office of the Committee of Buying and Warehouses of the Honorable East India Company London, Kelvedon Essex (Will TNA PROB 11/1913)	Y		1839

Coffin	Plate	Forename	Surname	M/F/Y/U	Age at Death	Inscription Text
3061		Adelaide	Wood	Y		Adel Wood | Born 31st May | 1830 | Died 31st Mar | 1831 [outer plate]
						Adelaide Wood | Born 31st May | 1830 | Died 31 Mar | 1831 [inner plate]
4032		Benjamin	Wood	M	46y	Benjamin Wood | Esqr |Died 16th Nov | 1838 | Aged 46 Years
	2070	Benjamin	Wood	M	46y	Benjamin Wood | Esq | Died 16th Novr | 1838 | aged 46 years
3034		Clementina Baron	Wood	Y	10m 13d	Miss Clementina | Baker Wood | Died 29 Dec 1828 | aged 10 mon & 13 days
1556		Philadelphia	Wood	F	87y	Mrs Philadelphia | Wood | Died 24th August | 1851 | aged 87 years
1110		Caroline	Woodham	F		Caroline Wood . . . | . . . ler | Died . . . January | 1842 [outer chest plate] Caroline | Woodham | 1842 [head plate]
2010		George Draper	Wright	Y	16m	Geoe Draper Wright | 1829
6031		Richard	Wroughton	M	72y	Mr | Richard Wroughton | Died 7 Feb | 1822 | Aged 72 Years
6087		Margaret	Wych	F	68y	Mrs | Margaret Wych | Died 12th March | 1829 | Aged 68 Years
3055		Anna	Wyndham	F	30y	Miss | Anna Wyndham | Died 31 Dec | 1818 | aged 30 years
3071		Sarah	Wyndham	F	80y	Mrs | Sarah Wyndham | obit 29 Oct | 1835 | aged 80 years
1125		Mary	Wynell Mayow	F		Mary Wynell Mayow | Widow of Mayow Wynell Mayow | . . . .
5037		Mayow	Wynell Mayow	M	54y	Mayow Wynell Mayow | Esq | Died 11th Jan | 1807 | in the 54th Year of his Life
	8080	Elizabeth Ann	Yardley	F	35y	Mrs Elizabeth | Ann Yardley | Obit 4th June | 1828 | Aetat 35 Years
1098		Mary	Yardley	F	76y	Mrs | Mary Yardley | Died 30th October | 1834 | in her 76th year
6074		William	Yardley	M		Mr | William Yardley | 1824
5020		John Hawden	Yates	Y	2m	Master John Hawden Yates | Died 5th August | 1830 | Aged 2 Months
1534		Elizabeth	Yenn	F	48y	M . . | Elizth Yenn | Died March . . . | 1806 | in her 48th year
1550		John	Yenn	M	71y	John Yenn | Esqr | Died 1st March | 1821 | aged 71 Yrs
1517		Susannah Mary	Yenn	F	59y	Susannah | Mary Yenn | Born 17 Jan | 1786 | Died 19 Jan | 1845 [inner plate]
	3111	Susannah Mary	Yenn	F	59y	Susannah | Mary Yenn | Born 1st Jany | 1786 | Died 19th Jan | 1845
1533		Anne	Young	F	91y	Anne | Dowager Lady Young | Relict of the Late | Admiral Sir George | Young K.C.B. | Died Oct 16th | 1830 | in the 91st year of her life
	1580	Sarah	. . . nny	F	50y	The remains of Sarah, the Wife of George . . . nny | Esqr | of . . . . . ort Street, Cavendish Square . . . . she died 3rd [or 8th] July 182 . | in the 50th year of her age
6098		Edn . . .	. . . nes	U	62y	Edn. . . . . nes | Died 24th Nov | Aged 62 Years | 1807
1130		? Jarim		U		. . . . . . Jarim . . . . .
5073		Charles		Y		Master Charles | . . . . | Died 29th July | 18 . . | Aged . . . . .
5047		Edward		M	25y	Mr | . . . . . . | Edward | . . . . hiky | 1819 | Aged 25 Years
4061		Eli		U		Eli . . . . . . | . . . . | . . . . | Died . . . . . | in . . . .
5046		Elizabeth		F		. . . Elizabeth . . . . . . | Died 20th . . . | 18 . . | . . . . . .
	8066	Elizabeth		F		Miss Elizabeth . . . . | Died 11th April . . . .
3058		Fran		M	84y	The Rev. | Fran . . . . | Died 23rd April | 1806 | aged 84 years
5069		Henry		Y	13m	. . . . | Henry . . . . . | Died . . . . | 1828 | Aged 13 months
1063		Horatio		Y		. . . | Horatio . . . . . | Died 7th Sept | 1816 | aged 7 mons
4036		John		M	55y	John . . . . . ids | Died . . . Decr | . . . . | . . . . 55 Years
5077		John		M		John . . . . | Esq | Died . . . . | 18 . . | Aged 6 . . . . .
1569		Thomas		M	71y	Thomas . . . . . . | Esqre | Died . . . . | 1811 | aged 71 years
4026				M		Master | H. W. . . . . | 1823
4047				U	49y	. . . . . | . . . . . | . . . . . | . . . . . | Aged 49 Years
4054				Y	17y	Mrs | . . . . | Died 10th June | 1818 | Aged 17 Years
4057				M	60y	. . . . | Died . . . . . . | 1824 | in his 60th Year
4085				Y	3m	. . . . | 1815 | Aged 3 months
5060				U	74y	. . . . . | . . . . | . . . . . | . . 23 Aug . . . . | . . . . . 74 years
6099				M	63y	. . . . | Esq | Died 25 . . . . . | 1827 | Aged 63 Years
6127				U	63y	. . . . | . . . . | Died . . . . Feb | 1807 | Aged 63 Yrs
7006				U	33y	. . . . | . . . . | Died . . . 17th | . . . . | Aged 33 Years
7011				F		. . . . | Wife of | W . . . . Esq | Died . . . . . | . . . . Yea

Notes/Sources	*will*	MI	*Year*
of Brunswick Sq, died of 'waterhead', aged 9 months, 2 Apr 1831 (LMA P82/GEO1/63)			1831
stock broker, City of London (Will TNA PROB 11/1903)	Y		1838
of Bloomsbury Sq, died of 'water on the head', aged 8 months, 31 Dec 1828 (LMA P82/GEO1/63)			- 1828
spinster, Mayfield, Sussex (Will TNA PROB 11/2140); fundholder, 28 Montague St, Bloomsbury (1851 Census)	Y		1851
spinster, St George Bloomsbury (Will TNA PROB 11/1958)	Y		1842
of Torrington St, died of measles, aged 16 months, 13 Apr 1829 (LMA P82/GEO1/63)			1829
gentleman, Berners St, Oxford St (Will TNA PROB 11/1654)	Y		1822
spinster, Warwick Sq, City of London (Will TNA PROB 11/1753)	Y		1829
of Charlotte St, died of dropsy, aged 30, 3 Jan 1819 (LMA P82/GEO1/63)			1818
widow, St George Bloomsbury (Will TNA PROB 11/1854)	Y		1835
widow, Sydenham, Kent (Will TNA PROB 11/1724; *List of Names 1815*)	Y		1827
of Lewisham, Kent (Will TNA PROB 11/1461); husband of Mary Wynell Mayow (1125)	Y		1807
of Thorney St, died of dropsy, aged 35, 4 Jun 1828 (LMA P82/GEO1/63)			1828
			1834
of Thorney St, died of 'inflammation', aged 67, 18 Aug 1824 (LMA P82/GEO1/63); possibly William Yardley, of St George Bloomsbury (TNA PROB 11/1696, 10 Feb 1825)	Y		1824
of Torrindton Sq, died of 'infammation' aged 2 months (LMA P82/GEO1/63)			1830
wife of John Yenn (1550), mother of Susannah Mary Yenn (1517); b. 1775		Y	1806
of Kensington Palace Green, Middx (Will TNA PROB 11/1642); Kensington Green (*List of Names 1815*); husband of Elizabeth Yenn (1534), father of Susannah Mary Yenn (1517)	Y	Y	1821
spinster, Gloucester Pl, Portman Sq (Will TNA PROB 11/2032); dau of John Yenn (1550) and Elizabeth Yenn (1534)	Y	Y	1845
of Bloomsbury (Will TNA PROB 11/1778); wife of Admiral Sir George Young, of Cookham, Berkshire (Will TNA PROB 11/1515); of Great Russell St, died of old age, aged 90, 20 Oct 1830 (LMA P82/GEO1/63)	Y		- 1830
could this be 2nd plate for Sarah Moneypenny? (1044)			-
			1807
			-
			1819
			-
			-
			1806
			1828
			1816
			-
			1811
			1823
			-
			1818
			1824
			1815
			-
			1827
			1807
			-

Appendix 2: Statistical testing of osteological dating methods

dating methods by Richard Wright

INTRODUCTION

One of the aims research aims of the project was to test the reliability of various osteological dating techniques on skeletons of known chronological age. The data is discussed in Chapter 7 above. The statistical tests undertaken as part of the work and their results are presented below.

AIM OF THE ANALYSIS

The aim of the analysis was to examine the correlation between known age at death derived from *departum* plates and six conventional age indicators. Table 7.3 gives the youngest and oldest implied age limits for each individual for each of the six age indicators. To simplify these data to a single number the average of the implied limits for each case was taken, but the averages between each of the six age indicators were not merged.

MULTIPLE LINEAR REGRESSION

The results for the six age indicators are available. Combining all six into a single Multiple Linear Regression equation (MLR) seems an obvious way to proceed (Draper and Smith 1998, chapter 9; Zar 1999, chapter 20). MLR simultaneously examines the correlation between known age at death (the independent variable) and all age indicators (the dependent variables).

Unfortunately MLR requires that each individual has a complete set of observations for each of the six ageing methods. The data is however, far from complete, and in fact only three of the 53 individuals has a complete set for the six age indicators. Yet by reducing the ageing methods to four it is possible to extract data for 13 of the 53 individuals of known age. MLR could be carried out on these 13 individuals and their four age indicators.

REGRESSION USING INDIVIDUAL AGE INDICATORS

In order not to sacrifice information latent in the incomplete sets of data for the remaining 40 individuals, the six age indicators were examined individually. None of these six analyses used all 53 individuals, but rather used different numbers and combinations of individuals (see Table 7.3).

All six individual analyses assume that the known age of death is the independent variable (i.e. the X axis) and the age implied by ageing indicators is the dependent variable (i.e. the Y axis). The lines of best fit considered for use in these analyses are of two types (Zar 1999, chapter 21):

The graph of a 1st degree polynomial, which is a linear function, as with a linear regression line.

The graph is a 2nd degree polynomial, which is a parabola.

Polynomials beyond a degree of two will fit the data points better, yet with such a small amount of data there is the risk of overfitting. For example, higher degree polynomials risk creating a curve that suggests age degeneration reverses itself in certain age groups, i.e. the curve rises then falls again. Yet enamel on the tooth crowns cannot repair itself after attrition, nor, so far as is known, can pubic symphisis reverse degenerative age changes. Because repair has not been reported in the relevant osteological studies such mathematical 'best fits' must be excluded.

To choose the lines of best fit a statistical package LeoStatistic has been used. This package can be downloaded from: http://www.leokrut.com/leostatistic/

Leostatistic was used specifically to search for the 'best formula'. The best formula may not be polynomial. If it is not, and to keep analyses consistent, it is necessary to look for a polynomial fit that is close enough to the 'best formula' as to make no substantive difference in the display. No problems were found in finding a suitable polynomial.

RESULTS

Multiple Linear Regression

The result for the MLR of 13 individuals has a correlation R of 0.836. The regression is statistically significant, with a probability of 0.031. These results mean that for the 13 individuals there is a high degree of correlation between known age at death and the four ageing indicators examined simultaneously.

Do all the indicators contribute equally to the MLR result? To answer this we can look at the weights of the age indicators:

Table A2.1: Age indicators: results of MLR

Age indicator	Standardised Beta coefficient	Probability
Pubic Symphysis (S and B)	0.199	0.369
Sternal rib end	0.087	0.693
Cranial suture closure	0.072	0.734
Auricular surface	0.731	0.012

This table shows that Auricular Surface, with a standardized beta coefficient of 0.731, has by far the greatest weight. It is followed, with a major gap, by Pubic Symphysis (S & B) at 0.199. Yet of these two indicators only Auricular Surface has a probability that is statistically significant at the 0.05 level.

In summary, this multiple linear regression (of 13 of the 53 individuals) suggests that more complete data would provide useful predictions of age by using the four age indicators in question. Auricular Surface is likely to have the main weight in the equation of age indication.

To judge by the distributions of the individual indicators (shown below) any future work using MLR is likely to benefit from normalisation of some of the indicators to create more linear distributions.

Regression for the individual age indicators

The use of LeoStatistic led to graphs for 2nd degree polynomial fits for all six indicators. Note however that the lines for sternal rib ends and attrition are virtually linear.

DISCUSSION

The distributions of the six indicators show that Auricular Surface has the highest correlation with known age at death. This result agrees with the MLR of a smaller number of individuals. Overall the results suggest that the age related changes of Pubic Symphysis and Auricular Surface stop around the age of 55. So there may be no value in expanding reference samples to include older people. Yet there is no such asymptote shown in the analysis of Sternal Rib End. They continue to degenerate into old age, though variance increases markedly with age. Suture closure shows virtually no positive slope and virtually no correlation. This unpromising result will be of no surprise to osteologists. Dental attrition increases exponentially with age. The explanation for this deviation from linearity is perhaps related to increasing tooth loss with age, the loss inflicting greater attritional load on the surviving teeth. None of the analyses shows a systematic over estimation of the age of young adults.

Comparison with Spitalfields

Comparisons can be made with the ageing results reported for Spitalfields. Use of the so-called Complex Method at Spitalfields showed major and systematic over estimation of the age of young adults and under estimation of the age of older adults (Molleson & Cox 1993, p.171). For St George's, Bloomsbury, we do not see systematic over estimation of the age of young adults. The results for ageing younger individuals are therefore much more encouraging than those from Spitalfields. Yet under estimation of the age of older adults does occur at St George's, and is perhaps to be explained by the stopping of the relevant degenerative changes around the age of 55 years old. It is interesting to note that by far the most successful ageing method for St George's, both in MLR and as an individual age indicator, is Auricular Surface. This method is not one of those used at Spitalfields.

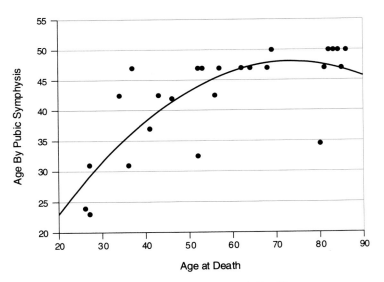

Coefficient of correlation = 0.378. N = 26.

Fig. A2.1   Regression: ageing using pubic symphysis (Todd)

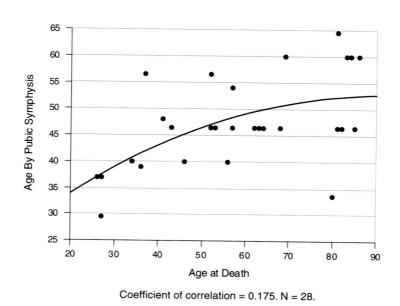

Coefficient of correlation = 0.175. N = 28.

Fig. A2.2   Regression: ageing using pubic symphysis (Suchey & Brooks)

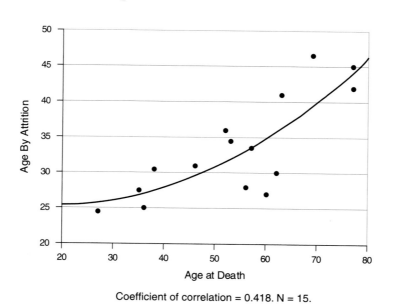

Coefficient of correlation = 0.418. N = 15.

Fig. A2.3   Regression: ageing using dental attrition

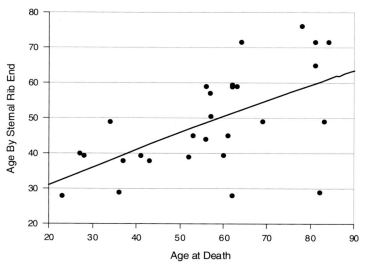

Coefficient of correlation = 0.191. N = 28.

Fig. A2.4   Regression: ageing using sternal rib end

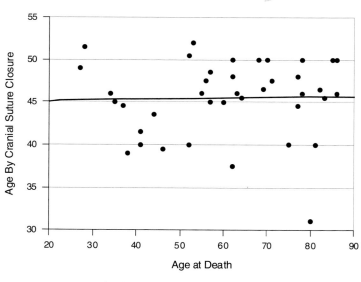

Coefficient of correlation = 0.002. N = 41.

Fig. A2.5   Regression: ageing using cranial suture closure

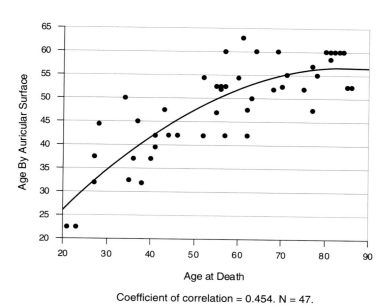

Coefficient of correlation = 0.454. N = 47.

Fig. A2.6   Regression: ageing using auricular surface

Bibliography and references

Manuscript sources

British Library

Asia, Pacific and Africa Collections

IOR/F/4/389/9876   May 1809-Nov 1820. Publication of the final orders of the Court of Directors regarding the Madras army officers suspended by the General Order of 1 May 1809 – Lieut Colonel John Doveton to resume his duties and rank – Major General Robert Bell re-appointed to the command of the Artillery and to a seat on the Military Board - memorial of General Bell regarding his allowances. (IOR/F - Records of the Board of Commissioners for the Affairs of India)

IOR/H/696   *1809.* Mutiny of European officers of the Madras Army. Includes: (17) General Orders by the Governor of Madras in Council. pp. 161-71, 1st May 1809, Censuring the Army officers for their Memorial to the Governor-General and the Address to Major Boles and punishing Lieut.-Col. St. Leger, Major John de Morgan, Capt. Josiah Marshall, Capt. James Grant, Lieut.-Col. Robert Bell, Lieut.-Col. J. M. Chalmers, Lieut.-Col. John Cuppage and Capt. J. M. Coombs; pp. 173-5, 1st May 1809, Making various appointments rendered necessary by the previous General Order; pp. 345-8, 26th and 30th Aug. 1809, Reappointment of Col. Barry Close to the command at Hyderabad, Good behaviour of the native troops during the disturbances in Mysore. (IOR/H - Home Miscellaneous [1600-1918])

IOR/H/700   1808-1810. Mutiny European officers of the Madras Army. Includes: Includes: (26) Lieut.-Col. Robert Bell (Artillery). pp. 259-87, to the Court of Directors 13th May 1809, with Papers on his case; pp. 289-99, to Lord Minto 6th Nov. 1809, with Papers. (IOR/H - Home Miscellaneous [1600-1918])

IOR/L/MAR/B/231A-F   *Hugh Inglis*: Journal (L/MAR/B – India Office Records: Marine Department Records, Ships' Journals 1702-1856)

     catalogue accessible online at www.nationalarchives.gov.uk/a2a/

London Metropolitan Archives

P82/GEO1/063   Searchers' Reports for Saint George's Bloomsbury, Jan 1771-Apr 1834
P82/GEO1/057 – /062   Register of burials, Mar 1761 – Sep 1855
P82/GEO1/064   Burial register giving details of graves Jan 1837-Sep 1856
P82/GEO1/065   Rough burial register Nov 1814-Aug 1827
P82/GEO1/069 – /072   Burial fee books January 1803 – February 1844
P82/GEO1/002 – /009   Registers of baptisms, Oct 1775 – Dec 1855
P82/GEO1/016 – /036   Registers of marriages, Feb 1767 – Jul 1856
P82/GEO1/054 – /055   Index to marriages, Jan 1730/1 – *c.* Dec 1855

Guildhall Library

MS 11936/444-560   Sun Assurance policy registers, 1808-1839. An online index to Sun policy registers Ms 11936/444 -560 (1808 – 1839) is available to search at www.nationalarchives.gov.uk/a2a/

Surrey Heritage

2843/4/20   Bond; Nicholas Winsland of Duke Street, Bloomsbury, Middlesex, builder to Sir Richard Frederick of Burwood Park, Walton upon Thames, bart, and Sir Henry

Fletcher of Ashley Park, bart. Nicholas Winsland agrees to erect a Chapel of Ease at Hersham according to specifications and drawings annexed to a contract of same date [not present] (Date 18 Mar 1839)

2843/4/35   Account of Nicholas Winsland, builder, for building the chapel, including work done by the bricklayer, carpenter, plumber, glazier, mason and smith (£2120 0s 10?d); receipt for balance of £750 attached (Date 15 Jun 1840)

(2843: Hersham, St Peter's: records (including of the former Holy Trinity Chapel of Ease), 1837-1981, catalogue accessible online at www.exploringsurreyspast.org.uk/

The National Archives

TNA ADM 36/12803   Ship: FORTITUDE, Type: PS (ADM 36: Admiralty: Royal Navy ships' musters [Series I])

TNA PROB 11   Prerogative Court of Canterbury wills, accessible online at www.nationalarchives.gov.uk/documentsonline/

TNA WORK 11/16/3   Heating, ventilation and lighting: House of Lords refreshment rooms: kitchen and scullery. Fixtures and fittings. Contract with Messrs. Jeakes. Heating and ventilation apparatus. Contracts A - D with Messrs. Jeakes. Date: 1847-1850. (Office of Works and successors: Houses of Parliament: Registered Files (1709-1973)

Abbreviations

Annals of Philosophy	*The Annals of Philosophy* (ed. Thomas Thomson), vol. 1 (Jan-Jun 1813) – vol. 1 (July-Dec 1820), London
Annual Register	*The Annual Register, or view of the history, politics, and literature for the Year . . . ,* (1758 – present) London
Blackwood's	*Blackwood's Edinburgh Magazine*, 1817-1905, Edinburgh and London
Colonial Gazette	*The Colonial Gazette*, 1838-1847 Clayton, London
Gazette	*The London Gazette*, 'published by authority', accessible online at www.gazettes-online.co.uk/home.aspx?geotype=London
GM	*Gentleman's Magazine*, 1736-1868, London
Holden's 1811	*Holden's Annual London and Country Directory. . for the Year 1811, First Volume, London Part.* London 1811
Kent's Directory 1794	*Kent's Directory for the Year 1794. Cities of London and Westminster, & Borough of Southwark.*
List of Names 1815	*A list of the names of the members of the United Company of Merchants of England, trading to the East-Indies, who appear qualified to vote at their general courts,* Cox and Son, Printers, Great Queen Street, 1815
London Magazine	*The London Magazine* (ed. John Scott), 1820-1829, London
Naval Chronicle	*The Naval Chronicle*, (ed. Mr Joyce Gold) 1799-1818, London
Pennsylvania Archives	*Pennsylvania Archives*, Colonial Records (1838-53) and Series 3 (1894-99), Series 4 (1900-02), and Series 6 (1906-07) accessible online at www/footnote.com/
Pigot's Glos 1830	*Pigot's Directory of Gloucestershire, 1830*
PO London 1808	*Post Office annual directory for 1808*
PO London 1829	*Post-Office London Directory for 1829.*
PO London 1841	*Post Office London Directory for 1841, Part 1: Street, Commercial & Trades; Part 2: Law, Court & Parliamentary*
PO London 1852	*Post Office Directory of London, with Essex, Hertfordshire, Kent, Middlesex, Surrey and Sussex*

Online sources

NPG British Artists' suppliers	National Portrait Gallery, British Artists' suppliers, 1650-1950: URL https://www.npg.org.uk/live/artistsupp_b.asp
Census 1841, 1851, etc	Census records for 1841-1901, accessible at www.ancestry.co.uk
Commissioned Officers	Commissioned Sea Officers of the Royal Navy, 1660-1815, 1954, typescript list National Maritime Museum, accessible online at www.ancestry.co.uk/
DNB	*Dictionary of National Bibliography*, Oxford, accessible online at www.oxforddnb.com/ (see **Printed and other secondary works** for individual citations)

IGI International Genealogical Index, Church of the Latter Day Saints, accessible online at www.familysearch.org/eng/default.asp

Old Bailey Proceedings accessible online at www.oldbaileyonline.org
Pallot's Marriage Index Pallot's Marriage Index 1780-1837, accessible at www.ancestry.co.uk/
Pallot's Baptism Index Pallot's Baptism Index 1780-1837, accessible at www.ancestry.co.uk/
The Times *The Times* digital archive 1785-1985, accessible online at archive.timesonline.co.uk/tol/archive/

Printed and other secondary works

Adjutant General's Office, 1798 *Lists of officers of His Majesty's and the Hon. Company's troops serving under the presidency of Bombay*, London

Allen, Joseph, 1852 *Battles of the British Navy, vol. 2*, revised edition, Henry G Bohn, London

Amery, C, 2002 Architecture of faith – the genius of Nicholas Hawksmoor, *Icon World Monuments*, Fall 2002, 30-35

Andry, Nicholas (Nicholas Andry de Bois-Regard), 1743 *Orthopaedia, or the art of correcting and preventing deformities in Children*, 2 vols, 1741, 1st English edition , printed for A Millar, London, 1743

Arrizabalaga, J, 2003 Syphilis, in Kiple (ed.) 2003, 312-17

Ashmead, Henry Graham, 1884 *History of Delaware County, Pennsylvania*, L. H. Everts & Co, Philadelphia

Aufderheide, A C and Rodríguez-Martín, C (eds) 1998 *The Cambridge encyclopedia of human paleopathology*, Cambridge

Bashford, L, and Pollard, T, 1998 'In the burying place'- the excavation of the Quaker burial ground, in Cox 1998, 154-166

Bass, W M, 1987 *Human osteology- a laboratory and field manual*, Missouri Archaeological Society Special Publication 2, 3rd edition, Columbia

Beck, S V, 1997a Syphilis: The great pox, in Kiple (ed.) 1997, 130-135

Beck, S V, 1997b Rickets: Where the sun doesn't shine, in Kiple (ed.) 1997, 110-115

Bevan, A (ed.), 1999 *Tracing your ancestors in the public records office*; PRO Handbook 19; 5th revised edition; PRO National Archives

Bishop, M, Gelbier, S, and Gibbons, D, 2001a Ethics – dental registration in the seventeenth and early eighteenth century , *British Dental Journal* **191 (7)** October 13, 2001, 395-400

Bishop, M, Gelbier, S, and Gibbons, D, 2001b Ethics – dentistry and tooth-drawing in the late eighteenth and early nineteenth centuries in England. Evidence of provision at all levels of society, *British Dental Journal* **191 (10)** November 24, 2001, 575-580

Boase, G C, 2004 Rogers, Francis James Newman (1791–1851), rev. Jonathan Harris, *Oxford Dictionary of National Biography*, Oxford University Press [http://www.oxforddnb.com/view/article/23973, accessed 5 Dec 2008]

Borrie, M, 2004a Ellis, Sir Henry (1777–1869), *Oxford Dictionary of National Biography*, Oxford University Press; online edn, Oct 2005 [http://www.oxforddnb.com/view/article/8696, accessed 10 Sept 2008]

Borrie, M, 2004b Madden, Sir Frederic (1801–1873), *Oxford Dictionary of National Biography*, Oxford University Press; online edn, Oct 2006 [http://www.oxforddnb.com/view/article/17751, accessed 10 Dec 2008]

Boulter, S, Robertson, D, and Start, H, 1998 The Newcastle Infirmary at the Forth, Newcastle Upon Tyne. Volume 2. The osteology: People, disease and surgery, unpublished report, Archaeology Research and Consultancy at the University of Sheffield

Boyle, A 1995 A catalogue of coffin fittings from St Nicholas, Sevenoaks, unpublished archive report, Oxford Archaeology

Boyle, A, 2002 St Bartholomew's church, Penn, Wolverhampton: results of investigations in the churchyard, unpublished client report, Oxford Archaeology

Boyle, A, 2004 What price compromise? Archaeological investigations at St Bartholomew's church, Penn, Wolverhampton, *Church Archaeology*, Vol. **5** and **6**, 69-78

Boyle, A, and Keevil, G, 1998 'To the praise of the dead and anatomie', The analysis of the post-medieval burials from St Nicholas', Sevenoaks, in Cox 1998, 85-99

Boyle, A, Boston, C, and Witkin, A, 2005 The archaeological experience at St Luke's Church, Old Street, Islington, unpublished client report, Oxford Archaeology

Bradley, L, 1982 Population studies from parish registers; in Drake, M (ed.): *Population studies from parish registers*; Nottingham: Local Population Studies

Brickley, M, Miles, A, and Stainer, H, 1999 *The Cross Bones burial ground, Redcross Way, Southwark, London, archaeological excavations (1991-1998) for the London Underground Limited Jubilee Line Extension Project*, MoLAS Monograph **3**, London

Brooks, S, and Suchey, J M, 1990 Skeletal age determination based on the os pubis: a comparison of the Acsádi-Nemeskéri and Suchey-Brooks methods, *Human Evolution* **5 (3)**, 227-238

Brothwell, D, 1981 *Digging up bones*, 3rd edition, New York

Buikstra, J E, and Ubelaker, D H, 1994 *Standards for data collection from human skeletal remains*, Arkansas Archaeological Survey Research Series No. **44**, Fayetteville, Arkansas, USA

Buckberry, J, and Chamberlain, A, 2002 Age estimation from the auricular surface of the ilium: a revised method, *American Journal of Physical Anthropology* 119 (3), 231-239

Burrows, George Man, 1828 *Commentaries on the causes, forms, symptoms and treatment, moral and medical, of insanity*, T & G Underwood, London 1828

Cannon, J, 2004 George III (1738–1820), *Oxford Dictionary of National Biography*, Oxford University Press; online edn, Jan 2008 [http://www.oxforddnb.com/view/article/105 40, accessed 17 Jan 2009]

Cansick, F T, 1869 *A Collection of Curious and Interesting Epitaphs, copied from the monuments of Distinguished and Noted Characters in The Ancient Church and Burial Grounds of Saint Pancras, Middlesex*, J Russell Smith, London

Carr, William, 2004 Taunton, Sir William Elias (1773–1835), rev. Eric Metcalfe, *Oxford Dictionary of National Biography*, Oxford University Press [http://www.oxforddnb.com/view/article/270 02, accessed 10 Sept 2008]

Carson, P, 2004 Grant, Charles (1746–1823), *Oxford Dictionary of National Biography*, Oxford University Press; online edn, Jan 2008 [http://www.oxford dnb.com/view/article/11248, accessed 01 Oct 2008]

Carter, K C, 2003 Pueperal fever, in Kiple (ed.) 2003, 265-7

Chamberlain, A T, 1994 *Human remains*, London

Cherry, B, and Pevsner, N, 1998 *The buildings of England, London 4, North*, London

Cooper, T, 2004 Lind, James (1736–1812), rev. Patrick Wallis, *Oxford Dictionary of National Biography*, Oxford University Press, [http://www.oxforddnb.com/view/article/16670, accessed 10 Sept 2008]

Cotton, Joseph, 1818 *Memoir on the Origin and Incorporation of the Trinity House of Deptford Strond*, London

Courtney, W P, 2004 Bingley, William (1774–1823), rev. P. E. Kell, *Oxford Dictionary of National Biography*, Oxford University Press; online edn, Oct 2005 [http://www.oxforddnb.com/view/article/2417, accessed 10 Sept 2008]

Cox, M, 1996 *Life and death at Spitalfields 1700-1850*, Council for British Archaeology, York

Cox, M (ed.) 1998 *Grave Concerns – death and burial in England 1700-1850*, CBA Research Report **113**, York

Cox, M, 2001 *Crypt archaeology: an approach*, IFA Paper No. **3**, Reading

Crawford, C, 1991 A scientific profession: medical reform and forensic medicine in British periodicals of the early nineteenth century, in French, R, and Wear, A (eds) 1991, 203-230

Curl, J S, 2003 *Death and architecture – an introduction to funerary and commemorative buildings in the Western European tradition, with some consideration of their settings*, Sutton Publishing

Davis, J, 2004 Munden, Joseph Shepherd (bap. 1758, d. 1832), *Oxford Dictionary of National Biography*, Oxford University Press, 2004 [http://www.oxforddnb.com/view/article/195 36, accessed 10 Sept 2008]

Davis, M T, 2004 Mansfield , Sir James (bap. 1734, d. 1821), *Oxford Dictionary of National Biography*, Oxford University Press; online edn, Jan 2008 [http://www.oxforddnb.com/view/article/179 95, accessed 11 Oct 2008]

Denko, C W, 2003 Osteoarthritis, in Kiple (ed.) 2003, 234-36

Dermigny, L (ed.), 1964 *Les memoires de Charles de Constant sur le Commerce a la Chine, par Charles de Constant*, SEVPEN, Paris

Ditchfield, G M, 2004 Heywood, Samuel (1753–1828), *Oxford Dictionary of National Biography*, Oxford University Press; online edn, Jan 2008 [http://www.oxforddnb.com/view/article/13189, accessed 10 Sept 2008]

Dobie, R, 1829 *The history of the united parishes of St Giles in the fields and St George Bloomsbury*, London

Dodwell, E, and Miles, J S, (eds) 1838 *Alphabetical list of the officers of the Madras Army, the dates of their respective promotion, retirement, resignation, or death . . . from the year 1760 to the years 1834 inclusive, corrected to September 30, 1837*, Longman, Orme, Brown, and Co., London

Donald, D, 1996 *The age of caricature: satirical prints in the reign of George III*, London

Donnelly, C J, and Murphy, E M, 2008 The origins of the *cillini* in Ireland, in Murphy, E M (ed,), *Deviant burial in the archaeological record*, Oxbow Books, Oxford

Dormandy, T, 1999 *The white death: a history of tuberculosis*, Hambledon Press, London

Draper, N R, and Smith, H, 1998 *Applied regression analysis*. John Wiley, Chichester

Dunlop, R, 2004 Hutchinson, Christopher Hely- (1767–1826), rev. Thomas Bartlett, *Oxford Dictionary of National Biography*, Oxford University Press; online edn, Jan 2008 [http://www.oxforddnb.com/view/article/12881, accessed 18 Oct 2008]

Elmes, J, 1831 *A topographical dictionary of London and its environs*, Whittaker, Treacher and Arnott, London

English, H, 1825 *A General Guide to the Companies formed for the working of Foreign Mines . . .*, Boosey & Sons, London

Estes, J W, 2003 Dropsy, in Kiple (ed.) 2003, 100-105

Fee, E, Brown, T M, Lazarus, J and Theermen, P, 2002 The effects of the corset, *American Journal of Public Health* **92 (7)** July 2002, 1085

Ferembach, D, Schwidetsky, I, and Stloukal, M, 1980 Recommendations for age and sex diagnoses of skeletons, *Journal of Human Evolution* **9**, 517-49

Forgan, S, 2004 Children, John George (1777–1852), *Oxford Dictionary of National Biography*, Oxford University Press, [http://www.oxforddnb.com/view/article/5299, accessed 10 Dec 2008]

French, R, and Wear, A (eds) 1991 *British medicine in an age of reform*, Wellcome Institute Series in the History of Medicine, London

Friar, S, 2003 *The Sutton companion to churches*, Sutton Publishing Ltd, Great Britain

Gardiner, J, and Wenborn, N 1995 *The History Today companion to British history*, Collins and Brown

Gelbier, Stanley, 2005 Dentistry and the University of London, *Medical History* **29**, 445-462

Goodman, A H, and Rose, J, 1990 Assessment of systemic physiological perturbations from dental enamel hypoplasias and associated histological structures, *Yearbook of Physical Anthropology* **33**, 59-110

Gray, John, 1837 *Dental Practice; or, Observations on the qualifications of the Surgeon-Dentist . . .*, London

Hamilton, J A, 2004 Littledale, Sir Joseph (1767–1842), rev. Hugh Mooney, *Oxford Dictionary of National Biography*, Oxford University Press, [http://www.oxforddnb.com/view/article/16777, accessed 10 Sept 2008]

Harris, P R, 2004 Planta, Joseph (1744–1827), *Oxford Dictionary of National Biography*, Oxford University Press; online edn, Jan 2008 [http://www.oxforddnb.com/view/article/22353, accessed 10 Sept 2008]

Hart, H G, 1841 *The new annual army list for 1841*, John Murray. London

Haslam, Fiona, 1996 *From Hogarth to Rowlandson: medicine in art in eighteenth-century Britain*, Liverpool UP

Haydn, J, 1851 *The book of dignities, containing rolls of the official personages of the British Empire, civil, ecclesiastical, judicial, military, naval, and municipal*. Longman, Brown, Green and Longmans, London

Healing, T D, Hoffman, P N, and Young, S E J, 1995 The infectious hazards of human cadavers, *Communicable Diseases Review* **5**, 61–68

Henderson, J 1987 Factors determining the state of preservation of human remains, in Boddington, A, Garland, A N, and Janaway, R C (eds) *Death, decay and reconstruction approaches to archaeology and forensic science*, Manchester University Press, Manchester, 43-54

Henderson, T F, 2004 Coxe, Peter (1753?–1844), rev. Jessica Hinings, *Oxford Dictionary of National Biography*, Oxford University Press; online edn, Jan 2008 [http://www.oxforddnb.com/view/article/6536, accessed 21 Dec 2008]

Hill, R, 1998 *The prizes of war: the naval prize system in the Napoleonic Wars 1793 -1815*, Sutton with Royal Naval Museum, Stroud

Hillam, C, 1990 *The roots of dentistry*, London

Hillary, Sir William, 1825 *An Appeal to the British Nation on the Humanity and Policy of forming a National Institution for the Preservation of Lives and property from Shipwreck*, 5th Edition, London

Hillson, S, 1996 *Dental anthropology*, 3rd edition, New York

Hoppa, R D, 1992 Evaluating human skeletal growth: an Anglo-Saxon example, *International Journal of Osteoarchaeology* 2 (4), 275-288

Hughes, Capt. R M, 1845 *The duties of judge advocates, compiled from her Majesty's and the hon. East India Company's military regulations . . .*, Smith, Elder & Co, London

Humphreys, M, 1997 Tuberculosis: The 'consumption' and civilisation, in Kiple (ed.) 1997, 136-141

Hunter, J, Roberts, C, and Martin, A (eds) 1997 *Studies in crime: an introduction to forensic archaeology*, Routledge, London

Iscan, M Y, and Kennedy, K A R (eds) 1989 *Reconstructing of life from the skeleton*, Alan R Liss, New York

Iscan, M Y, Loth, S R and Wright, R K, 1984 Age estimation from the ribs by phase analysis: white males, *Journal of Forensic Sciences* **29**, 1094-1104

Iscan, M Y, Loth, S R and Wright, R K, 1985 Age estimation from the ribs by phase analysis: white females, *Journal of Forensic Sciences* **30**, 853-863

James 1837 *The Naval History of Great Britain: From the Declaration of War by France in 1793 to the Accession of George IV, New edition with additions and notes by Captain Chamier*, Vol. 6, Richard Bentley, London

Janaway, R C, 1997 The decay of buried human remains and their associated materials, in Hunter, J, Roberts, C, and Martin, A (eds) 1997, 58-85

Janaway, R C, 1998 An introductory guide to textiles from 18th- and 19th-century burials, in Cox 1998, 17-32

Jurmain, R D, 1999 Osteoarthritis and activity: occupational and sports studies, in Jurmain, R D (ed.) *Stories from the skeleton- behavioural reconstruction in human osteology*, Gordon and Breach Publishers, Netherlands

Kiple, K F (ed.) 1997 *Plague, pox and pestilence – disease in history*, Weidenfeld and Nicolson, London

Kiple, K F (ed.) 2003 *The Cambridge historical dictionary of disease*; Cambridge UP, Cambridge

Klingerman, K M 2006 Binding femininity: an examination of the effects of tightlacing on the female pelvis, MA thesis, Louisiana State University and Agricultural and Mechanical College, accessible online at http://etd.lsu.edu/docs/available/etd-04072006-115441/unrestricted/Klingerman_thesis.pdf, accessed 14 Jan 2009

Kneller, P, 2003 Health and safety, in Cox, M, *Crypt archaeology: an approach*, IFA Paper No. **3**

Krogman, W M, and Iscan, M Y, 1986 *The human skeleton in forensic medicine,* 2nd edition, Charles C. Thomas, Springfield, USA

Levin, J, 2003 Peridontal disease (Pyorrhoea), in Kiple (ed.) 2003, 244-47

Lindsay, Lillian, 1927 The London dentist of the eighteenth century, *Proc Royal Society of Medicine* **20** (4), February 1927, 355–366

Litten, J, 1991 *The English way of death- the common funeral since 1450*, Robert Hale, London

Lovejoy, C O, Meindl, R S, Pryzbeck, T R, and Mensforth, R P, 1985 Chronological metamorphosis of the auricular surface of the ilium: a new method for the determination of adult skeletal age at death, *American Journal of Physical Anthropology* 68 (1),15-28

Lukasc, J R, 1989 Dental pathology: methods for reconstructing health status and dietary patterns in prehistory, in Iscan and Kennedy 1989, 261-286

Mahoney, D, 2004 The human bone assemblage from the Quaker burial ground, in Brown, R, Archaeological investigations at the Vancouver Centre, Kings Lynn, unpublished client report, Oxford Archaeology

Mangalwadi, V, 1997 *India: the grand experiment*

Maresh, M M, 1955 Linear growth of the long bones of the extremities from infancy through adolescence, *American Journal of diseases in childhood* **89**, 725-742

Maundrell, Henry, 1703 *A Journey from Aleppo to Jerusalem at Easter A.D. 1697*, Oxford

May, T, 1996 *The Victorian undertaker,* 28, Shire Album **330,** Shire Publications, Princes Risborough

Mays, S, 1998 *The archaeology of human bones*, Routledge, London

Mays, S, (ed.) 2005 *Guidance for best practice for treatment of human remains excavated from Christian burial grounds in England*, English Heritage, London

Mays, S, and Cox, M, 2000 Sex determination in skeletal remains, in Cox, M, and Mays, S (eds), *Human osteology: in archaeology and forensic science*, Greenwich Medical Media, London

McKinley J I and Roberts C, 1993 *Excavation and post-excavation treatment of cremated and inhumed human remains.* IFA Technical paper No 13, Birmingham

Meindl, R S and Lovejoy, C O, 1985 Ectocranial suture closure: A revised method for the determination of skeletal age at death based on the lateral-anterior sutures, *American Journal of Physical Anthropology* 68 (1), 57-66

Meindl, R S, Lovejoy, C O, Mensforth, R P, and Carlos, L D, 1985 Accuracy and direction of error in sexing the skeleton, implications for palaeodemography, *American Journal of Physical Anthropology* 68 (1), 79-85

Meller, H, 1975 *St George's Bloomsbury- an illustrated guide to the church*, St George's church and Bloomsbury Group, London

Miles, A, 1962 Assessment of age of a population of Anglo-Saxons from their dentition, *Proceedings of the Royal Society of Medicine* **55**, 881-886

Molleson, T and Cox, M, 1993 *The Spitalfields project: the middling sort*, CBA Research Report **86**

Moorees, C F A, Fanning, E A, and Hunt, E E, 1963a Age variation of formation stages for ten permanent teeth, *Journal of Dental Research* **42**, 1490-1502

Moorees, C F A, Fanning, E A, and Hunt, E E, 1963b Formation and resorption of three deciduous teeth in children, *American Journal of Physical Anthropology* **21 (2)**, 205-213

Munden, A F, 2004 Villiers, Henry Montagu (1813–1861), *Oxford Dictionary of National Biography*, Oxford University Press [http://www.oxforddnb.com/view/article/28298, accessed 10 Sept 2008]

Musgrave, T, and Musgrave, W, 2000 *An empire of plants – people and plants that changed the world*, Cassell, London

Nawrocki, 1995 Taphonomic processes in historical cemeteries, in Grauer, A L (ed.) *Bodies of evidence – reconstructing history through skeletal analysis*, Wiley Liss, 49-68

Noble, H W, 2002 Tooth transplantation: a controversial story, *History of Dentistry Research Group Newsletter* No. 11, October 2002

Nolan, J, 1997 The international centre for life: The archaeology and history of the Newcastle Infirmary, Newcastle City Archaeology Unit unpublished client report

Oldham, J, 2004 Dampier, Sir Henry (1758–1816), *Oxford Dictionary of National Biography*, Oxford University Press [http://www.oxforddnb.com/view/article/63080, accessed 10 Sept 2008]

Ortner, D J, and Putchar, W G J, 1981 *Identification of pathological conditions in human skeletal remains*, Smithsonian Institute Press, Washington

Phenice, T W 1969 A newly developed visual method of sexing the *os pubis, American Journal of Physical Anthropology* **30 (2)**, 297-302

Philippart, J (ed.), 1823 *The East India military calendar, containing the services of general and field officers of the Indian Army*, Kingsbury, Parbury and Allen, London

Philippart, J (ed.), 1828 *The East India military calendar, containing the services of general and field officers of the Indian Army, Vol 3,* Kingsbury, Parbury and Allen, London

Picard, L, 2000 *Dr Johnson's London, Life in London 1740-1770*, Weidenfeld and Nicolson, London

Polden, P, 2004 Hannen, James, Baron Hannen (1821–1894), *Oxford Dictionary of National Biography*, Oxford University Press, [http://www.oxforddnb.com/view/article/12216, accessed 10 Sept 2008]

Porter, R, 1994 *London – a social history*, Hamish Hamilton, London

Porter, R, 1997 *The greatest benefit to mankind – a medical history of humanity from antiquity to the present*, Harper Collins Publishers

Porter, R 2001 *Bodies politic-disease, death and doctors in Britain 1650-1900*, London

Privy Council, Great Britain, 1927 *In the matter of the boundary between the Dominion of Canada and the colony of Newfoundland in the Labrador Peninsula*, 13 vols King's Printer. Ottawa, 1927

Reeve J, 1998 A view from the metropolis: post medieval burials in London, in Cox 1998, 213–237

Reeve, J. and Adams, M. 1993 *The Spitalfields Project – across the Styx*, Vol.1 CBA Research Report **85**

Reeve, J, and Cox, M, 1999 Research and our recent ancestors: post-medieval burial grounds, in Downes, J, and Pollard, T (eds): *The loved body's corruption: archaeological contributions to the study of human mortality*, Cruithne Press

Richards, N David, 1968 Dentistry in England in the 1840s: the first indications of a movement towards professionalization, *Medical History* **12** (2) April 1968, 137–152

Richardson, R, 1991 'Trading assassins' and the licensing of anatomy, in French and Wear 1991, 74-91

Richmond, M, 1999 *Archaeologia Victoriana*: the archaeology of the Victorian funeral; in Downes, J and Pollard, T (eds), *The loved body's corruption*, 145-158

Rigg, J M, 2004 Wilde, Thomas, first Baron Truro (1782–1855)', rev. T. G. Watkin, *Oxford Dictionary of National Biography*, Oxford University Press; online edn, Jan 2008 [http://www.oxforddnb.com/view/article/29401, accessed 5 Dec 2008]

Roberts, C, 1997 Forensic anthropology 1: the contribution of biological anthropology to forensic contexts, in Hunter, J, Roberts, C, and Martin A (eds) 1997, 101-121

Roberts, C, Boylson, A, Buckley, L, Chamberlain, A C and Murphy, E M, 1998 Rib lesions and tuberculosis: the palaeopathological evidence; *Tubercle and Lung Disease* **79** (1), 55-60

Roberts, C, and Cox, M, 2003 *Health and disease in Britain from prehistory to present day*, Stroud

Roberts, C, and Manchester, K, 1995 *The archaeology of disease*, 2nd edition, New York

Roden, B, 1997 Dental attrition and age in Newcastle Blackgate and Newcastle infirmary populations, unpublished MSc dissertation, University of Sheffield

Rogers, J, and Waldron, T, 1995 *A field guide to joint disease in archaeology*, Chichester

Rubenhold, H (ed.), 2005 *Harris's list of Covent Garden ladies*, Tempus Books

Rugg, J, 1999 From reason to regulation- 1760-1850; in Jupp, P C, and Gittings, C, (eds) *Death in England – an illustrated history*, Manchester University Press, 202-229

St Hoyme, L E, and Iscan, M Y, 1989 Determination of sex and race: accuracy and assumptions, in Iscan, M Y, and Kennedy, K A R, (eds) 1989, 53-93

Sambrook, P, 2006 *A Country House at Work: Three Centuries of Dunham Massey*, National Trust

Saunders, S R, and Hoppa, R D, 1993 Growth deficits in survivors and non-survivors: biological mortality bias in subadult skeletal samples, *Yearbook of Physical Anthropology* **36**, 127-151

Scheuer, L, and Black, S, 2000 *Developmental juvenile osteology*, Elsevier Academic Press

Scheuer, J L, and Bowman, J E, 1995 Correlation of documentary and skeletal evidence in the St. Bride's crypt population, in *Grave reflections: portraying the past through cemetery studies* (Saunders, S, and Herring, A eds) Canadian Scholar's Press, 49-70

Schulte Beerbühl, M, 2008 The risk of bankruptcy among German merchants in Eighteenth-century England, in Grazter, K, and Stiefe, D, (eds) *History of insolvency and bankruptcy from an international perspective*, Södertörn Academic Studies **38**, 61-81

Schwarz, G S, 1979 Society, physicians, and the corset, *Bulletin of the New York Academy of Medicine* 55 (6), 551-590

Schwartz, J H, 1995 *Skeleton Keys*, Oxford UPs, Oxford

Smith, B H, 1991 Standards of human tooth formation and dental age assessment, in M A Kelley and C S Larsen (eds) *Advances in dental anthropology*, New York, 143-168

Start, H, and Kirk, M, 1998 The bodies of friends – the osteological analysis of a Quaker burial ground, in Cox 1998, 167-177

Stewart, F H, 1917 *Notes on old Gloucester County, New Jersey*, Historical Records published by the New Jersey Society of Pennsylvania, Vol. **1**, Camden, New Jersey

Strype, John, 1720 *A survey of the Cities of London and Westminster: containing the original, antiquity, increase, modern estate and government of those cities. Written at first in the year MDXCVIII. By John Stow, Citizen and native of London. Since reprinted and augmented . . .. Available online:* Strype, Survey of London (1720), [online] (hriOnline, Sheffield). Available from: URL: http://www.hrionline.ac.uk/strype/

Stuart-Macadam, P, 1991 Anaemia in Roman Britain: Poundbury Camp, in Bush, H and Zvelebil, M (eds) *Health in past societies: biocultural interpretations of human skeletal remains in archaeological contexts*, BAR International Series **257**, 101-14

Survey of London Grosvenor Square: Individual Houses built before 1926, *Survey of London: volume 40: The Grosvenor Estate in Mayfair, Part 2* (The Buildings) (1980), 117-166. URL: http://www.british-history.ac.uk/report.aspx?compid=42126 Date accessed: 18 January 2009.

Survey of London Piccadilly, South Side, *Survey of London: volumes 29 and 30: St James Westminster, Part 1* (1960), pp. 251-270. URL: http://www.british-history.ac.uk/report.aspx?compid=40571 Date accessed: 19 January 2009.

Sutherland, L D, and Suchey, J M, 1991 Use of the ventral arc in pubic sex determination, *Journal of Forensic Sciences*, 36, 501-511

Tarlow, S, 1998 Wormie clay and blessed sleep; in Tarlow, S and West, S: *The familiar past?*, 183- 198; Routledge

The Clerical guide or ecclesiastical directory, containing a complete register of the prelates and other dignitaries of the church, F C and J Rivington, St Paul's Yard, London 1817

The Clerical guide or ecclesiastical directory, containing a complete register of the prelates and other dignitaries of the church, 3rd edition (corrected by R Gilbert) CJ G and F Rivington, St Paul's Yard and Waterloo Place, Pall Mall, London 1829

Thorne, R, 2004 Hutchinson, Richard Hely-, first earl of Donoughmore (1756–1825), *Oxford Dictionary of National Biography*, Oxford University Press; online edn, Jan 2008 [http://www.oxforddnb.com/view/article/12885, accessed 18 Oct 2008]

Todd, T W, 1921a Age changes in the pubic bone. I: the male white pubis, *American Journal of Physical Anthropology* 3 (3), 285-335

Todd, T W, 1921b Age changes in the pubic bone III: the female white pelvis, *American Journal of Physical Anthropology* 4 (1), 26-39

Trollope, Rev W, 1834, *A History of the Royal Foundation of Christ's Hospital*, William Pickering London

Trotter, M, 1970 Estimations of stature from intact long limb bones, in Stewart, T D (ed.), *Personal identification in mass Disasters*, Washington, 71-83

Tulchinsky, G J J, 1966 Auldjo, Alexander, in Halpenny, F G (ed.) *Dictionary of Canadian Biography*, vol. **V1**, University of Toronto Press, 18-19. Available online at www.biographi.ca/

[http://www.biographi.ca/ accessed 17 Jan 2009]

Von Sömmerring, S T, 1793 *Über die Wirkungen der Schnürbrüste*, (On the effects of the Corset) Berlin

Weinglass, D H, 2004 Fuseli, Henry (1741–1825), *Oxford Dictionary of National Biography*, Oxford University Press; online edn, Jan 2007 [http://www.oxforddnb.com/view/article/10254, accessed 10 Sept 2008]

Weiss, E. and Jurmain, R 2007 Osteoarthritis revisited: a contemporary review of aetiology, *International Journal of Osteoarchaeology* **17 (5)**, 437-450.

Welch, Joseph (compiler) 1852 *The List of the Queen's scholars of St. Peter's College, Westminster, admitted to that foundation since 1663 . . .*, New Edn.

Wells, C, 1967 Pseudopathology, in Brothwell, D, and Sandison, A T (eds) *Disease in antiquity*, Illinois, 5-19

Werner, A, Conheeney, J and Fielder, K, 1998 Georgian and Victorian bodies, in Werner, A (ed.) *London bodies*, London, 82-101

White, J, 2008 *London in the 19th century. A human awful wonder of God*, 2007, Vintage Books, London

Wilson, R G, 2007 Meux family (per. 1757–1910), *Oxford Dictionary of National Biography*, online edn, Oxford University Press; online edn, Jan 2008 [http://www.oxforddnb.com/view/article/97889, accessed 11 Dec 2008]

Woodforde, J. 1968: *The strange story of false teeth;* Routledge and Kegan Paul, London

Wroth, W W, 2004 Nares, Robert (1753–1829), rev. M. K. C. MacMahon, *Oxford Dictionary of National Biography*, Oxford University Press [http://www.oxforddnb.com/view/article/19780, accessed 10 Sept 2008]

Young, S, 1998 Archaeology and smallpox, in Cox 1998, 190-196

Zar, J H, 1999 *Biostatistical analysis*. Prentice Hall International (UK), London